The Consolidated Asylum and Migration Acquis

THE EU DIRECTIVES IN AN EXPANDED EUROPE

The Consolidated
Asylum and Migration Acquis

THE EU DIRECTIVES IN AN EXPANDED EUROPE

Compiled and introduced by

Peter J. van Krieken

T·M·C·ASSER PRESS
The Hague

Published by T·M·C·ASSER PRESS
P.O.Box 16163, 2500 BD The Hague, The Netherlands
<www.asserpress.nl>

T·M·C·ASSER PRESS' English language books are distributed exclusively by:

Cambridge University Press, The Edinburgh Building, Shaftesbury Road,
Cambridge CB2 2RU, UK,
or
for customers in the USA, Canada and Mexico:
Cambridge University Press, 40 West 20th Street, New York, NY 10011-4211, USA
<www.cambridge.org>

to be cited as:
P.J. van Krieken, *The Consolidated Asylum and Migration Acquis* (The Hague, 2004)

ISBN 90-6704-180-7

PRINTED IN THE NETHERLANDS

PREFACE

The world is in turmoil. Yet, whereas some parts seem to fall apart, others are slowly but determinedly working towards greater cohesion and increased cooperation. Europe is a fitting illustration of the many advantages of joining hands to create an area of freedom, security and justice.

Like other continents, Europe has a long history and may enjoy a great future. The future depends not only on how Europeans themselves work and live together, but also on how they see their place and position in the global context. Europe owes it to other parts of the world to strive together for increased understanding, effective cooperation and for a world where all can make a decent living without fear, without want.

It is the issue of asylum and migration that challenges Europe in a fascinating manner. It covers human beings in need, in need of freedom, security and justice. The question of how best to react to that challenge will always have to be posed and answered. The last decade has increasingly shown that it is an illusion to think that we can help humankind or the globalization process by means of migration. An inward-looking approach – can we help them, should we help them, can we use their services – denies the urgency of a more holistic approach. Such an approach should reflect the preamble to the 1975 ILO Labour Migration Convention, in which the need was emphasized '...to avoid the excessive and uncontrolled or unassisted increase of migratory movements because of their negative social and human consequences...'. It was also considered '...that in order to overcome underdevelopment and structural and chronic unemployment, the governments of many countries increasingly stress the desirability of encouraging the transfer of capital and technology, rather than the transfer of workers...'.

Europe, like no other continent, should be aware of the continuous need to offer a safe haven to genuine refugees. Having produced millions of refugees itself, it should cater for the needs of the millions who are currently refugees, or the millions to come. This should be done in a truly global way, paying attention to the possibilities and realities on the ground in the many refugee-receiving countries as well as in Europe. The right to seek and enjoy asylum from persecution should never be tinkered with.

As for migration, the time has come to truly consider the advantages and disadvantages of migratory movements on the personal level, country level through to the global level. As indicated in the Declaration of The Hague on the Future of Refugee and Migration Policy – presented to UN Secretary-General Kofi Annan in November 2002 at the Peace Palace in The Hague – the concern for both refugees and migrants has to be located within the context of economic and political globalization, with all its potential for greater human development and prosperity, on the one hand, or alienation, disempowerment, impoverishment and polarisation on the other.

Refugees and migrants matter enormously to the international community. Their future is an essential element in the notion of peaceful international cooperation, stability and economic security. The aspirations and needs of people on the move deserve attention, without forgetting the absolute necessity to make the option to stay in one's own country the most important one.

Europe, too, needs to respond creatively to the various challenges. The recent debate and efforts to lay down minimum norms should be seen in the wider, global context. As such, the new EU Directives, compiled and introduced by Dr. Peter van Krieken who himself was actively involved with the process that resulted in the Declaration of The Hague, deserve to be studied in detail.

The first steps have been taken. That in itself is a positive move. The international norms, however, remain in place; leaning towards the edges thereof should be prevented at all costs. Moreover, Europe needs to look upon the European challenges involved in the broader context of global developments and global cooperation. Europe should think global. Appropriate further steps need to be taken.

With that in mind, I wholeheartedly recommend this Handbook on the Consolidated Asylum and Migration Acquis to be used and studied so that the Directives and further European legislation can be closely followed, debated, criticized, improved and/or lauded.

The Hague, June 2004

Frans BOUWEN MA
Senior International Consultant
to the The Hague Process on
Refugee and Migration Policy

ACKNOWLEDGEMENTS

This Volume is the logical follow-up to the *Asylum Acquis Handbook* (2000) and the *Migration Acquis Handbook* (2001) published by T.M.C. Asser Press. The asylum and migration debate is an ongoing one and it should hence come as no surprise that a great many new rules and regulations have meanwhile been agreed upon. Of particular importance, of course, was the Treaty of Amsterdam that entered into force on 1 May 1999. Under that Treaty it was decided to move the subjects of asylum and migration into the realm of the Treaty of the European Community. Moreover, it was determined that major legislative documents describing minimum norms should be agreed upon before the end of a 5-year transition period, that is before 1 May 2004. The latter date, also being the day on which the European Union was enlarged, carried special weight. And indeed, the Commission and Council more or less met the deadline.

Likewise, the T.M.C. Asser Press also imposed its deadline. A Volume containing the new Directives and supplementing the above-mentioned Handbooks should be on the market by the end of the summer of 2004. A race against time, that has only been won thanks to the kind and diligent assistance of Cristian Cartis. I am most grateful for his patience and involvement.

Moreover, I owe the team of T.M.C. Asser Press, Mr Peter Morris, the language editor, the indefatigable Frans Bouwen, ICMPD as well as the Röling Foundation and Johan Feitsma (*'still crazy after all these years'*) special thanks for their support.

Most of all, however, it is Diederik, Katrien and Sebastiaan who deserve praise for coping with a lack of attention and a dearth of sailing opportunities. Theirs is the new Europe. All together we should continue to build an area of veritable and viable freedom, security and justice.

The Hague, June 2004

TABLE OF CONTENTS

Part 1
ASYLUM

Part 3
MISCELLANEOUS

INTRODUCTION

The Introduction is divided into three parts:
Part A focuses on decision-making and the directives;
Part B deals with the question whether Europe is indeed in need of migrants; and
Part C of the introduction pays attention to forthcoming developments as well as the Danish approach.

A.   CONSOLIDATED

In this first part of the Introduction a description is given of the background to the directives as well as of the decision-making procedures concerned; also some attention is paid to the Schengen acquis. It is stressed that it concerns minimum norms only. Harmonization is not yet in the offing.

On the eve of the 1st of May 2004, the Commission issued a Press Release in which it welcomed the Council's Agreement on two asylum-related directives. António Vitorino, the EC Commissioner for Justice and Home Affairs submitted: 'Together with the formal adoption of the Qualification Directive, the agreement reached by the Council on the Asylum Procedures Directive effectively means that the first phase of the Common European Asylum System has now been established'. He also said: 'The importance of this agreement cannot be underestimated. Both Directives will significantly contribute to a common approach across all 25 EU Member States. The Directives will promote mutual confidence in Member States' asylum systems in the EU where only one Member State will be responsible for a particular application'.

This agreement was timely. Not just because the Union was about to receive 10 new members, but in particular because the transition period of 5 years foreseen under the Treaty of Amsterdam came to an end on the 1st of May 2004, – no coincidence indeed.

Under the Treaty of Amsterdam, the subjects of asylum and migration were formally 'moved' from the TEU to the TEC, from the Union Treaty to the Community Treaty, or, in Euro-speak, from the Third Pillar to the First Pillar.[1]

---

[1] Art. 63 of the thus amended Treaty establishing the European Community (official title: CONSOLIDATED VERSION OF THE TREATY ESTABLISHING THE EUROPEAN COMMUNITY) reads:
The Council, acting in accordance with the procedure referred to in Article 67, shall, within a period of five years after the entry into force of the Treaty of Amsterdam, adopt:

The Directives adopted are binding on current and new Member States except for Denmark. According to the Protocols agreed upon in 1997 Denmark, the UK and Ireland are not automatically bound by the measures taken under title IV of the TEC Treaty. However, the UK and Ireland have indicated in the case of each relevant directive that they would sign up to the Directives concerned. That was not the case with Denmark.

The drive to reach agreement before 1 May 2004, was based on the text of TEC Article 63 and was reflected in the *Scoreboard to review progress on the creation of an area of freedom, security and justice in the European Union* adopted by the Commission in March 2000 and approved by the Council. The Directives should also be seen in the light of the conclusions of the European Council in Tampere, October 1999, which called for the establishment of a Common European Asylum System which should include, in the short-term, a clear and workable determination of the State responsible for the examination of an asylum application, common standards for a fair and efficient asylum procedure, common minimum conditions of reception of asylum seekers, and the approximation of rules on the recognition and content of the refugee status. It should also be completed with measures on subsidiary forms of protection offering an appropriate status to any person in need of such protection.

---

1. measures on asylum, in accordance with the Geneva Convention of 28 July 1951 and the Protocol of 31 January 1967 relating to the status of refugees and other relevant treaties, within the following areas:
   a) criteria and mechanisms for determining which Member State is responsible for considering an application for asylum submitted by a national of a third country in one of the Member States,
   b) minimum standards on the reception of asylum seekers in Member States,
   c) minimum standards with respect to the qualification of nationals of third countries as refugees,
   d) minimum standards on procedures in Member States for granting or withdrawing refugee status
2. measures on refugees and displaced persons within the following areas:
   e) minimum standards for giving temporary protection to displaced persons from third countries who cannot return to their country of origin and for persons who otherwise need international protection,
   f) promoting a balance of effort between Member States in receiving and bearing the consequences of receiving refugees and displaced persons,
3. measures on immigration policy within the following areas:
   a) conditions of entry and residence, and standards on procedures for the issue by Member States of long-term visas and residence permits, including those for the purpose of family reunion,
   b) illegal immigration and illegal residence, including repatriation of illegal residents;
4. measures defining the rights and conditions under which nationals of third countries who are legally resident in a Member State may reside in other Member States
Measures adopted by the Council pursuant to points 3 and 4 shall not prevent any Member State from maintaining or introducing in the areas concerned national provisions which are compatible with this Treaty and with international agreements.
Measures to be adopted pursuant to points 2(b), 3(a) and 4 shall not be subject to the five-year period referred to above.

The drive to agree on minimum norms on asylum should also be seen in the light of the development to view 'asylum' as part of the broader migration challenge. It had become increasingly clear that many of the asylum-related movements were in fact migratory movements. Thus efforts to agree on norms in the asylum realm were combined with similar efforts on migration in general, including illegal migration. Major steps have indeed been taken. Return and integration, however, did not receive the attention they deserve. This is the more remarkable as asylum and migration should be seen as part of a broad picture of which return and integration are an inalienable part.

Visas, Immigration and Asylum

In terms of visas, immigration and asylum European law is now governed by a new institutional framework. The Qualification and Procedures Directives, together with the other legislative instruments on asylum and migration adopted by the Council at an earlier stage, guarantee a minimum level of protection and procedural safeguards in all Member States for those who are genuinely in need of international protection, whilst preventing abuses of asylum applications which undermine the credibility of the system. Moreover, important steps have also been taken in the field of migration, e.g., regulating the status of long-term immigrants. On the visa issue, the Schengen Agreement (part of the acquis) has become a 'trademark' as a Schengen visa is for many in this global world something worth striving for.

Chronological Overview

A. Political Developments[2]

1985: Schengen Agreement negotiated. Triggered by the absence of any movement on bringing down internal frontiers for the movement of people, which was hampering intra-EC movement of goods, a sub-group of 5 European Community Member States (Belgium, France, Germany, the Netherlands and Luxembourg) entered into the Schengen Agreement on the gradual abolition of checks at their mutual frontiers.

1986: Establishment of the Ad Hoc Working Group on Immigration and Asylum. This was the first, informal arena for discussing immigration and asylum issues in the European Communities of 12 Member States.

1990: Schengen Convention signed, preparing for the implementation of the 1985 Agreement, and putting practical matters in place for uniform visas, for example.

---

[2] Based on Van Selm and Tsolakis, MPI, policy brief, May 2004 No. 4.

1990: The Signing of the Inter-governmental Dublin Convention determining which Member State is responsible for assessing an asylum claim.

1992: Maastricht Treaty on European Union signed. Informal cooperation on asylum and migration issues was converted into formal cooperation among governments. They set out to discuss issues like the definition of a refugee, intending to make intergovernmental, as yet non-binding agreements.

1993: The Treaty on European Union (1992) enters into force.

1995: The Schengen Agreement (1985) and Schengen Convention (1990) come into effect, removing borders between the Schengen Members (the original five plus Spain and Portugal).

1997: Amsterdam Treaty is signed, moving asylum and immigration into 'semi-Community' activity, with unanimous voting required, and a shared right of initiative for the Council and Commission. Agreements would be binding, and should be the basis for a Common Policy. The UK and Ireland decide on a case to case basis to 'opt in'. Denmark has a full opt out.

1997: The Dublin Convention (1990) enters into force.

1998: The Vienna Action Plan focuses on how to best implement the provisions of the Treaty of Amsterdam on an area of freedom, security and justice.

1999: The Amsterdam Treaty (1997) enters into force. A timetable is set out for moving to full Community activity on asylum by 2004. An 'Area of Freedom, Security and Justice' is to be created for EU Member States, with free movement for citizens and a common asylum system. Various directives (binding agreements) should be agreed upon both in the field of asylum and migration. A five-year deadline is set for the first set of agreements.

1999: Schengen is incorporated into the European Union's basic laws ('acquis') as part of the Amsterdam Treaty, with special provisions for Denmark, and an opt out for the UK and Ireland. All other EU Member States have adopted Schengen, and Norway and Iceland also participate.

1999: The Tampere Summit meeting sets out a clear agenda with, as main elements, a common asylum system, managed migration and partnership with countries in regions of origin. This agenda is set out as 'Milestones for progress on the Area of Freedom, Security and Justice', promoting the project of developing an area of free movement, in which citizens would feel assured of an environment of security and justice.

2001: The Laeken Conclusions (Belgian Presidency) note the slow progress of building a common European asylum system. In the light of 9/11, the focus in Laeken in December 2001 was inevitably on security issues. Some governments pointed to the Commission as the cause of the slow progress on the asylum agenda items, although proposals were on the table and discussions within the Council were under way.

2002: The Seville Council (Spanish Presidency) decides to try to speed up the implementation of the Tampere Programme.

2002: The Danish Presidency draws up a 'Road Map' of the work ahead on border control, immigration, asylum and cooperation with third countries, in an attempt to reinforce the need for decisions and action.

2003: The UK introduces its 'Vision Paper' for processing asylum claims in 'transit' centres outside the EU, and returning asylum seekers to those centres or to reception centres in countries neighbouring their own in their regions of origin.

2003: The Thessaloniki Conclusions (Greek Presidency) ask the European Commission to look at new ideas such as an EU-wide resettlement programme, and pilot programmes for building capacity to better protect more refugees in their regions of origin. They also place the policy and political spotlight squarely on issues of immigrant integration.

2004: Under the Irish Presidency the missing directives are agreed upon, although some with 'political agreement' only, meaning that the formal agreement is supposed to be reached by the autumn of 2004.

B. Legal developments: Asylum

On 11 December 2000, the Council adopted a Regulation (2725/2000/EC) concerning the establishment of **'Eurodac'** for the comparison of fingerprints for the effective application of the Dublin Convention on the State responsible for examining applications for asylum lodged in one of the European Union Member States (*not included in this Volume*[3]).

On 20 July 2001, the Council adopted a Directive on minimum standards for giving **Temporary Protection** in the event of a mass influx of displaced persons and on measures promoting a balance of efforts between Member States in receiving such persons and bearing the consequences thereof (Chapter 1.6).

On 27 January 2003, the Council adopted a Directive on minimum standards on the **Reception** of applicants for asylum in Member States (Chapter 1.3).

On 18 February 2003, the Council adopted a Regulation establishing the criteria and mechanisms for determining the Member State responsible for examining an asylum application lodged in one of the Member States by a third country national (**Dublin Criteria**, Chapter 1.1).

---

[3] See *The Migration Acquis Handbook*, p. 279 ff.

In September 2003, the Commission adopted a regulation laying down detailed rules for the application of the Dublin Criteria (**Dublin Detailed Rules**, Chapter 1.2).

And finally, on 29 April 2004, the Council formally adopted the Directive on a common definition of who is a refugee or otherwise requires international protection and the rights and benefits which attach to each status (the **Qualification** Directive) (Chapter 1.5).

On that same day the Council also reached a political agreement on the Asylum **Procedures** Directive, in which Member States take a common approach to processing asylum applications in the EU (Chapter 1.4).

These Directives, together with the other legislative instruments on asylum already adopted by the Council, guarantee a minimum level of protection and procedural safeguards in all Member States for those who are genuinely in need of international protection, whilst preventing abuses of asylum applications which undermine the credibility of the system.

C. Legal developments: Migration

On 28 May 2001, the Council adopted a Directive on mutual recognition of decisions on the **Expulsion** of third-country nationals (Chapter 2.7).

On 11 July 2001, the Commission adopted a proposal for a Council Directive on conditions of entry and residence of third-country nationals for the purpose of paid **Employment** and self-employed economic activities. On 12 February 2003, the Commission reached partial agreement on European Parliament's amendments (Chapter 2.2).

On 14 May 2003, the Council adopted a Directive on **Social Security** schemes – extending the provisions of Regulation (EEC) No. 1408/71 and Regulation (EEC) No. 574/72 to nationals of third countries who are not already covered by those provisions solely on the ground of their nationality (Chapter 2.6).

On 22 September 2003, the Council adopted a Directive on **Family Reunification** (Chapter 2.5).

On 25 November 2003, the Council adopted a Directive on the status of third-country nationals who are **Long-term Residents** (Chapter 2.1).

On 30 March 2004, the Council reached political agreement on a Directive on conditions of entry and residence of third-country nationals for the purposes of studies, vocational training or voluntary service (**Students & Volunteers**, Chapter 2.3).

On 29 April 2004, the Council formally adopted a Directive on short-term residence permit issued to **Victims** of action to facilitate illegal immigration or trafficking in human beings who cooperate with the competent authorities (sic), (**Victims of trafficking**, Chapter 2.4).

These Directives represent important minimum norms. Approximation nor harmonization are as yet truly on offer. The need hereto, however, is obvious, as migrants, upon a couple of years of legal stay, may, like EU-citizens move freely in the Union. That should trigger the interest of one country in the policy and implementation of the other.

1st of May, 2004: decision-making

The 1st of May 2004 had triple relevance
1) Enlargement of the Union with 10 new Member States;
2) The end of the 5-year transition period under the Treaty of Amsterdam;
3) The assumed beginning of new decision-making procedures.

The first two aspects being obvious, it is the third point that deserves some elaboration, particularly as decision-making is a fairly sensitive and above all political and complex issue. Four dates are relevant: 1 May 1999 (the entry into force of the Treaty of Amsterdam); 1 February 2003 (the entry into force of the Treaty of Nice); 1 May 2004 (the end of the 5-year transition period as foreseen under the Treaty of Amsterdam)[4] and a future date related to the entry into force of a Convention/Constitution.

---

[4] Art. 67 as amended by the Treaty of Nice reads as follows:
Article 67
1. During a transitional period of five years following the entry into force of the Treaty of Amsterdam, the Council shall act unanimously on a proposal from the Commission or on the initiative of a Member State and after consulting the European Parliament.
2. After this period of five years:
   – the Council shall act on proposals from the Commission; the Commission shall examine any request made by a Member State that it submit a proposal to the Council,
   – the Council, acting unanimously after consulting the European Parliament, shall take a decision with a view to providing for all or parts of the areas covered by this title to be governed by the procedure referred to in Article 251 and adapting the provisions relating to the powers of the Court of Justice.
3. By derogation from paragraphs 1 and 2, measures referred to in Article 62(2)(b) (i) and (iii) shall, from the entry into force of the Treaty of Amsterdam, be adopted by the Council acting by a qualified majority on a proposal from the Commission and after consulting the European Parliament.

For most topics decision-making was and remains limited to (a) a Commission or Council proposal; (b) a unanimous Council decision; upon (c) consultation of the European Parliament. TEC, Article 67.1 clearly submits: During a transitional period of five years following the entry into force of the Treaty of Amsterdam, the Council shall act unanimously on a proposal from the Commission or on the initiative of a Member State and after consulting the European Parliament.

1 May 1999. This refers to TEC Article 67.3 in which *qualified majority* Council decisions are in place as from 1 May 1999 on two specific issues: 'measures referred to in Article 62(2)(b)(i) and (iii) shall, from the entry into force of the Treaty of Amsterdam, be adopted by the Council acting by a qualified majority on a proposal from the Commission and after consulting the European Parliament'. Article 62(2)(b)(i) refers to the list of third countries whose nationals must be in possession of visas when crossing the external borders and those whose nationals are exempt from that requirement; whereas paragraph (iii) refers to a uniform format for visas.

1 February 2003. With the entry into force of the Treaty of Nice a co-decision procedure under Article 251 TEC was introduced for some topics. By derogating from Article 67.1, the Council shall adopt, in accordance with the co-decision procedure referred to in Article 251, the measures provided for in Article 63(1) and (2)(a) provided that the Council has previously adopted, in accordance with paragraph 1 of this article, Community legislation defining the common rules and basic principles governing these issues and the measures provided for in Article 65 with the exception of aspects relating to family law.[5] Article 63.1 refers to

---

4. By derogation from paragraph 2, measures referred to in Article 62(2)(b) (ii) and (iv) shall, after a period of five years following the entry into force of the Treaty of Amsterdam, be adopted by the Council acting in accordance with the procedure referred to in Article 251.
5. By derogation from paragraph 1, the Council shall adopt, in accordance with the procedure referred to in Article 251:
   – the measures provided for in Article 63(1) and (2)(a) provided that the Council has previously adopted, in accordance with paragraph 1 of this article, Community legislation defining the common rules and basic principles governing these issues,
   – the measures provided for in Article 65 with the exception of aspects relating to family law.
PROTOCOL ON ARTICLE 67 OF THE TREATY ESTABLISHING THE EUROPEAN COMMUNITY THE HIGH CONTRACTING PARTIES HAVE AGREED UPON the following provision, which shall be annexed to the Treaty establishing the European Community (Sole Article):
From 1 May 2004, the Council shall act by a qualified majority, on a proposal from the Commission and after consulting the European Parliament, in order to adopt the measures referred to in Article 66 of the Treaty establishing the European Community.
   [5] TEC Art. 251:
   1. Where reference is made in this Treaty to this Article for the adoption of an act, the following procedure shall apply.
   2. The Commission shall submit a proposal to the European Parliament and the Council.
The Council, acting by a qualified majority after obtaining the opinion of the European Parliament:

'Dublin', the reception of asylum seekers, the qualification and the procedures, the very subjects of the directives contained in this Volume. The same is true for Article 63.2.a (conditions of entry and residence, and standards on procedures for the issue by Member States of long-term visas and residence permits, including those for the purpose of family reunion). In other words, now that common rules and basic principles have been agreed upon, further regulation is governed by the co-decision procedure under Article 251. This is indeed the case since 1 February 2003, not since 1 May 2004.

1 May 2004. The end of the transition period foreseen under the Treaty of Amsterdam is referred to in Article 67.2 TEC: After this period of five years (a)

---

if it approves all the amendments contained in the European Parliament's opinion, may adopt the proposed act thus amended; if the European Parliament does not propose any amendments, may adopt the proposed act; shall otherwise adopt a common position and communicate it to the European Parliament. The Council shall inform the European Parliament fully of the reasons which led it to adopt its common position. The Commission shall inform the European Parliament fully of its position.

If, within three months of such communication, the European Parliament: (a) approves the common position or has not taken a decision, the act in question shall be deemed to have been adopted in accordance with that common position; (b) rejects, by an absolute majority of its component members, the common position, the proposed act shall be deemed not to have been adopted; (c) proposes amendments to the common position by an absolute majority of its component members, the amended text shall be forwarded to the Council and to the Commission, which shall deliver an opinion on those amendments

3. If, within three months of the matter being referred to it, the Council, acting by a qualified majority, approves all the amendments of the European Parliament, the act in question shall be deemed to have been adopted in the form of the common position thus amended; however, the Council shall act unanimously on the amendments on which the Commission has delivered a negative opinion. If the Council does not approve all the amendments, the President of the Council, in agreement with the President of the European Parliament, shall within six weeks convene a meeting of the Conciliation Committee.

4. The Conciliation Committee, which shall be composed of the Members of the Council or their representatives and an equal number of representatives of the European Parliament, shall have the task of reaching agreement on a joint text, by a qualified majority of the Members of the Council or their representatives and by a majority of the representatives of the European Parliament. The Commission shall take part in the Conciliation Committee's proceedings and shall take all the necessary initiatives with a view to reconciling the positions of the European Parliament and the Council. In fulfilling this task, the Conciliation Committee shall address the common position on the basis of the amendments proposed by the European Parliament.

5. If, within six weeks of its being convened, the Conciliation Committee approves a joint text, the European Parliament, acting by an absolute majority of the votes cast, and the Council, acting by a qualified majority, shall each have a period of six weeks from that approval in which to adopt the act in question in accordance with the joint text. If either of the two institutions fails to approve the proposed act within that period, it shall be deemed not to have been adopted.

6. Where the Conciliation Committee does not approve a joint text, the proposed act shall be deemed not to have been adopted.

7. The periods of three months and six weeks referred to in this Article shall be extended by a maximum of one month and two weeks respectively at the initiative of the European Parliament or the Council.

the Council shall act on proposals from the Commission; the Commission shall examine any request made by a Member State that it submits a proposal to the Council; (b) the Council, acting unanimously after consulting the European Parliament, shall take a decision with a view to providing for all or parts of the areas covered by this title to be governed by the procedure referred to in Article 251 and adapting the provisions relating to the powers of the Court of Justice. The first of May 2004 has an impact on the 'initiative' rather than on the actual decision-making process.

New decision procedures can now be agreed upon by the Council itself. It may unanimously agree that certain topics will be covered by the qualified majority procedure. TEC Article 67.2 (2) reads: the Council, acting unanimously after consulting the European Parliament, shall take a decision with a view to providing for all or parts of the areas covered by this title to be governed by the procedure referred to in Article 251 and adapting the provisions relating to the powers of the Court of Justice. Moreover a/the forthcoming Convention/ Constitution will undoubtedly also shed new light on decision-making, the terms of 'qualified majority' in particular. In fact, neither the TEC nor the TEU with the Council as the main legislative body as yet live up to the *trias politica* principles as embedded in the Constitutions of the 25 EU Member States. Decision-making is a story that will be continued.

This Volume

The present Volume is meant to provide easy access to the Directives as they stand at the 1st of May, 2004. This indeed means that the two directives on which only political agreement had been reached (asylum procedures and students/ vocational training) have also been included. All efforts have been made to ensure that the text included here corresponds with the outcome of a lengthy procedure later in 2004. Yet, understandably perhaps, changes may occur and the reader is encouraged, when in doubt, to check with the Official Journal.

The texts of the Directives and a few other documents have been duly included, together with an extensive index.

To keep this Volume within limits, only the texts and the related memoranda have been included. The article by article explanation had to be omitted. The relevant Communications and the many other (often preceding) documents like Framework Decisions, London Resolutions, Joint Positions and Regulations can be found in the *Asylum Acquis Handbook* (2000), *The Migration Acquis Handbook* (2001) and the *Migration Acquis Update* (2002).[6] Also, for introduc-

---

[6] *Asylum Acquis Handbook:* ISBN 90 6704 122 X (Asser Press / Cambridge University Press); *Migration Acquis Handbook:* ISBN 90 6704 130 0 (Asser Press / Cambridge University Press); *Migration Acquis Update 2002*: without an ISBN number (it may be ordered through IOM Geneva or Vienna (e.g. <http://www.iomvienna.at/dynasite.php?mdsfid=73)>.

tions to the history of the acquis, JHA cooperation and so on, reference should be made to the *Asylum Acquis Handbook.*

This Volume does not touch upon the extensive Schengen Acquis. But for easy reference, some limited information is provided hereunder on the Schengen Acquis.

Finally, reference should also be made to the 1951 Refugee Convention, the UNHCR Handbook and the various UNHCR Executive Committee Conclusions on the one hand and e.g. the ILO Labour Migration Conventions and the 1990 Convention on Migrants Workers and Their Families on the other (texts and references to be found in the above-mentions *Handbooks*).

Schengen[7]

a) free movement

During the 1980s, a debate arose as to the meaning of the concept of free movement of persons. Some felt that this should apply to EU citizens only, which would involve retaining internal border checks in order to distinguish between citizens of the EU and non-EU nationals. Others argued in favour of free movement for everyone, which would mean an end to internal border checks altogether. Since the Member States found it impossible to reach an agreement, France, Germany, Belgium, Luxembourg and the Netherlands decided in 1985 to create a territory without internal borders. This became known as the Schengen area. The name was taken from the place in Luxembourg where the first agreements were signed. This intergovernmental cooperation expanded to include 13 countries in 1997. The 1997 Treaty of Amsterdam incorporated the decisions taken since 1985 by Schengen group members and the associated working structures into EU law on 1 May 1999.

As indicated, the first agreement between the five original group members was signed on 14 June 1985. A further convention was drafted and signed on 19 June 1990. When it came into effect in 1995, it abolished the internal borders of the signatory states and created a single external border where immigration checks for the Schengen area are carried out in accordance with a single set of rules. Common rules regarding visas, asylum rights and checks at external borders were adopted to allow the free movement of persons within the signatory states without disturbing law and order.

Accordingly, in order to reconcile freedom and security, this freedom of movement was accompanied by so-called compensatory measures. This involved improving coordination between the police, customs and the judiciary and taking the necessary measures to combat important problems such as terrorism and

---

[7] Based on: <http://www.europa.eu.int/scadplus/leg/en/lvb/l33020.htm>.

organised crime. In order to make this possible, a complex information system known as the Schengen Information System (SIS) was set up to exchange data on people's identities and descriptions of objects which are either stolen or lost.

Little by little the Schengen area has been extended to include 13 of the 15 Member States. Italy signed the agreement on 27 November 1990, Spain and Portugal joined on 25 June 1991, Greece followed on 6 November 1992, then Austria on 28 April 1995 and finally Denmark, Finland and Sweden joined on 19 December 1996.

Among the main measures are:

- the removal of checks at common borders, replacing them with external border control;
- a common definition of the rules for crossing external borders;
- separation in air terminals and ports of people travelling within the Schengen area from those arriving from countries outside the area;
- harmonisation of the rules regarding conditions of entry and visas for short stays;
- coordination between administrations on the surveillance of borders (liaison officers, harmonisation of instructions and staff training);
- defining the role of carriers in the fight against illegal immigration;
- the requirement for all non-EU nationals moving from one country to another to lodge a declaration;
- the drawing up of rules for asylum seekers (Dublin);
- the introduction of rights of surveillance and not pursuit;
- the strengthening of legal cooperation through a more expeditious extradition system and a quicker distribution of information concerning the implementation of criminal judgments;
- the creation of the Schengen Information System (SIS).[8]

---

[8] At present the Schengen Information System operates in 13 Member States and 2 non-Member States (Norway and Iceland). However, the system was not designed, and therefore lacks the capacity, to operate in as many Member States as there will be in the Union after enlargement. It is therefore necessary to develop a new second generation Schengen Information System (SIS II). The two decisions relating to SIS II (see hereunder) provide for the costs relating to the development of SIS II to be met by the general budget of the European Union, conforming to the Council conclusion of 29 May 2001.

To enable the future Member States to use the system, and to take account of the latest developments in information technology, the Council adopted on 6 December 2001 (a) Council Regulation (EC) No. 242/2001 on the development of the second generation Schengen information system (SIS II) based on Articles 66 of the Treaty establishing the European Community; (b) Council Decision 2001/866/JHA on the development of the second generation Schengen information system (SIS II) based on Articles 30(1), 31 and 34 of the Treaty on European Union. The reason for this distinction is that the purpose of the SIS is to improve police and judicial cooperation in criminal matters (covered by Title VI of the Treaty on European Union) and the policy on visas, immigration and the free movement of persons (covered by Title IV of the Treaty establishing the European Community). [Official Journal L 328 of 13.12.2001]. For more information on the SIS II functions regard could be had to e.g. 9715/04, 19 May 2004.

These measures, together with the decisions and declarations adopted by the Executive Committee set up by the 1990 implementing convention, the steps taken in order to implement the convention by the authorities on whom the Executive Committee conferred decision-making powers, the agreement signed on 14 June 1985, the convention implementing that agreement, signed on 19 June 1990, and the protocols and accession agreements which followed, constitute the Schengen acquis.

A protocol attached to the Treaty of Amsterdam incorporates the developments brought about by the Schengen agreement into the European Union framework. The Schengen area, which is the first concrete example of enhanced cooperation between 13 Member States, is now within the legal and institutional framework of the EU, thus coming under parliamentary and judicial scrutiny and attaining the objective of free movement of persons enshrined in the Single European Act of 1986 while ensuring democratic parliamentary control and providing citizens with accessible legal remedies when their rights are challenged (Court of Justice and/or national courts depending on the area of the law concerned).

In order to make this integration possible, the Council of the European Union took a number of decisions. First of all, as set out in the Treaty of Amsterdam, the Council took the place of the Executive Committee created under the Schengen agreement. On 1 May 1999, it established a procedure for incorporating the Schengen secretariat into the general secretariat of the Council including arrangements relating to Schengen secretariat staff [Official Journal L 119 of 07.05.1999]. Following this, new working groups were set up to help the Council manage the situation.[9]

b)   *The Schengen visa*

The entry into force of the Amsterdam Treaty in May 1999 incorporated the Schengen rules into the institutional framework of the European Union. Most of the matters in this field are decided by unanimity with the consultation of the European Parliament. Some matters, however, (visas issues and judicial cooperation in civil matters) are decided by qualified majority, in consultation or in co-decision with the European Parliament. Member States began to cooperate in the area of Justice and Home Affairs in the mid-1970s on an informal, intergovernmental basis outside the Community framework. In 1990, Germany, France and the Benelux countries signed the Schengen Agreement, which was an important step toward cooperation among the Member States in this area.

---

[9] A proposal, based on TEC art. 66 is contained in 9722/04 VISA COMIX 356. The Council adopted relevant conclusions on 19 February 2004 and on 8 June 2004 a Decision 'enabling the Commission to prepare the technical development of the Visa Information System' was formally adopted. See also COM (2003) 771.

In the following years, several Member States acceded to the Schengen Agreement. The aim of the agreement was to introduce genuine freedom of movement for persons without being controlled at internal borders, while providing for flanking measures in the fields of external border controls, visa policy, police cooperation and judicial cooperation in criminal matters.

Schengen stands for intensive and ever increasing cooperation. Related issues concern the following: the integration of the Schengen Acquis into the European Union, the Schengen catalogue on external borders, removal, and readmission, the Schengen Information Systems (SIS I and II), SIRENE (Supplément d'Informations Requis à l'Entrée Nationale, the national access to SIS systems; in the near future to be known as SISNET), police cooperation and indeed the issue of issuing visas.[10] For the visa system VIS will be set up, the Visa Information System.

A Schengen visa is a visa issued under the terms of the Schengen Agreement. Schengen is a small town in Luxembourg, close to the borders with France and Germany where a number of EU countries signed an agreement in 1985 in order to facilitate the free movement of persons within the EU area. The agreement came into force in 1995. Of the utmost importance is to note that membership of the EU does not automatically amount to partnership in the Schengen regime. It will last for a couple of years (2007, 2008) until the 10 new members will also fully embrace the Schengen membership.

A Schengen visa issued by any country under the Schengen rules will be valid for travel in all the Schengen countries. This means that one visa alone will enable the bearer to travel in all the 15 Schengen countries. The 15 Schengen countries are: Austria, Belgium, Denmark, Finland, France, Germany, Iceland, Italy, Greece, Luxembourg, the Netherlands, Norway, Portugal, Spain and Sweden. All these countries except Norway and Iceland are European Union members. The United Kingdom and Ireland are the two EU countries that do not implement the Schengen visa regime. Those wishing to travel to the United Kingdom or Ireland must thus apply for separate visas to enter those countries. However, in general, holders having valid Schengen visas will be issued with a visa for the United Kingdom or Ireland within a few days, or vice versa. A Schengen visa enables a person to visit one or several of the Schengen countries for business, tourism, visiting friends/relatives, etc., for a maximum of 90 days every six months.

Applications should be made to the Embassy/Consulate of the country which is the main destination of the journey. If the intention is to travel to several Schengen countries without having a main destination, one should apply for a visa to the Embassy/Consulate of the first country that one enters unless it is

---

[10] Details can be found on, e.g. <http://ue.eu.int/cms3_fo/showPage.asp?id=473&lang=EN&mode=g> and <http://www.eurovisa.info/BackgroundInfo.htm>.

merely a transit country. Honorary Consulates are not allowed to issue Schengen visas. All Schengen countries use the same type of visa sticker. The United Kingdom and Ireland also use the same type of sticker but it clearly states at the top of the sticker that its validity is only for Ireland or the United Kingdom, never the Schengen states. A holder of a residence permit to any of the Schengen countries may travel for three months to the other Schengen countries without having to obtain a Schengen visa. The processing time, especially for visas for businessmen, is normally no longer than a few days. Most Schengen Embassies have information about the Schengen visa, including requirements and application forms, on their websites.

A visa for business purposes will enable a person to visit business partners in order to discuss ongoing or future business relations, to market their products, take part in trade fairs, etc. Somebody who plans to take up a job or an assignment for a shorter or longer period of time will need a work/residence permit for that particular Schengen country.

Residence and work permits are still governed by the national law of each individual Schengen country. The work/residence permit will be processed by that country and under that country's law.[11]

B. EUROPE AND MIGRATION

Europe lacks a migration policy. Most actors seem to agree that migration should be considered as a given. Many submit that migration creates a win/ win situation, not only benefiting the individuals concerned but also the countries of origin and destination. They refer to ageing, the need for labour and the usefulness of remittances. In this part 2 of the Introduction it will be argued that non-migration may yield a far greater dividend than migratory movements.

'Citizens of the expanded European Union will begin to test the down to earth practicalities of 450 million people this week, after celebrations over the weekend marking the political unification of the Continent drew to a close.'

This was the front page leader story of the International Herald Tribune on Monday, 3 May 2004 (*'a new Europe gets ready for business'*). The report focused on companies now following the same rulebook and being able to sell their products throughout the Union. It also talked about EU residents shopping where they want. But of course, it underlined the main message of the enlargement, the lofty vision of cementing peace on a continent so often divided by conflict.

---

[11] This Volume does *not* contain the bulky Schengen Agreement *cum* Convention nor its various Implementation Agreements.

That same IHT issue (p. 2) also paid attention to the issue of migrants. It was argued that Western Europe should be eager to absorb workers from the new EU countries *as Europe needs more, not fewer, immigrants*. A UNFPA expert was quoted as saying that it is indeed rather difficult to explain why one needs immigrants when one does not have enough jobs to go around. The article focused on low fertility rates, the greying of the population at large, the baby-boomers on the eve of their retirement and the solution available: *European politicians already know what the real answer is: immigration*. Yet, it was acknowledged that the EU would need an average of 6.1 million immigrants a year and that by 2050 some 40% of the then EU population would be *recent immigrants or their offspring*. Craig Smith, a NYT journalist, submitted that *it would take concerted, discriminatory policies to prevent the natural demographic flow of the Arab world's excess labour to labour-hungry Europe*.

Indeed, the enlarged European Union woke up to a challenge. Is the question – as suggested in that IHT article – not so much whether Europe will be forced to accept more immigrants, but rather when, how many and from where? Are journalists, politicians and economists able to look beyond 2050, willing to face the consequences of reproductive health, social cohesion, globalization and freedom of movement? Has enough thought been given to the availability of alternatives?

It is not the case that the IHT opened new venues, or was innovative in any way. None other than Kofi Annan had presented similar views a few months earlier. Europe needs migrants to ensure a prosperous future and should stop using immigration as a scapegoat for its social problems, the UN Secretary-General told the European Parliament on 29 January 2004.[12] 'Migrants need Europe. But Europe also needs migrants. A closed Europe would be a meaner, poorer, weaker, older Europe. An open Europe will be a fairer, richer, stronger, younger Europe – provided you manage migration well', he said. He criticised the tone of the current debate on asylum and immigration in Europe, saying that migrants and asylum seekers were being vilified and dehumanised. Asylum systems were overburdened, said Mr Annan, because many people saw no other channel through which to migrate, sometimes resorting to human traffickers and falling into the hands of organised crime. Annan said that helping refugees was a legal and moral duty and urged the EU to set up a system of sharing res-ponsibility and ensuring asylum seekers receive fair treatment. He also urged the EU to offer greater avenues for legal immigration to Europe for skilled and unskilled workers, for family reunification and economic improvement – on a temporary and permanent basis.

---

[12] Kofi Annan received the Sakharov prize, EU's top human rights award, from the European Parliament on the same day. He accepted the prize on behalf of all the staff at the United Nations and in memory of special envoy Sergio Vieira de Mello and other officials who died as a result of the bomb attack at the UN office in Iraq in August 2003.

This Volume contains the Directives currently in place as of the 1ˢᵗ of May 2004. It concerns minimum norms, not harmonization as such. Neither do the Directives contain a clear-cut policy, not to mention a vision. The Directives were driven by the need to have some minimum norms in place by the end of the transition period foreseen under the Treaty of Amsterdam. The need for timely agreement was also obvious to prevent an even more cumbersome decision-making process as, in principle, 25 concurring votes are needed for a new directive, rather than 15. Moreover, once a Directive is in place, amendments and subsidiary regulations can be agreed upon with the qualified majority rule. Directives are now in place. Policies still need to be agreed upon.

lack of vision ('Immigration has always been easier to start than to stop'[13])

Asylum has changed over the last 50 years changed from a goal into a means, from badly needed protection into a safe haven from where the 'struggle' could be continued, organized, pursued and/or financed. Similarly, asylum also became the channel to be used in case legal migration was not an option, in other words not possible. Many of the asylum seekers were in fact migrants, looking for jobs and a better future, in itself a legitimate goal albeit that no (human) right to migration in general has been agreed upon. Now that most procedures have been streamlined (the *economy of procedures* stands central) and information on countries of origin has improved, resulting in restricted numbers of recognitions, possible profits from using the asylum channel for migratory purposes have diminished. The number of would-be migrants entering Europe, however, has remained stable. To put it bluntly, migrants no longer register as asylum seekers but join the growing army of illegals, irregulars, the numbers of which are now calculated at 5-8 million. Europe needs to determine exactly what it wants. Is migration the answer to its needs?

ageing

Coleman (Oxford) submitted at the Cairo+10 UNECE/UNFPA Conference (Geneva, January 2004) that there is no 'solution' to an ageing population short of a return to much higher rates of population growth or mass age-specific euthanasia. The problem is that the effect is not very great and immigration is an inefficient way of achieving this end. Immigrants themselves age and the country then requires more immigrants, as it were, to replace their number. Immigration cannot solve the problems of population ageing except at rates of immigration so high that they would generate economically and environmentally unsustainable

---

[13] Coleman's Cairo+10 contribution: (Keynote address on Population and Development in Europe during the last decade: an academic's overview): Facing the 21st Century. New developments, continuing problems (the full text can be found on the unece.org website).

population growth rates and permanently and radically change the cultural and ethnic composition of the host population. The population size consequent on the migration needed to preserve the current potential in the UK would double to 120 million by 2050 because the UK would be importing 1.2 million persons per year. By 2100, up to five million new immigrants would be needed every year and the UK population would have risen to 312 million.[14]

Of course, the retirement challenge needs to be addressed. Now that most experts agree that migration is not the answer, consideration must be given to (a) working up to the age of 65, 67 or even 70; (b) working longer hours (40 instead of 36); (c) salary decreases beyond the age of 55, possibly combined with less work (e.g., a 66% salary for a four-day working week, or a 50% salary for a three-day working week).[15] Most European Governments have understood the message. The Trade Unions, however, generally object. It is worth explaining that non-migration would ultimately improve the salaries and status of their members.

smaller populations

Apart from the idea that bigger populations mean more power (presumably through larger armed forces or a stronger economy), there is in principle nothing wrong with decreasing populations. Of course, people want to become richer, and the fear is justified that with less 'producers' less products will be on the market. It is then forgotten that productivity has increased steadily over the last 500 years or so, and there is no reason to suspect that productivity would suddenly stop doing so. Yet, two important conditions then need to be met: (i) sufficient creative and innovative engineering capabilities are to be available to replace labour with capital, that is to introduce new machineries; and (ii) qualified managers must introduce better processing and must continuously streamline procedures. Innovation is the key word, and Europe should invest heavily in ensuring that the replacement of labour by capital will remain a major option. Subject to that condition decreasing populations might still enjoy growing productivity. If only 'space' were not such a scarce commodity.[16]

Alternatively, it should be appreciated that a yearly increase in a population by a mere 1% will result in doubling the population in 72 years. For Europe that

---

[14] Coleman also refers to the *Korea Syndrome*: The *reductio ad absurdum* of all this is what one might call the 'Korea syndrome': the level of immigration required in order to preserve the current potential support ratio in the Republic of Korea and its consequences for population growth. In order to preserve Korea's present potential support ratio (10: 1) the population would need to increase to 6.2 billion people by the year 2050. Just by coincidence, this happens to be the entire population of the planet at the present time, so we would all have to go there.

[15] By 55, statistically speaking, most parents can 'breath': children leave school, the mortgage has been paid off, and some heritage money may be coming in.

[16] Remarkably, the Netherlands, in 2002-2003, combined increased unemployment with increased productivity.

would mean that by 2100 the EU-25 will have one billion inhabitants, and that the global population will reach the 25 billion mark by 2150. A prospect that deserves some thought?

jobs available, jobs needed

Europe has during the last two centuries moved from mainly agriculture to manufacturing and to service industries. Today, thanks to effective communication and transportation, most production can take place on far-away shores. What is needed nearby are health, education, infrastructure and retail. Infrastructure entails construction (roads, offices, housing) but also communication (trains, aircraft, cars, telecom) and general upkeep (repairs, cleaning). Of the four mentioned here, health and education are least prone to productivity increases.

agriculture

Moving agriculture, manufacturing and even, for instance, back-office jobs to countries outside Europe creates win/win situations.

Subsidies should be considered as the scourge of any international economic system: the EU alone spends, every day, $150 million on agricultural subsidies. This comes and goes at the cost of the economies of many developing or less developed countries. Countries that should be able to export their products are now forced to export their workforce. It is about tomatoes, not about the tomato-picker. Or, in other words, should the people move to where the capital is, or, rather, should capital move to where the people are?

The recent Brazil/WTO case (on subsidies paid to US cotton farmers) is of the utmost importance in this respect. More than ever, the migration 'lobby' should display an interest in such cases as it should in the subsidy issue at large. In the absence of subsidies, more producers will move production to low-income 'good weather' countries. This is already true for the Dutch flower industry, an industry without subsidies, and perfectly suitable to make use of the globalization processes, thereby benefiting producers, labour and consumers all at the same time.

manufacturing

As for manufacturing it can be submitted that once a manufacturer has reached the margins of profit, and is, e.g., faced with labourers who demand an increase in salary, three alternatives are available:
– by hiring migrant labour (including illegals) the manufacturer can avoid the demand/supply reality and can continue profitable production, thanks to relatively low labour costs

– by replacing labour with capital, the manufacturer can make a sound long-
  term investment, making use of the available innovation possibilities (thereby
  also promoting investments in innovative thinking at large)
– in the end the manufacturer can move the site of manufacturing to a low-
  labour-cost country.

Of the three alternatives, the first is by far the worst scenario as it delays the
introduction of innovative processes and procedures and because it delays
moving the site by a couple of years, at the cost of the consumer. The
introduction of innovative ideas or machinery benefits all, and the transfer of
production is an obvious blessing for Third World economies.

back-office

It is probably even more surprising to learn that also moving so-called back-
office activities (keeping files, administration, accounting, auditing) to low
income countries can be a very profitable exercise, that is: profitable to all. The
Economist, in its 13 December 2003 issue, calculated that the transfer of 1 dollar
worth of back office work from the USA to India would give India 33 dollar
cents and the USA no less than $1.12, making a total profit of 45%. This, it
should be added, includes re-employment.[17]

development aid

It is a well known yet staggering fact that the total of ODA (Official Development Assistance) covers a mere 35% of the total losses incurred by Third
World countries because of those countries not being able to export products to
the North/West as a result of tariffs and other export/import hindrances. It should
then be added that the OECD has allowed the reception costs of asylum seekers
who have come to the North/West to be considered as part of the ODA. It could
hence be argued that many countries would be better off without development
aid, but with their products having access to the markets of the North/West.

stell dich vor

In the 1970s quite a few cars in Germany had a bumper sticker that said *Stell dich
vor es gibt Krieg und keiner geht hin* (try and imagine, there is a war, and nobody

---

[17] India: labour: 0.10; profits retained in India: 0.10; suppliers 0.09; central government taxes
0.03; state government taxes: 0.01. Net benefit to India: 0.33. USA: savings accruing to US inves-
tors/customers: 0.58; imports of US goods and services by providers in India: 0.05; transfer of profits by US-based providers in India back to US: 0.04; Net direct benefit retained in US 0.67; Value
from US labour re-employed 0.45 – 0.47. Potential net benefit to US: 1.12-1.14. Source: The Economist, 13 December 2003.

joins[18]). Similarly, more research is needed into the alternative to non-migration ('migrants are needed and no one comes'). It is hereby submitted that in the case of migrants staying at home, all parties might be better off – the individuals as well as the countries of origin and destination. This is because the transfer of industries, agriculture and back-office jobs to low income or more productive countries would be much speedier, which ultimately substantially benefits the global economic development. It is about moving capital, rather than moving people.

remittances

Yet, there is much talk about the usefulness of remittances. Also the Worldbank subscribes to the idea that remittances represent significant numbers. Migrants provide huge flows of remittances to their countries, amounting to an estimated US$ 80 billion annually (in 2002), or the second largest source of external funding for developing countries. However, the total losses seem to become lost in the debate. Reference should be made to: (a) the use of the funds concerned; (b) the durability of those transfers; (c) the impact of 'dual loyalty' on integration and related processes; and (d) loss of human capital.

ad a) Many of the funds made available through remittances are used for consumption (cars, luxury goods, housing), often as part of a secondary pension fund. Of course, more often than not, the local economy benefits, but in some areas remittances used for the construction of housing often results in an increase in construction costs, which in turn disadvantages those who do not have migrants in their family.

ad b) The durability is questionable. Those who do not marry someone from the same area/country are not necessarily tempted to invest in the country of origin of just one partner; often emphasis on educating the children results in changing saving-patterns. In other words, the sustainability greatly depends on newcomers, on ongoing migratory patterns. Once no new migrants are welcome, remittances are bound to decrease. It would be surrealistic to insist on ongoing migration for the sake of remittances.

ad c) The idea behind remittances portrays an ongoing link between the migrant and the country of origin. In the case of permanent migration (contrary to temporary migration) this would be contrary to an all-integration approach, whereby the migrant focuses for the full 100% on the country of residence. It could hence be argued that supporting the transfer of savings to the country of origin rather than investing in the country of destination would be coun-terproductive to the all-integration-approach – although no results are available from research – if any – into this linkage.

---

[18] Originally from a Berthold Brecht poem/song. That poem, however takes a different turn: '... dann kommt der Krieg zu euch ... '

ad d) Migrants tend to work – at least during the first years – below their educational and skills levels. Recent studies in Canada have indicated that for that country alone the loss involved would amount to some CND$ 5 to 25 billion on a yearly basis. The inclusion of these 'fringe benefits' should enable us to draw a picture which is far more complete than hitherto provided.

dirty jobs

What remains to be done *in situ* is mainly limited to education, health, retail and infrastructure. The latter includes construction, communication and maintenance. Indeed, many of the jobs involved are the heavy and dirty ones, positions now often filled by migrants, legal and illegal. This is the case in spite of the significant unemployment rates in Europe as a whole. As usual, market mechanisms should be allowed to play its role. That means on the one hand that salaries for these jobs need to be appealing, but also that social welfare benefits need to be at such a level that actual work always acts as an incentive.

In migratory circles it is well known that a salary difference of 30% and more will trigger migration. It could be submitted that the difference between benefits and salaries should also be in the 30% range to make an impact on the individual decision- making process.

flexibility

In early May 2004, a conference on 'Co-ordination of Social Security in an Enlarged Europe' focused on a new employment regulation, under which unemployed people will be able to seek work in another EU country much more easily by 'exporting' their social welfare entitlements. Member States may allow unemployed people to bring their social welfare entitlements from their home country to the EU country where they are seeking work. This is an important piece of social legislation and it should have an impact on the employment, unemployment and intra-European migratory movements, as well as migration from third countries. This regulation protects the social security rights of people who move, for whatever reason, private or professional, from one Member State to another. If the fight against unemployment is indeed considered to be a priority for the Union, this new regulation represents a major achievement.

Europe is faced with an unemployment rate of probably well over 10%. The EU-15 at the time of the enlargement had an unemployment figure of almost 9%. Efforts need to be taken to ensure the highest possible labour market participation rate. This is of importance for the economy, demographic developments as well as financial aspects, like building up viable pension schemes.

If migration comes into this equation, consideration needs to be given to issues like the levels of social welfare, the need to accept jobs well below perceived levels and in particular training and education towards the needs of the labour market. Europe cannot afford the hiring of migrants as long as too many unemployed have no chance of finding employment. Indeed, intra-European migratory movements may have some impact on the European labour market as a whole. However, experiences in, e.g., Germany have shown that in spite of over 10% unemployment levels in some of the Eastern *Länder* and the need for labour in the South, intra-German movements have hitherto been minimal.

the need for highly skilled labour

Europe has become lazy. Most people enjoy early retirement, 36-hour working weeks and 6 weeks annual leave. Moreover, the educational systems have become the victims of their own success. They produce grades, diplomas and degrees, but not necessarily the skills and experts Europe truly needs. Europe needs engineers, not administrators. R&D budgets need to be increased. Of course, a service industry has different needs and needs different people than economies based on agriculture or manufacturing. Yet, at a time when over 400,000 experts found work in the USA, Europe should rethink its educational and R&D policies. Meanwhile, Europe might indeed be in need of some highly skilled experts to bail the European countries out. That type of utilitarian approach should result in flexibility as to the granting of visas, labour and residence permits. The successful migrants move on or move back. The unsuccessful ones more often than not stay put. Policies reflecting the above deserve to be developed.

trust

Economies tend to boom on the basis of trust. In 1995 Fukuyama, best known for his '*The End of History*' (1992) published an important book on '*Trust*'. Fukuyama argues that for an economy to boom and for a society to prosper aspects like trust and social cohesion are indispensable. Societal developments, interaction and group dynamics are far more important than hitherto believed:

'economic activity represents a crucial part of life and is knit together by a wide variety of norms, rules, moral obligations, and other habits that together shape the society (...); one of the most important lessons we can learn from an examination of economic life is that a nation's well-being, as well as its ability to compete, is conditioned by a single, pervasive characteristic: the level of *trust* inherent in the society' [p. 7].

'There are three paths to sociability: the first is based on family and kinship; the second on voluntary associations outside kinship such as schools, clubs, and professional organisations, and the third is the state. There are three forms of economic organisation corresponding to each path: the family business, the professionally managed corporation, and the state-owned or –sponsored enterprise. The first and third paths, it turns out, are closely related to one another: cultures in which the primary avenue toward sociability is family and kinship have a great deal of trouble creating large, durable economic organisations and therefore look to the state to initiate and support them' [p. 62].

In fact, Fukuyama displays his doubts concerning multicultural societies. And indeed, in the migration debate it is often forgotten that migrant workers do not only come to work, but are human beings with their own life-style and their own interests, goals and ideas. It is herewith submitted that due to the substantial numbers involved, actual segregation has in some cities taken place, is taking place in others or is about to take place altogether. This is bound to have a serious negative impact on interaction, intercultural relations and hence on trust, with all the negative results for society and the economy at large.

concluding remarks

Close to half of all migrants and refugees worldwide – or some 86 million adults – are economically active, employed or otherwise engaged in remunerative activity, according to the International Labour Office (ILO). The number of migrants crossing borders in search of employment and human security is expected to increase rapidly in the coming decades due to the failure of globalization to provide jobs and economic opportunities.

'If you look at the global economy from the perspective of people, its biggest structural failure is the inability to create enough jobs where people live', said ILO Director-General, Juan Somavia. 'We should consider ways of providing decent work to this vast flow of migrants through multilateral actions and policies'.

The issue of migration is now high on the international agenda. A recent report by the World Commission on the Social Dimension of Globalization placed migration at the top of its recommendations and a Global Commission on International Migration (GCIM) has begun work to prepare recommendations for the UN Secretary-General and other stakeholders. In 2006, the High-Level Dialogue of the United Nations General Assembly will be devoted to the issue of migration and development.

It is to be hoped that the 1975 dictum will be kept in mind and that the need will be emphasized '... to avoid the excessive and uncontrolled or unassisted increase of migratory movements because of their negative social and human consequences ...'. In order to overcome underdevelopment and structural and chronic unemployment, the governments of many countries increasingly and rightly stress '... the desirability of encouraging the transfer of capital and technology, rather than the transfer of workers...'.[19]

---

[19] From the Preamble of the 1975 ILO Labour Migration Convention (C159).

C.   BEYOND 2004

In this part C of the Introduction some attention is devoted to those articles of the Directives that will continue to give rise to debate. An effort has also been made to describe what can be expected in the years 2004-2010. Attention has been paid to the relevant June 2004 Communication and the UNHCR EU-pronged proposal. Also the Danish approach will be high-lighted.

Agreement

Above, it has been indicated that two of the Directives contained in this Volume have been the subject of political agreement only. Formal agreement will most probably be forthcoming in the autumn of 2004.

Regard should also be had to the very fact that the European Parliament has started a procedure at the European Court of Justice on the Family Reunification directive (see below). Of particular concern is that a maximum age may be agreed upon which is well below the age of majority. A similar fate may await the Directive on procedures, in particular the aspects dealing with the safe third country concept.

Amendments

The proof is in the eating. Most Directives contain an article to the effect that the Commission shall propose any amendments that are necessary. In fact such a proposal may already be part of the report which the Commission has to submit 2 years after the date of the adoption of the directive concerned to the European Parliament and the Council.

Such proposals, however, may greatly depend on the views and experiences of the Member States themselves. Each Member State shall appoint a national contact point with the aim of direct cooperation and exchange of information between the competent authorities. These national contact points should be considered to be instrumental towards evaluating the usefulness and effectiveness of the various directives. Any proposal to amend a directive should refer to or, as the case may be, be based on such evaluations. Needless to add that amendments are subject to the qualified majority decision-making.

Stand-still clause

Of great interest is the notion proposed by many to impose on certain countries a stand-still clause. That, in fact, would mean that that country would not be allowed to amend its national legislation in such a way that it would fall below the earlier standards in that country, even if the proposed standards would be well above the minimum norms as laid down in the directives. This, in fact is the case with the proviso to deal with children over 15 years of age as 'independent' applicants, not falling under the Family Reunification Directive (Art. 4.6). Also, the Procedures Directive (art. 35.2) is of relevance.

Such an approach might create misunderstandings and *de facto* inequality: it would make approximation a virtually impossible exercise as any new level should in that case be on or above the level of the country faced with such a stand-still obligation, well above the minimum levels agreed upon.

The Court

On 2 December 2003, the Legal Affairs Committee of the European Parliament decided to lodge a complaint to the European Court of Justice (ECJ) regarding the Family Reunification Directive (see chapter 2.5). The complaint concerns both procedure and contents. The ECJ is so empowered, based on the Treaty of Nice, in force since 1 February 2003, in conjunction with TEC Article 230.[20]

Political agreement on this Directive was reached on 27 February 2003. It was formally adopted by the Council on 22 September 2003. Formal agreement does not amount to 'adoption'. The European Parliament did not formally adopt its opinion until 9 April 2003. The Opinion concerned had no impact on the text: the Parliament's proposals, as is so often the case, were more or less ignored. The Parliament referred to both ECHR Article 8 and to the Charter of Fundamental Rights Article 7 and Article 33. The complaint shall deal with the contents. The outcome of the procedures will also be of great importance for the decision-making processes in general.

The outcome of the complaint procedure will be awaited with great interest. This is in particular the case as, for instance, the Procedures Directive may await a similar fate.

Main issues

The main issues that will be carefully scrutinized are most probably:
–   family reunification, the maximum age of the child (art. 4.6; every benchmark is discretionary, but it is a fact that the older the child, the more difficult the integration process will be)

---

[20] Art. 230, first part, reads as follows: The Court of Justice shall review the legality of acts adopted jointly by the European Parliament and the Council, of acts of the Council, of the Commission and of the ECB, other than recommendations and opinions, and of acts of the European Parliament intended to produce legal effects vis-à-vis third parties.

It shall for this purpose have jurisdiction in actions brought by a Member State, the European Parliament, the Council or the Commission on grounds of lack of competence, infringement of an essential procedural requirement, infringement of this Treaty or of any rule of law relating to its application, or misuse of powers.

- family reunification, the so-called dependents who are over 21 years old (art. 4.2.b, on adult unmarried children; art. 4.2.a on grandparents, ascending line)
- family formation: (art. 4.5; 21 or 24 as a minimum age?)
- the issue of travel documents for the ones who receive subsidiary protection (Qualification, art. 25).
- the concept of safe third countries
- accelerated and border procedures
- the administration as an appeal body v. the judiciary
- safe countries of origin (quod non)
- illegal residence and undeclared work
- the actual taking the fingerprints of those who do not apply for asylum but are found to be illegally present on the territory of a Member State and its various consequences.

Of greater importance, though, will be the debates on long-term policies, integration and return.

Policies

It should be stressed once again that the Directives represent minimum norms. The road towards approximation, not to speak of harmonization, is a long and winding one.[21] Of course, every now and then the Commission produces Communications, some of which even more relevant than others. A full list of these Communications has been given in Chapter 3.1.b. Although the Communications are very informative indeed and have been quite successful in that they were meant as discussion papers, no long-term vision has hitherto been presented. It is herewith submitted that before Europe can truly embark on the road towards harmonization, serious efforts need to be undertaken to agree on a long-term view on both asylum and migration in the European and global context. Issues like population and development, development and migration, population and growth, labour and entitlements all need to be tackled. A holistic approach is badly needed, in short linking migration issues with the social welfare policies of the various Member States.[22] It is in this respect to be regretted that the High Level Working Group (HLWG) has not been allowed to live up to the various expectations, as it was uniquely positioned to deal with migration and asylum in an environment where also security, foreign relations, trade and other global issues could be dealt with. Moreover, short-term solutions may create long-term problems.

---

[21] See for an overview through 2000, De Jong in *The Asylum Acquis Handbook*, p. 21 ff.

[22] In this context, the EU Employment and Social Policy reports are of relevance. See also the Council Decisions on Guidelines for Member States' employment policies.

Commission

In its *June 2004 Communication* on the assessment of the Tampere programme
and future orientations (a need for 'Tampere 2' ?), the Commission presents a
fairly neutral non-committal view. In all fairness it would appear to lack vision:

– Promote a genuine common policy for the management of migratory flows:
There must be a realistic approach taking account of economic and demographic
needs, to facilitate the legal admission of immigrants to the Union, in accordance
with a coherent policy respecting the principle of fair treatment of third-country
nationals. It is clear that the right of Member States to set the actual numbers of
third-country nationals admitted to work in an employed or self-employed
capacity will have to be maintained, within an overall framework including the
respect of Community preference. The interests of countries of origin should be
taken into account. Integration policy, concerning third-country nationals, will
have to be promoted and continued. In this perspective, the Union must put
adequate measures in place in order to support the action of Member States. The
credibility of a positive and open common approach to immigration will also
very much depend on the ability of the European Union to control illegal
immigration. Combating trafficking in human beings more strongly, and the
development of an effective policy on returns and readmission, will be facilitated
by the future Constitutional Treaty. Here, as elsewhere, the effectiveness of the
action will largely depend on strong solidarity.

– Develop a common European asylum policy on a fair basis:
A better balance between the efforts made by the Member States in the reception
of refugees and displaced persons will be achieved by means of the principle of
solidarity. An approach based on partnership and cooperation with third countries
of origin and of transit, countries of first asylum request and of destination, will
have to be established. The main objective of the common European asylum
system will be to determine a uniform asylum and subsidiary protection status, a
common procedure for granting and withdrawing this status, and a common
system of temporary protection. At the same time there is a need for an integrated
approach involving efficient administrative decision-making procedures on
returns, reintegration schemes and entry procedures that deter unfounded requests
and combat networks of people traffickers. This approach is all the more
important as the victims of abuses of the system are often genuine refugees.

– Establish a European judicial area respecting the legal traditions and systems of
the Member States, and closely associating those working in relevant areas:
The development of the European judicial area has neither the object nor the
effect of challenging the legal and judicial traditions of the Member States. This
approach, based on the proportionality and subsidiarity principles, is stated by the

draft Constitutional Treaty. The principle of mutual recognition has been placed at the heart of European integration in this field. However, mutual recognition requires a common basis of shared principles and minimum standards, in particular in order to strengthen mutual confidence. In order to ensure the effectiveness of the European policy on judicial matters it will remain necessary to maintain a high degree of involvement on the part of those working in this field.

UNHCR: the EU-pronged Proposal[23]

In the context of long-term policies, reference should be made and praise should be given to the UNHCR's prong approach. At the Dublin January 2004 meeting the High Commissioner for Refugees presented a forward-looking view on how the EU might face the various forthcoming challenges. In fact, the UNHCR proved to be far more visionary than the Commission or the Council for that matter, and it should be regretted that the Commission in its June 2004 Communication did not refer to the UNHCR's January 2004 prong approach.

In June 2003, the UNHCR presented a three-pronged proposal in the context of a dialogue with European Union Member States. The proposal contained elements on improving access to solutions in regions of origin and on improving domestic asylum systems, as well as a so-called 'EU-prong'. The latter aimed to encourage EU Member States to address the phenomenon of mixed movements of asylum-seekers and economic migrants by processing jointly presumed manifestly-unfounded asylum claims from selected non-refugee producing countries of origin. In light both of considerations relating to the earlier proposals and new thinking about asylum developments in Europe, the UNHCR revised its original proposal.

The proposed revision endeavours to take into account:
- the concerns of future EU States at the external borders of the enlarged EU likely to be most affected by the implementation of Dublin II and Eurodac;
- the concerns of EU Member States, particularly those relating to mixed migratory flows and the return of those not in need of international protection; and
- the longer-term objective of the EU harmonisation process to establish a common European asylum system.

The 'prong' is presented as a move towards responsibility-sharing within the EU in the provision of reception, decision-making and durable solutions for asylum-

---

[23] Based on the EU-prong text as found on <http://www.unhcr.ch/cgi-bin/texis/vtx/rsd/rsddocview.pdf? CATEGORY=RSDLEGAL&id=400e85b84&FILETYPE=pdf> and last consulted on 4 June 2004.

seekers and refugees. In short, it proposes the processing of certain categories of asylum claims in EU Reception Centres. Those recognised to be in need of international protection in this process would be settled in participating EU Member States in accordance with agreed burden-sharing criteria, whilst those found not to be in need of international protection would be returned promptly to their respective countries of origin under joint EU operations supported by an international organisation such as the International Organisation for Migration (IOM). Other categories of asylum seekers would continue to be assessed under the national system applicable in the Member State responsible for assessing the claim. These arrangements would be established in an incremental manner and are outlined in the paragraphs below. Structural elements include the creation of EU Reception Centres and an EU Asylum Agency, their legal basis being determined by one or more Council Regulations or Decisions.

Prong: Registration and pre-screening

The UNHCR's revised EU-pronged proposal recommends that registration and pre-screening be moved progressively from a matter implemented at national level to one that is carried out at the EU level. Initially, therefore, these processes would continue to be carried out by national officers, assisted if necessary by staff made available through the EU Asylum Agency, where capacity is lacking or systems become overwhelmed by an influx.

Prong: Categories of asylum claims to be assessed in EU Reception Centres

In order to determine which asylum applications should be assessed at EU Reception Centres, the UNHCR suggests that caseloads be identified either in relation to measures needed to ensure the effective implementation of Dublin II and Eurodac and/or on the basis of the asylum seekers' country of origin. Categories of asylum claims which EU Member States could consider processing in EU Reception Centres would include:
- caseloads in EU Member States where the number of transfers under Dublin II and the effect of Eurodac threaten to jeopardise the effective implementation of these instruments;
- caseloads present in several EU Member States from countries of origin whose asylum seekers are regularly rejected in high numbers in destination States; and/or
- caseloads present in several EU Member States from countries of origin, which warrant the pooling of resources to determine status because of their complexity.

In this way, States could pool and share their expertise and experience. If all asylum claims in the particular category concerned were determined at the same

Centre (or group of Centres if the numbers of applications warrant this), this should reduce pressure for irregular secondary movements.

Prong: Process to determine the claims of selected caseloads in EU Reception Centres

It is envisaged that decision-making in the EU Reception Centres would lead to a uniform status for those in need of international protection valid throughout the Union.

Procedures and decision-making would involve first instance decisions being made in an interim phase by national officers of the State concerned, supported by officials, interpreters, etc., seconded by the EU Asylum Agency and, at a later stage, directly by EU officers of the EU Asylum Agency; and appeals decided, in an interim phase, on the basis of the national system in place in the Member State concerned (if necessary, supported by the EU Asylum Agency) and, at a later stage, by an independent EU Asylum Review Board created under an appropriate instrument determining its composition and mandate.

Prong: Settlement through burden-sharing arrangements of those found to be in need of international protection

Settlement of those found to be in need of international protection in EU Member States on the basis of agreed criteria represents a key element of the UNHCR's proposal. Otherwise the potentially overwhelming burden of hosting *and* integrating persons in need of international protection is likely to fall largely on EU Member States at the external borders of the Union. Asylum seekers' awareness that cases recognised in EU Reception Centres would end up being settled among all Member States, rather than just in the Member State hosting the EU Reception Centre would represent an incentive for applicants to remain in the Reception Centre to which they have been assigned until a decision is taken, thus reducing pressure for onward irregular movement among Member States.

Prong: Return of those not in need of international protection to countries of origin

Collective action by EU Member States to ensure the prompt return of those found not to be in need of international protection to their countries of origin would allow the burden of returning rejected cases to be addressed jointly. Readmission agreements, complemented by the Directive on the mutual recognition of return decisions and other supportive incentives represent important components. Collective action by EU Member States is advantageous for the following reasons:

- prior negotiation of readmission agreements helps ensure rejected cases can be transferred promptly and under acceptable conditions;
- such negotiations are facilitated by the joint political weight of the EU and Member States;
- rejected asylum seekers from the same country of origin can be held together (and if likely to abscond, detained) before deportation and returned more easily as a group.

Prong: Role of international organisations and other actors

Collective EU action along the lines outlined above would enable the EU to take advantage of support and assistance from international organisations and non-governmental organisations (NGOs), including local civil society groups. It also includes the UNHCR's supervisory and monitoring role under its Statute in conjunction with Article 35 of the 1951 Refugee Convention.

EU Asylum Agency

The creation of an EU Asylum Agency represents an integral element of the UNHCR revised proposal. Like the recently agreed EU Agency for the Management of Operational Cooperation at External Borders, endorsed in November 2003 by the Council of Ministers, the EU Asylum Agency could set up offices in the different Member States as well as its headquarters in one Member State. Staff would initially be seconded from national immigration or asylum agencies and, as the Agency expands, then be independently recruited. The initial functions of the Agency would essentially be related to capacity building and the provision of support, with these functions expanding as it became established.

EU Reception Centres within the EU

The prong proposal also envisages the establishment of Reception Centres for asylum seekers
within the EU. A number of such centres could, for instance, be located close to the land and sea borders of the EU to facilitate reception and return. Asylum seekers would be hosted in such centres for the determination of their claims both from within the EU Member State where the Centre was situated and from other EU Member States on the basis of an appropriate arrangement.

Legal basis: EC Regulation(s) or Decision(s)

The legal basis for the proposals outlined above would need to be set out in one or more Council Regulations or Decisions. These would represent 'measures on refugees and displaced persons', which 'promote a balance of effort between Member States in receiving and bearing the consequences of receiving refugees and displaced persons', as envisaged in Article 63(2b) of the Consolidated Treaty. Two phases of implementation are envisaged, initially involving joint (inter-State) processing under the national law of the State where the EU Reception Centre is located and in conformity with EC Regulations and international standards. This pooling of decision-making and resources could later pave the way for collective EU processing by the EU Asylum Agency. As these mechanisms are gradually instituted, (an) instrument(s) will of course be needed to regulate the various matters.

Integration

The post-9/11 world is increasingly concerned about the non-integration of a great many migrants now residing in the EU. Multiculturalism, promoted during many years as the positive and constructive answer to migration in general, is now the subject of intense scrutiny. Marginalization in a labour market that appears to be focused on the skilled, rather than the unskilled, threatens to shake the fabric of some societies. Enzensbergers's doom-scenario is now no longer automatically referred to the trash can.[24]

When it boils down to the interpretation of TEC Article 63, it is recalled that it touches on the issue of conditions of residence. That could well mean that integration too will be the subject of a forthcoming Communication and Directive. The Member States have and will actively object to 'Brussels' dictating minimum norms on this sensitive issue. It is herewith nevertheless submitted that such steps can be expected in the fairly near future.

Return

Article 63.3.b refers to the repatriation of illegal residents. Those whose application for asylum has been rejected, the so-called *rejectees*, may sooner or later turn into illegal residents as well. Most observers now agree that return is of the utmost importance. On the international level there is no misunderstanding of the principles at stake.[25]

---

[24] See Enzensberger's *Aufsichten auf den Bürgerkrieg*, 1994.

[25] Cairo Program of Action (1994, par. 10.20): 'Governments of countries of origin of undocumented migrants and persons whose asylum claims have been rejected have the responsibility to accept the return and reintegration of those persons';

GA Resolution 56/137 (2001): '... Emphasizes the obligation of all States to accept the return of their nationals, calls upon all States to facilitate the return of their nationals who have been determined not to be in need of international protection ...';

UNHCR (ExCom), Conclusion C, 2003: '... Reaffirms [...] the obligation of States to receive back their own nationals, including the facilitation thereof, and remains seriously concerned, as re-

Yet most now also agree that measures promoting return (both 'encouraging' and 'repressive') will hardly have any impact as long as the individual concerned will enjoy *de facto* access to the labour market and/or public services. An integrated approach is hence being promoted whereby it is acknowledged that an approach based on aliens law and aliens policy alone cannot be successful. As the Netherlands Advisory Committee on Aliens Affairs has formulated it, not just aspects pertaining to laws regarding foreign nationals play a role in returning illegal immigrants and rejected asylum seekers but also – and mainly – socio-economic factors. It is an illusion that a return policy can be effective if millions of illegal immigrants find employment in the EU and, frequently, also have access to public facilities and provisions. For this reason it is important to put in place greater controls and impose more severe penalties, on a Europe-wide basis, on the hiring of illegal immigrants. As to the denial of public services reference, of course, has been made to the minimum norms as laid down in ECHR, Article 3.[26]

Of course, the Temporary Protection Directive pays ample attention to the subject of return. Yet, the spirit behind the articles concerned display a non-utilitarian attitude that should not be repeated in a forthcoming return directive.

The Danish experience

Following a June 1992 referendum in Denmark on the Treaty of the European Union, that country negotiated four reservations with its EU partners, including a reservation on Justice and Home Affairs (JHA). The reservation concerned, laid down in the Edinburgh Agreement of December 1992, states that Denmark will continue active cooperation, but only as long as it is on the inter-governmental level. That indeed meant that when the subjects of asylum and migration became incorporated into the TEC, Denmark would not be part of the new communal approach.[27] Denmark is hence not a party to the various Directives contained in this Volume. However, Denmark is a full-fledged member of and participates in 'Schengen'.

Denmark's special position may well prove to be a blessing in disguise. By not being bound to the communal rules and regulations, Denmark is able to set its own programme and to translate its very own views into law and policy. Three examples should suffice:

---

gards the return of persons found not to be in need of international protection, that some countries continue to restrict the return of their own nationals, either outright or through laws and practices which effectively block expeditious return ...'.

[26] *Terugkeer, de internationale aspecten.* ACVZ advies, 2004.

[27] For details, see Liebaut in *The Asylum Acquis Handbook*, p. 57 ff.

1) On family formation and family reunification, the Danes have agreed to impose strict criteria. The requirements may relate to the resident's housing and income conditions. Or it could be a requirement for both parties to a marriage to be over 24 years of age and have greater affiliation to Denmark than to any other country. One of the aims of these requirements is to protect very young people from being forced into marriage against their will, and to ensure the best possible basis for the integration process.

2) As for asylum law, the system in virtually all European countries used to consist of basically three levels: (i) the 1951 Refugee Convention; (ii) the ECHR's Article 3, protecting the war refugees; and (iii) so-called humanitarian cases, the residual group for whom returning home would create problems outside the parameters of the formal conventions. Denmark decided to stick to its international obligations (i and ii) and to skip the third category. It remains to be seen whether they will remain the odd man out, as the Qualification Directive would prima facie allow such a policy.

3) Lastly, reference should be made to the issue of labour migration. Denmark has in particular focused on access to public services (unemployment benefits, welfare). In short, it has been agreed that such access will only be possible after a lengthy stay (some seven years) only.

Similarly, the public debate focuses on the assimilation-integration divide.
— *assimilation*: this employs a culturalist and universalist human rights discourse, and legitimates a transgression of the public/private divide, whether called for in functional or moral terms. Politically, this position has by now been widely accepted across the political spectrum;
— *integration*: this employs an 'equal footing' and 'equal access' discourse, both as a set of demands on ethnic minorities and in defence of calls on employers to behave in a non-discriminatory manner. This liberal, republican and legalist discourse respects the public/private divide. It also involves market-oriented self-help and self-reliance measures.
— *pluriculturality*: this employs a diversity (management) discourse, reflecting the fact of ethnic diversity and a plural world, but within a pragmatic-instrumental modality ('let's take advantage of it'). This stance has traditionally been championed by political actors from the left of the political centre but the company-oriented instrumentality of diversity management strategies in other social sectors has allowed it to become broadly accepted.

Migration and asylum watchers alike should continue to look at Denmark. If not for innovative thinking, then at least for the laboratory aspects and the forthcoming cases at the ECHR Court in Strasbourg.

'Tampere 2'

The European Union will move on. A 'Tampere 2' will sooner or later be agreed upon. The June 2004 Communication, however, is too conservative a basis for a badly needed holistic approach. Issues like entry to the labour market, access to social welfare, integration and return need to be successfully embedded in a visionary, forward-looking policy document. The global context should also not be forgotten. Meanwhile, Europe should be ever so slightly ashamed that the UNHCR is far more courageous than the Europeans themselves when it comes to embarking on the road towards a European Asylum Agency, a European Appeals Board and an inner-European settlement scheme. Last but not least, there is also something interesting in the State of Denmark that the rest of the Union may wish to pay attention to. Europe, the Third World and the individuals concerned all need to be aware of the various costs and benefits.[28] To strike a balance between *emotion* and *ratio* is a challenging task indeed.

---

[28] IOM will focus on the cost-benefit aspects of migration in a forthcoming (2005) World Migration Report.

Part 1

ASYLUM

Chapter 1.1
DUBLIN CRITERIA

COUNCIL REGULATION
No. 343/2003 of 18 February 2003
establishing the criteria and mechanisms for determining the Member State responsible
for examining an asylum application lodged in one of the Member States by a third-
country national[1]

THE COUNCIL OF THE EUROPEAN UNION,
Having regard to the Treaty establishing the European Community, and in particular Article
63, first paragraph, point (1)(a),
Having regard to the proposal from the Commission,[2]
Having regard to the opinion of the European Parliament,[3]
Having regard to the opinion of the European Economic and Social Committee,[4]

Whereas:

(1) A common policy on asylum, including a Common European Asylum System, is a constituent part of the European Union's objective of progressively establishing an area of
freedom, security and justice open to those who, forced by circumstances, legitimately seek
protection in the Community.

(2) The European Council, at its special meeting in Tampere on 15 and 16 October 1999,
agreed to work towards establishing a Common European Asylum System, based on the full
and inclusive application of the Geneva Convention relating to the Status of Refugees of 28
July 1951, as supplemented by the New York Protocol of 31 January 1967, thus ensuring
that nobody is sent back to persecution, i.e. maintaining the principle of non-refoulement. In
this respect, and without affecting the responsibility criteria laid down in this Regulation,
Member States, all respecting the principle of non-refoulement, are considered as safe countries for third-country nationals.

(3) The Tampere conclusions also stated that this system should include, in the short term, a
clear and workable method for determining the Member State responsible for the examination of an asylum application.

---

[1] OJ L 50, 25.2.2003, p. 1.
[2] OJ C 304 E, 30.10.2001, p. 192.
[3] Opinion of 9 April 2002 (not yet published in the Official Journal).
[4] OJ C 125, 27.5.2002, p. 28.

(4) Such a method should be based on objective, fair criteria both for the Member States and for the persons concerned. It should, in particular, make it possible to determine rapidly the Member State responsible, so as to guarantee effective access to the procedures for determining refugee status and not to compromise the objective of the rapid processing of asylum applications.

(5) As regards the introduction in successive phases of a common European asylum system that should lead, in the longer term, to a common procedure and a uniform status, valid throughout the Union, for those granted asylum, it is appropriate at this stage, while making the necessary improvements in the light of experience, to confirm the principles underlying the Convention determining the State responsible for examining applications for asylum lodged in one of the Member States of the European Communities,[5] signed in Dublin on 15 June 1990 (hereinafter referred to as the Dublin Convention), whose implementation has stimulated the process of harmonizing asylum policies.

(6) Family unity should be preserved in so far as this is compatible with the other objectives pursued by establishing criteria and mechanisms for determining the Member State responsible for examining an asylum application.

(7) The processing together of the asylum applications of the members of one family by a single Member State makes it possible to ensure that the applications are examined thoroughly and the decisions taken in respect of them are consistent. Member States should be able to derogate from the responsibility criteria, so as to make it possible to bring family members together where this is necessary on humanitarian grounds.

(8) The progressive creation of an area without internal frontiers in which free movement of persons is guaranteed in accordance with the Treaty establishing the European Community and the establishment of Community policies regarding the conditions of entry and stay of third country nationals, including common efforts towards the management of external borders, makes it necessary to strike a balance between responsibility criteria in a spirit of solidarity.

(9) The application of this Regulation can be facilitated, and its effectiveness increased, by bilateral arrangements between Member States for improving communications between competent departments, reducing time limits for procedures or simplifying the processing of requests to take charge or take back, or establishing procedures for the performance of transfers.

(10) Continuity between the system for determining the Member State responsible established by the Dublin Convention and the system established by this Regulation should be ensured. Similarly, consistency should be ensured between this Regulation and Council Regulation (EC) No 2725/2000 of 11 December 2000 concerning the establishment of 'Eurodac' for the comparison of fingerprints for the effective application of the Dublin Convention.[6]

---

[5] OJ C 254, 19.8.1997, p. 1.
[6] OJ L 316, 15.12.2000, p. 1.

(11) The operation of the Eurodac system, as established by Regulation (EC) No 2725/2000 and in particular the implementation of Articles 4 and 8 contained therein should facilitate the implementation of this Regulation.

(12) With respect to the treatment of persons falling within the scope of this Regulation, Member States are bound by obligations under instruments of international law to which they are party.

(13) The measures necessary for the implementation of this Regulation should be adopted in accordance with Council Decision 1999/468/EC of 28 June 1999 laying down the procedures for the exercise of implementing powers conferred on the Commission.[7]

(14) The application of the Regulation should be evaluated at regular intervals.

(15) The Regulation observes the fundamental rights and principles which are acknowledged in particular in the Charter of Fundamental Rights of the European Union.[8] In particular, it seeks to ensure full observance of the right to asylum guaranteed by Article 18.

(16) Since the objective of the proposed measure, namely the establishment of criteria and mechanisms for determining the Member State responsible for examining an asylum application lodged in one of the Member States by a third-country national, cannot be sufficiently achieved by the Member States and, given the scale and effects, can therefore be better achieved at Community level, the Community may adopt measures in accordance with the principle of subsidiarity as set out in Article 5 of the Treaty. In accordance with the principle of proportionality, as set out in that Article, this Regulation does not go beyond what is necessary in order to achieve that objective.

(17) In accordance with Article 3 of the Protocol on the position of the United Kingdom and Ireland, annexed to the Treaty on European Union and to the Treaty establishing the European Community, the United Kingdom and Ireland gave notice, by letters of 30 October 2001, of their wish to take part in the adoption and application of this Regulation.

(18) In accordance with Articles 1 and 2 of the Protocol on the position of Denmark, annexed to the Treaty on European Union and to the Treaty establishing the European Community, Denmark does not take part in the adoption of this Regulation and is not bound by it nor subject to its application.

(19) The Dublin Convention remains in force and continues to apply between Denmark and the Member States that are bound by this Regulation until such time an agreement allowing Denmark's participation in the Regulation has been concluded,

HAS ADOPTED THIS REGULATION:

---

[7] OJ L 184, 17.7.1999, p. 23.
[8] OJ C 364, 18.12.2000, p. 1.

CHAPTER I
Subject Matter and Definitions

Article 1

This Regulation lays down the criteria and mechanisms for determining the Member State responsible for examining an application for asylum lodged in one of the Member States by a third-country national.

Article 2

For the purposes of this Regulation:

(a) 'third-country national' means anyone who is not a citizen of the Union within the meaning of Article 17(1) of the Treaty establishing the European Community;

(b) 'Geneva Convention' means the Convention of 28 July1951 relating to the status of refugees, as amended by the New York Protocol of 31 January 1967;

(c) 'application for asylum' means the application made by a third-country national which can be understood as a request for international protection from a Member State, under the Geneva Convention. Any application for international protection is presumed to be an application for asylum, unless a third-country national explicitly requests another kind of protection that can be applied for separately;

(d) 'applicant' or 'asylum seeker' means a third country national who has made an application for asylum in respect of which a final decision has not yet been taken;

(e) 'examination of an asylum application' means any examination of, or decision or ruling concerning, an application for asylum by the competent authorities in accordance with national law except for procedures for determining the Member State responsible in accordance with this Regulation;

(f) 'withdrawal of the asylum application' means the actions by which the applicant for asylum terminates the procedures initiated by the submission of his application for asylum, in accordance with national law, either explicitly or tacitly;

(g) 'refugee' means any third-country national qualifying for the status defined by the Geneva Convention and authorised to reside as such on the territory of a Member State;

(h) 'unaccompanied minor' means unmarried persons below the age of eighteen who arrive in the territory of the Member States unaccompanied by an adult responsible for them whether by law or by custom, and for as long as they are not effectively taken into the care of such a person; it includes minors who are left unaccompanied after they have entered the territory of the Member States;

(i) 'family members' means insofar as the family already existed in the country of origin, the following members of the applicant's family who are present in the territory of the Member States:

(i) the spouse of the asylum seeker or his or her unmarried partner in a stable relationship, where the legislation or practice of the Member State concerned treats unmarried couples in a way comparable to married couples under its law relating to aliens;

(ii) the minor children of couples referred to in point (i) or of the applicant, on condition that they are unmarried and dependent and regardless of whether they were born in or out of wedlock or adopted as defined under the national law;

(iii) the father, mother or guardian when the applicant or refugee is a minor and unmarried;

(j) 'residence document' means any authorisation issued by the authorities of a Member State authorising a third-country national to stay in its territory, including the documents substantiating the authorisation to remain in the territory under temporary protection arrangements or until the circumstances preventing a removal order from being carried out no longer apply, with the exception of visas and residence authorisations issued during the period required to determine the responsible Member State as established in this Regulation or during examination of an application for asylumor an application for a residence permit;

(k) 'visa' means the authorisation or decision of a Member State required for transit or entry for an intended stay in that Member State or in several Member States. The nature of the visa shall be determined in accordance with the following definitions:

(i) 'long-stay visa' means the authorisation or decision of a Member State required for entry for an intended stay in that Member State of more than three months;

(ii) 'short-stay visa' means the authorisation or decision of a Member State required for entry for an intended stay in that State or in several Member States for a period whose total duration does not exceed three months;

(iii) 'transit visa' means the authorisation or decision of a Member State for entry for transit through the territory of that Member State or several Member States, except for transit at an airport;

(iv) 'airport transit visa' means the authorisation or decision allowing a third-country national specifically subject to this requirement to pass through the transit zone of an airport, without gaining access to the national territory of the Member State concerned, during a stopover or a transfer between two sections of an international flight.

CHAPTER II
General Principles

Article 3

1. Member States shall examine the application of any third country national who applies at the border or in their territory to any one of them for asylum. The application shall be examined by a single Member State, which shall be the one which the criteria set out in Chapter III indicate is responsible.

2. By way of derogation from paragraph 1, each Member State may examine an application for asylum lodged with it by a third-country national, even if such examination is not its responsibility under the criteria laid down in this Regulation. In such an event, that Member State shall become the Member State responsible within the meaning of this Regulation and shall assume the obligations associated with that responsibility. Where appropriate, it shall inform the Member State previously responsible, the Member State conducting a procedure for determining the Member State responsible or the Member State which has been requested to take charge of or take back the applicant.

3. Any Member State shall retain the right, pursuant to its national laws, to send an asylum seeker to a third country, in compliance with the provisions of the Geneva Convention.

4. The asylum seeker shall be informed in writing in a language that he or she may reasonably be expected to understand regarding the application of this Regulation, its time limits and its effects.

Article 4

1. The process of determining the Member State responsible under this Regulation shall start as soon as an application for asylum is first lodged with a Member State.

2. An application for asylum shall be deemed to have been lodged once a form submitted by the applicant for asylum or a report prepared by the authorities has reached the competent authorities of the Member State concerned. Where an application is not made in writing, the time elapsing between the statement of intention and the preparation of a report should be as short as possible.

3. For the purposes of this Regulation, the situation of a minor who is accompanying the asylum seeker and meets the definition of a family member set out in Article 2, point (i), shall be in dissociable from that of his parent or guardian and shall be a matter for the Member State responsible for examining the application for asylum of that parent or guardian, even if the minor is not individually an asylum seeker. The same treatment shall be applied to children born after the asylum seeker arrives in the territory of the Member States, without the need to initiate a new procedure for taking charge of them.

4. Where an application for asylum is lodged with the competent authorities of a Member State by an applicant who is in the territory of another Member State, the determination of the Member State responsible shall be made by the Member State in whose territory the applicant is present. The latter Member State shall be informed without delay by the Member State which received the application and shall then, for the purposes of this Regulation, be regarded as the Member State with which the application for asylum was lodged. The applicant shall be informed in writing of this transfer and of the date on which it took place.

5. An asylum seeker who is present in another Member State and there lodges an application for asylum after withdrawing his application during the process of determining the Member State responsible shall be taken back, under the conditions laid down in Article 20, by the Member State with which that application for asylum was lodged, with a view to completing the process of determining the Member State responsible for examining the application for asylum. This obligation shall cease, if the asylum seeker has in the meantime left the territories of the Member States for a period of at least three months or has obtained a residence document from a Member State.

CHAPTER III
Hierarchy of Criteria

Article 5

1. The criteria for determining the Member State responsible shall be applied in the order in which they are set out in this Chapter.

2. The Member State responsible in accordance with the criteria shall be determined on the basis of the situation obtaining when the asylum seeker first lodged his application with a Member State.

Article 6

Where the applicant for asylum is an unaccompanied minor, the Member State responsible for examining the application shall be that where a member of his or her family is legally present, provided that this is in the best interest of the minor. In the absence of a family member, the Member State responsible for examining the application shall be that where the minor has lodged his or her application for asylum.

Article 7

Where the asylum seeker has a family member, regardless of whether the family was previously formed in the country of origin, who has been allowed to reside as a refugee in a Member State, that Member State shall be responsible for examining the application for asylum, provided that the persons concerned so desire.

Article 8

If the asylum seeker has a family member in a Member State whose application has not yet been the subject of a first decision regarding the substance, that Member State shall be responsible for examining the application for asylum, provided that the persons concerned so desire.

Article 9

1. Where the asylum seeker is in possession of a valid residence document, the Member State which issued the document shall be responsible for examining the application for asylum.

2. Where the asylum seeker is in possession of a valid visa, the Member State which issued the visa shall be responsible for examining the application for asylum, unless the visa was issued when acting for or on the written authorisation of another Member State. In such a case, the latter Member State shall be responsible for examining the application for asylum. Where a Member State first consults the central authority of another Member State, in particular for security reasons, the latter's reply to the consultation shall not constitute written authorisation within the meaning of this provision.

3. Where the asylum seeker is in possession of more than one valid residence document or visa issued by different Member States, the responsibility for examining the application for asylum shall be assumed by the Member States in the following order:
   (a) the Member State which issued the residence document conferring the right to the longest period of residency or, where the periods of validity are identical, the Member State which issued the residence document having the latest expiry date;
   (b) the Member State which issued the visa having the latest expiry date where the various visas are of the same type;
   (c) where visas are of different kinds, the Member State which issued the visa having the longest period of validity, or, where the periods of validity are identical, the Member State which issued the visa having the latest expiry date.

4. Where the asylum seeker is in possession only of one or more residence documents which have expired less than two years previously or one or more visas which have expired less than six months previously and which enabled him actually to enter the territory of a Member State, paragraphs 1, 2 and 3 shall apply for such time as the applicant has not left the territories of the Member States. Where the asylum seeker is in possession of one or more residence documents which have expired more than two years previously or one or more visas which have expired more than six months previously and enabled him actually to enter the territory of a Member State and where he has not left the territories of the Member States, the Member State in which the application is lodged shall be responsible.

5. The fact that the residence document or visa was issued on the basis of a false or assumed identity or on submission of forged, counterfeit or invalid documents shall not prevent responsibility being allocated to the Member State which issued it. However, the Member State issuing the residence document or visa shall not be responsible if it can establish that a fraud was committed after the document or visa had been issued.

Article 10

1. Where it is established, on the basis of proof or circumstantial evidence as described in the two lists mentioned in Article 18(3), including the data referred to in Chapter III of Regulation (EC) No. 2725/2000, that an asylum seeker has irregularly crossed the border into a Member State by land, sea or air having come from a third country, the Member State thus entered shall be responsible for examining the application for asylum. This responsibility shall cease 12 months after the date on which the irregular border crossing took place.

2. When a Member State cannot or can no longer be held responsible in accordance with paragraph 1, and where it is established, on the basis of proof or circumstantial evidence as described in the two lists mentioned in Article 18(3), that the asylum seeker – who has entered the territories of the Member States irregularly or whose circumstances of entry cannot be established – at the time of lodging the application has been previously living for a continuous period of at least five months in a Member State, that Member State shall be responsible for examining the application for asylum. If the applicant has been living for periods of time of at least five months in several Member States, the Member State where this has been most recently the case shall be responsible for examining the application.

Article 11

1. If a third-country national enters into the territory of a Member State in which the need for him or her to have a visa is waived, that Member State shall be responsible for examining his or her application for asylum.

2. The principle set out in paragraph 1 does not apply, if the third-country national lodges his or her application for asylum in another Member State, in which the need for him or her to have a visa for entry into the territory is also waived. In this case, the latter Member State shall be responsible for examining the application for asylum.

Article 12

Where the application for asylum is made in an international transit area of an airport of a Member State by a third-country national, that Member State shall be responsible for examining the application.

Article 13

Where no Member State responsible for examining the application for asylum can be designated on the basis of the criteria listed in this Regulation, the first Member State with which the application for asylum was lodged shall be responsible for examining it.

Article 14

Where several members of a family submit applications for asylum in the same Member State simultaneously, or on dates close enough for the procedures for determining the Member State responsible to be conducted together, and where the application of the criteria set out in this Regulation would lead to them being separated, the Member State responsible shall be determined on the basis of the following provisions:

(a) responsibility for examining the applications for asylum of all the members of the family shall lie with the Member State which the criteria indicate is responsible for taking charge of the largest number of family members;

(b) failing this, responsibility shall lie with the Member State which the criteria indicate is responsible for examining the application of the oldest of them.

CHAPTER IV
Humanitarian Clause

Article 15

1. Any Member State, even where it is not responsible under the criteria set out in this Regulation, may bring together family members, as well as other dependent relatives, on humanitarian grounds based in particular on family or cultural considerations. In this case that Member State shall, at the request of another Member State, examine the application for asylum of the person concerned. The persons concerned must consent.

2. In cases in which the person concerned is dependent on the assistance of the other on account of pregnancy or a newborn child, serious illness, severe handicap or old age, Member States shall normally keep or bring together the asylum seeker with another relative present in the territory of one of the Member States, provided that family ties existed in the country of origin.

3. If the asylum seeker is an unaccompanied minor who has a relative or relatives in another Member State who can take care of him or her, Member States shall if possible unite the minor with his or her relative or relatives, unless this is not in the best interests of the minor.

4. Where the Member State thus approached accedes to the request, responsibility for examining the application shall be transferred to it.

5. The conditions and procedures for implementing this Article including, where appropriate, conciliation mechanisms for settling differences between Member States concerning the need to unite the persons in question, or the place where this should be done, shall be adopted in accordance with the procedure referred to in Article 27(2).

CHAPTER V
Taking Charge and Taking Back

Article 16

1. The Member State responsible for examining an application for asylum under this Regulation shall be obliged to:

(a) take charge, under the conditions laid down in Articles 17 to 19, of an asylum seeker who has lodged an application in a different Member State;

(b) complete the examination of the application for asylum;

(c) take back, under the conditions laid down in Article 20, an applicant whose application is under examination and who is in the territory of another Member State without permission;

(d) take back, under the conditions laid down in Article 20, an applicant who has withdrawn the application under examination and made an application in another Member State;

(e) take back, under the conditions laid down in Article 20, a third-country national whose application it has rejected and who is in the territory of another Member State without permission.

2. Where a Member State issues a residence document to the applicant, the obligations specified in paragraph 1 shall be transferred to that Member State.

3. The obligations specified in paragraph 1 shall cease where the third-country national has left the territory of the Member States for at least three months, unless the third-country national is in possession of a valid residence document issued by the Member State responsible.

4. The obligations specified in paragraph 1(d) and (e) shall likewise cease once the Member State responsible for examining the application has adopted and actually implemented, following the withdrawal or rejection of the application, the provisions that are necessary before the third-country national can go to his country of origin or to another country to which he may lawfully travel.

Article 17

1. Where a Member State with which an application for asylum has been lodged considers that another Member State is responsible for examining the application, it may, as quickly as possible and in any case within three months of the date on which the application was lodged within the meaning of Article 4(2), call upon the other Member State to take charge of the applicant. Where the request to take charge of an applicant is not made within the period of three months, responsibility for examining the application for asylum shall lie with the Member State in which the application was lodged.

2. The requesting Member State may ask for an urgent reply in cases where the application for asylum was lodged after leave to enter or remain was refused, after an arrest for an unlawful stay or after the service or execution of a removal order and/or where the asylum seeker is held in detention. The request shall state the reasons warranting an urgent reply and the period within which a reply is expected. This period shall be at least one week.

3. In both cases, the request that charge be taken by another Member State shall be made using a standard form and including proof or circumstantial evidence as described in the two lists mentioned in Article 18(3) and/or relevant elements from the asylum seeker's statement, enabling the authorities of the requested Member State to check whether it is responsible on the basis of the criteria laid down in this Regulation. The rules on the preparation of and the procedures for transmitting requests shall be adopted in accordance with the procedure referred to in Article 27(2).

Article 18

1. The requested Member State shall make the necessary checks, and shall give a decision on the request to take charge of an applicant within two months of the date on which the request was received.

2. In the procedure for determining the Member State responsible for examining the application for asylum established in this Regulation, elements of proof and circumstantial evidence shall be used.

3. In accordance with the procedure referred to in Article 27(2) two lists shall be established and periodically reviewed, indicating the elements of proof and circumstantial evidence in accordance with the following criteria:
    (a) Proof:
        (i) This refers to formal proof which determines responsibility pursuant to this Regulation, as long as it is not refuted by proof to the contrary;
        (ii) The Member States shall provide the Committee provided for in Article 27 with models of the different types of administrative documents, in accordance with the typology established in the list of formal proofs.
    (b) Circumstantial evidence:
        (i) This refers to indicative elements which while being refutable may be sufficient, in certain cases, according to the evidentiary value attributed to them;
        (ii) Their evidentiary value, in relation to the responsibility for examining the application for asylum shall be assessed on a case-by-case basis.

4. The requirement of proof should not exceed what is necessary for the proper application of this Regulation.

5. If there is no formal proof, the requested Member State shall acknowledge its responsibility if the circumstantial evidence is coherent, verifiable and sufficiently detailed to establish responsibility.

6. Where the requesting Member State has pleaded urgency, in accordance with the provisions of Article 17(2), the requested Member State shall make every effort to conform to the

time limit requested. In exceptional cases, where it can be demonstrated that the examination of a request for taking charge of an applicant is particularly complex, the requested Member State may give the reply after the time limit requested, but in any case within one month. In such situations the requested Member State must communicate its decision to postpone a reply to the requesting Member State within the time limit originally requested.

7. Failure to act within the two-month period mentioned in paragraph 1 and the one-month period mentioned in paragraph 6 shall be tantamount to accepting the request, and entail the obligation to take charge of the person, including the provisions for proper arrangements for arrival.

Article 19

1. Where the requested Member State accepts that it should take charge of an applicant, the Member State in which the application for asylum was lodged shall notify the applicant of the decision not to examine the application, and of the obligation to transfer the applicant to the responsible Member State.

2. The decision referred to in paragraph 1 shall set out the grounds on which it is based. It shall contain details of the time limit for carrying out the transfer and shall, if necessary, contain information on the place and date at which the applicant should appear, if he is traveling to the Member State responsible by his own means. This decision may be subject to an appeal or a review. Appeal or review concerning this decision shall not suspend the implementation of the transfer unless the courts or competent bodies so decide on a case by case basis if national legislation allows for this.

3. The transfer of the applicant from the Member State in which the application for asylum was lodged to the Member State responsible shall be carried out in accordance with the national law of the first Member State, after consultation between the Member States concerned, as soon as practically possible, and at the latest within six months of acceptance of the request that charge be taken or of the decision on an appeal or review where there is a suspensive effect. If necessary, the asylum seeker shall be supplied by the requesting Member State with a laissez passer of the design adopted in accordance with the procedure referred to in Article 27(2). The Member State responsible shall inform the requesting Member State, as appropriate, of the safe arrival of the asylum seeker or of the fact that he did not appear within the set time limit.

4. Where the transfer does not take place within the six months' time limit, responsibility shall lie with the Member State in which the application for asylum was lodged. This time limit may be extended up to a maximum of one year if the transfer could not be carried out due to imprisonment of the asylum seeker or up to a maximum of eighteen months if the asylum seeker absconds.

5. Supplementary rules on carrying out transfers may be adopted in accordance with the procedure referred to in Article 27(2).

Article 20

1. An asylum seeker shall be taken back in accordance with Article 4(5) and Article 16(1)(c), (d) and (e) as follows:

(a) the request for the applicant to be taken back must contain information enabling the requested Member State to check that it is responsible;

(b) the Member State called upon to take back the applicant shall be obliged to make the necessary checks and reply to the request addressed to it as quickly as possible and under no circumstances exceeding a period of one month from the referral. When the request is based on data obtained from the Eurodac system, this time limit is reduced to two weeks;

(c) where the requested Member State does not communicate its decision within the one month period or the two weeks period mentioned in subparagraph (b), it shall be considered to have agreed to take back the asylum seeker;

(d) a Member State which agrees to take back an asylum seeker shall be obliged to readmit that person to its territory. The transfer shall be carried out in accordance with the national law of the requesting Member State, after consultation between the Member States concerned, as soon as practically possible, and at the latest within six months of acceptance of the request that charge be taken by another Member State or of the decision on an appeal or review where there is a suspensive effect;

(e) the requesting Member State shall notify the asylum seeker of the decision concerning his being taken back by the Member State responsible. The decision shall set out the grounds on which it is based. It shall contain details of the time limit on carrying out the transfer and shall, if necessary, contain information on the place and date at which the applicant should appear, if he is travelling to the Member State responsible by his own means. This decision may be subject to an appeal or a review. Appeal or review concerning this decision shall not suspend the implementation of the transfer except when the courts or competent bodies so decide in a case-by-case basis if the national legislation allows for this. If necessary, the asylum seeker shall be supplied by the requesting Member State with a laissez passer of the design adopted in accordance with the procedure referred to in Article 27(2). The Member State responsible shall inform the requesting Member State, as appropriate, of the safe arrival of the asylum seeker or of the fact that he did not appear within the set time limit.

2. Where the transfer does not take place within the six months' time limit, responsibility shall lie with the Member State in which the application for asylum was lodged. This time limit may be extended up to a maximum of one year if the transfer or the examination of the application could not be carried out due to imprisonment of the asylum seeker or up to a maximum of eighteen months if the asylum seeker absconds.

3. The rules of proof and evidence and their interpretation, and on the preparation of and the procedures for transmitting requests, shall be adopted in accordance with the procedure referred to in Article 27(2).

4. Supplementary rules on carrying out transfers may be adopted in accordance with the procedure referred to in Article 27(2).

CHAPTER VI
Administrative Cooperation

Article 21

1. Each Member State shall communicate to any Member State that so requests such personal data concerning the asylum seeker as is appropriate, relevant and non-excessive for:
    (a) the determination of the Member State responsible for examining the application for asylum;
    (b) examining the application for asylum;
    (c) implementing any obligation arising under this Regulation.

2. The information referred to in paragraph 1 may only cover:
    (a) personal details of the applicant, and, where appropriate, the members of his family (full name and where appropriate, former name; nicknames or pseudonyms; nationality, present and former; date and place of birth);
    (b) identity and travel papers (references, validity, date of issue, issuing authority, place of issue, etc.);
    (c) other information necessary for establishing the identity of the applicant, including fingerprints processed in accordance with Regulation (EC) No. 2725/2000;
    (d) places of residence and routes traveled;
    (e) residence documents or visas issued by a Member State;
    (f) the place where the application was lodged;
    (g) the date any previous application for asylum was lodged, the date the present application was lodged, the stage reached in the proceedings and the decision taken, if any.

3. Furthermore, provided it is necessary for the examination of the application for asylum, the Member State responsible may request another Member State to let it know on what grounds the asylum seeker bases his application and, where applicable, the grounds for any decisions taken concerning the applicant. The Member State may refuse to respond to the request submitted to it, if the communication of such information is likely to harm the essential interests of the Member State or the protection of the liberties and fundamental rights of the person concerned or of others. In any event, communication of the information requested shall be subject to the written approval of the applicant for asylum.

4. Any request for information shall set out the grounds on which it is based and, where its purpose is to check whether there is a criterion that is likely to entail the responsibility of the requested Member State, shall state on what evidence, including relevant information from reliable sources on the ways and means asylum seekers enter the territories of the Member States, or on what specific and verifiable part of the applicant's statements it is based. It is understood that such relevant information from reliable sources is not in itself sufficient to determine the responsibility and the competence of a Member State under this Regulation, but it may contribute to the evaluation of other indications relating to the individual asylum seeker.

5. The requested Member State shall be obliged to reply within six weeks.

6. The exchange of information shall be effected at the request of a Member State and may only take place between authorities whose designation by each Member State has been communicated to the Commission, which shall inform the other Member States thereof.

7. The information exchanged may only be used for the purposes set out in paragraph 1. In each Member State such information may, depending on its type and the powers of the recipient authority, only be communicated to the authorities and courts and tribunals entrusted with:
(a) the determination of the Member State responsible for examining the application for asylum;
(b) examining the application for asylum;
(c) implementing any obligation arising under this Regulation.

8. The Member State which forwards the information shall ensure that it is accurate and up-to-date. If it transpires that that Member State has forwarded information which is inaccurate or which should not have been forwarded, the recipient Member States shall be informed thereof immediately. They shall be obliged to correct such information or to have it erased.

9. The asylum seeker shall have the right to be informed, on request, of any data that is processed concerning him. If he finds that this information has been processed in breach of this Regulation or of Directive 95/46/EC of the European Parliament and the Council of 24 October 1995 on the protection of individuals with regard to the processing of personal data and on the free movement of such data,[9] in particular because it is incomplete or inaccurate, he is entitled to have it corrected, erased or blocked. The authority correcting, erasing or blocking the data shall inform, as appropriate, the Member State transmitting or receiving the information.

10. In each Member State concerned, a record shall be kept, in the individual file for the person concerned and/or in a register, of the transmission and receipt of information exchanged.

11. The data exchanged shall be kept for a period not exceeding that which is necessary for the purposes for which it is exchanged.

12. Where the data is not processed automatically or is not contained, or intended to be entered, in a file, each Member State should take appropriate measures to ensure compliance with this Article through effective checks.

Article 22

1. Member States shall notify the Commission of the authorities responsible for fulfilling the obligations arising under this Regulation and shall ensure that those authorities have the necessary resources for carrying out their tasks and in particular for replying within the

---

[9] OJ L 281, 23.11.1995, p. 31.

prescribed time limits to requests for information, requests to take charge of and requests to take back asylum seekers.

2. Rules relating to the establishment of secure electronic transmission channels between the authorities mentioned in paragraph 1 for transmitting requests and ensuring that senders automatically receive an electronic proof of delivery shall be established in accordance with the procedure referred to in Article 27(2).

Article 23

1. Member States may, on a bilateral basis, establish administrative arrangements between themselves concerning the practical details of the implementation of this Regulation, in order to facilitate its application and increase its effectiveness. Such arrangements may relate to:
   (a) exchanges of liaison officers;
   (b) simplification of the procedures and shortening of the time limits relating to transmission and the examination of requests to take charge of or take back asylum seekers;

2. The arrangements referred to in paragraph 1 shall be communicated to the Commission. The Commission shall verify that the arrangements referred to in paragraph 1(b) do not infringe this Regulation.

CHAPTER VII
Transitional Provisions and Final Provisions

Article 24

1. This Regulation shall replace the Convention determining the State responsible for examining applications for asylum lodged in one of the Member States of the European Communities, signed in Dublin on 15 June 1990 (Dublin Convention).

2. However, to ensure continuity of the arrangements for determining the Member State responsible for an application for asylum, where an application has been lodged after the date mentioned in the second paragraph of Article 29, the events that are likely to entail the responsibility of a Member State under this Regulation shall be taken into consideration, even if they precede that date, with the exception of the events mentioned in Article 10(2).

3. Where, in Regulation (EC) No. 2725/2000 reference is made to the Dublin Convention, such reference shall be taken to be a reference made to this Regulation.

Article 25

1. Any period of time prescribed in this Regulation shall be calculated as follows:
   (a) where a period expressed in days, weeks or months is to be calculated from the moment at which an event occurs or an action takes place, the day during which that event occurs or that action takes place shall not be counted as falling within the period in question;

(b) a period expressed in weeks or months shall end with the expiry of whichever day in the last week or month is the same day of the week or falls on the same date as the day during which the event or action from which the period is to be calculated occurred or took place. If, in a period expressed in months, the day on which it should expire does not occur in the last month, the period shall end with the expiry of the last day of that month;

(c) time limits shall include Saturdays, Sundays and official holidays in any of the Member States concerned.

2. Requests and replies shall be sent using any method that provides proof of receipt.

Article 26

As far as the French Republic is concerned, this Regulation shall apply only to its European territory.

Article 27

1. The Commission shall be assisted by a committee.

2. Where reference is made to this paragraph, Articles 5 and 7 of Decision 1999/468/EC shall apply. The period laid down in Article 5(6) of Decision 1999/468/EC shall be set at three months.

3. The Committee shall draw up its rules of procedure.

Article 28

At the latest three years after the date mentioned in the first paragraph of Article 29, the Commission shall report to the European Parliament and the Council on the application of this Regulation and, where appropriate, shall propose the necessary amendments. Member States shall forward to the Commission all information appropriate for the preparation of that report, at the latest six months before that time limit expires. Having submitted that report, the Commission shall report to the European Parliament and the Council on the application of this Regulation at the same time as it submits reports on the implementation of the Eurodac system provided for by Article 24(5) of Regulation (EC) No. 2725/2000.

Article 29

This Regulation shall enter into force on the 20th day following that of its publication in the Official Journal of the European Union. It shall apply to asylum applications lodged as from the first day of the sixth month following its entry into force and, from that date, it will apply to any request to take charge of or take back asylum seekers, irrespective of the date on which the application was made. The Member State responsible for the examination of an asylum application submitted before that date shall be determined in accordance with the criteria set out in the Dublin Convention.

This Regulation shall be binding in its entirety and directly applicable in the Member States in conformity with the Treaty establishing the European Community.

Explanatory Memorandum

1. **Criteria and mechanisms for determining the Member State responsible for examining an asylum application lodged in one of the member states by a third-country national**

The conclusions of the Tampere European Council of October 1999 state that a common European asylum system should include, in the short term, a clear and workable determination of the State responsible for the examination of an asylum application, common standards for a fair and efficient asylum procedure, common minimum conditions of reception of asylum seekers and the approximation of rules on the recognition and content of refugee status. The system should be complemented by measures on subsidiary forms of protection offering an appropriate status to any person in need of such protection. With a view to achieving that objective, the Commission has successively presented a proposal for a Council Directive on minimum standards for giving temporary protection in the event of a mass influx of displaced persons (COM(2000)303 final of 24 May 2000), a proposal for a Council Directive on minimum standards on procedures in Member States for granting and withdrawing refugee status (COM(2000)578 final of 20 September 2000) and a proposal for a Council Directive laying down minimum standards on the reception of applicants for asylum in Member States (COM(2001)181 final of 3 April 2001). With this proposal for a Regulation laying down the criteria and mechanisms for determining the Member State responsible for examining an asylum application lodged in one of the Member States by a third-country national, the Commission has added a block to the construction of a common European asylum system, in accordance with the programme provided for in the scoreboard to examine progress made in setting up an area of freedom, security and justice in the European Union, a document which was presented to the Council on 27 March 2000. The drafting of this proposal for a Regulation was preceded by a wide-ranging debate:

- Firstly, the debate was launched on the basis of the Commission's working paper entitled 'Revisiting the Dublin Convention: developing Community legislation for determining which Member State is responsible for considering an asylum application submitted in one of the Member States' (SEC(2000)522 final of 21 March 2000). That paper, which analyses some of the difficulties encountered in implementing the Convention, compares the results achieved with the objectives laid down in the introduction and with other potential objectives of a system for determining which Member State is responsible, and sets out a number of possible alternatives to the Convention, was discussed in the Council and has given rise to written contributions on the part of various interested organisations, including the HCR, ILPA/MPG, Amnesty International, the Conference of Churches on migrants in Europe and the European Council on Refugees and Exiles (ECRE).
- Secondly, as it had promised the Council, in autumn 2000 the Commission conducted an evaluation of the application of the Convention. The analysis of replies submitted by the Member States to a detailed questionnaire, together with discussions with

experts from the departments responsible for the day-to-day implementation of the Convention in the Member States, revealed the practical and legal difficulties encountered in implementing the Convention and enabled precise statistics to be produced. The conclusions drawn on that occasion were presented in the Commission staff working paper "Evaluation of the Dublin Convention" (SEC (2001) 756 final of 13 June 2001).

2. Objectives and scope of the proposal

2.1. *Objectives*

The Commission's aim in presenting this proposal is not merely to implement Article 63(1)(a) of the EC Treaty, but also to respond to the wish expressed by the Tampere European Council that the criteria and mechanisms for determining the Member State responsible for examining an asylum application would be based on a 'clear and workable method' forming part of 'a fair and efficient asylum procedure'. To that end, the proposal for a Regulation aims to:

- ensure that asylum seekers have effective access to the procedures for determining refugee status by making provision for the necessary links with those procedures as indicated in the proposal for a Directive on the minimum standards applicable to them and by laying down rules sanctioning failure to comply with timetables;
- prevent abuse of asylum procedures in the form of multiple applications for asylum submitted simultaneously or successively by the same person in several Member States with the sole aim of extending his stay in the European Union;
- close the loopholes and correct the inaccuracies detected in the Dublin Convention;
- adapt the system to the new realities resulting from the progress made as regards the establishment of an area without internal borders, in particular by drawing the consequences of the entry into force of Council Regulation (EC) No. 539/2001 of 15 March 2001 listing the third countries whose nationals must be in possession of visas when crossing the external borders and those whose nationals are exempt from that requirement;
- the Member State responsible to be determined as quickly as possible, partly by laying down a reasonable timetable for the various phases of proceedings and partly by providing clarifications on the standard of proof required to establish the responsibility of a Member State;
- increase the system's efficiency by granting the Member States a more realistic period in which to implement decisions on transfers of asylum seekers and by providing an appropriate framework for special implementing arrangements between Member States which jointly have to process a large number of cases involving the determination of the Member State responsible.

2.2. *Scope*

The working paper referred to above, 'Revisiting the Dublin Convention', reviewed several possible alternatives to the Dublin Convention system. It concluded that there did not appear to be many viable alternatives to the present system.

The most credible alternative scenario, in which responsibility would depend solely on where the application was lodged, would probably make it possible to set up a clear, viable system that meets a number of objectives: rapidity and certainty; no 'refugees in orbit'; resolution of the problem of multiple asylum applications; and a guarantee of family unity. However, as the Commission pointed out, it would require harmonisation in other areas such as asylum procedures, reception conditions, interpretation of the refugee definition and subsidiary protection in order to reduce any perceived incentives for asylum seekers to choose between the Member States when lodging their application. At this stage of the construction of the common European asylum system, there are significant differences between the Member States in terms of procedures for granting refugee status, reception conditions for asylum seekers and the administration of complementary forms of protection which could affect the destination chosen by asylum seekers. These differences will persist, albeit to a lesser degree, after the directives proposed by the Commission on those subjects have entered into force.

It would therefore not be realistic to envisage a system for determining the Member State responsible for examining an asylum application which diverges fundamentally from the Dublin Convention. As the Commission indicated in its communication to the Council and the European Parliament 'Towards a common asylum procedure and a uniform status, valid throughout the Union, for persons granted asylum' (COM(2000)755 final of 22 November 2000), a system based on different principles could probably only be envisaged in the context of establishing a common procedure and a uniform status, i.e. at a later stage. Consequently, this proposal for a Regulation is based on the same principles as the Dublin Convention and its scope is the same. In other words:

- the general principle is that responsibility for examining an asylum application lies with the Member State which played the greatest part in the applicant's entry into or residence on the territories of the Member States, subject to exceptions designed to protect family unity;
- the system for determining the State responsible applies only to persons requesting recognition of the status of refugee within the meaning of the Geneva Convention of 28 July 1951 relating to the Status of Refugees – to which all the Member States are parties – and does not cover the forms of subsidiary protection which have not yet been harmonised. However, so as to take the lessons of the past on board, the proposal includes a number of innovations:
- new provisions emphasising each Member State's responsibility *vis-à-vis* all its partners in the Union when it allows illegal residents to remain on its territory;
- much shorter procedural deadlines consistent with the proposed deadlines for granting and withdrawing refugee status, to ensure that applications for asylum are processed rapidly;
- extended deadlines for implementing transfers to the Member State responsible so as to allow for the practical difficulties arising in connection with such transfers;
- new provisions aimed at preserving the unity of asylum seekers' families, in so far as this is compatible with the other objectives of asylum and immigration policy, i.e. processing applications for asylum as rapidly as possible under a fair and efficient procedure, and ensuring that these provisions cannot be abused to get round the rules on family reunification put forward by the Commission in its proposal for a Council Directive on the right to family reunification (COM(1999)638 final – 1999/0258 (CNS)), which is currently being negotiated. This proposal for a Regulation, which is designed to replace the Dublin Convention, essentially sets out the Member States'

obligations *vis-à-vis* each other, which must apply to all parties on the same terms. It contains provisions on the Member States' obligations *vis-à-vis* asylum seekers whose applications are being examined with a view to determining which Member State is responsible only in so far as those provisions affect the course of proceedings between Member States or are necessary to ensure consistency with the proposal for a Directive on procedures for granting and withdrawing refugee status.

3. Overall assessment of provisions

3.1. *Criteria governing responsibility*

The proposal for a Regulation is based on the same principles as the Dublin Convention, namely the idea that, in an area within which free movement of persons is guaranteed by the Treaty, each Member State is answerable to all the others for its actions concerning the entry and residence of third-country nationals and must bear the consequences thereof in a spirit of solidarity and fair cooperation. The main criteria for allocating responsibility, and the hierarchical order in which they are presented, reflect this general approach by placing the burden of responsibility on the Member State which, by issuing him with a visa or residence document, being negligent in border control or admitting him without a visa, played the greatest part in the applicant's entry into or residence on the territories of the Member States. However, new criteria have been added:

The first group is designed to protect family unity. The Dublin Convention already provided for responsibility to be allocated to the State in which a member of the applicant's family is resident as a refugee, even if another criterion might also apply.

- This proposal adds a criterion for the purpose of uniting an unaccompanied minor, whatever the circumstances, with an adult member of his family who is already present in a Member State and is able to take charge of him.
- The proposal also provides for responsibility for examining applications for asylum to be vested in the Member State examining, under a normal procedure(within the meaning of the proposal for a Directive on minimum standards on procedures for granting refugee status), an application lodged by a family member who has arrived previously and who has not yet been the subject of a decision at first instance.
- Lastly, to prevent a literal application of responsibility criteria resulting in the members of a family group who have lodged applications in the same Member State being separated, there is a provision which lays down the rules for derogating from the normal application of criteria so as to maintain family unity within a given Member State.

A second group of criteria is designed to deal with the consequences of a Member State failing to meet its obligations in the fight against illegal immigration. The Dublin Convention already provided that a Member State in which an asylum seeker has stayed illegally for six months or more before lodging his asylum application cannot invoke the criterion of illegal entry to request the Member State through which the applicant entered the European Union to assume responsibility for examining the application. The provision signalled that a Member State which does not take effective action against the illegal presence of third-country nationals on its territory has an equivalent responsibility *vis-à-vis* its partners to that of a Member State which fails to control its borders properly. The proposal extends this

approach to several situations. Under the new criteria, where responsibility cannot be established on the basis of any of the higher-ranking criteria set out above:

- any Member State which knowingly tolerates the illegal presence of a third-country
  national on its territory (by not taking any measure to remove the individual or
  question or regularise his situation) must assume the consequences of the liability it
  has incurred vis-à-vis the other Member States by allowing that situation to continue;
- any Member State on whose territory a third-country national has remained illegally
  for more than six months must bear the consequences of its failure to combat illegal
  immigration.

3.2.   *Procedure for taking charge and taking back*

Arrangements for taking charge and taking back are similar to those in the Dublin Convention. The most significant differences with the Convention are as follows:

- the deadline for submitting requests to take charge is reduced from six months to
  sixty-five working days;
- the possibility of asking for an urgent reply;
- further clarification of the standard of proof required to establish a Member State's
  responsibility;
- the time limit for performing the transfer is six months: if it is exceeded, responsibility
  reverts to the Member State where the asylum application was lodged;
- the responsibility of the Member State responsible is discharged, where the asylum
  seeker has stayed for at least six months without permission in the Member State
  where he now is;
- the obligation to communicate to the asylum seeker a reasoned decision from which
  an appeal may lie, but, since a transfer to another Member State should not result in
  serious loss which is difficult to make good, the possibility of giving this appeal
  suspensive effect is withdrawn. This measure is designed to make proceedings faster
  and more efficient and to prevent appeals being lodged purely as stalling tactics.

3.3.   *Cooperation between Member States*

The mechanism for determining which Member State is responsible will not function unless
the Member States set up a system of fair cooperation with a view to collecting the necessary evidence, processing applications within the agreed time limits and organising transfers in the best conditions. The main form of cooperation between Member States consists
in exchanging the information necessary to determine responsibility, including personal
data in compliance with Directive 95/46/EC on the protection of individuals with regard to
the processing of personal data and on the free movement of such data. Where the purpose
of exchanges of information is to collect the requisite data to establish the responsibility of
a Member State, the Member State requested should be given a time in which to respond
that is compatible with the objective of determining responsibility rapidly (which was not
the case in the Dublin Convention). The proposed time limit is one month. The Member
States have a duty to make the necessary resources available to the departments required to
implement the mechanism for determining the Member State responsible.

Lastly, Member States may, on a bilateral basis, establish administrative arrangements between themselves to facilitate application of this proposal and increase its effectiveness.
Such arrangements may relate to exchanges of liaison officers, simplification of procedures

and shortening of response times, or mechanisms for rationalising transfers to prevent asylum seekers being shuttled between two Member States.

3.4.   *Final and transitional provisions*
Most of these are 'standard' provisions concerning discrimination, penalties and the Directive's entry into force.

The following should be noted:
- Provisions designed to ensure a smooth transition between the Dublin Convention and implementation of this proposal for a Regulation, particularly a clause laying down a time limit from the Regulation's entry into force until the date of its actual implementation;
- The setting-up of a regulatory committee to help the Commission draw up implementing measures for the proposal, and in particular rules on the production of evidence, the performance of transfers and standard forms for the Member States to submit requests for taking charge or taking back. Where necessary, this chapter could contain additional transitional provisions, if implementation of the Regulation were to precede implementation of the Directive on asylum procedures.

4.   **Legal basis**

Article 63(1)(a) of the EC Treaty specifically provides for the adoption of criteria and mechanisms for determining which Member State is responsible for considering an application asylum submitted by a national of a third country in one of the Member States.

Title IV of the Treaty is not applicable in the United Kingdom and Ireland, unless those two countries decide otherwise, in accordance with the provisions set out in the Protocol on the position of the United Kingdom and Ireland attached to the Treaties. Title IV does not apply to Denmark either, by virtue of the Protocol on the position of Denmark attached to the Treaties.

5.   **Subsidiarity and proportionality**

Subsidiarity
The purpose of this proposal is to lay down in Community law criteria and mechanisms for determining the Member State responsible for examining an asylum application which create mutual rights and obligations between the Member States. Clearly, by their very nature these rights and obligations cannot be created by the Member States acting in isolation and can, in view of the scope or the effects of the proposed measure, only be established at Community level.

Proportionality
The proposal is also designed to replace an instrument of international public law creating mutual rights and obligations between the Member States in identical terms for all Member States. The only instrument which meets these conditions in Community law is a regulation.

COMMISSION REGULATION (EC)
No. 1560/2003 of 2 September 2003
laying down detailed rules for the application of Council Regulation (EC) No. 343/2003
establishing the criteria and mechanisms for determining the Member State responsible
for examining an asylum application lodged in one of the Member States by a third-
country national[1]

THE COMMISSION OF THE EUROPEAN COMMUNITIES,
Having regard to the Treaty establishing the European Community,
Having regard to Council Regulation (EC) No. 343/2003 of 18 February 2003 establishing
the criteria and mechanisms for determining the Member State responsible for examining
an asylum application lodged in one of the Member States by a third-country national,[2] and
in particular Article 15(5), Article 17(3), Article 18(3), Article 19(3) and (5), Article 20(1),
(3) and(4) and Article 22(2) thereof,

Whereas:

(1) A number of specific arrangements must be established for the effective application of
Regulation (EC) No. 343/2003. Those arrangements must be clearly defined so as to facilitate cooperation between the authorities in the Member States competent for implementing
that Regulation as regards the transmission and processing of requests for the purposes of
taking charge and taking back, requests for information and the carrying out of transfers.

(2) To ensure the greatest possible continuity between the Convention determining the State
responsible for examining applications for asylum lodged in one of the Member States of
the European Communities,[3] signed in Dublin on 15 June 1990, and Regulation (EC) No.
343/2003, which replaces that Convention, this Regulation should be based on the common
principles, lists and forms adopted by the committee set up by Article18 of that Convention,
with the inclusion of amendments necessitated by the introduction of new criteria, the wording of certain provisions and of the lessons drawn from experience.

(3) The interaction between the procedures laid down in Regulation (EC) No. 343/2003 and
the application of Council Regulation (EC) No. 2725/2000 of 11 December 2000 concerning the establishment of 'Eurodac' for the comparison of fingerprints for the effective application of the Dublin Convention[4] must be taken into account.

---

[1]OJ L 222, 5.9.2003, p. 3.
[2] OJ L 50, 25.2.2003, p. 1.
[3] OJ C 254, 19.8.1997, p. 1.
[4] OJ L 316, 15.12.2000, p. 1.

(4) It is desirable, both for the Member States and the asylum seekers concerned, that there should be a mechanism for finding a solution in cases where Member States differ over the application of the humanitarian clause in Article 15 of Regulation (EC) No. 343/2003.

(5) The establishment of an electronic transmission network to facilitate the implementation of Regulation (EC) No. 343/2003 means that rules must be laid down relating to the technical standards applicable and the practical arrangements for using the network.

(6) Directive 95/46/EC of the European Parliament and of the Council of 24 October 1995 on the protection of individuals with regard to the processing of personal data and on the free movement of such data[5] applies to processing carried out pursuant to the present Regulation in accordance with Article 21 of Regulation (EC) No. 343/2003.

(7) In accordance with Articles 1 and 2 of the Protocol on the position of Denmark annexed to the Treaty on European Union and to the Treaty establishing the European Community, Denmark, which is not bound by Regulation (EC) No. 343/2003, is not bound by the present Regulation or subject to its application, until such time as an agreement allowing it to participate in Regulation (EC) No. 343/2003 is reached.

(8) In accordance with Article 4 of the Agreement of 19 January 2001 between the European Community and the Republic of Iceland and the Kingdom of Norway concerning the criteria and mechanisms for establishing the State responsible for examining an application for asylum lodged in a Member State or in Iceland or Norway,[6] this Regulation is to be applied by Iceland and Norway as it is applied by the Member States of the European Community. Consequently, for the purposes of this Regulation, Member States also include Iceland and Norway.

(9) It is necessary for the present Regulation to enter into force as quickly as possible to enable Regulation (EC) No. 343/2003 to be applied.

(10) The measures set out in this Regulation are in accordance with the opinion of the Committee set up by Article 27 of Regulation (EC) No. 343/2003,

HAS ADOPTED THIS REGULATION:

TITLE I
PROCEDURES

CHAPTER I
Preparation of Request

Article 1
Preparation of requests for taking charge

1. Requests for taking charge shall be made on a standard form in accordance with the model in Annex I. The form shall include mandatory fields which must be duly filled in and

---

[5] OJ L 281, 23.11.1995, p. 31.
[6] OJ L 93, 3.4.2001, p. 40.

other fields to be filled in if the information is available. Additional information may be entered in the field set aside for the purpose. The request shall also include:

(a) a copy of all the proof and circumstantial evidence showing that the requested Member State is responsible for examining the application for asylum, accompanied, where appropriate, by comments on the circumstances in which it was obtained and the probative value attached to it by the requesting Member State, with reference to the lists of proof and circumstantial evidence referred to in Article 18(3) of Regulation (EC) No. 343/2003, which are set out in Annex II to the present Regulation;

(b) where necessary, a copy of any written declarations made by or statements taken from the applicant.

2. Where the request is based on a positive result (hit) transmitted by the Eurodac Central Unit in accordance with Article 4(5) of Regulation (EC) No. 2725/2000 after comparison of the asylum seeker's fingerprints with fingerprint data previously taken and sent to the Central Unit in accordance with Article 8 of that Regulation and checked in accordance with Article 4(6) of that Regulation, it shall also include the data supplied by the Central Unit.

3. Where the requesting Member State asks for an urgent reply in accordance with Article 17(2) of Regulation (EC) No. 343/2003, the request shall describe the circumstances of the application for asylum and shall state the reasons in law and in fact which warrant an urgent reply.

Article 2
Preparation of requests for taking back

Requests for taking back shall be made on a standard form in accordance with the model in Annex III, setting out the nature of the request, the reasons for it and the provisions of Regulation (EC) No. 343/2003 on which it is based. The request shall also include the positive result (hit) transmitted by the Eurodac Central Unit, in accordance with Article 4(5) of Regulation EC) No. 2725/2000, after comparison of the applicant's fingerprints with fingerprint data previously taken and sent to the Central Unit in accordance with Article 4(1) and (2) of that Regulation and checked in accordance with Article 4(6) of that Regulation. For requests relating to applications dating from before Eurodac became operational, a copy of the fingerprints shall be attached to the form.

CHAPTER II
Reaction to Requests

Article 3
Processing requests for taking charge

1. The arguments in law and in fact set out in the request shall be examined in the light of the provisions of Regulation (EC) No. 343/2003 and the lists of proof and circumstantial evidence which are set out in Annex II to the present Regulation.

2. Whatever the criteria and provisions of Regulation (EC) No. 343/2003 that are relied on, the requested Member State shall, within the time allowed by Article 18(1) and (6) of that

Regulation, check exhaustively and objectively, on the basis of all information directly or indirectly available to it, whether its responsibility for examining the application for asylum is established. If the checks by the requested Member State reveal that it is responsible under at least one of the criteria of that Regulation, it shall acknowledge its responsibility.

Article 4
Processing of requests for taking back

Where a request for taking back is based on data supplied by the Eurodac Central Unit and checked by the requesting Member State, in accordance with Article 4(6) of Regulation (EC) No. 2725/2000, the requested Member State shall acknowledge its responsibility unless the checks carried out reveal that its obligations have ceased under the second subparagraph of Article 4(5) or under Article 16(2), (3) or (4) of Regulation (EC) No. 343/2003. The fact that obligations have ceased on the basis of those provisions may be relied on only on the basis of material evidence or substantiated and verifiable statements by the asylum seeker.

Article 5
Negative reply

1. Where, after checks are carried out, the requested Member State considers that the evidence submitted does not establish its responsibility, the negative reply it sends to the requesting Member State shall state full and detailed reasons for its refusal.

2. Where the requesting Member State feels that such a refusal is based on a misappraisal, or where it has additional evidence to put forward, it may ask for its request to be reexamined. This option must be exercised within three weeks following receipt of the negative reply. The requested Member State shall endeavour to reply within two weeks. In any event, this additional procedure shall not extend the time limits laid down in Article 18(1) and (6) and Article 20(1)(b) of Regulation (EC) No. 343/2003.

Article 6
Positive reply

Where the Member State accepts responsibility, the reply shall say so, specifying the provision of Regulation (EC) No. 343/2003 that is taken as a basis, and shall include practical details regarding the subsequent transfer, such as contact particulars of the department or person to be contacted.

CHAPTER III
Transfers

Article 7
Practical arrangements for transfers

1. Transfers to the Member State responsible may be carried out in one of the following ways:
   (a) at the request of the asylum seeker, by a certain specified date;

(b) by supervised departure, with the asylum seeker being accompanied to the point of embarkation by an official of the requesting Member State, the responsible Member State being notified of the place, date and time of the asylum seeker's arrival within an agreed time limit;

(c) under escort, the asylum seeker being accompanied by an official of the requesting Member State or by a representative of an agency empowered by the requesting Member State to act in that capacity and handed over to the authorities in the responsible Member State.

2. In the cases referred to in paragraph 1(a) and (b), the applicant shall be supplied with the laissez-passer referred to in Article 19(3) and Article 20(1)(e) of Regulation (EC) No. 343/2003, a model of which is set out in Annex IV to the present Regulation, to allow him to enter the Member State responsible and to identify himself on his arrival at the place and time indicated to him at the time of notification of the decision on taking charge or taking back by the Member State responsible. In the case referred to in paragraph 1(c), a laissez-passer shall be issued if the asylum seeker is not in possession of identity documents. The time and place of transfer shall be agreed in advance by the Member States concerned in accordance with the procedure set out in Article 8.

3. The Member State making the transfer shall ensure that all the asylum seeker's documents are returned to him before his departure, given into the safe keeping of members of the escort to be handed to the competent authorities of the Member State responsible, or sent by other appropriate means.

Article 8
Cooperation on transfers

1. It is the obligation of the Member State responsible to allow the asylum seeker's transfer to take place as quickly as possible and to ensure that no obstacles are put in his way. That Member State shall determine, where appropriate, the location on its territory to which the asylum seeker will be transferred or handed over to the competent authorities, taking account of geographical constraints and modes of transport available to the Member State making the transfer. In no case may a requirement be imposed that the escort accompany the asylum seeker beyond the point of arrival of the international means of transport used or that the Member State making the transfer meet the costs of transport beyond that point.

2. The Member State organising the transfer shall arrange the transport for the asylum seeker and his escort and decide, in consultation with the Member State responsible, on the time of arrival and, where necessary, on the details of the handover to the competent authorities. The Member State responsible may require that three working days' notice be given.

Article 9
Postponed and delayed transfers

1. The Member State responsible shall be informed without delay of any postponement due either to an appeal or review procedure with suspensive effect, or physical reasons such as ill health of the asylum seeker, non-availability of transport or the fact that the asylum seeker has withdrawn from the transfer procedure.

2. A Member State which, for one of the reasons set out in Article 19(4) and Article 20(2) of Regulation (EC) No. 343/2003, cannot carry out the transfer within the normal time limit of six months provided for in Article 19(3) and Article 20(1)(d) of that Regulation, shall inform the Member State responsible before the end of that time limit. Otherwise, the responsibility for processing the application for asylum and the other obligations under Regulation (EC) No. 343/2003 falls to the former Member State, in accordance with Article 19(4) and Article 20(2) of that Regulation.

3. When, for one of the reasons set out in Article 19(4) and Article 20(2) of Regulation (EC) No. 343/2003, a Member State undertakes to carry out the transfer after the normal time limit of six months, it shall make the necessary arrangements in advance with the Member State responsible.

Article 10
Transfer following an acceptance by default

1. Where, pursuant to Article 18(7) or Article 20(1)(c) of Regulation (EC) No. 343/2003 as appropriate, the requested Member State is deemed to have accepted a request to take charge or to take back, the requesting Member State shall initiate the consultations needed to organise the transfer.

2. If asked to do so by the requesting Member State, the Member State responsible must confirm in writing, without delay, that it acknowledges its responsibility as a result of its failure to reply within the time limit. The Member State responsible shall take the necessary steps to determine the asylum seeker's place of arrival as quickly as possible and, where applicable, agree with the requesting Member State the time of arrival and the practical details of the handover to the competent authorities.

CHAPTER IV
Humanitarian Clause

Article 11
Situations of dependency

1. Article 15(2) of Regulation (EC) No. 343/2003 shall apply whether the asylum seeker is dependent on the assistance of a relative present in another Member State or a relative present in another Member State is dependent on the assistance of the asylum seeker.

2. The situations of dependency referred to in Article 15(2) of Regulation (EC) No. 343/2003 shall be assessed, as far as possible, on the basis of objective criteria such as medical certificates. Where such evidence is not available or cannot be supplied, humanitarian grounds shall be taken as proven only on the basis of convincing information supplied by the persons concerned.

3. The following points shall be taken into account in assessing the necessity and appropriateness of bringing together the persons concerned:
    (a) the family situation which existed in the country of origin;

(b) the circumstances in which the persons concerned were separated;

(c) the status of the various asylum procedures or procedures under the legislation on aliens under way in the Member States.

4. The application of Article 15(2) of Regulation (EC) No. 343/2003 shall, in any event, be subject to the assurance that the asylum seeker or relative will actually provide the assistance needed.

5. The Member State in which the relatives will be reunited and the date of the transfer shall be agreed by the Member States concerned, taking account of:

(a) the ability of the dependent person to travel;

(b) the situation of the persons concerned as regards residence, preference being given to the bringing the asylum seeker together with his relative where the latter already has a valid residence permit and resources in the Member State in which he resides.

Article 12
Unaccompanied minors

1. Where the decision to entrust the care of an unaccompanied minor to a relative other than the mother, father or legal guardian is likely to cause particular difficulties, particularly where the adult concerned resides outside the jurisdiction of the Member State in which the minor has applied for asylum, cooperation between the competent authorities in the Member States, in particular the authorities or courts responsible for the protection of minors, shall be facilitated and the necessary steps taken to ensure that those authorities can decide, with full knowledge of the facts, on the ability of the adult or adults concerned to take charge of the minor in a way which serves his best interests.

Options now available in the field of cooperation on judicial and civil matters shall be taken account of in this connection.

2. The fact that the duration of procedures for placing a minor may lead to a failure to observe the time limits set in Article 18(1) and (6) and Article 19(4) of Regulation (EC) No. 343/2003 shall not necessarily be an obstacle to continuing the procedure for determining the Member State responsible or carrying out a transfer.

Article 13
Procedures

1. The initiative of requesting another Member State to take charge of an asylum seeker on the basis of Article 15 of Regulation (EC) No. 343/2003 shall be taken either by the Member State where the application for asylum was made and which is carrying out a procedure to determine the Member State responsible, or by the Member State responsible.

2. The request to take charge shall contain all the material in the possession of the requesting Member State to allow the requested Member State to assess the situation.

3. The requested Member State shall carry out the necessary checks to establish, where applicable, humanitarian reasons, particularly of a family or cultural nature, the level of

dependency of the person concerned or the ability and commitment of the other person concerned to provide the assistance desired.

4. In all events, the persons concerned must have given their consent.

Article 14
Conciliation

1. Where the Member States cannot resolve a dispute, either on the need to carry out a transfer or to bring relatives together on the basis of Article 15 of Regulation (EC) No. 343/2003, or on the Member State in which the persons concerned should be reunited, they may have recourse to the conciliation procedure provided for in paragraph 2 of this Article.

2. The conciliation procedure shall be initiated by a request from one of the Member States in dispute to the Chairman of the Committee set up by Article 27 of Regulation (EC) No. 343/2003. By agreeing to use the conciliation procedure, the Member States concerned undertake to take the utmost account of the solution proposed.

The Chairman of the Committee shall appoint three members of the Committee representing three Member States not connected with the matter. They shall receive the arguments of the parties either in writing or orally and, after deliberation, shall propose a solution within one month, where necessary after a vote.

The Chairman of the Committee, or his deputy, shall chair the discussion. He may put forward his point of view but he may not vote. Whether it is adopted or rejected by the parties, the solution proposed shall be final and irrevocable.

CHAPTER V
Common Provisions

Article 15
Transmission of requests

1. Requests, replies and all written correspondence between Member States concerning the application of Regulation (EC) No. 343/2003 shall where possible be sent through the 'DubliNet' electronic communications network, set up under Title II of the present Regulation.

By way of derogation from the first subparagraph, correspondence between the departments responsible for carrying out transfers and competent departments in the requested Member State regarding the practical arrangements for transfers, time and place of arrival, particularly where the asylum seeker is under escort, may be transmitted by other means.

2. Any request, reply or correspondence emanating from a National Access Point, as referred to in Article 19, shall be deemed to be authentic.

3. The acknowledgement issued by the system shall be taken as proof of transmission and of the date and time of receipt of the request or reply.

Article 16
Language of communication

The language or languages of communication shall be chosen by agreement between the Member States concerned.

Article 17
Consent of the persons concerned

1. For the application of Articles 7 and 8, Article 15(1) and Article 21(3) of Regulation (EC) No. 343/2003, which require the persons concerned to express a desire or give consent, their approval must be given in writing.

2. In the case of Article 21(3) of Regulation (EC) No. 343/2003, the applicant must know for what information he is giving his approval.

TITLE II
ESTABLISHMENT OF THE 'DUBLINET' NETWORK

CHAPTER I
Technical Standards

Article 18
Establishment of 'DubliNet'

1. The secure electronic means of transmission referred to in Article 22(2) of Regulation (EC) No. 343/2003 shall be known as 'DubliNet'.

2. DubliNet is based on the use of the generic IDA services referred to in Article 4 of Decision No. 1720/1999/EC.[7]

Article 19
National Access Points

1. Each Member State shall have a single designated National Access Point.

2. The National Access Points shall be responsible for processing incoming data and transmitting outgoing data.

3. The National Access Points shall be responsible for issuing an acknowledgement of receipt for every incoming transmission.

4. The forms of which the models are set out in Annexes I and III and the form for the request of information set out in Annex V shall be sent between National Access Points in

---

[7] OJ L 203, 3.8.1999, p. 9.

the format supplied by the Commission. The Commission shall inform the Member States of the technical standards required.

CHAPTER II
Rules for Use

Article 20
Reference number

1. Each transmission shall have a reference number making it possible unambiguously to identify the case to which it relates and the Member State making the request. That number must also make it possible to determine whether the transmission relates to a request for taking charge (type 1), a request for taking back (type 2) or a request for information (type 3).

2. The reference number shall begin with the letters used to identify the Member State in Eurodac. This code shall be followed by the number indicating the type of request, according to the classification set out in paragraph 1. If the request is based on data supplied by Eurodac, the Eurodac reference number shall be included.

Article 21
Continuous operation

1. The Member States shall take the necessary steps to ensure that their National Access Points operate without interruption.

2. If the operation of a National Access Point is interrupted for more than seven working hours the Member State shall notify the competent authorities designated pursuant to Article 22(1) of Regulation (EC) No. 343/2003 and the Commission and shall take all the necessary steps to ensure that normal operation is resumed as soon as possible.

3. If a National Access Point has sent data to a National Access Point that has experienced an interruption in its operation, the acknowledgement of transmission generated by the IDA generic services shall be used as proof of the date and time of transmission. The deadlines set by Regulation (EC) No. 343/2003 for sending a request or a reply shall not be suspended for the duration of the interruption of the operation of the National Access Point in question.

TITLE III
TRANSITIONAL AND FINAL PROVISIONS

Article 22
Laissez-passer produced for the purposes of the Dublin Convention

Laissez-passer printed for the purposes of the Dublin Convention shall be accepted for the transfer of applicants for asylum under Regulation (EC) No. 343/2003 for a period of no more than 18 months following the entry into force of the present Regulation.

Article 23
Entry into force

This Regulation shall enter into force on the day following that of its publication in the Official Journal of the European Union.

This Regulation shall be binding in its entirety and directly applicable in all Member States.

ANNEX I

STANDARD FORM FOR DETERMINING THE MEMBER STATE (¹) RESPONSIBLE OR EXAMINING AN APPLICATION FOR ASYLUM

Request for taking charge presented on the basis of the following Article of Council Regulation (EC) No 343/2003:

Article 6 (unaccompanied minor): ☐

Article 7 (family member resident in the Member State as a refugee): ☐

Article 8 (family member applying for asylum in a Member State): ☐

Article 9(1) or (3) (valid residence document): ☐

Article 9(2) or (3) (valid visa): ☐

Article 9(4) (residence document which expired less than two years previously or visa which expired less than six months previously): ☐

Article 10(1) (illegal entry at external frontier less than 12 months ago): ☐

Article 10(2) (residence of at least 5 months in the Member State): ☐

Article 11(1) (visa requirement waived for entry): ☐

Article 14 (keeping family groups together): ☐

Article 15 (humanitarian grounds): ☐

Eurodac data: ☐   Eurodac No: ....

Reply requested urgently: ☐   No later than: ....

Reason for urgency: ....
....

Photo

File number:

Personal particulars of applicant

1. Surname (*)   ....

   Maiden name   ....

2. Forename(s)   ....

3. Does the applicant use/has he/she used other names?   ☐ Yes   ☐ No

   What are/were they?   ....

4. Date of birth   ....

5. Place of birth   ....

   District/region   ....

   Country   ....

6. Nationality(ies)   ....

   (indicate all)   ....

   (a) current   ....

   (b) previous   ....

   (c) none/stateless   ....

7. Sex   ☐ Male   ☐ Female

8. Name of father   ....

9. Name of mother   ....

10. Marital status

☐ Single   ☐ Married   ☐ Widowed
☐ Divorced   ☐ Cohabitee

11. Language(s) of origin

....
....
....
....

Personal particulars of family members

12. Spouse Surname (*), maiden name, forename(s), sex, date of birth, place of birth, place of residence
   (if the spouse is seeking asylum a separate form should be completed; in this case include the reference number of the other member of the couple on all forms).

....
....

Reference number of spouse (if necessary): ....

13. Children Surname(*), forename(s), sex, date of birth, place of birth, place of residence
   (indicate all children; a separate form should be completed for children over 16 years of age if asylum is sought)

(a) ....
(b) ....
(c) ....
(d) ....
(e) ....

14. Place and date of the application for asylum in the country of residence: ....
....

Previous asylum procedures

15. Has the asylum applicant ever previously applied for asylum or recognition of refugee status in the country of residence or in another country?

☐ Yes   ☐ No

When and where?

....

Was any decision taken on the application?

☐ No   ☐ Don't know   ☐ Yes, application rejected

When was the decision taken?

....
....

Identity papers

16. National passport

☐ Yes   ☐ No

Number   ....
Issued on   ....
By   ....
Valid until   ....

17. Document replacing passport

☐ Yes   ☐ No

Number   ....
Issued on   ....
By   ....
Valid until   ....

18. Other document

☐ Yes   ☐ No

Number   ....
Issued on   ....
By   ....
Valid until   ....

19. In the absence of documents:
(specify whether they may have contained a valid visa or residence permit and, if so, indicate the issuing authority and date of issue as well as the period of validity)

☐ Left without documents ☐ Documents lost ☐ Documents stolen
(When? where? ....
....)

☐ Other reasons
(Please specify ....
....)

Residence documents/visas

20. Does the asylum applicant possess a residence document/ visa for the country of residence?

☐ Yes   ☐ No

Type of document

☐ Residence permit   ☐ Entry visa
☐ Transit visa

Issued on
By
Valid until

....
....
....

21. Does the asylum applicant possess a residence document/ visa for another EU Member State? (²)

☐ Yes   ☐ No

Which State?
Type of document

☐ Residence permit   ☐ Entry visa
☐ Transit visa

Issued on
By
Valid until

....
....
....

Travel route

22. Country in which the journey was begun (country of origin or of provenance)

....

— Route followed from country where journey was begun to point of entry into country in which asylum is requested

....

— Dates and times of travel

....

— Crossed border on

....

— At the authorised crossing point
or

....

— Avoided border controls (entered illegally)
— Means of transport used

☐ Public transport (what form? ....)
☐ Own vehicle ....
☐ Other means (how? ....)
....

23. Did the asylum applicant enter via another European Union Member State? (³)

☐ Yes   ☐ No

— Which was the first EU Member State entered?

....

— Crossed border at authorised crossing point,
or

....

— Avoided border controls at
— When?

....
....

Residence in another EU Member State (⁴)

24. Residence in another EU Member State or States after leaving country in which journey was begun (country of origin/ provenance)

☐ Yes   ☐ No

— In which State or States?
— From — to
— Place/exact address

....
....
....

— Residence was

☐ Authorised   ☐ Unauthorised

— Period of validity of residence permit

....
....

— Purpose of residence

....
....

Particulars of family members living in EU Member States (⁵)

25. (a) Is any family member residing in a Member State?   ☐ Yes   ☐ No
    — Name of family member   ....
    — Date of birth   ....
    — Marital status   ☐ Single   ☐ Married   ☐ Widowed
    ☐ Divorced
    — Relationship   ☐ spouse   ☐ father
    ☐ mother   ☐ child
    ☐ brother   ☐ sister
    ☐ guardian   ☐ other (please specify)
    — Member State   ....
    ....
    — Address in that State   ....
    — Residence status   ☐ recognised refugee   ☐ resident
    ☐ asylum applicant   ☐ illegal

    (b) Do any of those concerned object to the examination of
    the application for asylum in that Member State?   ☐ Yes   ☐ No

Other useful information
....
....
....
....
....

———

(¹) *Note:* Pursuant to the Agreement of 19 January 2001 between the European Community and the Republic of Iceland and the Kingdom of Norway, the words 'Member States' include Iceland and Norway.
(²) Including Iceland and Norway.
(³) Including Iceland and Norway.
(⁴) Including Iceland and Norway.
(⁵) Including Iceland and Norway.
(*) In block capitals.

ANNEX II
(References are to Articles of Council Regulation (EC) No. 343/2003)

LIST A
Means of Proof

I. Process of determining the State responsible for examining an application for asylum

1. Presence of a family member (father, mother, guardian) of an asylum applicant who is an unaccompanied minor (Article 6)

Probative evidence

— written confirmation of the information by the other Member State,
— extracts from registers,
— residence permits issued to the family member,
— evidence that the persons are related, if available,
— failing this, and if necessary, a DNA or blood test.

2. Legal residence in a Member State of a family member recognised as having refugee status (Article 7)

Probative evidence

— written confirmation of the information by the other Member State,
— extracts from registers,
— residence permits issued to the individual with refugee status,
— evidence that the persons are related, if available,
— consent of the persons concerned.

3. Presence of a family member applying for asylum whose application has not yet been the subject of a first decision regarding the substance in a Member State (Article 8)

Probative evidence

— written confirmation of the information by the other Member State,
— extracts from registers,
— temporary residence authorisations issued to the individual while the asylum application is being examined,
— evidence that the persons are related, if available,
— failing this, if necessary, a DNA or blood test,
— consent of the persons concerned.

4. Valid residence documents (Article 9(1) and (3) or residence documents which expired less than two years previously (and date of entry into force) (Article 9(4))

Probative evidence

— residence document,
— extracts from the register of aliens or similar registers,
— reports/confirmation of the information by the Member State which issued the residence document.

5. Valid visas (Article 9(2) and(3)) and visas which expired less than six months previously (and date of entry into force) (Article 9(4))

Probative evidence

— visa issued (valid or expired, as appropriate),
— extracts from the register of aliens or similar registers,
— reports/confirmation of the information by the Member State which issued the visa.

6. Legal entry into the territory at an external frontier (Article 11)

Probative evidence

— entry stamp in a passport,
— exit stamp from a country bordering on a Member State, bearing in mind the route taken by the asylum-seeker and the date the frontier was crossed,
— tickets conclusively establishing entry at an external frontier,
— entry stamp or similar endorsement in passport.

7. Illegal entry at an external frontier (Article 10(1))

Probative evidence

— positive match by Eurodac from a comparison of the fingerprints of the applicant with fingerprints taken pursuant to Article 8 of the 'Eurodac' Regulation,
— entry stamp in a forged or falsified passport,
— exit stamp from a country bordering on a Member State, bearing in mind the route taken by the asylum-seeker and the date the frontier was crossed,
— tickets conclusively establishing entry at an external frontier,
— entry stamp or similar endorsement in passport.

8. Residence in a Member State for at least five months (Article 10(2))

Probative evidence

— residence authorisations issued while the application for a residence permit is being examined,
— requests to leave the territory or expulsion order issued on dates at least five months apart or that have not been enforced,
— extracts from the records of hospitals, prisons, detention centres.

9. Departure from the territory of the Member States (Article 16(3))

Probative evidence

— exit stamp,
— extracts from third-country registers (substantiating residence),
— tickets conclusively establishing departure from or entry at an external frontier,
— report/confirmation by the Member State from which the asylum-seeker left the territory of the Member States,
— stamp of third country bordering on a Member State, bearing in mind the route taken by the asylum-seeker and the date the frontier was crossed.

II. Obligation on the Member State responsible for examining the application for asylum to readmit or take back the asylum-seeker

1. Process of determining the Member State responsible is under way in the Member State where the asylum application was lodged (Article 4(5))

Probative evidence

— positive match by Eurodac from a comparison of the fingerprints of the applicant with fingerprints taken pursuant to Article 4 of the 'Eurodac' Regulation,
— form submitted by the asylum-seeker,
— official report drawn up by the authorities,
— fingerprints taken in connection with an asylum application,
— extracts from relevant registers and files,
— written report by the authorities attesting that an application has been made.

2. Application for asylum is under examination or was lodged previously (Article 16(1)(c)(d) and (e))

Probative evidence

— positive match by Eurodac from a comparison of the fingerprints of the applicant with fingerprints taken pursuant to Article 4 of the 'Eurodac' Regulation,
— form submitted by the asylum-seeker,
— official report drawn up by the authorities,
— fingerprints taken in connection with an asylum application,
— extracts from relevant registers and files,
— written report by the authorities attesting that an application has been made.

3. Departure from the territory of the Member States (Article 4(5), Article 16(3))

Probative evidence
— exit stamp,
— extracts from third-country registers (substantiating residence),
— exit stamp from a third country bordering on a Member State, bearing in mind the route taken by the asylum seeker and the date on which the frontier was crossed,
— written proof from the authorities that the alien has actually been expelled.

4. Expulsion from the territory of the Member States (Article 16(4))

Probative evidence

— written proof from the authorities that the alien has actually been expelled,
— exit stamp,
— confirmation of the information regarding expulsion by the third country.

LIST B
Circumstantial Evidence

I. Process of determining the State responsible for examining an application for asylum

1. Presence of a family member (father, mother, guardian) of an asylum applicant who is an unaccompanied minor (Article 6)

Indicative evidence[1]

— verifiable information from the asylum applicant,
— statements by the family members concerned,
— reports/confirmation of the information by an international organisation, such as UNHCR.

2. Legal residence in a Member State of a family member recognised as having refugee status (Article 7)

Indicative evidence

— verifiable information from the asylum applicant,
— reports/confirmation of the information by an international organisation, such as UNHCR.

3. Presence of a family member applying for asylum whose application has not yet been the subject of a first decision regarding the substance in a Member State (Article 8)

Indicative evidence

— verifiable information from the asylum applicant,
— reports/confirmation of the information by an international organisation, such as UNHCR.

4. Valid residence documents (Article 9(1) and (3)) or residence documents which expired less than two years previously (and date of entry into force) (Article 9(4))

Indicative evidence

— detailed and verifiable statements by the asylum applicant,
— reports/confirmation of the information by an international organisation, such as UNHCR,
— reports/confirmation of the information by the Member State which did not issue the residence permit,
— reports/confirmation of the information by family members, travelling companions, etc.

5. Valid visas (Article 9(2) and (3)) and visas which expired less than six months previously (and date of entry into force) (Article 9(4))

Indicative evidence

— detailed and verifiable statements by the asylum applicant,
— reports/confirmation of the information by an international organisation, such as UNHCR,
— reports/confirmation of the information by the Member State which did not issue the residence permit,
— reports/confirmation of the information by family members, travelling companions, etc.

6. Legal entry into the territory at an external frontier (Article 11)

Indicative evidence

— detailed and verifiable statements by the asylum applicant,
— reports/confirmation of the information by an international organisation, such as UNHCR,

---

[1] This indicative evidence must always be followed by an item of probative evidence as defined in list A.

— reports/confirmation of the information by another Member State or third country,
— reports/confirmation of the information by family members, travelling companions, etc.
— fingerprints, except in cases where the authorities decided to take fingerprints when the alien crossed the external frontier. In such cases, they constitute probative evidence as defined in list A,
— tickets,
— hotel bills,
— entry cards for public or private institutions in the Member States,
— appointment cards for doctors, dentists, etc.,
— information showing that the asylum applicant has used the services of a travel agency,
—   other circumstantial evidence of the same kind.

7. Illegal entry into the territory at an external frontier (Article 10(1))

Indicative evidence

— detailed and verifiable statements by the asylum applicant,
— reports/confirmation of the information by an international organisation, such as UNHCR,
— reports/confirmation of the information by another Member State or third country,
— reports/confirmation of the information by family members, travelling companions, etc.,
— fingerprints, except in cases where the authorities decided to take fingerprints when the alien crossed the external frontier. In such cases, they constitute probative evidence as defined in list A,
— tickets,
— hotel bills,
— entry cards for public or private institutions in the Member States,
— appointment cards for doctors, dentists, etc.,
— information showing that the asylum applicant has used the services of a courier or a travel agency,
— other circumstantial evidence of the same kind.

8. Residence in a Member State for at least five months (Article 10(2))

Indicative evidence

— detailed and verifiable statements by the asylum applicant,
— reports/confirmation of the information by an international organisation, such as UNHCR,
— reports/confirmation of the information by a non-governmental organisation, such as an organisation providing accommodation for those in need,
— reports/confirmation of the information by family members, travelling companions, etc.,
— fingerprints,
— tickets,
— hotel bills,
— entry cards for public or private institutions in the Member States,
— appointment cards for doctors, dentists, etc.,
— information showing that the asylum applicant has used the services of a courier or a travel agency,
— other circumstantial evidence of the same kind.

9. Departure from the territory of the Member States (Article 16(3))

Indicative evidence

— detailed and verifiable statements by the asylum applicant,
— reports/confirmation of the information by an international organisation, such as UNHCR,
— reports/confirmation of the information by another Member State,
— re Article 3(7) and Article 10(3): exit stamp where the asylum applicant concerned has left the

territory of the Member States for a period of at least three months,
— reports/confirmation of the information by family members, travelling companions, etc.,
— fingerprints, except in cases where the authorities decided to take fingerprints when the alien crossed the external frontier. In such cases, they constitute probative evidence as defined in list A,
— tickets,
— hotel bills,
— appointment cards for doctors, dentists, etc. in a third country,
— information showing that the asylum applicant has used the services of a courier or a travel agency,
— other circumstantial evidence of the same kind.

II. Obligation on the Member State responsible for examining the application for asylum to readmit or take back the asylum-seeker

1. Process of determining the Member State responsible is under way in the Member State where the asylum application was lodged (Article 4(5))

Indicative evidence

— verifiable statements by the asylum applicant,
— reports/confirmation of the information by an international organisation, such as UNHCR,
— reports/confirmation of the information by family members, travelling companions, etc.,
— reports/confirmation of the information by another Member State.

2. Application for asylum is under examination or was lodged previously (Article 16(1) (c)(d)(e))

Indicative evidence

— verifiable statements by the asylum applicant,
— reports/confirmation of the information by an international organisation, such as UNHCR,
— reports/confirmation of the information by another Member State.

3. Departure from the territory of the Member States (Article 4(5), Article 16(3))

Indicative evidence

— detailed and verifiable statements by the asylum applicant,
— reports/confirmation of the information by an international organisation, such as UNHCR,
— reports/confirmation of the information by another Member State,
— exit stamp where the asylum applicant concerned has left the territory of the Member States for a period of at least three months,
— reports/confirmation of the information by family members, travelling companions, etc.,
— fingerprints, except in cases where the authorities decided to take fingerprints when the alien crossed the external frontier. In such cases, they constitute probative evidence as defined in list A,
— tickets,
— hotel bills,
— appointment cards for doctors, dentists, etc. in a third country,
— information showing that the asylum applicant has used the services of a courier or a travel agency,
— other circumstantial evidence of the same kind.

4. Expulsion from the territory of the Member States (Article 16(4))

Indicative evidence

— verifiable statements by the asylum applicant,
— reports/confirmation of the information by an international organisation, such as UNHCR,
— exit stamp where the asylum applicant concerned has left the territory of the Member States for a period of at least three months,
— reports/confirmation of the information by family members, travelling companions, etc.,
— fingerprints, except in cases where the authorities decided to take fingerprints when the alien crossed the external frontier. In such cases, they constitute probative evidence as defined in list A,
— tickets,
— hotel bills,
— appointment cards for doctors, dentists, etc.,
— information showing that the asylum applicant has used the services of a courier or a travel agency,
— other circumstantial evidence of the same kind.

ANNEX III

STANDARD FORM FOR REQUESTS FOR TAKING BACK

Request for taking back presented on the basis of the following Article of Council Regulation (EC) No 343/2003:

Article 4(5) (process of determining the Member State responsible is under way in the Member State where the application was lodged): □

Article 16(1)(c) (applicant is in the Member State without permission and his application is being examined in the Member State responsible): □

Article 16(1)(d) (applicant has made an application after withdrawing his application in the Member State responsible): □

Article 16(1)(e) (applicant is in the Member State without permission and his application has been rejected in the Member State responsible): □

Eurodac data: □   Eurodac No: ....

Reply requested urgently: □   No later than: ....

Reason for urgency: ....
....

```



          Photo



```

File number:

Personal particulars of applicant

1. Surname (*) ....

   Maiden name ....

2. Forename(s) ....

3. Does the applicant use/has he/she used other names?   □ Yes   □ No

   What are/were they? ....

4. Date of birth ....

5. Place of birth ....

   District/region ....

   Country ....

6. Nationality(ies) ....

   (indicate all) ....

   (a) current ....

   (b) previous ....

   (c) none/stateless ....

7. Sex   □ Male   □ Female

8. Name of father ....

9. Name of mother ....

10. Marital status   □ Single   □ Married   □ Widowed
    □ Divorced   □ Cohabitee

(*) In block capitals.

Previous asylum procedures

11. Has the applicant ever previously applied for asylum or recognition of refugee status in the country of residence or in another country?

☐ Yes   ☐ No

When and where?

....
....

Was any decision taken on the application?

☐ No   ☐ Don't know   ☐ Yes, application rejected

When was the decision taken

....
....

12. Does the applicant state that he left the territory of the Member States?

☐ Yes   ☐ No

If yes:

Date of departure: ....

Date of return: ....

Which country(ies) did he go to?

....

Travel route:

....
....
....

13. Documents submitted by the applicant

Please enclose a list:

....
....
....
....
....
....

Comments:

ANNEX IV

Specimen laissez-passer for transfer of asylum applicants

LAISSEZ-PASSER

Reference No (*):

Issued pursuant to Articles 19 and 20 of Council Regulation (EC) No 343/2003 of 18 February 2003 establishing the criteria and mechanisms for determining the Member State responsible for examining an asylum application lodged in one of the Member States ([1]) by a third-country national.

Valid only for transfer from .... ([2]) to .... ([3]) with the asylum applicant required to present him/herself at

.... ([4]) by .... ([5]).

Issued at:

SURNAME: ....

FORENAMES: ....

PLACE AND DATE OF BIRTH: ....

NATIONALITY: ....

Date of issue: ....

Photo

For the Ministry for the Interior: ....

Seal

The bearer of this laissez-passer has been identified by the authorities .... ([6]) ([7]).

This document is issued pursuant to Articles 19 and 20 of Regulation (EC) No 343/2003 only and cannot under any circumstances be regarded as equivalent to a travel document permitting the external frontier to be crossed or to a document proving the individual's identity.

———

(*) Reference number to be given by the country from which the transfer takes place.
([1]) *NB.* Pursuant to the Agreement of 19 January 2001 between the European Community and the Republic of Iceland and the Kingdom of Norway, the words 'Member States' include Iceland and Norway.
([2]) Member State from which transferred.
([3]) Member State to which transferred.
([4]) Place where the asylum applicant has to present him/herself upon arrival in the Member State responsible.
([5]) Deadline by which the asylum applicant has to present him/herself upon arrival in the Member State responsible.
([6]) On the basis of the following travel or identity documents presented to the authorities.
([7]) On the basis of a statement by the asylum applicant or of documents other than a travel or identity document.

ANNEX V

REQUEST FOR INFORMATION PURSUANT TO ARTICLE 21 OF COUNCIL REGULATION (EC) No 343/2003

Date: ____/____/_____

Reference No: ....

Individual concerned:

— Surname: ....

— Forename: ....

— Date of birth: ....

— Place of birth: ....

— Nationality: ....

Indicative evidence enclosed: ☐ Yes: ☐ No

(please specify) ....

....

....

This request for information concerns:

residence document:	☐	appeal:	☐
travel document:	☐	decision:	☐
visa:	☐	expulsion:	☐
application for asylum:	☐	other:	☐

Details: ....

....

....

....

....

....

....

————————

Chapter 1.3
RECEPTION

COUNCIL DIRECTIVE 2003/9/EC
of 27 January 2003
laying down minimum standards for the reception of asylum seekers[1]

THE COUNCIL OF THE EUROPEAN UNION,
Having regard to the Treaty establishing the European Community, and in particular point (1)(b) of the first subparagraph of Article 63 thereof,
Having regard to the proposal from the Commission,[2]
Having regard to the opinion of the European Parliament,[3]
Having regard to the opinion of the Economic and Social Committee,[4]
Having regard to the opinion of the Committee of the Regions,[5]

Whereas:

(1) A common policy on asylum, including a Common European Asylum System, is a constituent part of the European Union's objective of progressively establishing an area of freedom, security and justice open to those who, forced by circumstances, legitimately seek protection in the Community.

(2) At its special meeting in Tampere on 15 and 16 October 1999, the European Council agreed to work towards establishing a Common European Asylum System, based on the full and inclusive application of the Geneva Convention relating to the Status of Refugees of 28 July 1951, as supplemented by the New York Protocol of 31 January 1967, thus maintaining the principle of non-refoulement.

(3) The Tampere Conclusions provide that a Common European Asylum System should include, in the short term, common minimum conditions of reception of asylum seekers.

(4) The establishment of minimum standards for the reception of asylum seekers is a further step towards a European asylum policy.

(5) This Directive respects the fundamental rights and observes the principles recognised in particular by the Charter of Fundamental Rights of the European Union. In particular, this

---

[1] OJ L 31, 6.2.2003, p. 18.
[2] OJ C 213 E, 31.7.2001, p. 286.
[3] Opinion delivered on 25 April 2002 (not yet published in the Official Journal).
[4] OJ C 48, 21.2.2002, p. 63.
[5] OJ C 107, 3.5.2002, p. 85.

Directive seeks to ensure full respect for human dignity and to promote the application of Articles 1 and 18 of the said Charter.

(6) With respect to the treatment of persons falling within the scope of this Directive, Member States are bound by obligations under instruments of international law to which they are party and which prohibit discrimination.

(7) Minimum standards for the reception of asylum seekers that will normally suffice to ensure them a dignified standard of living and comparable living conditions in all Member States should be laid down.

(8) The harmonisation of conditions for the reception of asylum seekers should help to limit the secondary movements of asylum seekers influenced by the variety of conditions for their reception.

(9) Reception of groups with special needs should be specifically designed to meet those needs.

(10) Reception of applicants who are in detention should be specifically designed to meet their needs in that situation.

(11) In order to ensure compliance with the minimum procedural guarantees consisting in the opportunity to contact organisations or groups of persons that provide legal assistance, information should be provided on such organisations and groups of persons.

(12) The possibility of abuse of the reception system should be restricted by laying down cases for the reduction or withdrawal of reception conditions for asylum seekers.

(13) The efficiency of national reception systems and cooperation among Member States in the field of reception of asylum seekers should be secured.

(14) Appropriate coordination should be encouraged between the competent authorities as regards the reception of asylum seekers, and harmonious relationships between local communities and accommodation centres should therefore be promoted.

(15) It is in the very nature of minimum standards that Member States have the power to introduce or maintain more favourable provisions for third-country nationals and stateless persons who ask for international protection from a Member State.

(16) In this spirit, Member States are also invited to apply the provisions of this Directive in connection with procedures for deciding on applications for forms of protection other than that emanating from the Geneva Convention for third country nationals and stateless persons.

(17) The implementation of this Directive should be evaluated at regular intervals.

(18) Since the objectives of the proposed action, namely to establish minimum standards on the reception of asylum seekers in Member States, cannot be sufficiently achieved by the

Member States and can therefore, by reason of the scale and effects of the proposed action, be better achieved by the Community, the Community may adopt measures in accordance with the principles of subsidiarity as set out in Article 5 of the Treaty. In accordance with the principle of proportionality, as set out in that Article, this Directive does not go beyond what is necessary in order to achieve those objectives.

(19) In accordance with Article 3 of the Protocol on the position of the United Kingdom and Ireland, annexed to the Treaty on European Union and to the Treaty establishing the European Community, the United Kingdom gave notice, by letter of 18 August 2001, of its wish to take part in the adoption and application of this Directive.

(20) In accordance with Article 1 of the said Protocol, Ireland is not participating in the adoption of this Directive. Consequently, and without prejudice to Article 4 of the aforementioned Protocol, the provisions of this Directive do not apply to Ireland.

(21) In accordance with Articles 1 and 2 of the Protocol on the position of Denmark, annexed to the Treaty on European Union and to the Treaty establishing the European Community, Denmark is not participating in the adoption of this Directive and is therefore neither bound by it nor subject to its application,

HAS ADOPTED THIS DIRECTIVE:

CHAPTER I
Purpose, Definitions and Scope

Article 1
Purpose

The purpose of this Directive is to lay down minimum standards for the reception of asylum seekers in Member States.

Article 2
Definitions

For the purposes of this Directive:

(a) 'Geneva Convention' shall mean the Convention of 28 July 1951 relating to the status of refugees, as amended by the New York Protocol of 31 January 1967;

(b) 'application for asylum' shall mean the application made by a third-country national or a stateless person which can be understood as a request for international protection from a Member State, under the Geneva Convention. Any application for international protection is presumed to be an application for asylum unless a third-country national or a stateless person explicitly requests another kind of protection that can be applied for separately;

(c) 'applicant' or 'asylum seeker' shall mean a third country national or a stateless person who has made an application for asylum in respect of which a final decision has not yet been taken;

(d) 'family members' shall mean, in so far as the family already existed in the country of origin, the following members of the applicant's family who are present in the same Member State in relation to the application for asylum:

(i) the spouse of the asylum seeker or his or her unmarried partner in a stable relationship, where the legislation or practice of the Member State concerned treats unmarried couples in a way comparable to married couples under its law relating to aliens;

(ii) the minor children of the couple referred to in point (i) or of the applicant, on condition that they are unmarried and dependent and regardless of whether they were born in or out of wedlock or adopted as defined under the national law;

(e) 'refugee' shall mean a person who fulfils the requirements of Article 1(A) of the Geneva Convention;

(f) 'refugee status' shall mean the status granted by a Member State to a person who is a refugee and is admitted as such to the territory of that Member State;

(g) 'procedures' and 'appeals', shall mean the procedures and appeals established by Member States in their national law;

(h) 'unaccompanied minors' shall mean persons below the age of eighteen who arrive in the territory of the Member States unaccompanied by an adult responsible for them whether by law or by custom, and for as long as they are not effectively taken into the care of such a person; it shall include minors who are left unaccompanied after they have entered the territory of Member States;

(i) 'reception conditions' shall mean the full set of measures that Member States grant to asylum seekers in accordance with this Directive;

(j) 'material reception conditions' shall mean the reception conditions that include housing, food and clothing, provided in kind, or as financial allowances or in vouchers, and a daily expenses allowance;

(k) 'detention' shall mean confinement of an asylum seeker by a Member State within a particular place, where the applicant is deprived of his or her freedom of movement;

(l) 'accommodation centre' shall mean any place used for collective housing of asylum seekers.

Article 3
Scope

1. This Directive shall apply to all third country nationals and stateless persons who make an application for asylum at the border or in the territory of a Member State as long as they are allowed to remain on the territory as asylum seekers, as well as to family members, if they are covered by such application for asylum according to the national law.

2. This Directive shall not apply in cases of requests for diplomatic or territorial asylum submitted to representations of Member States.

3. This Directive shall not apply when the provisions of Council Directive 2001/55/EC of 20 July 2001 on minimum standards for giving temporary protection in the event of a mass influx of displaced persons and on measures promoting a balance of efforts between Member States in receiving such persons and bearing the consequences thereof [6] are applied.

4. Member States may decide to apply this Directive in connection with procedures for deciding on applications for kinds of protection other than that emanating from the Geneva

---

[6] OJ L 212, 7.8.2001, p. 12.

Convention for third-country nationals or stateless persons who are found not to be refugees.

Article 4
More favourable provisions

Member States may introduce or retain more favourable provisions in the field of reception conditions for asylum seekers and other close relatives of the applicant who are present in the same Member State when they are dependent on him or for humanitarian reasons insofar as these provisions are compatible with this Directive.

CHAPTER II
General Provisions on Reception Conditions

Article 5
Information

1. Member States shall inform asylum seekers, within a reasonable time not exceeding fifteen days after they have lodged their application for asylum with the competent authority, of at least any established benefits and of the obligations with which they must comply relating to reception conditions. Member States shall ensure that applicants are provided with information on organisations or groups of persons that provide specific legal assistance and organisations that might be able to help or inform them concerning the available reception conditions, including health care.

2. Member States shall ensure that the information referred in paragraph 1 is in writing and, as far as possible, in a to language that the applicants may reasonably be supposed to understand. Where appropriate, this information may also be supplied orally.

Article 6
Documentation

1. Member States shall ensure that, within three days after an application is lodged with the competent authority, the applicant is provided with a document issued in his or her own name certifying his or her status as an asylum seeker or testifying that he or she is allowed to stay in the territory of the Member State while his or her application is pending or being examined. If the holder is not free to move within all or a part of the territory of the Member State, the document shall also certify this fact.

2. Member States may exclude application of this Article when the asylum seeker is in detention and during the examination of an application for asylum made at the border or within the context of a procedure to decide on the right of the applicant legally to enter the territory of a Member State. In specific cases, during the examination of an application for asylum, Member States may provide applicants with other evidence equivalent to the document referred to in paragraph 1.

3. The document referred to in paragraph 1 need not certify the identity of the asylum seeker.

4. Member States shall adopt the necessary measures to provide asylum seekers with the document referred to in paragraph1, which must be valid for as long as they are authorised to remain in the territory of the Member State concerned or at the border thereof.

5. Member States may provide asylum seekers with a travel document when serious humanitarian reasons arise that require their presence in another State.

Article 7
Residence and freedom of movement

1. Asylum seekers may move freely within the territory of the host Member State or within an area assigned to them by that Member State. The assigned area shall not affect the unalienable sphere of private life and shall allow sufficient scope for guaranteeing access to all benefits under this Directive.

2. Member States may decide on the residence of the asylum seeker for reasons of public interest, public order or, when necessary, for the swift processing and effective monitoring of his or her application.

3. When it proves necessary, for example for legal reasons or reasons of public order, Member States may confine an applicant to a particular place in accordance with their national law.

4. Member States may make provision of the material reception conditions subject to actual residence by the applicants in a specific place, to be determined by the Member States. Such a decision, which may be of a general nature, shall be taken individually and established by national legislation.

5. Member States shall provide for the possibility of granting applicants temporary permission to leave the place of residence mentioned in paragraphs 2 and 4 and/or the assigned area mentioned in paragraph 1. Decisions shall be taken individually, objectively and impartially and reasons shall be given if they are negative. The applicant shall not require permission to keep appointments with authorities and courts if his or her appearance is necessary.

6. Member States shall require applicants to inform the competent authorities of their current address and notify any change of address to such authorities as soon as possible.

Article 8
Families

Member States shall take appropriate measures to maintain as far as possible family unity as present within their territory, if applicants are provided with housing by the Member State concerned. Such measures shall be implemented with the asylum seeker's agreement.

Article 9
Medical screening

Member States may require medical screening for applicants on public health grounds.

Article 10
Schooling and education of minors

1. Member States shall grant to minor children of asylum seekers and to asylum seekers who are minors access to the education system under similar conditions as nationals of the host Member State for so long as an expulsion measure against them or their parents is not actually enforced. Such education may be provided in accommodation centres. The Member State concerned may stipulate that such access must be confined to the State education system. Minors shall be younger than the age of legal majority in the Member State in which the application for asylum was lodged or is being examined. Member States shall not withdraw secondary education for the sole reason that the minor has reached the age of majority.

2. Access to the education system shall not be postponed for more than three months from the date the application for asylum was lodged by the minor or the minor's parents. This period may be extended to one year where specific education is provided in order to facilitate access to the education system.

3. Where access to the education system as set out in paragraph 1 is not possible due to the specific situation of the minor, the Member State may offer other education arrangements.

Article 11
Employment

1. Member States shall determine a period of time, starting from the date on which an application for asylum was lodged, during which an applicant shall not have access to the labour market.

2. If a decision at first instance has not been taken within one year of the presentation of an application for asylum and this delay cannot be attributed to the applicant, Member States shall decide the conditions for granting access to the labour market for the applicant.

3. Access to the labour market shall not be withdrawn during appeals procedures, where an appeal against a negative decision in a regular procedure has suspensive effect, until such time as a negative decision on the appeal is notified.

4. For reasons of labour market policies, Member States may give priority to EU citizens and nationals of States parties to the Agreement on the European Economic Area and also to legally resident third-country nationals.

Article 12
Vocational training

Member States may allow asylum seekers access to vocational training irrespective of whether they have access to the labour market. Access to vocational training relating to an employment contract shall depend on the extent to which the applicant has access to the labour market in accordance with Article 11.

Article 13
General rules on material reception conditions and health care

1. Member States shall ensure that material reception conditions are available to applicants when they make their application for asylum.

2. Member States shall make provisions on material reception conditions to ensure a standard of living adequate for the health of applicants and capable of ensuring their subsistence. Member States shall ensure that that standard of living is met in the specific situation of persons who have special needs, in accordance with Article 17, as well as in relation to the situation of persons who are in detention.

3. Member States may make the provision of all or some of the material reception conditions and health care subject to the condition that applicants do not have sufficient means to have a standard of living adequate for their health and to enable their subsistence.

4. Member States may require applicants to cover or contribute to the cost of the material reception conditions and of the health care provided for in this Directive, pursuant to the provision of paragraph 3, if the applicants have sufficient resources, for example if they have been working for a reasonable period of time. If it transpires that an applicant had sufficient means to cover material reception conditions and health care at the time when these basic needs were being covered, Member States may ask the asylum seeker for a refund.

5. Material reception conditions may be provided in kind, or in the form of financial allowances or vouchers or in a combination of these provisions. Where Member States provide material reception conditions in the form of financial allowances or vouchers, the amount thereof shall be determined in accordance with the principles set out in this Article.

Article 14
Modalities for material reception conditions

1. Where housing is provided in kind, it should take one or a combination of the following forms:
    (a) premises used for the purpose of housing applicants during the examination of an application for asylum lodged at the border;
    (b) accommodation centres which guarantee an adequate standard of living;
    (c) private houses, flats, hotels or other premises adapted for housing applicants.

2. Member States shall ensure that applicants provided with the housing referred to in paragraph 1(a), (b) and (c) are assured:

(a) protection of their family life;

(b) the possibility of communicating with relatives, legal advisers and representatives of the United Nations High Commissioner for Refugees (UNHCR) and non-governmental organisations (NGOs) recognised by Member States. Member States shall pay particular attention to the prevention of assault within the premises and accommodation centres referred to in paragraph 1(a) and (b).

3. Member States shall ensure, if appropriate, that minor children of applicants or applicants who are minors are lodged with their parents or with the adult family member responsible for them whether by law or by custom.

4. Member States shall ensure that transfers of applicants from one housing facility to another take place only when necessary. Member States shall provide for the possibility for applicants to inform their legal advisers of the transfer and of their new address.

5. Persons working in accommodation centres shall be adequately trained and shall be bound by the confidentiality principle as defined in the national law in relation to any information they obtain in the course of their work.

6. Member States may involve applicants in managing the material resources and non-material aspects of life in the centre through an advisory board or council representing residents.

7. Legal advisors or counsellors of asylum seekers and representatives of the United Nations High Commissioner for Refugees or non-governmental organisations designated by the latter and recognised by the Member State concerned shall be granted access to accommodation centres and other housing facilities in order to assist the said asylum seekers. Limits on such access may be imposed only on grounds relating to the security of the centres and facilities and of the asylum seekers.

8. Member States may exceptionally set modalities for material reception conditions different from those provided for in this Article, for a reasonable period which shall be as short as possible, when:

– an initial assessment of the specific needs of the applicant is required,

– material reception conditions, as provided for in this Article, are not available in a certain geographical area,

– housing capacities normally available are temporarily exhausted,

– the asylum seeker is in detention or confined to border posts.

These different conditions shall cover in any case basic needs.

Article 15
Health care

1. Member States shall ensure that applicants receive the necessary health care which shall include, at least, emergency care and essential treatment of illness.

2. Member States shall provide necessary medical or other assistance to applicants who have special needs.

CHAPTER III
Reduction or Withdrawal of Reception Conditions

Article 16
Reduction or withdrawal of reception conditions

1. Member States may reduce or withdraw reception conditions in the following cases:
    (a) where an asylum seeker:
        – abandons the place of residence determined by the competent authority without informing it or, if requested, without permission, or
        – does not comply with reporting duties or with requests to provide information or to appear for personal interviews concerning the asylum procedure during a reasonable period laid down in national law, or
        – has already lodged an application in the same Member State.
When the applicant is traced or voluntarily reports to the competent authority, a duly motivated decision, based on the reasons for the disappearance, shall be taken on the reinstallation of the grant of some or all of the reception conditions;
    (b) where an applicant has concealed financial resources and has therefore unduly benefited from material reception conditions.

If it transpires that an applicant had sufficient means to cover material reception conditions and health care at the time when these basic needs were being covered, Member States may ask the asylum seeker for a refund.

2. Member States may refuse conditions in cases where an asylum seeker has failed to demonstrate that the asylum claim was made as soon as reasonably practicable after arrival in that Member State.

3. Member States may determine sanctions applicable to serious breaching of the rules of the accommodation centres as well as to seriously violent behaviour.

4. Decisions for reduction, withdrawal or refusal of reception conditions or sanctions referred to in paragraphs 1, 2 and 3 shall be taken individually, objectively and impartially and reasons shall be given. Decisions shall be based on the particular situation of the person concerned, especially with regard to persons covered by Article 17, taking into account the principle of proportionality. Member States shall under all circumstances ensure access to emergency health care.

5. Member States shall ensure that material reception conditions are not withdrawn or reduced before a negative decision is taken.

CHAPTER IV
Provisions for Persons with Special Needs

Article 17
General principle

1. Member States shall take into account the specific situation of vulnerable persons such as minors, unaccompanied minors, disabled people, elderly people, pregnant women, single parents with minor children and persons who have been subjected to torture, rape or other serious forms of psychological, physical or sexual violence, in the national legislation implementing the provisions of Chapter II relating to material reception conditions and health care.

2. Paragraph 1 shall apply only to persons found to have special needs after an individual evaluation of their situation.

Article 18
Minors

1. The best interests of the child shall be a primary consideration for Member States when implementing the provisions of this Directive that involve minors.

2. Member States shall ensure access to rehabilitation services for minors who have been victims of any form of abuse, neglect, exploitation, torture or cruel, inhuman and degrading treatment, or who have suffered from armed conflicts, and ensure that appropriate mental health care is developed and qualified counselling is provided when needed.

Article 19
Unaccompanied minors

1. Member States shall as soon as possible take measures to ensure the necessary representation of unaccompanied minors by legal guardianship or, where necessary, representation by an organisation which is responsible for the care and well-being of minors, or by any other appropriate representation. Regular assessments shall be made by the appropriate authorities.

2. Unaccompanied minors who make an application for asylum shall, from the moment they are admitted to the territory to the moment they are obliged to leave the host Member State in which the application for asylum was made or is being examined, be placed:
   (a) with adult relatives;
   (b) with a foster-family;
   (c) in accommodation centres with special provisions for minors;
   (d) in other accommodation suitable for minors.

Member States may place unaccompanied minors aged 16 or over in accommodation centres for adult asylum seekers. As far as possible, siblings shall be kept together, taking into account the best interests of the minor concerned and, in particular, his or her age and degree of maturity. Changes of residence of unaccompanied minors shall be limited to a minimum.

3. Member States, protecting the unaccompanied minor's best interests, shall endeavour to trace the members of his or her family as soon as possible. In cases where there may be a threat to the life or integrity of the minor or his or her close relatives, particularly if they have remained in the country of origin, care must be taken to ensure that the collection, processing and circulation of information concerning those persons is undertaken on a confidential basis, so as to avoid jeopardising their safety.

4. Those working with unaccompanied minors shall have had or receive appropriate training concerning their needs, and shall be bound by the confidentiality principle as defined in the national law, in relation to any information they obtain in the course of their work.

Article 20
Victims of torture and violence

Member States shall ensure that, if necessary, persons who have been subjected to torture, rape or other serious acts of violence receive the necessary treatment of damages caused by the aforementioned acts.

CHAPTER V
Appeals

Article 21
Appeals

1. Member States shall ensure that negative decisions relating to the granting of benefits under this Directive or decisions taken under Article 7 which individually affect asylum seekers may be the subject of an appeal within the procedures laid down in the national law. At least in the last instance the possibility of an appeal or a review before a judicial body shall be granted.

2. Procedures for access to legal assistance in such cases shall be laid down in national law.

CHAPTER VI
Actions to Improve the Efficiency of the Reception System

Article 22
Cooperation

Member States shall regularly inform the Commission on the data concerning the number of persons, broken down by sex and age, covered by reception conditions and provide full information on the type, name and format of the documents provided for by Article 6.

Article 23
Guidance, monitoring and control system

Member States shall, with due respect to their constitutional structure, ensure that appropriate guidance, monitoring and control of the level of reception conditions are established.

Article 24
Staff and resources

1. Member States shall take appropriate measures to ensure that authorities and other organisations implementing this Directive have received the necessary basic training with respect to the needs of both male and female applicants.

2. Member States shall allocate the necessary resources in connection with the national provisions enacted to implement this Directive.

CHAPTER VII
Final Provisions

Article 25
Reports

By 6 August 2006, the Commission shall report to the European Parliament and the Council on the application of this Directive and shall propose any amendments that are necessary. Member States shall send the Commission all the information that is appropriate for drawing up the report, including the statistical data provided for by Article 22 by 6 February 2006. After presenting the report, the Commission shall report to the European Parliament and the Council on the application of this Directive at least every five years.

Article 26
Transposition

1. Member States shall bring into force the laws, regulations and administrative provisions necessary to comply with this Directive by 6 February 2005. They shall forthwith inform the Commission thereof. When the Member States adopt these measures, they shall contain a reference to this Directive or shall be accompanied by such a reference on the occasion of their official publication. Member States shall determine how such a reference is to be made.

2. Member States shall communicate to the Commission the text of the provisions of national law which they adopt in the field relating to the enforcement of this Directive.

Article 27
Entry into force

This Directive shall enter into force on the day of its publication in the *Official Journal of the European Union*.

Article 28
Addressees

This Directive is addressed to the Member States in accordance with the Treaty establishing the European Union.

1. **Minimum standards on the reception of applicants for asylum in Member States: a further step ahead towards the common european asylum system**

According to the Conclusions of the Presidency at the Tampere European Council in October 1999, a Common European Asylum System is to include, in the short term, a clear and workable determination of the State responsible for the examination of an asylum application, common standards for a fair and efficient asylum procedure, common minimum conditions of reception of asylum seekers and the approximation of rules on the recognition and content of the refugee status. This is to be supplemented with measures on subsidiary forms of protection offering an appropriate status to any person in need of such protection. In addition, the Conclusions make clear that, in the longer term, Community rules should lead to a common asylum procedure and a uniform status for those who are granted asylum valid throughout the Union. Finally, the European Council, in Tampere, urged the Council to step up its efforts to reach agreement on the issue of temporary protection for displaced persons on the basis of solidarity between Member States.

On 28 September 2000, the Council adopted a Decision (2000/596/EC) establishing a European Refugee Fund as a solidarity measure to promote a balance in the efforts made by Member States in receiving and bearing the consequences of receiving refugees and displaced persons.

On 11 December 2000, the Council adopted a Regulation (2725/2000/EC) concerning the establishment of 'Eurodac' for the comparison of fingerprints for the effective application of the Dublin Convention on the State responsible for examining applications for asylum lodged in one of the European Union Member States.

In addition to the proposals for the above mentioned acts approved by the Council, the Commission has adopted:
 – On 24 May 2000, a proposal for a Council Directive on minimum standards for giving temporary protection in the event of a mass influx of displaced persons based on solidarity between Member States;
 – On 20 September 2000, a proposal for a Council Directive on minimum standards on procedures in Member States for granting and withdrawing refugee status;
 – On 22 November 2000, a Communication on a common asylum procedure and a uniform status for those who are granted asylum valid throughout the Union.

As indicated in the scoreboard to review progress on the creation of an area for freedom, security and justice in the European Union, approved by the Council on 27 March 2000, the Commission is now, in early 2001, proposing a Council Directive on minimum standards on the reception of applicants for asylum in Member States. This proposal has been drafted on the basis of a number of preparatory activities and background materials.

The Commission commissioned a Study, delivered at the beginning of November 2000, 'on the legal framework and administrative practices in the Member States of the European Union regarding reception conditions for asylum seekers, displaced persons and other persons seeking international protection'.

In June 2000, the French delegation presented a discussion paper on conditions for the reception of asylum seekers that was followed by the adoption of Conclusions by the December Council. At the end of July 2000, the United Nations High Commissioner for Refugees published an important study on the same issue.

In December 2000, the Commission thought it appropriate to have bilateral consultations with Member States, on the basis of a discussion paper concerning the future Community instrument on reception conditions for applicants for asylum in the European Union. As well as the Member States, the Commission specifically consulted the UNHCR and some of the more relevant non-governmental organisations.

The December Council Conclusions, the Reception Conditions Study and the written and oral comments expressed on the Commission's discussion paper have been the 'foundation' material that has been used to draft this proposal. The UNHCR Study, the Danish Refugee Council Fourth Report on Legal and Social Conditions for asylum seekers and Refugees in Western European Countries, the existing soft law (principally the 1997 Council Resolution on unaccompanied minors who are nationals of third countries) have also been taken into account. Finally, attention has been paid to the draft joint action on conditions for reception of asylum seekers, tabled by the Spanish Presidency in 1995 but never approved.

2. The objectives of the proposal

With this proposal for a Directive, the Commission is pursuing the following aims:
  1. Implementing point (1)(b) of the first paragraph of Article 63 of the Treaty, paragraph 36(b)(V) of the Vienna Action Plan, Conclusion 14 of the Tampere European Council and the second part of the paragraph on a fair and efficient asylum procedure of the Scoreboard presented to the Council and the Parliament in March 2000;
  2. Setting out the minimum standards of reception conditions for applicants for asylum in the European Union, normally sufficient to ensure them a dignified standard of living;
  3. Identifying the different reception conditions available to applicants for asylum at the various stages or types of asylum procedures as well as for groups with special needs including minors, and cases for their exclusion, reduction and review;
  4. Outlining the possible actions to improve the efficiency of the national reception systems;
  5. Limiting secondary movements of applicants for asylum influenced solely by the diversity of the applicable rules on reception conditions;
  6. Ensuring that applicants for asylum are afforded comparable living conditions in all Member States as, according to the Dublin Convention, they do not have the right to choose the Member State that should examine their application.

3. An overview of the standards in the proposal

This proposal is composed of five main sets of rules:
  (a) The first group of provisions concerns the most general provisions of the proposal, including its objective and scope as well as the definitions of the concepts that are relevant for a clear understanding of the proposal.
  (b) The second set of rules focuses on the reception conditions that should be granted, in principle, at all stages and in all kinds of asylum procedures (information, documentation,

freedom of movement, housing, food, clothing, daily expenses allowance, unity of the family, health care, schooling for minors). In addition, the consideration that no-one should be deprived of ordinary living conditions for too long is the basis for the provisions to the effect that Member States should not on a general basis deny certain reception conditions when applicants for asylum are not responsible for the length of the procedure and they have been in the procedure for a long period of time (access to labour market and vocational training).

(c) A third group of rules sets the requirements (or minimum standards) of some reception conditions (material reception conditions and health care) which Member States are required to ensure. The approach suggested in the proposal is flexible enough to allow

each Member State to retain considerable room for manoeuvre when implementing these minimum standards. The general approach is that the living conditions of applicants for asylum must always be dignified but that they should be improved as long as applications can be considered admissible and not manifestly unfounded or the procedure in place is too long. When asylum applicants belong to groups with special needs, or when they are in detention, reception conditions should be designed to meet their specific needs.

(d) The fourth group of rules includes the provisions for reducing or withdrawing access to some or all reception conditions as well as the possibility of review before a court of a decision on reduction or withdrawal of reception conditions. These rules are meant to ensure that the reception system is not abused. However, as the reduction or withdrawal of reception conditions can affect the standard of living of applicants and their ability to effectively pursue procedural guarantees, it is of the utmost importance that decisions on these issues are subject to review.

(e) Finally, the proposal outlines several rules to ensure its complete implementation as well as the improvement of the national reception systems. If the final aims of the future directive are to be met, the instruments that are put in place to reach these aims have to be checked, revised and adjusted to be sure they are going to produce the expected results. This has to be done at different levels. At *national level*, there is the need for guiding, monitoring and controlling the system and for the possibility of improving it and remedying sources of inefficiency. In addition, it is important that a national contact point is designated and that appropriate measures are enacted to establish direct cooperation and an exchange of information between the competent authorities. At *Community level*, it is important to assess whether the purposes of this Directive are met or if there is room for improvement. The reporting system envisaged in this proposal should meet this need. Finally, as far as the general attitude of public opinion towards applicants for asylum is concerned, it is clear that the political and social perception of asylum-related issues by public opinion in general and by local communities in particular plays a major role in the quality of life of applicants for asylum. This Directive does not impose detailed obligations on Member States but sets the aims to be pursued (to promote harmonious relationships between the local communities and the reception and accommodation centres that are located in their territory).

The Commission, for its part, envisages to introduce a Contact Committee. The Contact Committee will facilitate the transposition and the subsequent implementation of the Directive through regular consultations on all practical problems arising from its application. It will help avoid duplication of work where common standards are set. In addition, the Committee will facilitate consultation between the Member States on standards for reception of applicants for asylum that they may lay down at national level. This would greatly help the construction of a Common European Asylum System as envisaged by the Conclusions of the Presidency at the Tampere European Council in October 1999. Lastly, the Committee will advise the Commission, if necessary, on any supplements or amendments to be made to this Directive or on any adjustments deemed necessary.

4. The choice of legal basis

The choice of legal basis is consistent with the amendments made to the Treaty establishing the European Community by the Amsterdam Treaty, which entered into force on 1 May 1999. Point (1)(b) of the first paragraph of Article 63 of the EC Treaty provides that the Council shall adopt measures on asylum in accordance with the Geneva Convention of 28 July 1951, the Protocol of 31 January 1967 relating to the status of refugees and other relevant treaties within the area of minimum standards on the reception of asylum seekers in Member States. Article 63 is accordingly the proper legal basis for a proposal to establish minimum standards for reception conditions for applicants for asylum in Member States.

Title IV of the EC Treaty is not applicable to the United Kingdom and to Ireland, unless those Member States decide otherwise in accordance with the procedure laid down in the Protocol on the position of the United Kingdom and Ireland annexed to the Treaties. Title IV is likewise not applicable to Denmark, by virtue of the Protocol on the position of Denmark annexed to the Treaties.

5. Subsidiarity and proportionality: justification and value added

Subsidiarity
The insertion of the new Title IV (Visas, asylum, immigration and other policies related to free movement of persons) in the Treaty establishing the European Community demonstrates the will of the High Contracting Parties to confer powers in these matters on the European Community. But the European Community does not have exclusive powers here. Consequently, even with the political will to implement a common policy on asylum and immigration, it must act in accordance with Article 5 of the EC Treaty, i.e. the Community may take action only if and insofar as the objectives of the proposed action cannot be sufficiently achieved by the Member States and can therefore, by reason of the scale or effects of the proposed action, be better achieved by the Community. The proposed Directive satisfies these criteria.

The establishment of an area of freedom, security and justice entails the adoption of measures relating to asylum. The specific objective of this initiative is to lay down minimum standards on reception conditions for applicants for asylum in Member States. The standards laid down in this proposal must be capable of being applied through minimum conditions in all the Member States. Minimum Community standards have to be laid down by the kind of action proposed here. They will help to limit secondary movements of asylum applicants as resulting from disparities in reception conditions in Member States. Henceforth, applicants for asylum will be less inclined than before to decide on their country of destination on the basis of the reception conditions there. The continued absence of standards on reception conditions would have a negative effect on the effectiveness of other instruments relating to asylum. Conversely, once minimum standards on reception conditions are in place, the operation of, *inter alia*, an effective system for determining which Member State is responsible for considering an asylum application is fully justified. Applicants for asylum who cannot choose in complete freedom where to lodge their application should be granted the same minimum standards in reception in any Member State of the European Union. The idea of a single Member State responsible for examining an application for asylum becomes fairer to applicants for asylum if the same minimum standards in reception conditions are granted to them in all Member States. At the same time, minimum standards in reception conditions could limit the importance of one of the factors that determine secondary movements within the Union and, in this way, would help to establish the effectiveness of the mechanisms according to which the responsible Member State is chosen. To establish common minimum standards in reception conditions for applicants for asylum is a fundamental tool to make national asylum systems more effective and a Common European Asylum System more concrete.

Proportionality
The form taken by Community action must be the simplest form allowing the proposal to attain its objectives and to be implemented as efficiently as possible. In this spirit, the legal instrument chosen is a directive, which allows minimum standards to be laid down, while leaving national authorities the choice of the most appropriate form and methods for implementing it in their national welfare system and general context. The proposal concentrates on a set of minimum standards that are strictly necessary for the coherence of the planned action without laying down standards relating to other aspects of asylum. On several occasions different models are proposed allowing Member States to choose the one that is most appropriate to the national situation. In other cases, the proposal sets deadlines corresponding to those set in the proposal for a directive on minimum standards on common asylum procedures (COM(2000)578) to ensure consistency within the Common European Asylum System. Finally, several rules require Member States only to comply with certain aims (e.g. they are asked to integrate considerations specific to the protection of persons having special needs in the national rules concerning their psychological and health care and material reception conditions) but leave Member States completely free to choose the means used to achieve this aim. The proposal, therefore, does not go beyond what is necessary to achieve the objective of the Directive.

Chapter 1.4
PROCEDURES

COUNCIL DIRECTIVE[1]
on minimum standards on procedures in Member States for granting and withdrawing refugee status [2]

[Editor: here follow recitals the Council / Commission agreed to be included in the Preamble:]

It is in the interest of both Member States and applicants for asylum to decide as soon as possible on applications for asylum. The organisation of the processing of applications for asylum is left to the discretion of Member States, so that they may, in accordance with their national needs, prioritize or accelerate the processing of any application, taking into account the standards in this Directive.

The notion of public order may cover a conviction for committing a serious crime.

This Directive does not deal with procedures governed by Council Regulation (EC) No. 343/2003 of 18 February 2003 (Dublin) establishing the criteria and mechanisms for determining the Member state responsible for examining an asylum application lodged in one of the Member States by a third country national.

It results from the status of Bulgaria and Romania as candidate countries for the accession to the European Union and the progress made by these countries for membership that they should be regarded as constituting safe countries of origin for the purposes of this Directive until the date of their accession to the European Union.

The designation of a third country as a safe country of origin for the purposes of this Directive cannot establish an absolute guarantee of safety for nationals of that country. By its very nature, the assessment underlying the designation can only take into account the general civil, legal and political circumstances in that country and whether actors of persecution, torture or inhuman or degrading treatment or punishment are subject to sanction in practice when found liable in the country concerned. For this reason, it is important that, where an applicant shows that there are serious reasons to consider the country not to be safe in his/her particular circumstances, the designation of the country as safe can no longer be considered relevant for him/her.

---

[1] Editor: NB the numbering of the articles is not final; changes may occur.

[2] 2000/0238 (CNS) dated 30 April 2004; this directive received political agreement only; formal agreement expected for autumn 2004.

Border procedures mainly apply to those applicants which to not meet the conditions for entry into the territory of the Member States.

According to Article 64 TEU, this Directive does not affect the exercise of the responsibilities incumbent upon Member States with regard to the maintenance of law and order and the safeguarding of internal security.

It reflects a basic principle of Community law that the decisions taken on an application for asylum must be subject to an effective remedy before a court or tribunal in the meaning of Article 234 TEC. The effectiveness of the remedy, also with regard to the examination of the relevant facts, depends on the administrative and judicial system of each Member State seen as a whole.

With respect to the treatment of persons falling within the scope of this Directive, Member States are bound by obligations under instruments of international law to which they are party and which prohibit discrimination.

CHAPTER I
General Provisions

Article 1
Purpose

The purpose of this Directive is to establish minimum standards on procedures in Member States for granting and withdrawing refugee status.

Article 2
Definitions

For the purposes of this Directive:

(a) 'Geneva Convention' means the Convention of 28 July 1951 relating to the status of refugees, as amended by the New York Protocol of 31 January 1967;

(b) 'Application for asylum' means an application made by a third country national or stateless person which can be understood as a request for international protection from a Member State under the Geneva Convention. Any application for international protection is presumed to be an application for asylum, unless the person concerned explicitly requests another kind of protection that can be applied for separately;

(c) 'Applicant' or 'applicant for asylum' means a third country national or stateless person who has made an application for asylum in respect of which a final decision has not yet been taken;

(d) A final decision is a decision whether the third country national or stateless person be granted refugee status by virtue of Council Directive on minimum standards for the qualification and status of third country nationals or stateless persons as refugees or as persons who otherwise need international protection and the content of the protection granted and which is no longer subject to a remedy within the framework of Chapter V irrespective of whether such remedy has the effect of allowing applicants to remain in the Member States concerned pending its outcome, subject to Annex III;

(e) 'Determining authority' means any quasi-judicial or administrative body in a Member State responsible for examining applications for asylum and competent to take decisions at first instance in such cases, subject to Annex I;

(f) 'Refugee' means a third country national or a stateless person who fulfils the requirements of Article 1 of the Geneva Convention as set out in Council Directive on minimum standards for the qualification and status of third country nationals or stateless persons as refugees or as persons who otherwise need international protection and the content of the protection granted;

(g) 'Refugee Status' means the recognition by a Member State of a third country national or stateless person as a refugee;

(h) 'Unaccompanied minor' means a person below the age of eighteen who arrives in the territory of the Member States unaccompanied by an adult responsible for him/her whether by law or by custom, and for as long as he/she is not effectively taken into the care of such a person; it includes a minor who is left unaccompanied after he/she has entered the territory of the Member States;

(i) 'Representative' means a person acting on behalf of an organisation representing an unaccompanied minor as legal guardian, a person acting on behalf of a national organisation which is responsible for the care and well-being of minors, or any other appropriate representation appointed to ensure his/her best interests;

(j) 'Withdrawal of refugee status' means the decision by a competent authority to revoke, end or refuse to renew the refugee status of a person in accordance with Council Directive on minimum standards for the qualification and status of third country nationals or stateless persons as refugees or as persons who otherwise need international protection and the content of the protection granted;

(k) 'Remain in the Member State' means to remain in the territory, including at the border or in transit zones of the Member State in which the application for asylum has been made or is being examined.

Article 3[3]
Scope

1. This Directive shall apply to all applications for asylum made in the territory, including at the border, or in the transit zones of the Member States and to the withdrawal of refugee status.

2. This Directive shall not apply in cases of requests for diplomatic or territorial asylum submitted to representations of Member States.

---

[3] Editor: 'The Council is of the view that the Member States which apply the provisions of Article 3(3) of the Directive can, where they suspend an examination of an application for asylum in accordance with Article 17 of Council Directive 2001/55/EC (on minimum standards for giving temporary protection in the event of a mass influx of displaced persons and on measures promoting a balance of efforts between Member States in receiving such persons and bearing the consequences thereof), also suspend the examination of the application for other kinds of international protection covered by the procedure referred to in Article 3(3) until such time as that suspension no longer applies.'

3. Where Member States employ or introduce a procedure in which asylum applications are examined both as applications on the basis of the Geneva Convention, and as applications for other kinds of international protection as defined by Article 15 of Council Directive on minimum standards for the qualification and status of third country nationals or stateless persons as refugees or as persons who otherwise need international protection and the content of the protection granted, they shall apply this Directive throughout their procedure.

4. Moreover, Member States may decide to apply this Directive in procedures for deciding on applications for any kind of international protection.

Article 4
Responsible authorities

1. Member States shall designate for all procedures a determining authority which will be responsible for an appropriate examination of the applications in accordance with the provisions of this Directive, in particular Articles 8(2) and 9.

In accordance with Article 4(4) of Council Regulation (EC) No. 343/2003, applications for asylum made in a Member State to the authorities of another Member State carrying out immigration controls there shall be dealt with by the Member State on whose territory the application is made.

2. However, Member States may provide that another authority is responsible in the following cases for the purpose of:
    (a) processing cases in which it is considered to transfer the applicant to another State according to the rules establishing criteria and mechanisms for determining which state is responsible for considering an application for asylum, until such time as the transfer takes place or the requested State has refused to take charge or take over the applicant;
    (b) taking a decision on the application in the light of national security provisions, provided a determining authority is consulted prior to this decision as to whether the applicant qualifies as a refugee by virtue of Council Directive on minimum standards for the qualification and status of third country nationals or stateless persons as refugees or as persons who otherwise need international protection and the content of the protection granted;
    (c) conducting a preliminary examination pursuant to Article 32, provided this authority has access to the applicant's file regarding the previous application;
    (d) processing cases in the framework of the procedures provided for in Article 35(1);
    (e) refusing permission to enter in the framework of the procedure provided for in Article 35(2) to (5), subject to the conditions and as set out in these paragraphs;
    (f) establishing that an applicant is seeking to enter or has entered in the Member State from a safe third country pursuant to Article 36, subject to the conditions and as set out in this Article.

3. Member States shall ensure that where authorities are designated in accordance with paragraph 2, the personnel of such authorities have the appropriate knowledge or receive the necessary training to fulfil their obligations when implementing this Directive.

Article 5
More favourable provisions

Member States may introduce or maintain more favourable standards on procedures for granting and withdrawing refugee status, insofar as those standards are compatible with this Directive.

CHAPTER II
Basic Principles and Guarantees

Article 6
Access to the procedure

1. Member States may require that applications for asylum be made in person and/or at a designated place.

2. Member States shall ensure that each adult having legal capacity has the right to make an application for asylum on his/her own behalf.

3. Member States may provide that an application may be made by an applicant on behalf of his/her dependants. In such cases Member States shall ensure that dependant adults consent to the lodging of the application on their behalf, failing which they shall have an opportunity to make an application on their own behalf. Consent shall be requested at the time the application is lodged or, at the latest, when the personal interview with the dependant adult is conducted.

4. Member States may determine, in national legislation
    (a) the cases in which a minor can make an application on his/her own behalf;
    (b) the cases in which the application of an unaccompanied minor has to be lodged by a representative as provided for in Article 17(1)(a);
    (c) the cases in which the lodging of an application for asylum is deemed to constitute also the lodging of an application for asylum for any unmarried minor.

5. Member States shall ensure that authorities likely to be addressed by someone who wishes to make an asylum application are able to advise that person how and where he/she may make such an application and/or may require these authorities to forward the application to the competent authority.

Article 7
Right to remain in the Member State pending the examination of the application

1. Applicants shall be allowed to remain in the Member State, for the sole purpose of the procedure, until such time as the determining authority has made a decision in accordance with the procedures at first instance set out in Chapter III. This right to remain shall not constitute an entitlement to a residence permit.

2. Member States can make an exception only where, in accordance with Articles 32 and 34, a subsequent application will not be further examined or where they will surrender or extradite, as appropriate, a person either to another Member State pursuant to obligations in accordance with a European Arrest Warrant or otherwise, or to a third country, or to international criminal courts or tribunals.

Article 8
Requirements for the examination of applications

1. Without prejudice to Article 23(4)(i), Member States shall ensure that applications for asylum are neither rejected nor excluded from examination on the sole ground that they have not been made as soon as possible.

2. Member States shall ensure that decisions by the determining authority on applications for asylum are taken after an appropriate examination. To that end, Member States shall ensure that

(a) applications are examined and decisions are taken individually, objectively and impartially;

(b) precise and up-to-date information is obtained from various sources, such as information from the United Nations High Commissioner for Refugees (UNHCR), as to the general situation prevailing in the countries of origin of applicants for asylum and, where necessary, in countries through which they have transited, and that such information is made available to the personnel responsible for examining applications and taking decisions;

(c) the personnel examining applications and taking the decisions have the knowledge with respect to relevant standards applicable in the field of asylum and refugee law.

3. The authorities referred to in Chapter V shall, through the determining authority or the applicant or otherwise, have access to the general information referred to in paragraph 2(b), necessary for the fulfillment of their task.

4. Member States may provide for rules concerning the translation of documents relevant for the examination of applications.

Article 9
Requirements for a decision by the determining authority

1. Member States shall ensure that decisions on applications for asylum are given in writing.

2. Member States shall also ensure that, where an application is rejected, the reasons in fact and in law are stated in the decision and information on how to challenge a negative decision is given in writing.

Member States need not state the reasons for not granting the refugee status in the decision where the applicant is granted a status, which offers the same rights and benefits under national and Community law as the refugee status by virtue of Council Directive on minimum standards for the qualification and status of third country nationals or stateless persons as refugees or as persons who otherwise need international protection and the content of the protection granted. In these cases, Member States shall ensure that the reasons for not granting the refugee status are stated in the applicant's file, and that the applicant has, upon request, access to his/her file.

Moreover, Member States need not provide information on how to challenge a negative decision in writing in conjunction with that decision where the applicant has been informed at an earlier stage either in writing or by electronic means accessible to the applicant of how to challenge such a decision.

3. For the purposes of Article 6(3), and whenever the application is based on the same grounds, Member States may take one single decision, covering all dependants.

Article 10
Guarantees for applicants for asylum

1. With respect to the procedures provided for in Chapter III of this Directive, Member States shall ensure that all applicants for asylum enjoy the following guarantees:

(a) they must be informed in a language which they may reasonably be supposed to understand of the procedure to be followed and of their rights and obligations during the procedure and the possible consequences of not complying with their obligations and not co-operating with the authorities. They must be informed about the time-frame, as well as the means at their disposal to fulfil the obligation to submit the elements as referred to in Article 4 of Council Directive on minimum standards for the qualification and status of third country nationals or stateless persons as refugees or as persons who otherwise need international protection and the content of the protection granted. The information must be given in time to enable them to exercise the rights guaranteed in this Directive and to comply with the obligations described in Article 11;

(b) they must receive the services of an interpreter for submitting their case to the competent authorities whenever necessary. Member States shall consider it necessary to give these services at least when the determining authority calls upon the applicant to be interviewed as referred to in Articles 12 and 13 and appropriate communication cannot be ensured without such services. In this case and in other cases where the competent authorities call upon the applicant, the services shall be paid for out of public funds;

(c) they must not be denied the opportunity to communicate with the UNHCR or with any other organisation working on behalf of the UNHCR in the territory of the Member State pursuant to an agreement with that Member State;

(d) they must be given notice in reasonable time of the decision by the determining authority on their application for asylum. If a legal adviser or other counsellor is legally representing the applicant, Member States may choose to give notice of the decision to him/her instead of to the applicant for asylum;

(e) they must be informed about the result of the decision by the determining authority in a language that they may reasonably be supposed to understand when they are not assisted or represented by a legal adviser or other counsellor and when free legal assistance is not available. The information provided shall include information on how to challenge a negative decision in accordance with the provisions of Article 9(2).

2. With respect to the procedures provided for in Chapter V, Member States shall ensure that all applicants for asylum enjoy equivalent guarantees to the ones listed in paragraph 1(b), (c) and (d).

Article 11
Obligations of the applicants for asylum

1. Member States may impose upon applicants for asylum obligations to cooperate with the competent authorities insofar as these obligations are necessary for the processing of the application.

2. In particular, Member States may provide that
    (a) applicants for asylum are required to report to the competent authorities or to appear there in person, either without delay or at a specified time;
    (b) applicants for asylum have to hand over documents in their possession relevant to the examination of the application, such as their passports;
    (c) applicants for asylum are required to inform the competent authorities of their current place of residence or address and inform them of change of this place of residence or address as soon as possible. Member States may provide that the applicant shall have to accept any communication at the most recent place of residence or address which he/she indicated accordingly;
    (d) the competent authorities may search the applicant and the items he/she carries with him/her;
    (e) the competent authorities may take a photograph of the applicant; and
    (f) the competent authorities may record the applicant's oral statements, provided he/she has previously been informed thereof.

Article 12
Persons invited to a personal interview

1. Before a decision is taken by the determining authority, the applicant for asylum shall be given the opportunity of a personal interview on his/her application for asylum with a person competent under national law to conduct such an interview. Member States may also give the opportunity of a personal interview to each adult among the dependants referred to in Article 6(3). Member States may determine in national legislation the cases in which a minor shall be given the opportunity of a personal interview.

2. The personal interview may be omitted where :
    (a) the determining authority is able to take a positive decision on the basis of evidence available; or
    (b) the competent authority has already had a meeting with the applicant for the purpose of assisting him/her with filling his/her application and submitting the essential information regarding the application, in terms of Article 4(2) of Council Directive on minimum standards for the qualification and status of third country nationals or stateless persons as refugees or as persons who otherwise need international protection and the content of the protection granted; or
    (c) the determining authority, on the basis of a complete examination of information provided by the applicant, considers the application as unfounded in the cases where the circumstances mentioned in Article 23(4)(a), (c), (g), (h) and (j) apply.

3. The personal interview may also be omitted, where it is not reasonably practicable, in particular where the competent authority is of the opinion that the applicant is unfit or un-

able to be interviewed owing to enduring circumstances beyond his/her control. When in doubt, Member States may require a medical or psychological certificate. Where the Member State does not provide the opportunity for a personal interview pursuant to this paragraph, or where applicable, to the dependant, reasonable efforts must be made to allow the applicant or the dependant to submit further information.

4. The absence of a personal interview in accordance with this Article shall not prevent the determining authority from taking a decision on an application for asylum.

5. The absence of a personal interview pursuant to paragraph 2(b) and (c) and paragraph 3 shall not adversely affect the decision of the determining authority.

6. Irrespective of Article 20(1), Member States, when deciding on the application for asylum, may take into account the fact that the applicant failed to appear for the personal interview, unless he or she had good reasons for the failure to appear.

Article 13
Requirements for a personal interview

1. A personal interview shall normally take place without the presence of family members unless the determining authority considers it necessary for an appropriate examination to have other family members present.

2. A personal interview must take place under conditions which ensure appropriate confidentiality.

3. Member States shall take appropriate steps to ensure that personal interviews are conducted in conditions which allow applicants to present the grounds for their applications in a comprehensive manner. To that end, Member States shall
    (a) ensure that the person who conducts the interview is sufficiently competent to take account of the personal or general circumstances surrounding the application, including the applicant's cultural origin or vulnerability, insofar as it is possible to do so, and
    (b) select an interpreter who is able to ensure appropriate communication between the applicant and the person who conducts the interview. The communication need not necessarily take place in the language preferred by the applicant for asylum if there is another language which he/she may reasonably be supposed to understand and in which he/she is able to communicate in.

4. Member States may provide for rules concerning the presence of third parties at the personal interview.

5. This Article is also applicable to the meeting referred to in Article 12(2)(b).

Article 14
Status of the report of a personal interview in the procedure

1. Member States shall ensure that a written report is made of every personal interview, containing at least the essential information regarding the application, as presented by the

applicant, in terms of Article 4(2) of Council Directive on minimum standards for the qualification and status of third country nationals or stateless persons as refugees or as persons who otherwise need international protection and the content of the protection granted.

2. Member States shall ensure that applicants have timely access to the report of the personal interview. Where access is only granted after the decision of the determining authority, Member States shall ensure that access is possible as soon as necessary for allowing an appeal to be prepared and lodged in due time.

3. Member states may request the applicant's approval on the contents of the report of the personal interview. Where an applicant refuses to approve the contents of the report, the reasons for this refusal shall be entered into the applicant's file. The refusal of an applicant to approve the contents of the report of the personal interview shall not prevent the determining authority from taking a decision on his/her application.

4. This Article is also applicable to the meeting referred to in Article 12(2)(b).

Article 15
Right to legal assistance and representation

1. Member States shall allow applicants for asylum at their own cost the opportunity to consult in an effective manner a legal adviser or other counsellor, admitted or permitted as such under national law, on matters relating to their asylum applications.

2. In the event of a negative decision by a determining authority, Member States shall ensure that free legal assistance and/or representation be granted on request subject to the provisions of paragraph 3.

3. Member States may provide in their national legislation that free legal assistance and/or representation be granted :
    (a) only for the procedures before a court or tribunal in accordance with Chapter V and not to any onward appeals or reviews provided for under national law, including a rehearing of an appeal following an onward appeal or review; and/or
    (b) only to those who lack sufficient resources; and/or
    (c) only to legal advisers or other counsellors specifically designated by national law to assist and/or represent applicants for asylum; and/or
    (d) only if the appeal or review is likely to succeed.
    Member States shall ensure that legal assistance and/or representation granted under subparagraph (d) is not arbitrarily restricted.

4. Rules concerning the modalities for filing and processing such requests may be provided by Member States.

5. Moreover, Member States may
    (a) impose monetary and/or time limits on the provision of free legal assistance and /or representation provided that such limits do not arbitrarily restrict access to legal assistance and/or representation.

(b) provide that, as regards fees and other costs, the treatment shall not be more favourable than the treatment generally accorded to their nationals in matters pertaining to legal assistance.

6. Member States may demand to be reimbursed wholly or partially for any expenses granted if and when the applicant's financial situation has improved considerably or if the decision to grant such benefits was taken on the basis of false information supplied by the applicant.

Article 16
Scope of legal assistance and representation

1. Member States shall ensure that a legal adviser or other counsellor admitted or permitted as such under national law who assists or represents an applicant for asylum under the terms of national law shall enjoy access to such information in the applicant's file as is liable to be examined by the authorities referred to in Chapter V, insofar as the information is relevant to the examination of the application.

Member States may make an exception where disclosure of information or sources would jeopardise national security, the security of the organisations or persons providing the information or the security of the person(s) to whom the information relates or where the investigative interests relating to the examination of applications of asylum by the competent authorities of the Member States or the international relations of the Member States would be compromised. In these cases, access to the information or sources in question must be available to the authorities referred to in Chapter V, except where such access is precluded in national security cases.

2. Member States shall ensure that the legal adviser or other counsellor who assists or represents an applicant for asylum has access to closed areas, such as detention facilities and transit zones, for the purpose of consulting that applicant. Member States may only limit the possibility to visit applicants in closed areas where such limitation is, by virtue of national legislation, objectively necessary for the security, public order or administrative management of the area or to ensure an efficient examination of the application, provided that access by the legal adviser or other counsellor is not thereby severely limited or rendered impossible.

3. Member States may provide rules covering the presence of legal advisers or other counsellors at all interviews in the procedure, without prejudice to this Article or to Article 17(1)(b).

4. Member States may provide that the applicant is allowed to bring with him/her to the personal interview the legal adviser or other counsellor, admitted as such under national law. Member States may require the presence of the applicant at the personal interview even if he/she is represented under the terms of national law by such a legal adviser or counsellor and may require the applicant to respond in person to the questions asked. The absence of the legal adviser or other counsellor shall not prevent the competent authority from conducting the personal interview with the applicant.

Article 17
Guarantees for unaccompanied minors

1. With respect to all procedures provided for in this Directive and without prejudice to the provisions of Articles 12 and 14, Member States shall:

(a) as soon as possible take measures to ensure that a representative represents and/or assists the unaccompanied minor with respect to the examination of the application. This representative can also be the representative referred to in Article 19 of Council Directive 2003/9/EC laying down minimum standards for the reception of asylum seekers;

(b) ensure that the representative is given the opportunity to inform the unaccompanied minor about the meaning and possible consequences of the personal interview and, where appropriate, how to prepare himself/herself for the personal interview. Member States shall allow the representative to be present at that interview and to ask questions or make comments, within the framework set by the person who conducts the interview. Member States may require the presence of the unaccompanied minor at the personal interview even if the representative is present.

2. Member States may refrain from appointing a representative where the unaccompanied minor:

(a) will in all likelihood reach the age of maturity before a decision at first instance is taken; or

(b) can avail himself, free of charge, of a legal adviser or other counsellor, admitted as such under national law to fulfil the tasks assigned above to the representative; or

(c) is married or has been married.

3. Member States may, in accordance with laws and regulations in force at the time of the adoption of this Directive, also refrain from appointing a representative where the unaccompanied minor is 16 years old or older, unless he/she is unable to pursue his/her application without a representative.

4. Member States shall ensure that:

(a) if an unaccompanied minor has a personal interview on his/her application for asylum as referred to in Articles 12, 13 and 14, that interview is conducted by a person who has the necessary knowledge of the special needs of minors;

(b) an official who has the necessary knowledge of the special needs of minors prepares the decision by the determining authority on the application of an unaccompanied minor.

5. Member States may use medical examinations to determine the age of unaccompanied minors within the framework of the examination of an application for asylum. In cases where medical examinations are used, Member States shall ensure that:

(a) unaccompanied minors are informed prior to the examination of their application for asylum, and in a language which they may reasonably be supposed to understand, about the possibility of age determination by a medical examination. This shall include information on the method of examination and the possible consequences of the result of the medical examination for the examination of the application for asylum, as well as the consequences of refusal on the part of the unaccompanied minor to undergo the medical examination;

(b) unaccompanied minors and/or their representatives consent to carry out an examination to determine the age of the minors concerned, and

(c) the decision to reject an application for asylum from an unaccompanied minor who refused to undergo this medical examination shall not be based solely on that refusal. The fact that an unaccompanied minor has refused to undergo such a medical examination shall not prevent the determining authority from taking a decision on the application for asylum.

6. The best interests of the child shall be a primary consideration for Member States when implementing the provisions of this Article.

Article 18
Detention

1. Member States shall not hold a person in detention for the sole reason that he/she is an applicant for asylum.

2. Where an applicant for asylum is held in detention, Member States shall ensure that there is the possibility of speedy judicial review.

Article 19
Procedure in case of withdrawal of the application

1. Insofar as the Member States foresee the possibility of explicit withdrawal of the application under national law, when an applicant for asylum explicitly withdraws his/her application for asylum, Member States shall ensure that the determining authority takes a decision either to discontinue the examination or to reject the application.

2. Member States may also decide that the determining authority can decide to discontinue the examination without taking a decision. In this case, Member States shall ensure that the determining authority shall enter a notice in the applicant's file.

Article 20
Procedure in case of implicit withdrawal or abandonment of the application

1. When there is reasonable cause to consider that an applicant for asylum has implicitly withdrawn or abandoned his/her application for asylum, Member States shall ensure that the determining authority takes a decision either to discontinue the examination or to reject the application on the basis that the applicant has not established an entitlement to refugee status in accordance with Council Directive on minimum standards for the qualification and status of third country nationals or stateless persons as refugees or as persons who otherwise need international protection and the content of the protection granted. Member States may assume that the applicant has implicitly withdrawn or abandoned his/her application for asylum in particular when it is ascertained that:
(a) he/she has failed to respond to requests to provide information essential to his/her application in terms of Article 4 of Council Directive on minimum standards for the qualification and status of third country nationals or stateless persons as refugees or as persons who otherwise need international protection and the content of the protection granted or has not appeared for an personal interview as provided for in Articles 12, 13 and 14, unless the applicant demonstrates within a reasonable time that his failure was due to circumstances beyond his control;

(b) he/she has absconded or left without authorisation the place where he/she lived or was held, without contacting the competent authority within a reasonable time or he/she has not within a reasonable time complied with reporting duties or other obligations to communicate. For the purpose of implementing these provisions, Member States may lay down time limits or guidelines.

2. Member States shall ensure that the applicant who reports again to the competent authority after a decision to discontinue as referred to in paragraph 1 is taken, is entitled to request that his/her case be re-opened, unless the request is examined in accordance with Articles 32 and 34. Member States may provide for a time limit after which the applicant's case can no longer be reopened.

Member States shall ensure that such a person is not removed contrary to the principle of non-refoulement. Member States may allow the determining authority to take up the examination at the stage which the application was discontinued.

Article 21
The role of UNHCR

1. Member States shall allow the UNHCR:
(a) to have access to applicants for asylum, including those in detention and in airport or port transit zones;
(b) to have access to information on individual applications for asylum, on the course of the procedure and on the decisions taken, provided that the applicant for asylum agrees thereto;
(c) to present its views, in the exercise of its supervisory responsibilities under Article 35 of the Geneva Convention, to any competent authorities regarding individual applications for asylum at any stage of the procedure.

2. Paragraph 1 shall also apply to an organisation which is working in the territory of the Member State on behalf of the UNHCR pursuant to an agreement with that Member State.

Article 22
Collection of information on individual cases

For the purpose of examining individual cases, Member States shall not:
(a) directly disclose the information regarding individual applications for asylum, or the fact that an application has been made, to the alleged actor(s) of persecution of the applicant for asylum;
(b) obtain any information from the alleged actor(s) of persecution in a manner that would result in such actor(s) being directly informed of the fact that an application has been made by the applicant in question, and would jeopardise the physical integrity of the applicant and his/her dependants, or the liberty and security of his/her family members still living in the country of origin.

CHAPTER III
Procedures at First Instance

Section I

Article 23
Examination procedure

1. Member States shall process applications for asylum in an examination procedure in accordance with the basic principles and guarantees of Chapter II.

2. Member States shall ensure that such a procedure is concluded as soon as possible, with-out prejudice to an adequate and complete examination. Member States shall ensure that, when no decision can be taken within six months,

(a) the applicant concerned shall either be informed of the delay: or

(b) receive, upon his/her request, information on the time-frame within which the decision on his/her application is to be expected. Such information shall not constitute an obligation for the Member State towards the applicant concerned to take a decision within that time frame.

3. Member States may prioritise or accelerate any examination in accordance with the basic principles and guarantees of Chapter II including where the application is likely to be well-founded or where the applicant has special needs.

4. Moreover, Member States may lay down that an examination procedure in accordance with the basic principles and guarantees of Chapter II be prioritised or accelerated if:

(a) the applicant in submitting his/her application and presenting the fact, has only raised issues that are not relevant or of minimal relevance to the examination of whether he/she qualifies as a refugee by virtue of Council Directive on minimum standards for the qualification and status of third country nationals or stateless persons as refugees or as persons who otherwise need international protection and the content of the protection granted; or

(b) the applicant clearly does not qualify as a refugee or for refugee status in a Member State under Council Directive on minimum standards for the qualification and status of third country nationals or stateless persons as refugees or as persons who otherwise need international protection and the content of the protection granted; or

(c) the application for asylum is considered to be unfounded:

– because the applicant is from a safe country of origin within the meaning of Articles 29, 30 and 31 of this Directive, or

– because the country which is not a Member State is considered to be a safe third country for the applicant, without prejudice to Article 28(1); or

(d) the applicant has misled the authorities by presenting false information or documents or by withholding relevant information or documents with respect to his/her identity and/or nationality that could have had a negative impact on the decision; or

(e) the applicant has filed another application for asylum stating other personal data; or

(f) the applicant has not produced information to establish with a reasonable degree of certainty his/her identity or nationality, or, it is likely that, in bad faith, he/she has destroyed or disposed of an identity or travel document that would have helped establish his/her identity or nationality; or

(g) the applicant has made inconsistent, contradictory, unlikely or insufficient representations which make his/her claim clearly unconvincing in relation to his/her having being the object of persecution under Council Directive on minimum standards for the qualification and status of third country nationals or stateless persons as refugees or as persons who otherwise need international protection and the content of the protection granted; or

(h) the applicant has submitted a subsequent application raising no relevant new elements with respect to his/her particular circumstances or to the situation in his/her country of origin; or

(i) the applicant has failed without reasonable cause to make his/her application earlier, having had opportunity to do so; or

(j) the applicant is making an application merely in order to delay or frustrate the enforcement of an earlier or imminent decision which would result in his/her removal; or

(k) the applicant failed without good reasons to comply with obligations referred to in Articles 4(1) and (2) of Council Directive on minimum standards for the qualification and status of third country nationals or stateless persons as refugees or as persons who otherwise need international protection and the content of the protection granted or in Articles 11(2)(a) and (b) and 20(1) of this Directive; or

(l) the applicant entered the territory of the Member State unlawfully or prolonged his/her stay unlawfully and, without good reason, has either not presented himself/herself to the authorities and/or filed an application for asylum as soon as possible given the circumstances of his/her entry; or

(m) the applicant is a danger to the national security or the public order of the Member State; or the applicant has enforceably been expelled for serious reasons of public security and public order under national law; or

(n) the applicant refuses to comply with an obligation to have his/her fingerprints taken in accordance with relevant Community and/or national legislation; or

(o) the application was made by an unmarried minor to whom Article 6(4)(c) applies after the application of the parents or parent responsible for the minor has been rejected by a decision and no relevant new elements were raised with respect to his/her particular circumstances or to the situation in his/her country of origin.

Article 24
Specific procedures

1. Member States may moreover provide for the following specific procedures derogating from the basic principles and guarantees of Chapter II:

(a) a preliminary examination for the purpose of processing cases considered within the framework of the provisions set out in Section IV;

(b) procedures for the purpose of processing cases considered within the framework set out in Section V.

2. Member States may also provide a derogation in respect of Section VI.

Section II

Article 25
Cases of inadmissible applications

1. In addition to cases in which an application is not examined in accordance with the provisions of Council Regulation 343/2003 establishing the criteria and mechanisms for determining the Member State responsible for examining an asylum application lodged in one of the Member States by a third country national, Member States are not required to examine whether the applicant qualifies as a refugee in accordance with Council Directive on minimum standards for the qualification and status of third country nationals or stateless persons as refugees or as persons who otherwise need international protection and the content of the protection granted where an application is considered inadmissible pursuant to the present Article.

2. Member States may consider an application for asylum as inadmissible pursuant to this Article if:
 (a) another Member State has granted refugee status;
 (b) a country which is not a Member State is considered as a first country of asylum for the applicant, pursuant to Article 26;
 (c) a country which is not a Member State is considered as a safe third country for the applicant, pursuant to Article 27;
 (d) the applicant is allowed to remain in the Member State concerned on some other ground and as result of this he/she has been granted a status equivalent to the rights and benefits of the refugee status by virtue of Council Directive on minimum standards for the qualification and status of third country nationals or stateless persons as refugees or as persons who otherwise need international protection and the content of the protection granted;
 (e) the applicant is allowed to remain in the territory of the Member State concerned on some other grounds which protect him/her against refoulement pending the outcome of a procedure for the determination of a status pursuant to (d);
 (f) the applicant has lodged an identical application after a final decision;
 (g) a dependant of the applicant lodges an application, after he/she has in accordance with Article 6(3), consented to have his/her case be part of an application made on his/her behalf and there are no facts relating to the dependant's situation justifying a separate application.

Article 26
Application of the concept of first country of asylum

A country can be considered to be a first country of asylum for a particular applicant for asylum if:
 (a) he/she has been recognised in that country as a refugee and he/she can still avail himself/herself of that protection; or
 (b) he/she enjoys otherwise sufficient protection in that country, including benefiting from the principle of non-refoulement, provided that he/she will be re-admitted to that country.

In applying the concept of first country of asylum to the particular circumstances of an applicant for asylum, Member States may take into account the content of Article 27(1).

Article 27[4]
The safe third country concept

1. Member States may apply the safe third country concept only where the competent authorities are satisfied that a person seeking asylum will be treated in accordance with the following principles in the third country concerned:

(a) life and liberty are not threatened on account of race, religion, nationality, membership of a particular social group or political opinion; and

(b) the principle of non-refoulement in accordance with the Geneva Convention is respected; and

(c) the prohibition on removal in breach of the right to freedom from torture and cruel, inhuman or degrading treatment as laid down in international law is respected; and

(d) the possibility exists to request refugee status and, if found to be a refugee, to receive protection in accordance with the Geneva Convention.

2. The application of the safe third country concept shall be subject to rules laid down in national legislation, including:

(a) rules requiring a connection between the person seeking asylum and the third country concerned based on which it would be reasonable for that person to go to that country;

(b) rules on the methodology by which the competent authorities satisfy themselves that the safe third country concept may be applied to a particular country or to a particular applicant. Such methodology shall include case by case consideration of the safety of the country

---

[4] Editor: 'The Council recalls the conclusions of the European Council at Thessaloniki which, *inter alia,* invited the Council to examine *"the possibilities to further reinforce the asylum procedures in order to make them more efficient with a view to accelerating, as much as possible, the processing of non-international protection-related applications"*.

The Council considers that it is necessary to identify quickly and effectively those persons in need of protection, and in parallel, to provide for mechanisms to prevent abuse in order to maintain the credibility of the institution of asylum. The establishment of a minimum common list of safe countries of origin is such a mechanism. Identification of countries for inclusion on this list is based on: the experiences of Member States with regard to the national application of the safe country of origin principle and the cessation clauses of the Geneva Convention; their fulfilment of the criteria in Annex II of the draft Directive; and the number of asylum applications lodged in the Member States by nationals of those countries.

The Council considers, having regard to the preparatory work already conducted, that apart from Romania and Bulgaria, the following countries may also be suitable for inclusion on a minimum common list of safe countries of origin to be adopted as part of this Directive:

Benin, Botswana, Cape Verde, Chile, Costa Rica, Ghana, Mali, Mauritius, Senegal, Uruguay.

The Council undertakes, prior to the date on which the European Parliament will be reconsulted with regard to this draft Directive, to conduct during the coming months an in-depth assessment of these countries to ensure that they fulfil the criteria in Annex II. When conducting this assessment, regard shall be had to a range of information sources, including information from the Member States, the UNHCR, the Council of Europe and other international organisations.

Where, following this assessment, a country is considered not to fulfil the criteria in Annex II, that country shall not be included on the minimum common list of safe countries of origin.'

for a particular applicant and/or national designation of countries considered to be generally safe;

(c) rules, in accordance with international law, allowing an individual examination of whether the third country concerned is safe for a particular applicant which, as a minimum, shall permit the applicant to challenge the application of the safe third country concept on the grounds that he/she would be subjected to torture, cruel, inhuman or degrading treatment or punishment.

3. When implementing a decision solely based on this Article, Member States shall:

(a) inform the applicant accordingly; and

(b) provide him/her with a document informing the authorities of the third country, in the language of that country, that the application has not been examined in substance.

4. Where the third country does not permit the applicant for asylum in question to enter its territory, Member States shall ensure that access to a procedure is given in accordance with the basic principles and guarantees described in Chapter II.

5. Member States shall inform the Commission periodically of the countries to which this concept is applied in accordance with the provisions of this Article.

Section III

Article 28
Cases of unfounded applications

1. Without prejudice to Articles 19 and 20, Member States may only consider an application for asylum as unfounded if the determining authority has established that the applicant does not qualify for refugee status pursuant to Council Directive on minimum standards for the qualification and status of third country nationals or stateless persons as refugees or as persons who otherwise need international protection and the content of the protection granted.

2. In the cases mentioned in Article 23(4)(b) and in cases of unfounded applications for asylum in which any of the circumstances listed in Article 23(4)(a) and (c) to (o) apply, Member States may also consider an application, if it is so defined in the national legislation, as manifestly unfounded.

Article 29
Minimum common list of third countries as safe countries of origin

1. The third countries designated in the minimum common list of third countries as contained in Annex II shall be regarded by Member States as safe countries of origin.

2. The Council may, acting by a qualified majority on a proposal from the Commission and after consultation of the European Parliament, amend the minimum common list by adding or removing third countries, in accordance with Annex II. The Commission shall examine any request made by the Council or by a Member State that it submit a proposal to amend the minimum common list. When making its proposal, the Commission shall make use of

information from the Member States, its own information and, where necessary, information from UNHCR, the Council of Europe and other relevant international organisations.

3. Where the Council requests the Commission to submit a proposal for removing a third country from the minimum common list, the obligation of Member States pursuant to Article 31(2) shall be suspended with regard to this third country as of the day following the Council decision requesting such a submission.

4. Where a Member State requests the Commission to submit a proposal to the Council for removing a third country from the minimum common list, that Member State shall notify the Council in writing of the request made to the Commission. The obligation of this Member State pursuant to Article 31(2) shall be suspended with regard to the third country as of the day following the notification of the request to the Council.

5. The European Parliament shall be informed of the suspensions under paragraphs 3 and 4.

6. The suspensions under paragraphs 3 and 4 shall end after three months, unless the Commission makes a proposal, before the end of this period, to withdraw the third country from the minimum common list. The suspensions shall end in any case where the Council rejects, a proposal by the Commission to withdraw the third country from the list.

7. Upon request by the Council, the Commission shall report to the Council and the European Parliament on whether the situation of a country on the minimum common list is still in conformity with Annex II. When presenting its report to the Council and the European Parliament, the Commission may make such recommendations or proposals as it deems appropriate.

Article 30
National designation of third countries as safe countries of origin

1. Without prejudice to Article 29, Member States may retain or introduce legislation that allows, in accordance with Annex II, for the national designation of third countries other than those appearing on the minimum common list, as safe countries of origin for the purpose of examining applications for asylum. This may include designation of part of a country as safe where the conditions in Annex II are fulfilled in relation to that part.

2. By derogation to paragraph 1, Member States may retain legislation in force at the time of adoption of this Directive that allows for the national designation of third countries, other than those appearing on the minimum common list, as safe countries of origin for the purposes of examining applications for asylum where they are satisfied that persons in the third countries concerned are generally1 neither subject to:

   (a) persecution as defined in Article 9 of Council Directive on minimum standards for the qualification and status of third country nationals or stateless persons as refugees or as persons who otherwise need international protection and the content of the protection granted; nor

   (b) torture or inhuman or degrading treatment or punishment.

3. Member States may also retain legislation in force at the time of the adoption of this Directive that allows for the national designation of part of a country as safe or a country or part of a country as safe for a specified group of persons in that country where the conditions in paragraph 2 are fulfilled in relation to that part or group.

4. In assessing whether a country is a safe country of origin in accordance with paragraphs 2 and 3, Member States shall have regard to the legal situation, the application of the law and the general political circumstances in the third country concerned.

5. The assessment of whether a country is a safe country of origin in accordance with this Article shall be based on a range of sources of information, including in particular information from other Member States, the UNHCR, the Council of Europe and other relevant international organisations.

6. Member States shall notify to the Commission the countries that are designated as safe countries of origin in accordance with the provisions of this Article.

Article 31
Application of the safe country of origin concept

1. A third country designated as a safe country of origin either in accordance with the provisions of Article 29 or 30 can, after an individual examination of the application, be considered as a safe country of origin for a particular applicant for asylum only if:
  (a) he/she has the nationality of that country; or
  (b) he/she is a stateless person and was formerly habitually resident in that country; and he/she has not submitted any serious grounds for considering the country not to be a safe country of origin in his/her particular circumstances in terms of his/her qualification as a refugee in accordance with Council Directive on minimum standards for the qualification and status of third country nationals or stateless persons as refugees or as persons who otherwise need international protection and the content of the protection granted.

2. Member States shall, in accordance with paragraph 1, consider the application for asylum as unfounded where the third country is designated as safe pursuant to Article 29.

3. Member States shall lay down in national legislation further rules and modalities for the application of the safe country of origin concept.

Section IV

Article 32
Cases of subsequent applications

1. Where a person who has applied for asylum in a Member State makes further representations or a subsequent application in the same Member State, that Member State may examine these further representations or the elements of the subsequent application in the framework of the examination of the previous application or in the framework of the examination of the decision under review or appeal insofar as the competent authorities can take into

account and consider all the elements underlying the further representations or subsequent application within this framework.

2. Moreover, Member States may apply a specific procedure as referred to in paragraph 3, where a person makes a subsequent application for asylum:
(a) after his/her previous application has been withdrawn by virtue of Articles 19 or 20;
(b) after a decision has been taken on the previous application. Member States may also decide to apply this procedure only after a final decision has been taken.

3. A subsequent application for asylum shall be subject first to a preliminary examination as to whether, after the withdrawal of the previous application or after the decision referred to in paragraph 2(b) on this application has been reached, new elements or findings relating to the examination of whether he/she qualifies as a refugee by virtue of Council Directive on minimum standards for the qualification and status of third country nationals or stateless persons as refugees or as persons who otherwise need international protection and the content of the protection granted have arisen or have been presented by the applicant.

4. If, following the preliminary examination referred to in paragraph 3, new elements or findings arise or are presented by the applicant which significantly add to the likelihood of the applicant qualifying as a refugee by virtue of Council Directive on minimum standards for the qualification and status of third country nationals or stateless persons as refugees or as persons who otherwise need international protection and the content of the protection granted, the application shall be further examined in conformity with Chapter II.

5. Member States may, in accordance with national legislation, further examine a subsequent application where there are other reasons according to which a procedure has to be reopened.

6. Member States may decide to further examine the application only if the applicant concerned was, through no fault of his/her own, incapable of asserting the situations set forth in paragraphs 3, 4 and 5 in the previous procedure, in particular by exercising his/her right to an effective remedy pursuant to Article 39.

7. This procedure may also be applicable in the case of a dependant who lodges an application, after he/she has in accordance with Article 6(3), consented to have his/her case be part of an application made on his/her behalf. In this case the preliminary examination referred to in paragraph 3 will consist of examining whether there are facts relating to the dependant's situation justifying a separate application.

Article 33
(Negligence)

Member States may retain or adopt the procedure provided for in Article 32 in the case of an application for asylum filed at a later date by an applicant who, either intentionally or owing to gross negligence, fails to go to a reception centre or to appear before the competent authorities at a specified time.

Article 34
Procedural rules

1. Member States shall ensure that applicants for asylum whose application is subject to a preliminary examination pursuant to Article 32 enjoy the guarantees listed in Article 10(1).

2. Member States may lay down in national law rules on the preliminary examination pursuant to Article 32. Those rules may inter alia:

(a) oblige the applicant concerned to indicate facts and substantiate evidence which justify a new procedure;

(b) require submission of the new information by the applicant concerned within a time limit after which it has been obtained by him or her;

(c) permit the preliminary examination to be conducted on the sole basis of written submissions without a personal interview.

The conditions shall not render the access of applicants for asylum to a new procedure impossible nor result in the effective annulment or severe curtailment of such access.

3. Member States shall ensure that

(a) the applicant is informed in an appropriate manner of the outcome of the preliminary examination and, in case the application will not be further examined, of the reasons and of the possibilities of seeking an appeal or review of the decision;

(b) if one of the situations referred to in Article 32(2) applies, the determining authority shall further examine the subsequent application in conformity with the provisions of Chapter II as soon as possible.

Section V

Article 35
Cases of border procedures

1. Member States may provide for procedures, in accordance with the basic principles and guarantees of Chapter II, in order to decide, at the border or transit zones of the Member State, on the applications made at such locations.

2. However, when procedures as set out in paragraph 1 do not exist, Member States may maintain, subject to the provisions of this Article and in accordance with the laws or regulations in force at the time of the adoption of this Directive, procedures derogating from the basic principles and guarantees described in Chapter II, in order to decide, at the border or in transit zones, on the permission to enter their territory of applicants for asylum who have arrived and made an application for asylum at such locations.

3. The procedures referred to in paragraph 2 shall ensure in particular that the persons concerned:

– shall be allowed to remain at the border or transit zones of the Member State, without prejudice to Article 7; and

– must be immediately informed of their rights and obligations, as described in Article 10(1)(a); and

– have access, if necessary, to the services of an interpreter, as described in Article 10(1)(b); and

– are interviewed, before the competent authority takes a decision in such procedures, in relation to their application for asylum by persons with appropriate knowledge of the relevant standards applicable in the field of asylum and refugee law, as described in Articles 12 to 14; and

– can consult a legal adviser or counsellor admitted or permitted as such under national law, as described in Article 15(1); and

– have a representative appointed in the case of unaccompanied minors, as described in Article 17(1), unless Article 17(2) or (3) applies.

Moreover, in case permission to enter is refused by a competent authority, this competent authority shall state the reasons in fact and in law why his/her application for asylum is considered as unfounded or as inadmissible.

4. Member States shall ensure that a decision in the framework of the procedures provided for in paragraph 2 is taken within a reasonable time. When a decision has not been taken within four weeks, the applicant for asylum shall be granted entry to the territory of the Member State in order for his/her application to be processed in accordance with the other provisions of this Directive.

5. In the event of particular types of arrivals or arrivals involving a large number of third country nationals or stateless persons lodging applications for asylum at the border or in a transit zone, which makes it practically impossible to apply there the provisions of paragraph 1 or the specific procedure set out in paragraphs 2 and 3, those procedures may also be applied where and for as long as these third country nationals or stateless persons are accommodated normally at locations in proximity to the border or transit zone.

Section VI

Article 36
(Illegal entry from a safe third country)

1. Member States may provide that no, or no full, examination of the asylum application and of the safety of the applicant in his/her particular circumstances as described in Chapter II takes place in cases where a competent authority has established, on the basis of the facts, that the applicant for asylum is seeking to enter or has entered illegally into its territory from a safe third country according to paragraph 2.

2. A third country can only be considered as a safe third country for the purpose of paragraph 1 where:

(a) it has ratified and observes the provisions of the Geneva Convention without any geographical limitations; and

(b) it has in place an asylum procedure prescribed by law; and

(c) it has ratified the European Convention for the Protection of Human Rights and Fundamental Freedoms and it observes its provisions, including the standards relating to effective remedies; and

(d) it has been so designated by the Council in accordance with paragraph 3.

3. The Council shall, acting by qualified majority on the proposal of the Commission and after consultation of the European Parliament, adopt or amend a common list of third countries that shall be regarded as safe third countries for the purposes of paragraph 1.

4. Member States concerned shall lay down in national law the modalities for implementing the provisions of paragraph 1 and the consequences of decisions pursuant to those provisions in accordance with the principle of non-refoulement under the Geneva Convention including providing for exceptions from the application of this Article for humanitarian or political reasons or for reasons of public international law.

5. When implementing a decision solely based on this Article, Member States concerned shall:
(a) inform the applicant accordingly; and
(b) provide him/her with a document informing the authorities of the third country, in the language of that country, that the application has not been examined in substance.

6. Where the safe third country does not readmit the applicant for asylum in question, Member States shall ensure that access to a procedure is given in accordance with the basic principles and guarantees described in Chapter II.

7. Member States which have designated third countries as safe countries in accordance with national legislation in force at the date of the adoption of this Directive and on the basis of the criteria in paragraph 2(a) to (c), may apply paragraph 1 to these third countries until such time as the Council has adopted the common list pursuant to paragraph 3.

CHAPTER IV
Procedures for the Withdrawal of Refugee Status

Article 37
Withdrawal of refugee status

Member States shall ensure that an examination may be started to withdraw the refugee status of a particular person when new elements or findings arise indicating that there are reasons to reconsider the validity of his/her refugee status.

Article 38
Procedural rules

1. Member States shall ensure that, where the competent authority is considering to withdraw the refugee status of a third country national or stateless person in accordance with Article 14 of Council Directive on minimum standards for the qualification and status of third country nationals or stateless persons as refugees or as persons who otherwise need international protection and the content of the protection granted, the person concerned shall enjoy the following guarantees:
(a) to be informed in writing that the competent authority is reconsidering his or her qualification for refugee status and the reasons for such a reconsideration; and
(b) to be given the opportunity to submit, in a personal interview in accordance with Article 10(1)(b) and Articles 12 to 14 or in a written statement, reasons as to why his/her

refugee status should not be withdrawn. In addition, Member States shall ensure that within the framework of such a procedure:

(c) the competent authority is able to obtain precise and up to date information from various sources, such as, where appropriate, information from the United Nations High Commissioner for Refugees (UNHCR), as to the general situation prevailing in the countries of origin of the persons concerned; and

(d) where information is collected on the individual case for the purpose of reconsidering the refugee status, it is not obtained from the actor(s) of persecution in a manner that would result in such actor(s) being directly informed of the fact that the person concerned is a refugee, whose status is under reconsideration, nor jeopardise the physical integrity of the person and his/her dependants, or the liberty and security of his/her family members still living in the country of origin.

2. Member States shall ensure that the decision of the competent authority to withdraw the refugee status is given in writing. The reasons in fact and in law shall be stated in the decision and information on how to challenge the decision shall be given in writing.

3. Once the competent authority has taken the decision to withdraw the refugee status, Articles 15, paragraph 2, 14, paragraph 1 and 21 are equally applicable.

4. By derogation to paragraphs 1, 2 and 3, Member States may decide that the refugee status lapses by law in case of cessation in accordance with Article 11(1), sub-paragraphs (a), (b), (c) and (d) of Council Directive on minimum standards for the qualification and status of third country nationals or stateless persons as refugees or as persons who otherwise need international protection and the content of the protection granted or if the refugee has unequivocally renounced his/her recognition as a refugee.

CHAPTER V
Appeals Procedures

Article 39
The right to an effective remedy

1. Member States shall ensure that applicants for asylum have the right to an effective remedy before a court or tribunal, against the following:

(a) a decision taken on their application for asylum, including a decision:

(i) to consider an application inadmissible pursuant to Article 25(2);

(ii) at the border or in the transit zones of a Member State as described in Article 35(1);

(iii) not to conduct an examination pursuant to Article 36;

(b) a refusal to re-open the examination of an application after its discontinuation pursuant to Articles 19 and 20;

(c) a decision not to further examine the subsequent application pursuant to Articles 32 and 34;

(d) a decision refusing entry within the framework of the procedures provided for under Article 35(2);

(e) a decision for the withdrawal of the refugee status pursuant to Article 38.

2. Member States shall provide for time limits and other necessary rules for the applicant to exercise his/her right to an effective remedy pursuant to paragraph 1.

3. Member States shall, where appropriate, provide for rules in accordance with their international obligations dealing with:
(a) the question of whether the remedy pursuant to paragraph 1 shall have the effect of allowing applicants to remain in the Member State concerned pending its outcome; and
(b) the possibility of legal remedy or protective measures where the remedy pursuant to paragraph 1 does not have the effect of allowing applicants to remain in the Member State concerned pending its outcome. Member States may also provide for an ex officio remedy; and
(c) the grounds of challenge to a decision under Article 25(2)(c) in accordance with the methodology applied under Article 27(2)(b) and (c).

4. Member States may lay down time limits for the court or tribunal pursuant to paragraph 1 to examine the decision of the determining authority.

5. Where an applicant has been granted a status, which offers the same rights and benefits under national and Community law as the refugee status by virtue of Council Directive .../... on minimum standards for the qualification and status of third country nationals or stateless persons as refugees or as persons who otherwise need international protection and the content of the protection granted, the applicant may be considered to have an effective remedy where a court or tribunal decides that the remedy pursuant to paragraph 1 is inadmissible or unlikely to succeed on the basis of insufficient interest on the part of the applicant in maintaining the proceedings.

6. Member States may also lay down in national legislation the conditions under which it can be assumed that an applicant has implicitly withdrawn or abandoned his/her remedy pursuant to paragraph 1, together with the rules on the procedure to be followed.

CHAPTER VI
General and Final Provisions

Article 40
(Authorities challenging decisions)

This Directive does not affect the possibility for public authorities of challenging the administrative and/or judicial decisions as provided for in national legislation.

Article 41
Confidentiality

Member States shall ensure that authorities implementing this Directive are bound by the confidentiality principle, as defined in national law, in relation to any information they obtain in the course of their work.

Article 42
Report

No later than two years after the date specified in Article 43, the Commission shall report to the European Parliament and the Council on the application of this Directive in the Member States and shall propose any amendments that are necessary. Member States shall send the Commission all the information that is appropriate for drawing up this report. After presenting the report, the Commission shall report to the European Parliament and the Council on the application of this Directive in the Member States at least every two years.

Article 43
Transposal

Member States shall bring into force the laws, regulations and administrative provisions necessary to comply with this Directive by [24 months after the date of its adoption]. Concerning Article 15, Member States shall bring into force the laws, regulations and administrative provisions necessary to comply with this Directive by [36 months after the date of its adoption]. They shall forthwith inform the Commission thereof.

When Member States adopt those provisions, they shall contain a reference to this Directive or be accompanied by such a reference on the occasion of their official publication. Member States shall determine how such reference is to be made.

Member States shall communicate to the Commission the text of the provisions of national law, which they adopt in the field covered by this Directive.

Article 44
Transition

Member States shall apply the laws, regulations and administrative provisions set out in Article 43 to applications for asylum lodged after [date mentioned in Article 43] and to procedures for the withdrawal of refugee status started after [date mentioned in Article 43].

Article 45
Entry into force

This Directive shall enter into force on the twentieth day following that of its publication in the *Official Journal of the European Union*.

Article 46
Addressees

This Directive is addressed to the Member States in conformity with the Treaty establishing the European Community.

ANNEX I
DEFINITION OF 'DETERMINING AUTHORITY'

When implementing the provision of this Directive, Ireland may, insofar as the provisions of section17(1) of the Refugee Act 1996 (as amended) continues to apply, consider that:

'***determining authority***' provided for in Article 2(e) of this Directive shall, insofar as the examination of whether an applicant should or, as the case may be, should not be declared to be a refugee is concerned, mean the Office of the Refugee Applications Commissioner; and

'***decisions at first instance***' provided for in Article 2(e) of this Directive shall include recommendations of the Refugee Applications Commissioner as to whether an applicant should or, as the case may be, should not be declared to be a refugee. Ireland will notify the European Commission of any amendments to the provisions of section 17(1) of the Refugee Act 1996 (as amended).

ANNEX II
DESIGNATION OF SAFE COUNTRIES OF ORIGIN FOR THE PURPOSES OF ARTICLES 29 AND 30(1)[5]

A country is considered as a safe country of origin where, on the basis of the legal situation, the application of the law within a democratic system and the general political circumstances, it can be shown that there is generally and consistently no persecution as defined in Article 9 of Council Directive on minimum standards for the qualification and status of third country nationals or stateless persons as refugees or as persons who otherwise need international protection and the content of the protection granted; no torture or inhuman or degrading treatment or punishment; and no threat by reason of indiscriminate violence in situations of international or internal armed conflict.

In making this assessment, account shall be taken, *inter alia*, of the extent to which protection is provided against persecution or mistreatment through:

(a) the relevant laws and regulations of the country and the manner in which they are applied;

(b) observance of the rights and freedoms laid down in the European Convention for the Protection of Human Rights and Fundamental Freedoms and/or the International Covenant for Civil and Political Rights and/or the Convention against Torture, in particular the rights from which derogation cannot be made under Article 15(2) of the said European Convention;

(c) respect of the non-refoulement principle according to the Geneva Convention;

(d) provision for a system of effective remedies against violations of these rights and freedoms.

ANNEX III
DEFINITION OF 'APPLICANT' OR 'APPLICANT FOR ASYLUM'

When implementing the provisions of this Directive Spain may, insofar as the provisions of

---

[5] Editor: See also the recital on Bulgaria and Romania.

'*Ley de procedimiento administrativo*' of [date] and '*Ley de la jurisdicción contencioso administrativa*' of [date] continues to apply, consider that, for the purposes of Chapter V, the definition of 'applicant' or 'applicant for asylum' in Article 2(c) of the Directive shall include an 'appellant' as established in the above mentioned Acts.

The 'appellant' shall be entitled to the same guarantees as an 'applicant' or an 'applicant for asylum' as set out in the Directive for the purposes of exercising his/her right to an effective remedy in Chapter V. Spain will notify the European Commission of any relevant amendments to the above mentioned Act.

EXPLANATORY MEMORANDUM

A. As provided for by COM(2002)326 final

1. Background

On 20 September 2000 the Commission adopted a draft Council Directive on minimum standards on procedures in Member States for granting and withdrawing refugee status.[6]

The proposal was sent to the Council, the European Parliament and the Economic and Social Committee.

The Economic and Social Committee delivered a favourable opinion on 25 and 26 April 2001 (CES 530/2001).

On 20 September 2001 the European Parliament adopted its Opinion in plenary, approving the Commission proposal subject to amendments and calling on the Commission to amend its proposal accordingly. On the basis of a report presented to the plenary by Mr Watson, chairperson of the Committee on Citizen's Freedoms and Rights, Justice and Home Affairs, the European Parliament has adopted 106 amendments (A5-0291/2001).[7] In the Council the proposal has been the subject of negotiations in the course of 2001. During the Belgian Presidency, the December 2001 Council adopted Conclusions with regard to the approach taken by the future Directive.[8] The declaration of the Laeken European Council requested the Commission to bring forward a modified proposal.

2. An overview of the new proposal

In conformity with the Council Conclusions, this proposal sets out a different structure for asylum procedures in Member States and amends a considerable number of the minimum standards proposed by the Commission. In addition, it takes over a number of the amendments of the European Parliament, either in the recitals or in the text of the proposal.
The following key changes have been made:

---

[6] COM(2000)578 final, OJ C 62 E, 27.2.2001, 231.

[7] OJ C 77E, 28.3.2002, 94.

[8] (15107/1/REV 1). Press release 14581/01 (Presse 444), 2396th Council Meeting Justice, Home Affairs and Civil Protection, Brussel, 6 and 7 December 2001.

1. Following suggestions from certain Member States and the European Parliament, most if not all guarantees in Chapter II have been modified, i.e. either upgraded in terms of the level of protection accorded to applicants for asylum or qualified, to take into account specific circumstances or exceptions occurring in practice, methods or safe guards against abuse and certain national conditions or particularities;

2. In accordance with the Council Conclusions the classification of procedures of former chapters III and IV has been re-organised. Instead of a separate admissibility procedure, applications considered as inadmissible may be processed in accelerated procedures;

3. Following suggestions from some Member States special standards on two new types of accelerated procedures are introduced: a procedure to examine applications lodged at the border or on the entry to the territory and a procedure in which the need to initiate a new procedure for a subsequent application is assessed;

4. New cases of inadmissible applications are introduced, whilst other cases of applications, where there is evidence of misconduct by the applicant or abuse of the procedure, may also be processed in accelerated procedures;

5. Obligations to set a reasonable time limit for taking a decision under the regular procedure, to consider non-compliance with this time limit as a negative decision against which an applicant can lodge an appeal, as well as obligations for appeal bodies to take decisions within a reasonable time limit have been deleted;

6. The obligation to introduce a two level appeal system, in which a court of law is competent at least once to review a decision is replaced, in accordance with general principles of Community law, by the right of every applicant for asylum to have an effective remedy before a court of law against a decision on his application, leaving the institutional arrangements for review or appeal to national discretion.

7. Following an amendment from the European Parliament, it is proposed that the implementation of this particular asylum Directive should be evaluated at regular intervals not exceeding two years.

B.   *As provided for by COM(2000)578 final*

1.   **Minimum standards on procedures in Member States for granting and withdrawing refugee status: a first measure to build the common european asylum system**

According to the Conclusions of the Presidency at the Tampere European Council in October 1999, a common European asylum system is to include, in the short term, a clear and workable determination of the State responsible for the examination of an asylum application, common standards for a fair and efficient asylum procedure, common minimum conditions of reception of asylum seekers and the approximation of rules on the recognition and content of the refugee status. This is to be supplemented with measures on subsidiary forms of protection offering an appropriate status to any person in need of such protection. On 24

May 2000, the Commission adopted a proposal for a Council Directive on temporary protection in the event of a mass influx of displaced persons based on solidarity between Member States as a tool in the service of a common European asylum system.

The Commission is now, in the autumn of 2000, proposing a draft Council Directive on minimum standards on procedures in Member States for granting and withdrawing refugee status as a means to establish a fair and efficient asylum procedure, as indicated in the scoreboard to review progress on the creation of an area for freedom, security and justice in the European Union, approved by the Council on 27 March 2000.

In March 1999, the Commission began work on asylum procedures with its working paper 'Towards common standards for asylum procedures'. This document was discussed in the Council both at Ministerial level and among officials. Thirteen Member States subsequently submitted written comments. The European Parliament adopted Resolution A5-0123/2000 on the working document in the plenary session of 13 to 16 June 2000. In addition, the Commission specifically consulted the UNHCR, ECRE, Amnesty International and Save the Children on the working document. All four organisations submitted written comments, as did three other NGOs (the Refugee Legal Centre, the Medical Foundation for the Care of Victims of Torture and the Immigration Law Practitioners' Association). Following an analysis of these replies, the Commission has drafted its proposal, taking into account, where necessary, the existing soft law, principally the 1995 Council Resolution on minimum guarantees for asylum procedures, the 1992 London Council Resolutions on manifestly unfounded applications, host third countries and countries in which there is generally no serious risk of persecution and the 1997 Council Resolution on unaccompanied minors who are nationals of third countries.

The proposal takes into account the approach envisaged by the Conclusions of the Presidency at the Tampere European Council in October 1999 that a common European asylum system, while including in the short term the abovementioned measures on asylum in accordance with the Geneva Convention of 28 July 1951 and the Protocol of 31 January 1967 relating to the status of refugees and other treaties, should lead, in the longer term, to a common asylum procedure and a uniform status for those granted asylum valid throughout the Union.

2.   Scope of the proposal

As an essential first measure on asylum procedures for the purpose of achieving a common asylum policy on the basis of Title IV of the Treaty establishing the European Community, as amended by the Amsterdam Treaty, the proposal sets out the requisite measures for a simple and quick system for dealing with asylum applications. It focuses on all the legislative tools and mechanisms which Member States can use to operate a system that processes cases swiftly and correctly. Common standards and time-limits are set in order to dismiss quickly inadmissible and manifestly unfounded cases so that each national system can operate smoothly for the benefit of Geneva Convention refugees. Aligning national systems on the basis of these standards will enable Member States to build efficient asylum procedures for the future within the framework of a common European asylum system.

This measure will not require Member States to apply uniform procedures. Nor will it oblige them to adopt common concepts and practices which they do not wish to apply. For example, if a Member State does not wish to apply the safe third-country concept to reject asylum applications, the measure will not oblige this Member State to adopt the concept. Moreover, all standards for operating a fair and efficient procedure are laid down without prejudice to Member States' discretionary power to prioritise cases on the basis of national policies.

The measure also allows Member States to derogate from certain rules it they so wish, as this is a first measure on asylum procedures. For instance, it is proposed that Member States should be able to derogate from the principle that appeal has suspensive effect in, *inter alia*, manifestly unfounded cases. The issue of suspensive effect is a complex one and Member States appear to hold very divergent views on the advantages and disadvantages of suspensive effect. The Commission would welcome Member States that choose to adopt these and other derogations permitted at this stage, to introduce additional safeguards, such as the adoption by law of the derogations or supplementary procedural guarantees in individual cases.

Moreover, the proposal is limited to the minimum standards necessary for granting and withdrawing refugee status. Consequently, it does not include minimum standards for determining whether persons qualify for protection under some other international instrument or are otherwise in need of protection. Nonetheless, if the Member States were to apply the standards in this proposal in deciding on applications for kinds of protection other than that emanating from the Geneva Convention, this would be welcomed by the Commission. Accordingly, the proposal provides that Member States may decide to apply the provisions of the Directive to these other procedures.

The proposal does not prejudge other measures on a common asylum policy as laid down in the Vienna Action Plan and the Scoreboard. Articles 63(1) and 63(2) provide for the adoption of measures on asylum regarding the criteria and mechanisms for determining which Member State is responsible for considering an asylum application, minimum standards on the reception of asylum applicants, minimum standards with respect to the qualification of nationals of third countries as refugees and measures for persons who otherwise need international protection. The Commission will put forward proposals on these particular areas in accordance with the Scoreboard.

Neither does this particular proposal prejudge any measures that have not been envisaged in the Vienna Action Plan and the Scoreboard. Several other measures with respect to procedures for the admission of refugees by the Member States of the European Union could be considered within the scope of point (1)(d) of the first paragraph of Article 63 of the EC Treaty. For one thing, the present proposal confines itself to procedures for cases of spontaneous applicants at the border or on the territory of the Member States in Europe. It is therefore without prejudice to a possible measure on procedures for admitting to Member States third-country nationals who qualify as Geneva Convention refugees, but have not yet been able to reach the external frontiers of the European Union.

The Communication on common asylum procedures and a uniform status for those who are granted asylum valid throughout the Union will outline what measures may be taken next on asylum procedures for the purpose of achieving a common asylum policy on the basis of Title IV of the Treaty establishing the European Community, as amended by the Amsterdam Treaty, including those that could be taken on the basis of point (1)(d) of the first paragraph of Article 63.

3. The objectives of the proposal

With this proposal for a Directive, the Commission is pursuing the following aims:

1. implementing point (1)(d) of the first paragraph of Article 63 of the Treaty, paragraph 36(b)(iii) of the Vienna Action Plan, Conclusion 14 of the Tampere European Council and the first part of the paragraph on a fair and efficient asylum procedure of the Scoreboard presented to the Council and Parliament in March 2000;

2. providing for measures that are essential to the efficiency of Member States' procedures for granting and withdrawing refugee status;

3. laying down common definitions of, and common requirements for inadmissible and manifestly unfounded cases, including the safe country concepts in order to achieve a common approach among those Member States that apply these practices and concepts;

4. laying down time-limits for deciding in first instance and in appeal in these cases, empowering Member States to effectively process them as soon as possible;

5. enhancing thereby the ability of Member States to examine the asylum applications of persons that may be Geneva Convention refugees;

6. laying down a minimum level of procedural safeguards for asylum applicants in the procedures in Member States to ensure a common level of procedural fairness in the European Community;

7. laying down specific safeguards for fair procedures for persons with special needs;

8. setting minimum requirements for decisions and decision-making authorities with a view to reducing disparities in examination processes in Member States and ensuring a good standard of decision making throughout the European Community.

4. An overview of the standards in the proposal

The proposal basically consists of three different sets of provisions.

The first set deals with procedural guarantees for asylum applicants. These provisions relate to situations found throughout all stages of the asylum procedures and are designed to approximate notions of procedural fairness among Member States. Every applicant for asylum must:

– have the right to appeal against a decision in first instance, irrespective of the nature of the decision;

– be informed at decisive moments in the course of the procedure, in a language which he understands, of his legal position in order to be able to consider possible next steps. For instance, when receiving the decision in first instance, an applicant must be informed of its contents and of the possibility to appeal this decision. In addition, specific guarantees are laid down for persons with special needs, such as (unaccompanied) minors.

A second set of provisions concerns minimum requirements regarding the decision-making process. While Member States may retain their national systems, decision making has to meet certain minimum requirements in the interests of developing a comprehensive common European asylum policy. It will generally suffice for Member States to have in place a three-tier system: an authority determining refugee status, an authority to hear administrative or judicial appeals and an Appellate Court. Furthermore, decision-making authorities should have access to information on country of origin and be able to seek expert advice whenever necessary. Personnel should have received the requisite initial training, decision making should follow certain investigative standards, decisions are to be taken individually, objectively and impartially, and full reasons should be stated for adverse decisions.

A final set of provisions concerns common standards for the application of certain concepts and practices. These concepts or practices ('inadmissible applications', 'manifestly unfounded applications', 'safe country of origin'; 'safe third country') are already in place in many Member States, but application and interpretation vary significantly. With a view to limiting secondary movements between Member States, the Commission proposes that they be made subject to common standards. Each Member State may decide whether or not to apply a concept or practice, but if it does, its national application would have to follow the common framework for all Member States. Accordingly, while there is no obligation to apply an accelerated procedure to dismiss manifestly unfounded applications, Member States will have to abide by the common definitions and maximum time-limits if they do so. Similarly, where Member States wish to dismiss an application as inadmissible on the basis of the safe third-country concept, they must abide by the common principles for designating a country as a safe third country as laid down in Annex I to the proposal as well as the common requirements for applying the concept in individual cases. Member States will be able to dismiss applications as inadmissible if:
    – another Member State is responsible for examining the application, according to the criteria and mechanisms for determining which Member State is responsible;
    – a country is considered as a first country of asylum for the applicant;
    – a country is considered as a safe third country for the applicant.

As a procedure to determine whether another Member State is responsible for examining an asylum application may take place in parallel with or in the context of a more comprehensive examination of the asylum application in Member States, the general procedural guarantees in the proposal will also apply to the former procedure.

However, the only guarantee included in the proposal which is specifically related to the procedure for determining whether another Member State is responsible for examining an asylum application is one that is based upon a principle of procedural fairness at the heart of this proposal: the principle that an applicant is informed of his legal position at all decisive moments in the course of the procedure. The Commission will come forward with a proposal for a Community instrument on a clear and workable determination of the Member State responsible for the examination of an application for asylum at the beginning of 2001.

Member States will be able to dismiss applications as manifestly unfounded if:
    – the applicant has, without reasonable cause, submitted a fraudulent application with respect to his identity or nationality;

– the applicant has produced no identity or travel document and has not provided the determining authority with sufficient or sufficiently convincing information to determine his identity or nationality, and there are serious reasons for considering that the applicant has in bad faith destroyed or disposed of an identity or travel document that would help determine his identity or nationality;

– an application is made at the last stage of a procedure to deport the person and could have been made earlier;

– in submitting and explaining his application, the applicant does not raise issues that justify international protection on the basis of the Geneva Convention or Article 3 of the 1950 European Convention for the Protection of Human Rights and Fundamental Freedoms;

– the applicant is from a safe country of origin;

– the applicant has submitted a new application raising no relevant new facts with respect to his particular circumstances or to the situation in his country of origin.

Finally, the proposal lays down a common approach for the concepts of both safe third country and safe country of origin on the basis of an analysis of the positions of the Member States, the Resolution of the European Parliament and the views expressed by the UNHCR and other relevant organisations. This approach consists of:

– the use of common principles to determine what these concepts should mean;

– national lists of safe countries for those Member States that so wish, subject to notification to the Commission;

– common requirements for applying the concepts in individual cases;

– regular exchanges of views among Member States on the designation of safe countries, national lists and the application of the concepts in individual cases under the umbrella of a Community procedure in a so-called Contact Committee (see below).

The Commission, for its part, envisages to introduce a Contact Committee. The Contact Committee will facilitate the transposition and the subsequent harmonised implementation of the Directive through regular consultations on all practical problems arising from its application. It will help avoid duplication of work where common standards are set, notably with respect to the situation in safe third countries and safe countries of origin. Secondly, the Committee will facilitate consultation between the Member States on more stringent or additional guarantees and obligations that they may lay down at national level. This would help prepare the ground for a common asylum procedure as envisaged by the Conclusions of the Presidency at the Tampere European Council in October 1999. Lastly, the Committee will advise the Commission, if necessary, on any supplements or amendments to be made to this Directive or on any adjustments deemed necessary.

5.   The choice of legal basis

The choice of legal basis is consistent with the amendments made to the Treaty establishing the European Community by the Amsterdam Treaty, which entered into force on 1 May 1999. Point (1)(d) of the first paragraph of Article 63 of the EC Treaty provides that the Council shall adopt measures on asylum in accordance with the Geneva Convention of 28 July 1951 and the Protocol of 31 January 1967 relating to the status of refugees and other relevant treaties within the area of minimum standards on procedures in Member States for granting or withdrawing refugee status. Article 63 is accordingly the proper legal basis for a proposal to establish minimum standards for procedures in Member States to grant and withdraw refugee status.

Title IV of the EC Treaty is not applicable to the United Kingdom and to Ireland, unless those Member States decide otherwise in accordance with the procedure laid down in the Protocol on the position of the United Kingdom and Ireland annexed to the Treaties. Title IV is likewise not applicable to Denmark, by virtue of the Protocol on the position of Denmark annexed to the Treaties.

6.   Subsidiarity and proportionality: justification and value added

Subsidiarity
The insertion of the new Title IV (Visas, asylum, immigration and other policies related to free movement of persons) in the Treaty establishing the European Community demonstrates the will of the High Contracting Parties to confer powers in these matters on the European Community. But the European Community does not have exclusive powers here. Consequently, even with the political will to implement a common policy on asylum and immigration, it must act in accordance with Article 5 of the EC Treaty, i.e. the Community may only take action if, and in so far as the objectives of the proposed action cannot be sufficiently achieved by the Member States and can therefore, by reason of the scale or effects of the proposed action, be better achieved by the Community. The proposed Directive satisfies these criteria.

The establishment of an area of freedom, security and justice entails the adoption of measures relating to asylum. The specific objective of this initiative is to lay down minimum standards on procedures in Member States for granting and withdrawing refugee status. The standards laid down in this proposal must be capable of being applied through minimum measures in all the Member States. The situation regarding the procedural guarantees for asylum applicants, the requirements for decision making and the standards for applying concepts and practices such as accelerated procedures vary considerably from one Member State to another. Minimum Community standards have to be laid down by the kind of action proposed here. They will help to limit secondary movements of asylum applicants as resulting from disparities in procedures in Member States. Henceforth, applicants for asylum will decide on their country of destination less on the basis of the procedural rules and practices in place than before.

The continued absence of standards on the procedures for granting and withdrawing refugee status would have a negative effect on the effectiveness of other instruments relating to asylum. Conversely, once minimum standards on asylum procedures are in place, the operation of, *inter alia*, an effective system for determining which Member State is responsible for considering an asylum application is fully justified.

Proportionality
The form taken by Community action must be the simplest form allowing the proposal to attain its objectives and to be implemented as efficiently as possible. In this spirit, the legal instrument chosen is a Directive, which allows minimum standards to be laid down, while

leaving national authorities the choice of the most appropriate form and methods for implementing it in their national legal system and general context. The proposal concentrates on a set of minimum standards that are strictly necessary for the coherence of the planned action without laying down standards relating to other aspects of asylum.

Chapter 1.5
QUALIFICATION

COUNCIL DIRECTIVE
on minimum standards for the qualification and status of third country nationals or
stateless persons as refugees or as persons who otherwise need international protection
and the content of the protection granted[1]

THE COUNCIL OF THE EUROPEAN UNION,
Having regard to the Treaty establishing the European Community, and in particular
points 1(c), 2(a) and 3(a) of Article 63 thereof,
Having regard to the proposal from the Commission,
Having regard to the Opinion of the European Parliament,[2]
Having regard to the Opinion of the Economic and Social Committee,[3]
Having regard to the Opinion of the Committee of the Regions,[4]

Whereas:

(1) A common policy on asylum, including a Common European Asylum System, is a
constituent part of the European Union's objective of progressively establishing an area of
freedom, security and justice open to those who, forced by circumstances, legitimately seek
protection in the Community.

(2) The European Council at its special meeting in Tampere on 15 and 16 October 1999
agreed to work towards establishing a Common European Asylum System, based on the full
and inclusive application of the Geneva Convention relating to the Status of Refugees of
28 July 1951 ('Geneva Convention'), as supplemented by the New York Protocol of
31 January 1967 (Protocol), thus affirming the principle of non-refoulement and ensuring
that nobody is sent back to persecution.

(3) The Geneva Convention and Protocol provide the cornerstone of the international legal
regime for the protection of refugees.

(4) The Tampere Conclusions provide that a Common European Asylum System should
include, in the short term, the approximation of rules on the recognition of refugees and the
content of refugee status.

---

[1] This Directive has been formally adopted on 29 April 2004.
[2] OJ C 300E, 11.12.2003, p. 25.
[3] OJ C 221, 17.9.2002, p. 43.
[4] OJ C 278, 14.11.2002, p. 44.

(5) The Tampere Conclusions also provide that rules regarding refugee status should be complemented by measures on subsidiary forms of protection, offering an appropriate status to any person in need of such protection.

(6) The main objective of this Directive is, on the one hand, to ensure that Member States apply common criteria for the identification of persons genuinely in need of international protection, and, on the other hand, to ensure that a minimum level of benefits is available for these persons in all Member States.

(7) The approximation of rules on the recognition and content of refugee and subsidiary protection status should help to limit the secondary movements of applicants for asylum between Member States, where such movement is purely caused by differences in legal frameworks.

(8) It is in the very nature of minimum standards that Member States should have the power to introduce or maintain more favourable provisions for third country nationals or stateless persons who request international protection from a Member State, where such a request is understood to be on the grounds that the person concerned is either a refugee within the meaning of Article 1(A) of the Geneva Convention, or a person who otherwise needs international protection.

(9) Those third country nationals or stateless persons, who are allowed to remain in the territories of the Member States for reasons not due to a need for international protection but on a discretionary basis on compassionate or humanitarian grounds, fall outside the scope of this Directive.

(10) This Directive respects the fundamental rights and observes the principles recognised in particular by the Charter of Fundamental Rights of the European Union. In particular this Directive seeks to ensure full respect for human dignity and the right to asylum of applicants for asylum and their accompanying family members.

(11) With respect to the treatment of persons falling within the scope of this Directive, Member States are bound by obligations under instruments of international law to which they are party and which prohibit discrimination.

(12) The 'best interests of the child' should be a primary consideration of Member States when implementing this Directive.

(13) This Directive is without prejudice to the Protocol on asylum for nationals of Member States of the European Union as annexed to the Treaty Establishing the European Community.

(14) The recognition of refugee status is a declaratory act.

(15) Consultations with the United Nations High Commissioner for Refugees may provide valuable guidance for Member States when determining refugee status according to Article 1 of the Geneva Convention.

(16) Minimum standards for the definition and content of refugee status should be laid down to guide the competent national bodies of Member States in the application of the Geneva Convention.

(17) It is necessary to introduce common criteria for recognising applicants for asylum as refugees within the meaning of Article 1 of the Geneva Convention.

(18) In particular, it is necessary to introduce common concepts of protection needs arising *sur place;* sources of harm and protection; internal protection; and persecution, including the reasons for persecution.

(19) Protection can be provided not only by the State but also by parties or organisations, including international organisations, meeting the conditions of this Directive, which control a region or a larger area within the territory of the State.

(20) It is necessary, when assessing applications from minors for international protection, that Member States should have regard to child-specific forms of persecution.

(21) It is equally necessary to introduce a common concept of the persecution ground 'membership of a particular social group'.

(22) Acts contrary to the purposes and principles of the United Nations are set out in the Preamble and Articles 1 and 2 of the Charter of the United Nations and are, amongst others, embodied in the United Nations Resolutions relating to measures combating terrorism, which declare that 'acts, methods and practices of terrorism are contrary to the purposes and principles of the United Nations' and that 'knowingly financing, planning and inciting terrorist acts are also contrary to the purposes and principles of the United Nations'.

(23) As referred to in Article 14, "status" can also include refugee status.

(24) Minimum standards for the definition and content of subsidiary protection status should also be laid down. Subsidiary protection should be complementary and additional to the refugee protection enshrined in the Geneva Convention.

(25) It is necessary to introduce criteria on the basis of which applicants for international protection are to be recognised as eligible for subsidiary protection. Those criteria should be drawn from international obligations under human rights instruments and practices existing in Member States.

(26) Risks to which a population of a country or a section of the population is generally exposed do normally not create in themselves an individual threat which would qualify as serious harm.

(27) Family members, merely due to their relation to the refugee, will normally be vulnerable to acts of persecution in such a manner that could be the basis for refugee status.

(28) The notion of national security and public order also covers cases in which a third country national belongs to an association which supports international terrorism or supports such an association.

(29) While the benefits provided to family members of beneficiaries of subsidiary protection status do not necessarily have to be the same as those provided to the qualifying beneficiary, they need to be fair in comparison to those enjoyed by beneficiaries of subsidiary protection status.

(30) Within the limits set out by international obligations, Member States may lay down that the granting of benefits with regard to access to employment, social welfare, health care and access to integration facilities requires the prior issue of a residence permit.

(31) This Directive does not apply to financial benefits from the Member States which are granted to promote education and training.

(32) The practical difficulties encountered by beneficiaries of refugee or subsidiary protection status concerning the authentication of their foreign diplomas, certificates or other evidence of formal qualification should be taken into account.

(33) Especially to avoid social hardship, it is appropriate, for beneficiaries of refugee or subsidiary protection status, to provide without discrimination in the context of social assistance the adequate social welfare and means of subsistence.

(34) With regard to social assistance and health care, the modalities and detail of the provision of core benefits to beneficiaries of subsidiary protection status should be determined by national law. The possibility of limiting the benefits for beneficiaries of subsidiary protection status to core benefits is to be understood in the sense that this notion covers at least minimum income support, assistance in case of illness, pregnancy and parental assistance, insofar as they are granted to nationals according to the legislation of the Member State concerned.

(35) Access to health care, including both physical and mental health care, should be ensured to beneficiaries of refugee or subsidiary protection status.

(36) The implementation of this Directive should be evaluated at regular intervals, taking into consideration in particular the evolution of the international obligations of Member States regarding non-refoulement, the evolution of the labour markets in the Member States as well as the development of common basic principles for integration.

(37) Since the objectives of the proposed Directive, namely to establish minimum standards for the granting of international protection to third country nationals and stateless persons by Member States and the content of the protection granted, cannot be sufficiently achieved by the Member States and can therefore, by reason of the scale and effects of the Directive, be better achieved at Community level, the Community may adopt measures, in accordance with the principle of subsidiarity as set out in Article 5 of the Treaty. In accordance with the principle of proportionality, as set out in that Article, this Directive does not go beyond what is necessary in order to achieve those objectives.

(38) In accordance with Article 3 of the Protocol on the position of the United Kingdom and Ireland, annexed to the Treaty on European Union and to the Treaty establishing the European Community, the United Kingdom has notified, by letter of 28 January 2002, its wish to take part in the adoption and application of this Directive.

(39) In accordance with Article 3 of the Protocol on the position of the United Kingdom and Ireland, annexed to the Treaty on European Union and to the Treaty establishing the European Community, Ireland has notified, by letter of 13 February 2002, its wish to take part in the adoption and application of this Directive.

(40) In accordance with Articles 1 and 2 of the Protocol on the position of Denmark, annexed to the Treaty on European Union and to the Treaty establishing the European Community, Denmark is not taking part in the adoption of this Directive and is not bound by it or subject to its application,

HAVE ADOPTED THIS DIRECTIVE,

CHAPTER I
General Provisions

Article 1
Subject matter and scope

The purpose of this Directive is to lay down minimum standards for the qualification of third country nationals or stateless persons as refugees or as persons who otherwise need international protection and the content of the protection granted.

Article 2
Definitions

For the purposes of this Directive:

(a) 'International protection' means the refugee and subsidiary protection status as defined in (d) and (f);

(b) 'Geneva Convention' means the Convention relating to the status of refugees done at Geneva on 28 July 1951, as amended by the New York Protocol of 31 January 1967;

(c) 'Refugee' means a third country national who, owing to a well-founded fear of being persecuted for reasons of race, religion, nationality, political opinion or membership of a particular social group, is outside the country of nationality and is unable or, owing to such fear, is unwilling to avail himself or herself of the protection of that country, or a stateless person, who, being outside of the country of former habitual residence for the same reasons as mentioned above, is unable or, owing to such fear, unwilling to return to it, and to whom Article 12 does not apply;

(d) 'Refugee status' means the recognition by a Member State of a third country national or a stateless person as a refugee;

(e) 'Person eligible for subsidiary protection' means a third country national or a stateless person who does not qualify as a refugee but in respect of whom substantial grounds have been shown for believing that the person concerned, if returned to his or her country of origin, or in the case of a stateless person, to his or her country of former habitual residence, would face a real risk of suffering serious harm as defined in Article 15, and to whom Article 17(1) and (2) do not apply, and is unable, or, owing to such risk, unwilling to avail himself or herself of the protection of that country;

(f) 'Subsidiary protection status' means the recognition by a Member State of a third country national or a stateless person as a person eligible for subsidiary protection;

(g) 'Application for international protection' means a request made by a third country national or a stateless person for protection from a Member State, who can be understood to seek refugee status or subsidiary protection status, and who does not explicitly request another kind of protection, outside the scope of this Directive, that can be applied for separately;

(h) 'Family members' means, insofar as the family already existed in the country of origin, the following members of the family of the beneficiary of refugee or subsidiary protection status who are present in the same Member State in relation to the application for international protection:

– the spouse of the beneficiary of refugee or subsidiary protection status or his or her unmarried partner in a stable relationship, where the legislation or practice of the Member State concerned treats unmarried couples in a way comparable to married couples under its law relating to aliens;

– the minor children of the couple referred to in the first indent or of the beneficiary of refugee or subsidiary protection status, on condition that they are unmarried and dependent and regardless of whether they were born in or out of wedlock or adopted as defined under the national law;

(i) 'Unaccompanied minors' means third-country nationals or stateless persons below the age of eighteen, who arrive on the territory of the Member States unaccompanied by an adult responsible for them whether by law or custom, and for as long as they are not effectively taken into the care of such a person; it includes minors who are left unaccompanied after they have entered the territory of the Member States;

(j) 'Residence permit' means any permit or authorisation issued by the authorities of a Member State, in the form provided for under that State's legislation, allowing a third country national or stateless person to reside on its territory;

(k) 'Country of origin' means the country or countries of nationality or, for stateless persons, of former habitual residence.

Article 3
More favourable standards

Member States may introduce or retain more favourable standards for determining who qualifies as a refugee or as a person eligible for subsidiary protection, and for determining the content of international protection, in so far as those standards are compatible with this Directive.

CHAPTER II
Assessment of Applications for International Protection

Article 4
Assessment of facts and circumstances

1. Member States may consider it the duty of the applicant to submit as soon as possible all elements needed to substantiate the application for international protection. In cooperation with the applicant it is the duty of the Member State to assess the relevant elements of the application.

2. The elements referred to in of paragraph 1 consist of the applicant's statements and all documentation at the applicants disposal regarding the applicant's age, background, including that of relevant relatives, identity, nationality(ies), country(ies) and place(s) of previous residence, previous asylum applications, travel routes, identity and travel documents and the reasons for applying for international protection.

3. The assessment of an application for international protection is to be carried out on an individual basis and includes taking into account:

(a) all relevant facts as they relate to the country of origin at the time of taking a decision on the application; including laws and regulations of the country of origin and the manner in which they are applied;

(b) the relevant statements and documentation presented by the applicant including information on whether the applicant has been or may be subject to persecution or serious harm;

(c) the individual position and personal circumstances of the applicant, including factors such as background, gender and age, so as to assess whether, on the basis of the applicant's personal circumstances, the acts to which the applicant has been or could be exposed would amount to persecution or serious harm;

(d) whether the applicant's activities since leaving the country of origin were engaged in for the sole or main purpose of creating the necessary conditions for applying for international protection, so as to assess whether these activities will expose the applicant to persecution or serious harm if returned to that country;

(e) whether the applicant could reasonably be expected to avail himself of the protection of another country where he could assert citizenship.

4. The fact that an applicant has already been subject to persecution or serious harm or to direct threats of such persecution or such harm, is a serious indication of the applicant's well-founded fear of persecution or real risk of suffering serious harm, unless there are good reasons to consider that such persecution or serious harm will not be repeated.

5. Where Member States apply the principle according to which it is the duty of the applicant to substantiate the application for international protection and where aspects of the applicant's statements are not supported by documentary or other evidence, those aspects shall not need confirmation, when the following conditions are met:

(a) the applicant has made a genuine effort to substantiate his application;

(b) all relevant elements, at the applicant's disposal, have been submitted, and a satisfactory explanation regarding any lack of other relevant elements has been given;

(c) the applicant's statements are found to be coherent and plausible and do not run counter to available specific and general information relevant to the applicant's case;

(d) the applicant has applied for international protection at the earliest possible time, unless the applicant can demonstrate good reason for not having done so; and

(e) the general credibility of the applicant has been established.

Article 5
International protection needs arising *sur place*

A well-founded fear of being persecuted or a real risk of suffering serious harm may be based on events which have taken place since the applicant left the country of origin.

A well-founded fear of being persecuted or a real risk of suffering serious harm may be based on activities which have been engaged in by the applicant since he left the country of origin, in particular where it is established that the activities relied upon constitute the expression and continuation of convictions or orientations held in the country of origin.

Without prejudice to the Geneva Convention, Member States may determine that an applicant who files a subsequent application shall normally not be granted refugee status, if the risk of persecution is based on circumstances which the applicant has created by his own decision since leaving the country of origin.

Article 6
Actors of persecution or serious harm

Actors of persecution or serious harm include:
– the State;
– parties or organisations controlling the State or a substantial part of the territory of the State;
– non-State actors, if it can be demonstrated that the actors mentioned in (a) and (b), including international organisations, are unable or unwilling to provide protection against persecution or serious harm as defined in Article 7.

Article 7
Actors of protection

1. Protection can be provided by:
(a) the State; or
(b) parties or organisations, including international organisations, controlling the State or a substantial part of the territory of the State.

2. Protection is generally provided when the actors mentioned in paragraph 1 take reasonable steps to prevent the persecution or suffering of serious harm, *inter alia*, by operating an effective legal system for the detection, prosecution and punishment of acts constituting persecution or serious harm, and the applicant has access to such protection.

3. When assessing whether an international organisation controls a State or a substantial part of its territory and provides protection as described in paragraph 2, Member States shall take into account any guidance which may be provided in relevant Council acts.

Article 8
Internal protection

1. As part of the assessment of the application for international protection, Member States may determine that an applicant is not in need of international protection if in a part of the country of origin there is no well-founded fear of being persecuted or no real risk of suffering serious harm and the applicant can reasonably be expected to stay in that part of the country.

2. In examining whether a part of the country of origin is in accordance with paragraph 1, Member States shall at the time of taking the decision on the application have regard to the general circumstances prevailing in that part of the country and to the personal circumstances of the applicant.

3. Paragraph 1 may apply notwithstanding technical obstacles to return to the country of origin.

CHAPTER III
Qualification for Being a Refugee

Article 9
Acts of persecution

1. Acts of persecution within the meaning of Article 1(A) of the Geneva Convention must:
    (a) be sufficiently serious by their nature or repetition as to constitute a severe violation of basic human rights, in particular the rights from which derogation cannot be made under Article 15(2) of the European Convention for the Protection of Human Rights and Fundamental Freedoms; or
    (b) be an accumulation of various measures, including violations of human rights which is sufficiently severe as to affect an individual in a similar manner as mentioned in (a).

2. Acts of persecution as qualified in paragraph 1, can, *inter alia*, take the form of:
    (a) acts of physical or mental violence, including acts of sexual violence;
    (b) legal, administrative, police, and/or judicial measures which are in themselves discriminatory or which are implemented in a discriminatory manner;
    (c) prosecution or punishment, which is disproportionate or discriminatory;
    (d) denial of judicial redress resulting in a disproportionate or discriminatory punishment;
    (e) prosecution or punishment for refusal to perform military service in a conflict, where performing military service would include crimes or acts falling under the exclusion clauses as set out in Article 12(2);
    (f) acts of a gender-specific or child-specific nature.

3. In accordance with Article 2(c), there must be a connection between the reasons mentioned in Article 10 and the acts of persecution as qualified in paragraph 1.

Article 10
Reasons for persecution

1. Member States shall take the following elements into account when assessing the reasons for persecution:

(a) the concept of race shall in particular include considerations of colour, descent, or membership of a particular ethnic group;

(b) the concept of religion shall in particular include the holding of theistic, non-theistic and atheistic beliefs, the participation in, or abstention from, formal worship in private or in public, either alone or in community with others, other religious acts or expressions of view, or forms of personal or communal conduct based on or mandated by any religious belief;

(c) the concept of nationality shall not be confined to citizenship or lack thereof but shall in particular include membership of a group determined by its cultural, ethnic, or linguistic identity, common geographical or political origins or its relationship with the population of another State;

(d) a group shall be considered to form a particular social group where in particular:

– members of that group share an innate characteristic, or a common background that cannot be changed, or share a characteristic or belief that is so fundamental to identity or conscience that a person should not be forced to renounce it; and

– that group has a distinct identity in the relevant country, because it is perceived as being different by the surrounding society;

Depending on the circumstances in the country of origin, a particular social group might include a group based on a common characteristic of sexual orientation. Sexual orientation cannot be understood to include acts considered to be criminal in accordance with national law of the Member States: Gender related aspects might be considered, without by themselves alone creating a presumption for the applicability of this Article;

(e) the concept of political opinion shall in particular include the holding of an opinion, thought or belief on a matter related to the potential actors of persecution mentioned in Article 6 and to their policies or methods, whether or not that opinion, thought or belief has been acted upon by the applicant.

2. When assessing if an applicant has a well-founded fear of being persecuted it is immaterial whether the applicant actually possesses the racial, religious, national, social or political characteristic which attracts the persecution, provided that such a characteristic is attributed to the applicant by the actor of persecution.

Article 11
Cessation

1. A third country national or a stateless person shall cease to be a refugee, if he or she:

(a) has voluntarily re-availed himself or herself of the protection of the country of nationality; or

(b) having lost his or her nationality, has voluntarily re-acquired it; or

(c) has acquired a new nationality, and enjoys the protection of the country of his or her new nationality; or

(d) has voluntarily re-established himself or herself in the country which he or she left or outside which he or she remained owing to fear of persecution; or

(e) can no longer, because the circumstances in connection with which he or she has been recognised as a refugee have ceased to exist, continue to refuse to avail himself or herself of the protection of the country of nationality;

(f) being a stateless person with no nationality, he or she is able, because the circumstances in connection with which he or she has been recognised as a refugee have ceased to exist, to return to the country of former habitual residence.

2. In considering points (e) and (f) of paragraph 1, Member States shall have regard to whether the change of circumstances is of such a significant and non-temporary nature that the refugee's fear of persecution can no longer be regarded as well-founded.

Article 12
Exclusion

1. A third country national or a stateless person is excluded from being a refugee, if:

(a) he or she falls within the scope of Article 1(D) of the Geneva Convention, relating to protection or assistance from organs or agencies of the United Nations other than the United Nations High Commissioner for Refugees. When such protection or assistance has ceased for any reason, without the position of such persons being definitely settled in accordance with the relevant resolutions adopted by the General Assembly of the United Nations, these persons shall ipso facto be entitled to the benefits of this Directive;

(b) he or she is recognised by the competent authorities of the country in which he or she has taken residence as having the rights and obligations which are attached to the possession of the nationality of that country; or rights and obligations equivalent to those.

2. A third country national or a stateless person is excluded from being a refugee where there are serious reasons for considering that:

(a) he or she has committed a crime against peace, a war crime, or a crime against humanity, as defined in the international instruments drawn up to make provision in respect of such crimes;

(b) he or she has committed a serious non-political crime outside the country of refuge prior to his or her admission as a refugee; which means the time of issuing a residence permit based on the granting of refugee status; particularly cruel actions, even if committed with an allegedly political objective, may be classified as serious non-political crimes;

(c) he or she has been guilty of acts contrary to the purposes and principles of the United Nations as set out in the Preamble and Articles 1 and 2 of the Charter of the United Nations.

3. Paragraph 2 applies to persons who instigate or otherwise participate in the commission of the crimes or acts mentioned therein.

CHAPTER IV
Refugee Status

Article 13
Granting of refugee status

Member States shall grant refugee status to a third country national or a stateless person, who qualifies as a refugee in accordance with Chapters II and III.

Article 14
Revocation of, ending of or refusal to renew refugee status

1. Concerning applications for international protection filed after the entry into force of this Directive, Member States shall revoke, end or refuse to renew the refugee status of a third country national or a stateless person granted by a governmental, administrative, judicial or quasi-judicial body, if he or she has ceased to be a refugee in accordance with Article 11.

2. Without prejudice to the duty of the refugee in accordance with Article 4(1) to disclose all relevant facts and provide all relevant documentation at his/her disposal, the Member State, which has granted refugee status, shall on an individual basis demonstrate that the person concerned has ceased to be or has never been a refugee in accordance with paragraph 1 of this Article.

3. Member States shall revoke, end or refuse to renew the refugee status of a third country national or a stateless person, if, after he or she has been granted refugee status, it is established by the Member State concerned that:
   (a) he or she should have been or is excluded from being a refugee in accordance with Article 12;
   (b) his or her misrepresentation or omission of facts, including the use of false documents, were decisive for the granting of refugee status.

4. Member States may revoke, end or refuse to renew the status granted to a refugee by a governmental, administrative, judicial or quasi-judicial body, when:
   (a) there are reasonable grounds for regarding him or her as a danger to the security of the Member State in which he or she is present;
   (b) he or she, having been convicted by a final judgement of a particularly serious crime, constitutes a danger to the community of that Member State.

5. In situations described in paragraph 4, Member States may decide not to grant status to a refugee, where such a decision has not yet been taken.

6. Persons to whom paragraphs 4 or 5 apply are entitled to rights set out in or similar to those set out in Articles 3, 4, 16, 22, 31 and 32 and 33 of the Geneva Convention insofar as they are present in the Member State.

CHAPTER V
Qualification for Subsidiary Protection

Article 15
Serious harm

Serious harm consists of:
   (a) death penalty or execution; or
   (b) torture or inhuman or degrading treatment or punishment of an applicant in the country of origin, or
   (c) serious and individual threat to a civilian's life or person by reason of indiscriminate violence in situations of international or internal armed conflict.

Article 16
Cessation

1. A third country national or a stateless person shall cease to be eligible for subsidiary protection when the circumstances which led to the granting of subsidiary protection status have ceased to exist or have changed to such a degree that protection is no longer required.

2. In applying paragraph 1, Member States shall have regard to whether the change of circumstances is of such a significant and non-temporary nature that the person eligible for subsidiary protection no longer faces a real risk of serious harm.

Article 17
Exclusion

1. A third country national or a stateless person is excluded from being eligible for subsidiary protection where there are serious reasons for considering that:
   (a) he or she has committed a crime against peace, a war crime, or a crime against humanity, as defined in the international instruments drawn up to make provision in respect of such crimes;
   (b) he or she has committed a serious crime;
   (c) he or she has been guilty of acts contrary to the purposes and principles of the United Nations as set out in the Preamble and Articles 1 and 2 of the Charter of the United Nations;
   (d) he or she constitutes a danger to the community or to the security of the Member State in which he or she is present.

2. Paragraph 1 applies to persons who instigate or otherwise participate in the commission of the crimes or acts mentioned therein.

3. Member States may exclude a third country national or a stateless person from being eligible for subsidiary protection, if he or she prior to his or her admission to the Member State has committed one or more crimes, outside the scope of paragraph 1, which would be punishable by imprisonment, had they been committed in the Member State concerned, and if he or she left his or her country of origin solely in order to avoid sanctions resulting from these crimes.

CHAPTER VI
Subsidiary Protection Status

Article 18
Granting of subsidiary protection status

Member States shall grant subsidiary protection status to a third country national or a stateless person eligible for subsidiary protection in accordance with Chapters II and V.

Article 19
Revocation of, ending of or refusal to renew subsidiary protection status

1. Concerning applications for international protection filed after the entry into force of this Directive, Member States shall revoke, end or refuse to renew the subsidiary protection status of a third country national or a stateless person granted by a governmental, administrative, judicial or quasi-judicial body, if he or she has ceased to be eligible for subsidiary protection in accordance with Article 16.

2. Member States may revoke, end or refuse to renew the subsidiary protection status of a third country national or a stateless person granted by a governmental, administrative, judicial or quasi-judicial body, if after having been granted subsidiary protection status, he or she should have been excluded from being eligible for subsidiary protection in accordance with Article 17(3).

3. Member States shall revoke, end or refuse to renew the subsidiary protection status of a third country national or a stateless person, if:
    (a) he or she, after having been granted subsidiary protection status, should have been or is excluded from being eligible for subsidiary protection in accordance with Article 17(1) and (2);
    (b) his or her misrepresentation or omission of facts, including the use of false documents, were decisive for the granting of subsidiary protection status.

4. Without prejudice to the duty of the third country national or stateless person in accordance with Article 4(1) to disclose all relevant facts and provide all relevant documentation at his/her disposal, the Member State, which has granted the subsidiary protection status, shall on an individual basis demonstrate that the person concerned has ceased to be or is not eligible for subsidiary protection in accordance with paragraphs 1, 2 and 3 of this Article.

CHAPTER VII
Content of International Protection

Article 20
General rules

1. This Chapter shall be without prejudice to the rights laid down in the Geneva Convention.

2. This Chapter shall apply both to refugees and persons eligible for subsidiary protection unless otherwise indicated.

3. When implementing this Chapter, Member States shall take into account the specific situation of vulnerable persons such as minors, unaccompanied minors, disabled people, elderly people, pregnant women, single parents with minor children and persons who have been subjected to torture, rape or other serious forms of psychological, physical or sexual violence.

4. Paragraph 3 shall apply only to persons found to have special needs after an individual evaluation of their situation.

5. The best interest of the child shall be a primary consideration for Member States when implementing the provisions of this Chapter that involve minors.

6. Within the limits set out by the Geneva Convention, Member States may reduce the benefits of this Chapter, granted to a refugee whose refugee status has been obtained on the basis of activities engaged in for the sole or main purpose of creating the necessary conditions for being recognised as a refugee.

7. Within the limits set out by international obligations of Member States, Member States may reduce the benefits of this Chapter, granted to a person eligible for subsidiary protection, whose subsidiary protection status has been obtained on the basis of activities engaged in for the sole or main purpose of creating the necessary conditions for being recognised as a person eligible for subsidiary protection.

Article 21
Protection from refoulement

1. Member States shall respect the principle of non-refoulement in accordance with their international obligations.

2. Where not prohibited by the international obligations mentioned in paragraph 1, Member States may refoule a refugee, whether formally recognised or not, when:
(a) there are reasonable grounds for considering him or her as a danger to the security of the Member State in which he or she is present; or
(b) he or she, having been convicted by a final judgement of a particularly serious crime, constitutes a danger to the community of that Member State.

3. Member States may revoke, end or refuse to renew or to grant the residence permit of (or to) a refugee to whom paragraph 2 applies.

Article 22
Information

Member States shall provide persons recognised as being in need of international protection, as soon as possible after the respective protection status has been granted, with access to information, in a language likely to be understood by them, on the rights and obligations relating to that status.

Article 23
Maintaining family unity

1. Member States shall ensure that family unity can be maintained.

2. Member States shall ensure that family members of the beneficiary of refugee or subsidiary protection status, who do not individually qualify for such status, are entitled to claim the benefits referred to in Articles 24 to 34, in accordance with national procedures and as far as it is compatible with the personal legal status of the family member.

Insofar as the family members of beneficiaries of subsidiary protection status are concerned, Member States may define the conditions applicable to such benefits.

In these cases, Member States shall ensure that any benefits provided guarantee an adequate standard of living.

3. Paragraphs 1 and 2 are not applicable where the family member is or would be excluded from refugee or subsidiary protection status pursuant to Chapters III and V.

4. Notwithstanding paragraphs 1 and 2, Member States may refuse, reduce or withdraw the benefits referred therein for reasons of national security or public order.

5. Member States may decide that this Article also applies to other close relatives who lived together as part of the family at the time of leaving the country of origin, and who were wholly or mainly dependent on the beneficiary of refugee or subsidiary protection status at that time.

Article 24
Residence permits

1. As soon as possible after their status has been granted, Member States shall issue to beneficiaries of refugee status a residence permit which must be valid for at least three years and renewable unless compelling reasons of national security or public order otherwise require, and without prejudice to Article 21(3).

Without prejudice to Article 23(1), the residence permit to be issued to the family members of the beneficiaries of refugee status may be valid for less than three years and renewable.

2. As soon as possible after the status has been granted, Member States shall issue to beneficiaries of subsidiary protection status a residence permit which must be valid for at least one year and renewable, unless compelling reasons of national security or public order otherwise require.

Article 25
Travel document

1. Member States shall issue to beneficiaries of refugee status travel documents in the form set out in the Schedule to the Geneva Convention, for the purpose of travel outside their territory unless compelling reasons of national security or public order otherwise require.

2. Member States shall issue to beneficiaries of subsidiary protection status who are unable to obtain a national passport, documents which enable them to travel, at least when serious humanitarian reasons arise that require their presence in another State, unless compelling reasons of national security or public order otherwise require.

Article 26
Access to employment

1. Member States shall authorise beneficiaries of refugee status to engage in employed or self-employed activities subject to rules generally applicable to the profession and to the public service, immediately after the refugee status has been granted.

2. Member States shall ensure that activities such as employment-related education opportunities for adults, vocational training and practical workplace experience are offered to beneficiaries of refugee status, under equivalent conditions as nationals.

3. Member States shall authorise beneficiaries of subsidiary protection status to engage in employed or self-employed activities subject to rules generally applicable to the profession and to the public service immediately after the subsidiary protection status has been granted. The situation of the labour market in the Member States may be taken into account, including for possible prioritisation of access to employment for a limited period of time to be determined in accordance with national law. Member States shall ensure that the beneficiary of subsidiary protection status has access to a post for which the beneficiary has received an offer in accordance with national rules on prioritisation in the labour market.

4. Member States shall ensure that beneficiaries of subsidiary protection status have access to activities such as employment-related education opportunities for adults, vocational training and practical workplace experience, under conditions to be decided by the Member States.

5. The law in force in the Member States applicable to remuneration, access to social security systems relating to employed or self-employed activities and other conditions of employment shall apply.

Article 27
Access to education

1. Member States shall grant full access to the education system to all minors granted refugee or subsidiary protection status, under the same conditions as nationals.

2. Member States shall allow adults granted refugee or subsidiary protection status access to the general education system, further training or retraining, under the same conditions as third country nationals legally resident.

3. Member States shall ensure equal treatment between beneficiaries of refugee or subsidiary protection status and nationals in the context of the existing recognition procedures for foreign diplomas, certificates and other evidence of formal qualifications.

Article 28
Social welfare

1. Member States shall ensure that beneficiaries of refugee or subsidiary protection status receive, in the Member State that has granted such statuses, the necessary social assistance, as provided to nationals of that Member State.

2. By exception to the general rule laid down in paragraph 1, Member States may limit social assistance granted to beneficiaries of subsidiary protection status to core benefits which will then be provided at the same levels and under the same eligibility conditions as nationals.

Article 29
Health care

1. Member States shall ensure that beneficiaries of refugee or subsidiary protection status have access to health care under the same eligibility conditions as nationals of the Member State that has granted such statuses.

2. By exception to the general rule laid down in paragraph 1, Member States may limit health care granted to beneficiaries of subsidiary protection to core benefits which will then be provided at the same levels and under the same eligibility conditions as nationals.

3. Member States shall provide, under the same eligibility conditions as nationals of the Member State that has granted the status, adequate health care to beneficiaries of refugee or subsidiary protection status who have special needs, such as pregnant women, disabled people, persons who have undergone torture, rape or other serious forms of psychological, physical or sexual violence or minors who have been victims of any form of abuse, neglect, exploitation, torture, cruel, inhuman and degrading treatment or who have suffered from armed conflict.

Article 30
Unaccompanied minors

1. As soon as possible after the granting of refugee or subsidiary protection status Member States shall take the necessary measures, to ensure the representation of unaccompanied minors by legal guardianship or, where necessary, by an organisation responsible for the care and well-being of minors, or by any other appropriate representation including that based on legislation or Court order.

2. Member States shall ensure that the minor's needs are duly met in the implementation of this Directive by the appointed guardian or representative. The appropriate authorities shall make regular assessments.

3. Member States shall ensure that unaccompanied minors are placed either:
   (a) with adult relatives; or
   (b) with a foster family; or
   (c) in centres specialised in accommodation for minors; or
   (d) in other accommodation suitable for minors.

In this context, the views of the child shall be taken into account in accordance with his or her age and degree of maturity.

4. As far as possible, siblings shall be kept together, taking into account the best interests of the minor concerned and, in particular, his or her age and degree of maturity. Changes of residence of unaccompanied minors shall be limited to a minimum.

5. Member States, protecting the unaccompanied minor's best interests, shall endeavour to trace the members of the minor's family as soon as possible. In cases where there may be a threat to the life or integrity of the minor or his or her close relatives, particularly if they have remained in the country of origin, care must be taken to ensure that the collection, processing and circulation of information concerning those persons is undertaken on a confidential basis.

6. Those working with unaccompanied minors shall have had or receive appropriate training concerning their needs.

Article 31
Access to accommodation

The Member States shall ensure that beneficiaries of refugee or subsidiary protection status have access to accommodation under equivalent conditions as other third country nationals legally resident in their territories.

Article 32
Freedom of movement within the Member State

Member States shall allow freedom of movement within their territory to beneficiaries of refugee or subsidiary protection status, under the same conditions and restrictions as those provided for other third country nationals legally resident in their territories.

Article 33
Access to integration facilities

1. In order to facilitate the integration of refugees into society, Member States shall make provision for integration programmes which they consider to be appropriate or create pre-conditions which guarantee access to such programmes.

2. Where it is considered appropriate by Member States, beneficiaries of subsidiary protection status shall be granted access to integration programmes.

Article 34
Repatriation

Member States may provide assistance to beneficiaries of refugee or subsidiary protection status who wish to repatriate.

CHAPTER VIII
Administrative Cooperation

Article 35
Cooperation

Member States shall each appoint a national contact point, whose address they shall communicate to the Commission, which shall communicate it to the other Member States. Member States shall, in liaison with the Commission, take all appropriate measures to establish direct cooperation and an exchange of information between the competent authorities.

Article 36
Staff

Member States shall ensure that authorities and other organisations implementing this Directive have received the necessary training and shall be bound by the confidentiality principle, as defined in the national law, in relation to any information they obtain in the course of their work.

CHAPTER IX
Final Provisions

Article 37
Reports

By .... ,[5] the Commission shall report to the European Parliament and the Council on the application of this Directive and shall propose any amendments that are necessary. These proposals for amendments shall be made by way of priority in relation to Articles 15, 26 and 33. Member States shall send the Commission all the information that is appropriate for drawing up that report by ....[6]

After presenting the report, the Commission shall report to the European Parliament and the Council on the application of this Directive at least every five years.

Article 38
Transposition

1. The Member States shall bring into force the laws, regulations and administrative provisions necessary to comply with this Directive before ....[7] They shall forthwith inform the Commission thereof.

When the Member States adopt those measures, they shall contain a reference to this Directive or shall be accompanied by such a reference on the occasion of their official publication. The methods of making such reference shall be laid down by Member States.

---

[5] 18 months after the date provided for in Article 38(1).
[6] 12 months after the date provided for in Article 38(1).
[7] 24 months after the date of entry into force of this Directive.

2. Member States shall communicate to the Commission the text of the provisions of national law which they adopt in the field covered by this Directive.

Article 39
Entry into force

This Directive shall enter into force on the twentieth day following that of its publication in the Official Journal of the European Union.

Article 40
Addressees

This Directive is addressed to the Member States in accordance with the Treaty establishing the European Community.

EXPLANATORY MEMORANDUM

1. **Minimum standards for the qualification and status of third country nationals and stateless persons as refugees or as persons who otherwise need international protection**

50 years after the Geneva Convention: creating the heart of the Common European Asylum System

According to the Conclusions of the Presidency at the Tampere European Council in October 1999, a Common European Asylum System is to include, in the short term, a clear and workable determination of the State responsible for the examination of an asylum application, common standards for a fair and efficient asylum procedure, common minimum conditions of reception for asylum seekers and the approximation of rules on the recognition and content of refugee status. This is to be supplemented with measures on subsidiary forms of protection offering an appropriate status to any person in need of such protection. In addition, the Conclusions make clear that, in the longer term, Community rules should lead to a common asylum procedure and a uniform status for those who are granted asylum valid throughout the Union. Finally, the European Council, in Tampere, urged the Council to step up its efforts to reach agreement on the issue of temporary protection for displaced persons on the basis of solidarity between Member States.

- On 28 September 2000, the Council adopted a Decision (2000/596/EC) establishing a European Refugee Fund as a solidarity measure to promote a balance in the efforts made by Member States in receiving and bearing the consequences of receiving refugees and displaced persons.
- On 11 December 2000, the Council adopted a Regulation (2725/2000/EC) concerning the establishment of 'Eurodac' for the comparison of fingerprints for the effective application of the Dublin Convention on the State responsible for examining applications for asylum lodged in one of the European Union Member States.
- On 20 July 2001, the Council adopted a Directive (2001/55/EC) on minimum standards for giving temporary protection in the event of a mass influx of displaced persons and on measures promoting a balance of efforts between Member States in receiving such persons and bearing the consequences thereof;

In addition to the Proposals for the above mentioned acts approved by the Council, the Commission has adopted:
- On 20 September 2000, a Proposal for a Council Directive on minimum standards on procedures in Member States for granting and withdrawing refugee status;
- On 22 November 2000, a Communication on a common asylum procedure and a uniform status for those who are granted asylum valid throughout the Union.
- On 3 April 2001, a Proposal for a Council Directive on minimum standards on the reception of applicants for asylum in Member States.
- On 26 July 2001 a Proposal for a Council Regulation establishing the criteria and mechanisms for determining the Member State responsible for examining an asylum application lodged in one of the Member States by a third country national

As indicated in the scoreboard to review progress on the creation of an area for freedom, security and justice in the European Union, approved by the Council on 27 March 2000, the Commission is now, in the second half of 2001, proposing a Council Directive on minimum standards on the qualification and status of third country nationals and stateless persons as refugees and as persons otherwise in need of international protection. This will complete the Commission's work on a proposed set of 'building blocks', which jointly constitute the first step of the 'Common European Asylum System' called for by the Tampere European Council.

This Proposal has been drafted on the basis of a number of preparatory activities and background materials.

In the preparatory phases of the legislative process leading to the current Proposal, the Commission organised a series of bilateral consultations with Member States. These consultations were held on the basis of a discussion paper, drafted with a view to facilitating discussions with Member States on how best to legislate in EC legal instruments, rules on the recognition and content of refugee and subsidiary protection status.

In its November 2000 Communication, entitled 'Towards a common asylum procedure and a uniform status, valid throughout the Union for persons granted asylum' (the Asylum Communication), the Commission wrote that *representatives of civil society, associations, non-governmental organisations and local authorities and communities must also be partners in the new system as actors and vectors of asylum values in Europe'*. Within this context the Commission consulted in addition to Member States, UNHCR, expert non-governmental organisations in the field such as the European Council on Refugees and Exiles (ECRE) and Amnesty International, specialised non-governmental organisations such as the European Women's Lobby and Save the Children, academic experts such as the ODYSSEUS academic network for legal studies on immigration and asylum in Europe, and representatives of the judiciary such as the International Association of Refugee Law Judges, on the basis of the aforementioned discussion paper.

On 23 and 24 April 2001 a Seminar, held in Norrköping, and entitled 'International protection within one single asylum procedure' was organised by the Swedish Presidency of the European Union. This seminar dealt with the following three issues: the interpretation of the refugee definition, subsidiary forms of protection and a single asylum procedure. The discussion held there and the main findings of the seminar, as well as the different background papers prepared for this Seminar were important sources of inspiration in drafting the current Proposal.

Where it relates to the issue of the refugee definition, the present Proposal also draws on a recent academic study undertaken by the Refugee Studies Centre, University of Oxford for the European Commission. This Proposal incorporates the findings of an expert meeting that was organised to discuss this study as well as various relevant national, European and international texts and jurisprudence. It also reflects various recent comparative Council and CIREA overviews of Member States practices regarding the issue of subsidiary protection.

2. **Scope of the proposal**

With regard to the Common European Asylum System, it was agreed at the Tampere European Council that it 'should include *the approximation of rules on the recognition and content of the refugee status* and should be complemented by *measures on subsidiary forms of protection offering an appropriate status to any person in need of such protection*'. The main aim being to ensure that a minimum level of protection is available in all Member States for those genuinely in need and to reduce disparities between Member States' legislation and practice in these areas. Any differences not solely connected with family, cultural or historical factors, likely to influence in one way or another the flows of asylum applicants, should as far as possible disappear between the Member States, where such movement is purely caused by differences in legal frameworks.

This Proposal relates to an instrument for part of the 'first-step' of a Common European Asylum System, which is to be 'based on the full and inclusive application of the Geneva Convention, thus ensuring that nobody is sent back to persecution, i.e. maintaining the principle of non-refoulement'. The Proposal therefore lays down rules for determining which applicants for international protection qualify for refugee status and which qualify for subsidiary protection status. It does not extend to cover those third country national or stateless persons present in the territory of Member States who Member States currently allow to remain in their territory for reasons not related to a need for international protection, such as compassionate or humanitarian ones.

In the interests of greater harmonisation and limiting unwarranted secondary movement of asylum seekers, this Directive includes provisions on the minimum rights and benefits to be enjoyed by the beneficiaries of refugee and subsidiary protection status. In the main, the rights and benefits attached to both international protection statuses are the same, to reflect the fact that the needs of all persons in need of international protection are broadly similar. However, some differentiation has been made, in recognition of the primacy of the Geneva Convention and the fact that the regime of subsidiary protection starts from the premise that the need for such protection is temporary in nature, notwithstanding the fact that in reality the need for subsidiary protection often turns out to be more lasting. In order to reflect this underlying premise and reality entitlement to some important rights and benefits has been made incremental, requiring that a brief qualification period be served before a beneficiary of subsidiary protection status becomes eligible to claim them.

This Proposal does not address the procedural aspects of granting and withdrawing refugee status or subsidiary protection status. The procedures for asylum applicants are laid out in the Proposal for a Council Directive on minimum standards on procedures in Member States for granting and withdrawing refugee status. Article 3 of that Directive makes the applicability of the Directive to applications for international protection, not made specifically in relation to the Geneva Convention, optional. This leaves a potential gap in the European protection regime and allows for differences in Member State practice in this area to continue with a possible negative affect on the goal of limiting unwarranted secondary movement of asylum seekers within the European Union. Member States are therefore encouraged to apply the optional Article 3 of the Proposal for a Council Directive on minimum standards on procedures in Member States for granting and withdrawing refugee status to all applications for international protection in a similar manner in the interests of harmonisation. In the Asylum Communication the Commission states that at the end of this first step of the harmonisation process of EU asylum policy, and whatever the result, it will be necessary to consider whether mechanisms can be developed to correct certain differences that might remain or to prevent the phenomenon of divergent interpretation of Community rules. Specific questions related to the issues covered in this Proposal were also already identified in the Communication as being in need of further clarification, such as: should the EU aim for transposing the Geneva Convention status into Community law, should the EU envisage one or more uniform personal statuses and what kind of documents, rights, freedom of movement and right of residence in another Member State should refugees and others in need of international protection have. These questions are not covered by this Proposal because it is envisaged that they will be tackled in the second step of the harmonisation process.

3. Guiding principles

The Charter of fundamental rights of the European Union reiterated the right to asylum in its Article 18. Flowing from this the Proposal reflects that the cornerstone of the system should be the full and inclusive application of the Geneva Convention, complemented by measures offering subsidiary protection to those persons not covered by the Convention but who are nonetheless in need of international protection. It is argued that the wording of the definition of who is a refugee, as contained in Article 1(A)(2) of the 1951 Geneva Convention, as well as the Convention itself, remains relevant today and is sufficiently flexible, full and inclusive to offer a guarantee of international protection to a significant proportion of those persons in need of it. This approach is in accordance with the principles of interpretation as codified in Article 31(1) of the 1969 Vienna Convention on the Law of Treaties, requiring that a 'treaty shall be interpreted in good faith in accordance with the ordinary meaning to be given to the terms of the treaty in their context and in the light of its object and purpose'. The Directive takes as a starting point the '*Joint Position of 4 March 1996 defined by the Council on the basis of Article K.3 of the Treaty on European Union on the harmonised application of the definition of the term "refugee" in Article 1 of the Geneva Convention of 28 July 1951 relating to the status of refugee*'. (hereinafter the Joint Position). Other sources of reference were the '*Handbook on procedures and criteria for determining refugee status*' of the office of the United Nations High Commissioner for Refugees (hereinafter the Handbook), drafted with a view to assisting States party to the Convention in interpreting the Convention's refugee definition, and the EXCOM Conclusions. However, the primary point of reference is the Geneva Convention itself.

The subsidiary protection measures proposed are considered complementary to the protection regime enshrined in the Geneva Convention and its 1967 Protocol and are to be implemented in such a manner that they do not undermine but instead complement the existing refugee protection regime. The definition of subsidiary protection employed in this Proposal is based largely on international human rights instruments relevant to subsidiary protection. The most pertinent of them being (Article 3 of) the European Convention on Human Rights and Fundamental Freedoms (hereinafter the ECHR), (Article 3 of) the UN Convention against Torture and other Cruel, Inhuman or Degrading Treatment, and (Article 7 of) the International Covenant on Civil and Political Rights.

Though no specific EU acquis on the issue of subsidiary protection exists, the ECHR and the case law of the European Court on Human Rights provide for a legally binding framework, informing the Commission's legislative work on this issue. Partly in response to the case law of the European Court of Human Rights and general principles of international humanitarian law, Member States have developed schemes of 'subsidiary' or 'complementary' protection.

This Proposal has drawn from the disparate Member State systems and has attempted to adopt and adapt the best ones. Rather then creating new ratione personae protection obligations incumbent on Member States, the Proposal is clarifying and codifying existing international and Community obligations and practice.

4.   **The objectives of the proposal**

With this Proposal for a Directive, the Commission is pursuing the following aims:
  1. Implementing point (1)(c), 2(a), and 3(a) of the first paragraph of Article 63 of the Treaty, paragraph 38(b)(i and ii) of the Vienna Action Plan, Conclusion 14 of the Tampere European Council and relevant references in the Scoreboard presented to the Council and the Parliament in March 2000;
  2. Setting out minimum standards on the qualification and status of applicants for international protection as refugees or beneficiaries of subsidiary protection status;
  3. Ensuring that a minimum level of protection is available in all Member States for those genuinely in need of international protection and to reduce disparities between Member States' legislation and practice in these areas as the first step towards full harmonisation.
  4. Limiting secondary movements of applicants for international protection influenced solely by the diversity of the applicable rules on recognising refugee status and granting subsidiary protection status;
  5. To guarantee a high level of protection for those who genuinely need it, whilst at the same time preventing abuses of asylum applications which undermine the credibility of the system, often to the detriment of applicants in genuine need of protection.

5.   **An overview of the standards in the proposal**

This Proposal is composed of seven Chapters:
  (a) The first group of provisions concerns the most general aspects of the Proposal, including its objective and scope as well as the definitions of the concepts that are relevant for a clear understanding of the Proposal.
  (b) The second set of rules focuses on the general nature of international protection, identifying the many common characteristics of its two constitutive elements, refugee status and subsidiary protection status. It outlines general rules on establishing how to determine

whether a claim for international protection is well founded or not. Its guiding principle is that international protection of any sort is a type of surrogate protection to be provided in lieu of national protection only when the realistic possibility of obtaining protection from an applicant's country of origin is absent.

(c) A third group of rules is specific to the qualification as a refugee. It focuses in particular on the definition of 'persecution' and offers an interpretation of this central notion, including the five grounds on which it can be predicated, based on Article 1(A) of the Geneva Convention. It also contains rules laying down the circumstances in which Member States may withdraw refugee status when such status is found no longer to be required as well as rules for excluding applicants from such status.

(d) The fourth group of rules provides a framework for identifying three categories of applicants for international protection who do not qualify as refugees but are eligible for the supplementary status of subsidiary protection. The three categories are based on Member States existing obligations under human rights instruments, as well as existing Member State practice in this area, and are designed to complement the refugee protection regime. It also contains rules laying down the circumstances in which Member States may withdraw subsidiary protection status when such status is found no longer to be required as well as rules for excluding applicants from such status.

(e) A fifth set of rules lays down the minimum obligations that Member States shall have towards those to whom they grant international protection. These obligations include the duration and content of the status flowing from recognition as a refugee or as a beneficiary of subsidiary protection status. The benefits accruing to both categories of international protection status shall be very similar with a few important exceptions with regard to the duration of the status, and certain rights which depend on a qualification period in the case of beneficiaries of subsidiary protection to reflect the potentially more temporary nature of this category.

(f) Finally, the Proposal outlines in its two final Chapters several rules to ensure the Directive's complete implementation. If the final aims of the future directive are to be met, the instruments that are put in place to reach these aims have to be checked, revised and adjusted to be sure they are going to produce the expected results. It is important that a national contact point is designated and that appropriate measures are enacted to establish direct cooperation and an exchange of information between the competent authorities. At Community level, it is important to assess whether the purposes of this Directive are met or if there is room for improvement.

The Commission, for its part, envisages the introduction of one Contact Committee. This Contact Committee will facilitate the transposition and the subsequent implementation of this and other Directives in the field of asylum through regular consultations on all practical problems arising from its application. It will help avoid duplication of work where common standards are set and to adopt complementary strategies in combating abuse of the protection regime. In addition, the Committee will facilitate consultation between the Member States on reaching similar interpretations of the rules laid down on international protection that they may lay down at national level. This would greatly help the construction of a Common European Asylum System as envisaged by the Conclusions of the Presidency at the Tampere European Council in October 1999. Lastly, the Committee will advise the Commission, if necessary, on any supplements or amendments to be made to this Directive or on any adjustments deemed necessary.

6.   **The choice of legal basis**

The choice of legal basis is consistent with the amendments made to the Treaty establishing the European Community by the Amsterdam Treaty, which entered into force on 1 May 1999.

Points (1)(c) and 2(a) of the first paragraph of Article 63 of the EC Treaty provides that the Council shall adopt measures on asylum in accordance with the Geneva Convention of 28 July 1951, the Protocol of 31 January 1967 and other relevant human rights instruments, relating to minimum standards on the qualification and status of refugees and persons who otherwise need international protection. Point (3)(a) of the first paragraph of Article 63 of the EC Treaty provides that the Council is to adopt measures relating to 'conditions of entry and residence, and standards on procedures for the issue by Member States of long-term visas and residence permits, including those for the purpose of family reunion'. As this Article applies equally to refugees as to other categories of third country nationals, it constitutes the legal basis for the inclusion in this Proposal of the conditions of residence of refugees, including their rights such as employment and education. Article 63 is accordingly the proper legal basis for a Proposal to establish minimum standards for the qualification and status of refugees and persons who otherwise need international protection in Member States.

Title IV of the EC Treaty is not applicable to the United Kingdom and to Ireland, unless those Member States decide otherwise in accordance with the procedure laid down in the Protocol on the position of the United Kingdom and Ireland annexed to the Treaties. Title IV is likewise not applicable to Denmark, by virtue of the Protocol on the position of Denmark annexed to the Treaties.

7.   **Subsidiarity and proportionality: justification and value added**

Subsidiarity
The insertion of the new Title IV (Visas, asylum, immigration and other policies related to free movement of persons) in the Treaty establishing the European Community demonstrates the will of the High Contracting Parties to confer powers in these matters on the European Community. But the European Community does not have exclusive powers here. Consequently, even with the political will to implement a common policy on asylum and immigration, it must act in accordance with Article 5 of the EC Treaty, i.e. the Community may take action only if and insofar as the objectives of the proposed action cannot be sufficiently achieved by the Member States and can therefore, by reason of the scale or effects of the proposed action, be better achieved by the Community. The proposed Directive satisfies these criteria.

The establishment of an area of freedom, security and justice entails the adoption of measures relating to asylum. The specific objective of this initiative is to lay down minimum standards on the qualification and status of refugees and persons who otherwise need international protection in Member States. The standards laid down in this Proposal must be capable of being applied through minimum conditions in all the Member States. Minimum Community standards have to be laid down by the kind of action proposed here. They will help to limit secondary movements of asylum applicants that result from disparities in Member States practices and legislation. Henceforth, applicants for asylum will be less inclined than before to decide on their country of destination on the basis of different protection regimes. They will also be less inclined than before to choose their country of destination on the different level of rights and benefits that Member States attach to recognition of a form of international protection. The continued absence of approximated rules on the qualification and status of refugees and persons who otherwise need international protection would have a negative effect on the effectiveness of other instruments relating to asylum. Conversely, once minimum standards on the qualification and status of refugees and persons who otherwise need international protection are in place, the operation of, *inter alia*, an effective system for determining which Member State is responsible for considering an asylum application is fully justified. Applicants for international protection who cannot choose in complete freedom where to lodge their application should expect their claims for international protection to be assessed in a similar way in any Member State of the European Union and for successful recognition of such a claim to result in a comparable set of rights and benefits. The idea of a single Member State responsible for examining an application for international protection becomes fairer to applicants if the same minimum standards exist across all Member States. At the same time, minimum standards on the qualification and content of the two protection regimes should limit the importance of factors that determine secondary movements within the Union and, in this way, would help to establish the effectiveness of the mechanisms according to which the responsible Member State is chosen. Establishing common minimum standards on the qualification and status of refugees and persons who otherwise need international protection is a fundamental tool in making national asylum systems more effective and a Common European Asylum System more credible.

Proportionality
The form taken by Community action must be the simplest form allowing the Proposal to attain its objectives and to be implemented as efficiently as possible. In this spirit, the legal instrument chosen is a Directive, which allows minimum standards to be laid down, while leaving national authorities the choice of the most appropriate form and methods for implementing it in their national system. The Proposal concentrates on a set of minimum standards that are strictly necessary for the coherence of the planned action without laying down standards relating to other aspects of asylum. The Proposal refers to the Proposal for a directive on minimum standards on common asylum procedures (COM(2000)578), to the Proposal for a Directive laying down minimum standards on the reception of applicants for asylum in Member States (COM(2001)181), the Proposal for a Council Regulation establishing the criteria and mechanisms for determining the Member State responsible for examining an asylum application lodged in one of the Member States by a third country national (COM(2001)447), the Council Directive (2001/55/EC) on minimum standards for giving temporary protection in the event of a mass influx of displaced persons and on measures promoting a balance of efforts between Member States in receiving such persons and bearing the consequences thereof , the amended Proposal for a Council Directive on the right to family reunification (COM(2000)624) and to the Proposal for a Council Directive concerning the status of third country nationals who are long term residents(COM(2001) 127) to ensure consistency within the Common European Asylum System and with other Proposals for Community instruments in the field of immigration. Finally, several rules require Member States only to comply with certain aims (e.g. they are asked to integrate considerations specific to the applications for international protection from persons having special needs) but leave Member States completely free to choose the means used to achieve this aim. The Proposal, therefore, does not go beyond what is necessary to achieve the objective of the Directive.

Chapter 1.6
TEMPORARY PROTECTION

COUNCIL DIRECTIVE 2001/55/EC

of 20 July 2001

on minimum standards for giving temporary protection in the event of a mass influx of displaced persons and on measures promoting a balance of efforts between Member States in receiving such persons and bearing the consequences thereof[1]

THE COUNCIL OF THE EUROPEAN UNION,

Having regard to the Treaty establishing the European Community, and in particular point 2(a) and (b) of Article 63 thereof,

Having regard to the proposal from the Commission,[2]

Having regard to the opinion of the European Parliament,[3]

Having regard to the opinion of the Economic and Social Committee,[4]

Having regard to the opinion of the Committee of the Regions,[5]

Whereas:

(1) The preparation of a common policy on asylum, including common European arrangements for asylum, is a constituent part of the European Union's objective of establishing progressively an area of freedom, security and justice open to those who, forced by circumstances, legitimately seek protection in the European Union.

(2) Cases of mass influx of displaced persons who cannot return to their country of origin have become more substantial in Europe in recent years. In these cases it may be necessary to set up exceptional schemes to offer them immediate temporary protection.

(3) In the conclusions relating to persons displaced by the conflict in the former Yugoslavia adopted by the Ministers responsible for immigration at their meetings in London on 30 November and 1 December 1992 and Copenhagen on 1 and 2 June 1993, the Member States and the Community institutions expressed their concern at the situation of displaced persons.

(4) On 25 September 1995 the Council adopted a Resolution on burden-sharing with regard to the admission and residence of displaced persons on a temporary basis,[6] and, on 4 March

---

[1] OJ L 212, 7.8.2001, p.12.

[2] OJ C 311 E, 31.10.2000, p. 251.

[3] Opinion delivered on 13 March 2001 (not yet published in the Official Journal).

[4] OJ C 155, 29.5.2001, p. 21.

[5] Opinion delivered on 13 June 2001 (not yet published in the Official Journal).

[6] OJ C 262, 7.10.1995, p. 1.

1996, adopted Decision 96/198/JHA on an alert and emergency procedure for burden-sharing with regard to the admission and residence of displaced persons on a temporary basis.[7]

(5) The Action Plan of the Council and the Commission of 3 December 1998[8] provides for the rapid adoption, in accordance with the Treaty of Amsterdam, of minimum standards for giving temporary protection to displaced persons from third countries who cannot return to their country of origin and of measures promoting a balance of effort between Member States in receiving and bearing the consequences of receiving displaced persons.

(6) On 27 May 1999 the Council adopted conclusions on displaced persons from Kosovo. These conclusions call on the Commission and the Member States to learn the lessons of their response to the Kosovo crisis in order to establish the measures in accordance with the Treaty.

(7) The European Council, at its special meeting in Tampere on 15 and 16 October 1999, acknowledged the need to reach agreement on the issue of temporary protection for displaced persons on the basis of solidarity between Member States.

(8) It is therefore necessary to establish minimum standards for giving temporary protection in the event of a mass influx of displaced persons and to take measures to promote a balance of efforts between the Member States in receiving and bearing the consequences of receiving such persons.

(9) Those standards and measures are linked and interdependent for reasons of effectiveness, coherence and solidarity and in order, in particular, to avert the risk of secondary movements. They should therefore be enacted in a single legal instrument.

(10) This temporary protection should be compatible with the Member States' international obligations as regards refugees. In particular, it must not prejudice the recognition of refugee status pursuant to the Geneva Convention of 28 July 1951 on the status of refugees, as amended by the New York Protocol of 31 January 1967, ratified by all the Member States.

(11) The mandate of the United Nations High Commissioner for Refugees regarding refugees and other persons in need of international protection should be respected, and effect should be given to Declaration No. 17, annexed to the Final Act to the Treaty of Amsterdam, on Article 63 of the Treaty establishing the European Community which provides that consultations are to be established with the United Nations High Commissioner for Refugees and other relevant international organisations on matters relating to asylum policy.

(12) It is in the very nature of minimum standards that Member States have the power to introduce or maintain more favourable provisions for persons enjoying temporary protection in the event of a mass influx of displaced persons.

---

[7] OJ L 63, 13.3.1996, p. 10.
[8] OJ C 19, 20.1.1999, p. 1.

(13) Given the exceptional character of the provisions established by this Directive in order to deal with a mass influx or imminent mass influx of displaced persons from third countries who are unable to return to their country of origin, the protection offered should be of limited duration.

(14) The existence of a mass influx of displaced persons should be established by a Council Decision, which should be binding in all Member States in relation to the displaced persons to whom the Decision applies. The conditions for the expiry of the Decision should also be established.

(15) The Member States' obligations as to the conditions of reception and residence of persons enjoying temporary protection in the event of a mass influx of displaced persons should be determined. These obligations should be fair and offer an adequate level of protection to those concerned.

(16) With respect to the treatment of persons enjoying temporary protection under this Directive, the Member States are bound by obligations under instruments of international law to which they are party and which prohibit discrimination.

(17) Member States should, in concert with the Commission, enforce adequate measures so that the processing of personal data respects the standard of protection of Directive 95/46/EC of the European Parliament and the Council of 24 October 1995 on the protection of individuals with regard to the processing of personal data and on the free movement of such data.[9]

(18) Rules should be laid down to govern access to the asylum procedure in the context of temporary protection in the event of a mass influx of displaced persons, in conformity with the Member States' international obligations and with the Treaty.

(19) Provision should be made for principles and measures governing the return to the country of origin and the measures to be taken by Member States in respect of persons whose temporary protection has ended.

(20) Provision should be made for a solidarity mechanism intended to contribute to the attainment of a balance of effort between Member States in receiving and bearing the consequences of receiving displaced persons in the event of a mass influx. The mechanism should consist of two components. The first is financial and the second concerns the actual reception of persons in the Member States.

(21) The implementation of temporary protection should be accompanied by administrative cooperation between the Member States in liaison with the Commission.

(22) It is necessary to determine criteria for the exclusion of certain persons from temporary protection in the event of a mass influx of displaced persons.

---

[9] OJ L 281, 23.11.1995, p. 31.

(23) Since the objectives of the proposed action, namely to establish minimum standards for giving temporary protection in the event of a mass influx of displaced persons and measures promoting a balance of efforts between the Member States in receiving and bearing the consequences of receiving such persons, cannot be sufficiently attained by the Member States and can therefore, by reason of the scale or effects of the proposed action, be better achieved at Community level, the Community may adopt measures in accordance with the principle of subsidiarity as set out in Article 5 of the Treaty. In accordance with the principle of proportionality as set out in that Article, this Directive does not go beyond what is necessary in order to achieve those objectives.

(24) In accordance with Article 3 of the Protocol on the position of the United Kingdom and Ireland, annexed to the Treaty on European Union and to the Treaty establishing the European Community, the United Kingdom gave notice, by letter of 27 September 2000, of its wish to take part in the adoption and application of this Directive.

(25) Pursuant to Article 1 of the said Protocol, Ireland is not participating in the adoption of this Directive. Consequently and without prejudice to Article 4 of the aforementioned Protocol, the provisions of this Directive do not apply to Ireland.

(26) In accordance with Articles 1 and 2 of the Protocol on the position of Denmark, annexed to the Treaty on European Union and to the Treaty establishing the European Community, Denmark is not participating in the adoption of this Directive, and is therefore not bound by it nor subject to its application,

HAS ADOPTED THIS DIRECTIVE:

CHAPTER I
General Provisions

Article 1

The purpose of this Directive is to establish minimum standards for giving temporary protection in the event of a mass influx of displaced persons from third countries who are unable to return to their country of origin and to promote a balance of effort between Member States in receiving and bearing the consequences of receiving such persons.

Article 2

For the purposes of this Directive:

(a) 'temporary protection' means a procedure of exceptional character to provide, in the event of a mass influx or imminent mass influx of displaced persons from third countries who are unable to return to their country of origin, immediate and temporary protection to such persons, in particular if there is also a risk that the asylum system will be unable to process this influx without adverse effects for its efficient operation, in the interests of the persons concerned and other persons requesting protection;

(b) 'Geneva Convention' means the Convention of 28 July 1951 relating to the status of refugees, as amended by the New York Protocol of 31 January 1967;

(c) 'displaced persons' means third-country nationals or stateless persons who have had to leave their country or region of origin, or have been evacuated, in particular in response to an appeal by international organisations, and are unable to return in safe and durable conditions because of the situation prevailing in that country, who may fall within the scope of Article 1(A) of the Geneva Convention or other international or national instruments giving international protection, in particular:

(i) persons who have fled areas of armed conflict or endemic violence;

(ii) persons at serious risk of, or who have been the victims of, systematic or generalised violations of their human rights;

(d) 'mass influx' means arrival in the Community of a large number of displaced persons, who come from a specific country or geographical area, whether their arrival in the Community was spontaneous or aided, for example through an evacuation programme;

(e) 'refugees' means third-country nationals or stateless persons within the meaning of Article 1(A) of the Geneva Convention;

(f) 'unaccompanied minors' means third-country nationals or stateless persons below the age of eighteen, who arrive on the territory of the Member States unaccompanied by an adult responsible for them whether by law or custom, and for as long as they are not effectively taken into the care of such a person, or minors who are left unaccompanied after they have entered the territory of the Member States;

(g) 'residence permit' means any permit or authorisation issued by the authorities of a Member State and taking the form provided for in that State's legislation, allowing a third country national or a stateless person to reside on its territory;

(h) 'sponsor' means a third-country national enjoying temporary protection in a Member State in accordance with a decision taken under Article 5 and who wants to be joined by members of his or her family.

Article 3

1. Temporary protection shall not prejudge recognition of refugee status under the Geneva Convention.

2. Member States shall apply temporary protection with due respect for human rights and fundamental freedoms and their obligations regarding non-refoulement.

3. The establishment, implementation and termination of temporary protection shall be the subject of regular consultations with the Office of the United Nations High Commissioner for Refugees (UNHCR) and other relevant international organisations.

4. This Directive shall not apply to persons who have been accepted under temporary protection schemes prior to its entry into force.

5. This Directive shall not affect the prerogative of the Member States to adopt or retain more favourable conditions for persons covered by temporary protection.

CHAPTER II
Duration and Implementation of Temporary Protection

Article 4

1. Without prejudice to Article 6, the duration of temporary protection shall be one year. Unless terminated under the terms of Article 6(1)(b), it may be extended automatically by six monthly periods for a maximum of one year.

2. Where reasons for temporary protection persist, the Council may decide by qualified majority, on a proposal from the Commission, which shall also examine any request by a Member State that it submit a proposal to the Council, to extend that temporary protection by up to one year.

Article 5

1. The existence of a mass influx of displaced persons shall be established by a Council Decision adopted by a qualified majority on a proposal from the Commission, which shall also examine any request by a Member State that it submit a proposal to the Council.

2. The Commission proposal shall include at least:
    (a) a description of the specific groups of persons to whom the temporary protection will apply;
    (b) the date on which the temporary protection will take effect;
    (c) an estimation of the scale of the movements of displaced persons.

3. The Council Decision shall have the effect of introducing temporary protection for the displaced persons to which it refers, in all the Member States, in accordance with the provisions of this Directive. The Decision shall include at least:
    (a) a description of the specific groups of persons to whom the temporary protection applies;
    (b) the date on which the temporary protection will take effect;
    (c) information received from Member States on their reception capacity;
    (d) information from the Commission, UNHCR and other relevant international organisations.

4. The Council Decision shall be based on:
    (a) an examination of the situation and the scale of the movements of displaced persons;
    (b) an assessment of the advisability of establishing temporary protection, taking into account the potential for emergency aid and action on the ground or the inadequacy of such measures;
    (c) information received from the Member States, the Commission, UNHCR and other relevant international organisations.

5. The European Parliament shall be informed of the Council Decision.

Article 6

1. Temporary protection shall come to an end:

(a) when the maximum duration has been reached; or

(b) at any time, by Council Decision adopted by a qualified majority on a proposal from the Commission, which shall also examine any request by a Member State that it submit a proposal to the Council.

2. The Council Decision shall be based on the establishment of the fact that the situation in the country of origin is such as to permit the safe and durable return of those granted temporary protection with due respect for human rights and fundamental freedoms and Member States' obligations regarding non-refoulement. The European Parliament shall be informed of the Council Decision.

Article 7

1. Member States may extend temporary protection as provided for in this Directive to additional categories of displaced persons over and above those to whom the Council Decision provided for in Article 5 applies, where they are displaced for the same reasons and from the same country or region of origin. They shall notify the Council and the Commission immediately.

2. The provisions of Articles 24, 25 and 26 shall not apply to the use of the possibility referred to in paragraph 1, with the exception of the structural support included in the European Refugee Fund set up by Decision 2000/596/EC,[10] under the conditions laid down in that Decision.

CHAPTER III
Obligations of the Member States Towards Persons Enjoying Temporary Protection

Article 8

1. The Member States shall adopt the necessary measures to provide persons enjoying temporary protection with residence permits for the entire duration of the protection. Documents or other equivalent evidence shall be issued for that purpose.

2. Whatever the period of validity of the residence permits referred to in paragraph 1, the treatment granted by the Member States to persons enjoying temporary protection may not be less favourable than that set out in Articles 9 to 16.

3. The Member States shall, if necessary, provide persons to be admitted to their territory for the purposes of temporary protection with every facility for obtaining the necessary visas, including transit visas. Formalities must be reduced to a minimum because of the urgency of the situation. Visas should be free of charge or their cost reduced to a minimum.

---

[10] OJ L 252, 6.10.2000, p. 12.

Article 9

The Member States shall provide persons enjoying temporary protection with a document, in a language likely to be understood by them, in which the provisions relating to temporary protection and which are relevant to them are clearly set out.

Article 10

To enable the effective application of the Council Decision referred to in Article 5, Member States shall register the personal data referred to in Annex II, point (a), with respect to the persons enjoying temporary protection on their territory.

Article 11

A Member State shall take back a person enjoying temporary protection on its territory, if the said person remains on, or, seeks to enter without authorisation onto, the territory of another Member State during the period covered by the Council Decision referred to in Article 5. Member States may, on the basis of a bilateral agreement, decide that this Article should not apply.

Article 12

The Member States shall authorise, for a period not exceeding that of temporary protection, persons enjoying temporary protection to engage in employed or self-employed activities, subject to rules applicable to the profession, as well as in activities such as educational opportunities for adults, vocational training and practical workplace experience. For reasons of labour market policies, Member States may give priority to EU citizens and citizens of States bound by the Agreement on the European Economic Area and also to legally resident third country nationals who receive unemployment benefit. The general law in force in the Member States applicable to remuneration, access to social security systems relating to employed or self-employed activities and other conditions of employment shall apply.

Article 13

1. The Member States shall ensure that persons enjoying temporary protection have access to suitable accommodation or, if necessary, receive the means to obtain housing.

2. The Member States shall make provision for persons enjoying temporary protection to receive necessary assistance in terms of social welfare and means of subsistence, if they do not have sufficient resources, as well as for medical care. Without prejudice to paragraph 4, the assistance necessary for medical care shall include at least emergency care and essential treatment of illness.

3. Where persons enjoying temporary protection are engaged in employed or self-employed activities, account shall be taken, when fixing the proposed level of aid, of their ability to meet their own needs.

4. The Member States shall provide necessary medical or other assistance to persons enjoying temporary protection who have special needs, such as unaccompanied minors or persons who have undergone torture, rape or other serious forms of psychological, physical or sexual violence.

Article 14

1. The Member States shall grant to persons under 18 years of age enjoying temporary protection access to the education system under the same conditions as nationals of the host Member State. The Member States may stipulate that such access must be confined to the state education system.

2. The Member States may allow adults enjoying temporary protection access to the general education system.

Article 15

1. For the purpose of this Article, in cases where families already existed in the country of origin and were separated due to circumstances surrounding the mass influx, the following persons shall be considered to be part of a family:

(a) the spouse of the sponsor or his/her unmarried partner in a stable relationship, where the legislation or practice of the Member State concerned treats unmarried couples in a way comparable to married couples under its law relating to aliens; the minor unmarried children of the sponsor or of his/her spouse, without distinction as to whether they were born in or out of wedlock or adopted;

(b) other close relatives who lived together as part of the family unit at the time of the events leading to the mass influx, and who were wholly or mainly dependent on the sponsor at the time.

2. In cases where the separate family members enjoy temporary protection in different Member States, Member States shall reunite family members where they are satisfied that the family members fall under the description of paragraph 1(a), taking into account the wish of the said family members. Member States may reunite family members where they are satisfied that the family members fall under the description of paragraph1(b), taking into account on a case by case basis the extreme hardship they would face if the reunification did not take place.

3. Where the sponsor enjoys temporary protection in one Member State and one or some family members are not yet in a Member State, the Member State where the sponsor enjoys temporary protection shall reunite family members, who are in need of protection, with the sponsor in the case of family members where it is satisfied that they fall under the description of paragraph 1(a). The Member State may reunite family members, who are in need of protection, with the sponsor in the case of family members where it is satisfied that they fall under the description of paragraph 1(b), taking into account on a case by case basis the extreme hardship which they would face if the reunification did not take place.

4. When applying this Article, the Member States shall taken into consideration the best interests of the child.

5. The Member States concerned shall decide, taking account of Articles 25 and 26, in which Member State the reunification shall take place.

6. Reunited family members shall be granted residence permits under temporary protection. Documents or other equivalent evidence shall be issued for that purpose. Transfers of family members onto the territory of another Member State for the purposes of reunification under paragraph 2, shall result in the withdrawal of the residence permits issued, and the termination of the obligations towards the persons concerned relating to temporary protection, in the Member State of departure.

7. The practical implementation of this Article may involve cooperation with the international organisations concerned.

8. A Member State shall, at the request of another Member State, provide information, as set out in Annex II, on a person receiving temporary protection which is needed to process a matter under this Article.

Article 16

1. The Member States shall as soon as possible take measures to ensure the necessary representation of unaccompanied minors enjoying temporary protection by legal guardianship, or, where necessary, representation by an organisation which is responsible for the care and well-being of minors, or by any other appropriate representation.

2. During the period of temporary protection Member States shall provide for unaccompanied minors to be placed:
   (a) with adult relatives;
   (b) with a foster-family;
   (c) in reception centres with special provisions for minors, or in other accommodation suitable for minors;
   (d) with the person who looked after the child when fleeing.
The Member States shall take the necessary steps to enable the placement. Agreement by the adult person or persons concerned shall be established by the Member States. The views of the child shall be taken into account in accordance with the age and maturity of the child.

CHAPTER IV
Access to the Asylum Procedure in the Context of Temporary Protection

Article 17

1. Persons enjoying temporary protection must be able to lodge an application for asylum at any time.

2. The examination of any asylum application not processed before the end of the period of temporary protection shall be completed after the end of that period.

Article 18

The criteria and mechanisms for deciding which Member State is responsible for considering an asylum application shall apply. In particular, the Member State responsible for examining an asylum application submitted by a person enjoying temporary protection pursuant to this Directive, shall be the Member State which has accepted his transfer onto its territory.

Article 19

1. The Member States may provide that temporary protection may not be enjoyed concurrently with the status of asylum seeker while applications are under consideration.

2. Where, after an asylum application has been examined, refugee status or, where applicable, other kind of protection is not granted to a person eligible for or enjoying temporary protection, the Member States shall, without prejudice to Article 28, provide for that person to enjoy or to continue to enjoy temporary protection for the remainder of the period of protection.

CHAPTER V
Return and Measures after Temporary Protection has Ended

Article 20

When the temporary protection ends, the general laws on protection and on aliens in the Member States shall apply, without prejudice to Articles 21, 22 and 23.

Article 21

1. The Member States shall take the measures necessary to make possible the voluntary return of persons enjoying temporary protection or whose temporary protection has ended. The Member States shall ensure that the provisions governing voluntary return of persons enjoying temporary protection facilitate their return with respect for human dignity. The Member State shall ensure that the decision of those persons to return is taken in full knowledge of the facts. The Member States may provide for exploratory visits.

2. For such time as the temporary protection has not ended, the Member States shall, on the basis of the circumstances prevailing in the country of origin, give favourable consideration to requests for return to the host Member State from persons who have enjoyed temporary protection and exercised their right to a voluntary return.

3. At the end of the temporary protection, the Member States may provide for the obligations laid down in Chapter III to be extended individually to persons who have been covered by temporary protection and are benefiting from a voluntary return programme. The extension shall have effect until the date of return.

Article 22

1. The Member States shall take the measures necessary to ensure that the enforced return of persons whose temporary protection has ended and who are not eligible for admission is conducted with due respect for human dignity.

2. In cases of enforced return, Member States shall consider any compelling humanitarian reasons which may make return impossible or unreasonable in specific cases.

Article 23

1. The Member States shall take the necessary measures concerning the conditions of residence of persons who have enjoyed temporary protection and who cannot, in view of their state of health, reasonably be expected to travel; where for example they would suffer serious negative effects if their treatment was interrupted. They shall not be expelled so long as that situation continues.

2. The Member States may allow families whose children are minors and attend school in a Member State to benefit from residence conditions allowing the children concerned to complete the current school period.

CHAPTER VI
Solidarity

Article 24

The measures provided for in this Directive shall benefit from the European Refugee Fund set up by Decision 2000/596/EC, under the terms laid down in that Decision.

Article 25

1. The Member States shall receive persons who are eligible for temporary protection in a spirit of Community solidarity. They shall indicate – in figures or in general terms – their capacity to receive such persons. This information shall be set out in the Council Decision referred to in Article 5. After that Decision has been adopted, the Member States may indicate additional reception capacity by notifying the Council and the Commission. This information shall be passed on swiftly to UNHCR.

2. The Member States concerned, acting in cooperation with the competent international organisations, shall ensure that the eligible persons defined in the Council Decision referred to in Article 5, who have not yet arrived in the Community have expressed their will to be received onto their territory.

3. When the number of those who are eligible for temporary protection following a sudden and massive influx exceeds the reception capacity referred to in paragraph 1, the Council shall, as a matter of urgency, examine the situation and take appropriate action, including recommending additional support for Member States affected.

Article 26

1. For the duration of the temporary protection, the Member States shall cooperate with each other with regard to transferral of the residence of persons enjoying temporary protection from one Member State to another, subject to the consent of the persons concerned to such transferral.

2. A Member State shall communicate requests for transfers to the other Member States and notify the Commission and UNHCR. The Member States shall inform the requesting Member State of their capacity for receiving transferees.

3. A Member State shall, at the request of another Member State, provide information, as set out in Annex II, on a person enjoying temporary protection which is needed to process a matter under this Article.

4. Where a transfer is made from one Member State to another, the residence permit in the Member State of departure shall expire and the obligations towards the persons concerned relating to temporary protection in the Member State of departure shall come to an end. The new host Member State shall grant temporary protection to the persons concerned.

5. The Member States shall use the model pass set out in Annex I for transfers between Member States of persons enjoying temporary protection.

CHAPTER VII
Administrative Cooperation

Article 27

1. For the purposes of the administrative cooperation required to implement temporary protection, the Member States shall each appoint a national contact point, whose address they shall communicate to each other and to the Commission. The Member States shall, in liaison with the Commission, take all the appropriate measures to establish direct cooperation and an exchange of information between the competent authorities.

2. The Member States shall, regularly and as quickly as possible, communicate data concerning the number of persons enjoying temporary protection and full information on the national laws, regulations and administrative provisions relating to the implementation of temporary protection.

CHAPTER VIII
Special Provisions

Article 28

1. The Member States may exclude a person from temporary protection if:
    (a) there are serious reasons for considering that:

(i) he or she has committed a crime against peace, a war crime, or a crime against humanity, as defined in the international instruments drawn up to make provision in respect of such crimes;

(ii) he or she has committed a serious non-political crime outside the Member State of reception prior to his or her admission to that Member State as a person enjoying temporary protection. The severity of the expected persecution is to be weighed against the nature of the criminal offence of which the person concerned is suspected. Particularly cruel actions, even if committed with an allegedly political objective, may be classified as serious non-political crimes. This applies both to the participants in the crime and to its instigators;

(iii) he or she has been guilty of acts contrary to the purposes and principles of the United Nations;

(b) there are reasonable grounds for regarding him or her as a danger to the security of the host Member State or, having been convicted by a final judgment of a particularly serious crime, he or she is a danger to the community of the host Member State.

2. The grounds for exclusion referred to in paragraph 1 shall be based solely on the personal conduct of the person concerned. Exclusion decisions or measures shall be based on the principle of proportionality.

CHAPTER IX
Final Provisions

Article 29

Persons who have been excluded from the benefit of temporary protection or family reunification by a Member State shall be entitled to mount a legal challenge in the Member State concerned.

Article 30

The Member States shall lay down the rules on penalties applicable to infringements of the national provisions adopted pursuant to this Directive and shall take all measures necessary to ensure that they are implemented. The penalties provided for must be effective, proportionate and dissuasive.

Article 31

1. Not later than two years after the date specified in Article 32, the Commission shall report to the European Parliament and the Council on the application of this Directive in the Member States and shall propose any amendments that are necessary. The Member States shall send the Commission all the information that is appropriate for drawing up this report.

2. After presenting the report referred to at paragraph 1, the Commission shall report to the European Parliament and the Council on the application of this Directive in the Member States at least every five years.

Article 32

1. The Member States shall bring into force the laws, regulations and administrative provisions necessary to comply with this Directive by 31 December 2002 at the latest. They shall forthwith inform the Commission thereof.

2. When the Member States adopt these measures, they shall contain a reference to this Directive or shall be accompanied by such reference on the occasion of their official publication. The methods of making such a reference shall be laid down by the Member States.

Article 33

This Directive shall enter into force on the day of its publication in the *Official Journal of the European Communities*.

Article 34

This Directive is addressed to the Member States in accordance with the Treaty establishing the European Community.

ANNEX I

Model pass for the transfer of persons enjoying temporary protection

PASS

Name of the Member State delivering the pass:

Reference number (*):

Issued under Article 26 of Directive 2001/55/EC of 20 July 2001 on minimum standards for giving temporary protection in the event of a mass influx of displaced persons and on measures promoting a balance of effort between Member States in receiving such persons and bearing the consequences thereof.

Valid only for the transfer from .... (¹) to .... (²).

The person in question must present himself/herself at .... (³) by .... (⁴).

Issued at: ....

SURNAME: ....

FORENAMES: ....

PLACE AND DATE OF BIRTH: ....

In case of a minor, name(s) of responsible adult: ....

SEX: ....

NATIONALITY: ....

Date issued: ....

```
PHOTO
```

SEAL

Signature of the beneficiary: ....   For the competent authorities: ....

The pass-holder has been identified by the authorities .... (⁵) (⁶)

The identity of the pass-holder has not been established ....

This document is issued pursuant to Article 26 of Directive 2001/55/EC only and in no way constitutes a document which can be equated to a travel document authorising the crossing of the external border or a document proving the individual's identity.

(*) The reference number is allocated by the country from which the transfer to another Member State is made.
(¹) Member State from which the transfer is being made.
(²) Member State to which the transfer is being made.
(³) Place where the person must present himself/herself on arrival in the second Member State.
(⁴) Deadline by which the person must present himself/herself on arrival in the second Member State.
(⁵) On the basis of the following travel or identity documents, presented to the authorities.
(⁶) On the basis of documents other than a travel or identity document.

ANNEX II

The information referred to in Articles 10, 15 and 26 of the Directive includes to the extent necessary one or more of the following documents or data:

(a) personal data on the person concerned (name, nationality, date and place of birth, marital status, family relationship);

(b) identity documents and travel documents of the person concerned;

(c) documents concerning evidence of family ties (marriage certificate, birth certificate, certificate of adoption);

(d) other information essential to establish the person's identity or family relationship;

(e) residence permits, visas or residence permit refusal decisions issued to the person concerned by the Member State, and documents forming the basis of decisions;

(f) residence permit and visa applications lodged by the person concerned and pending in the Member State, and the stage reached in the processing of these.

The providing Member State shall notify any corrected information to the requesting Member State.

EXPLANATORY MEMORANDUM

1. **A tool in the service of a common European asylum system and of the full operation of the Geneva Convention: temporary protection in the event of a mass influx of displaced persons based on solidarity between the Member States**

1.1. As envisaged by the conclusions of the Presidency at the Tampere European Council in October 1999, a common European asylum system must be based on the full and inclusive application of the Geneva Convention, maintaining the principle of non-refoulement. It is to include, in the short term, a clear and workable determination of the State responsible for the examination of an asylum application, common standards for a fair and efficient asylum procedure, common minimum conditions of reception of asylum seekers, and the approximation of rules on the recognition and content of the refugee status. It should also be completed with measures on subsidiary forms of protection offering an appropriate status to any person in need of such protection. In the longer term, Community rules should lead to a common asylum procedure and a uniform status for those who are granted asylum valid throughout the Union. The Commission was asked to prepare a communication on this matter in 2000. An agreement on the issue of temporary protection in situations of mass influx of displaced persons on the basis of solidarity between Member States is to be reached rapidly.

1.2. The Commission is now, in the spring of 2000, proposing a draft Council Directive on temporary protection in the event of a mass influx, based on solidarity between the Member States, as indicated in the scoreboard for the evaluation of progress in the establishment of an area of freedom, security and justice in the European Union, approved by the Council on 27 March 2000.

The Commission is aware of the difficulties of the temporary protection project. It has drawn the conclusions from three consecutive years of failed negotiations in the Council. Even so, acting on the basis of the mandate given by the Tampere European Council and of the Treaty, it has not abandoned its ambitions. It hopes that the Council, which gave an undertaking in Tampere and approved the scoreboard, will assume its responsibilities and welcome the Commission's offer in the proposed legislative instrument. The Commission's new proposal is more than a mere formal 'Amsterdamisation' of its old proposals for joint actions. It reflects all the consequences of the entry into force of the Amsterdam Treaty, discussions in the Council, notably during the German and Finnish Presidencies, and the Member States' response to the Kosovo refugee crisis.

1.3. The proposal is part of a series of recent and forthcoming Commission initiatives on asylum policy under the new Treaty establishing the European Community. In March 1999, it began work on asylum procedures with its working paper 'Towards common standards for asylum procedures'. In May 1999, it proposed a draft Council Regulation concerning the Eurodac system for comparing the fingerprints of asylum-seekers and certain other foreign nationals, the objective of which is to improve the effectiveness of the Dublin Convention. In December 1999, it presented a proposal for a Council Decision establishing a European Refugee Fund. It is proposing a comprehensive financial approach based on solidarity to support the Member States' efforts in asylum matters. Still in December 1999, the Commission presented a proposal for a Council Directive on family reunification, which includes the situation of refugees and persons enjoying subsidiary protection. In March 2000, a document to facilitate strategic discussion on the replacement of the Dublin Convention by Community legislation was tabled. In the next few months, a legislative proposal concerning asylum procedures will also be presented.

1.4. The consequences of a mass influx of displaced persons in the Union impose such pressures on the asylum system that special arrangements are necessary to give immediate protection to the persons who need it and avoid blocking up the asylum system, which would be against the interests not only of States but also of other persons seeking protection outside the mass influx. Temporary protection in the event of a mass influx as proposed by the Commission is not a third form of protection, alongside refugee status on the basis of the Geneva Convention and subsidiary protection, the consequence of which would be to undermine the Member States' international obligations or to prejudice efforts to harmonise and consolidate forms of subsidiary protection in Europe. On the contrary, minimum standards for giving temporary protection in the event of a mass influx and measures promoting a balance of efforts between the Member States on a basis of solidarity are a component of the system, and more specifically a tool enabling the system to operate smoothly and not collapse under a mass influx. It is accordingly a tool in the service of a common European asylum system and of the full operation of the Geneva Convention.

1.5. The definition of minimum standards for the grant of temporary protection in the event of a mass influx of displaced persons does not exhaust the scope of Article 63(2)(a) of the EC Treaty, and the Community will subsequently take the initiatives needed to adopt minimum standards for the grant of other forms of protection to which that provision applies.

2.   Temporary protection and the national and international situation

2.1. In the context of the large-scale movement of people fleeing the conflict in the former Yugoslavia and the dangers that it caused, Europe was, for the first time since the second world war, directly involved in forced movements of people which are not comparable to previous waves of refugees in either quantitative or qualitative terms.

2.2. Temporary protection has been developed by several Member States as a response to the challenge raised by the mass influx to the asylum system. Special provisions on an autonomous basis have been adopted to speed up decision-making as regards temporary admission so as to avoid or delay the application of the lengthy procedures laid down for asylum requests. These provisions allow the grant of immediate protection and well-defined rights. They also seek to avoid destabilising the relevant administrative and/or judicial authorities with powers in matters of asylum and, consequently, penalising applicants for refugee status under the Geneva Convention or for subsidiary protection, outside the context of the specific influx, to whom the system is no longer equipped to pay the same attention. Temporary protection is by definition confined to a specified limited period during which the situation in the country of origin is such that the persons concerned cannot return there in adequate conditions of safety and dignity. Although the Geneva Convention does not automatically exclude the grant of refugee status to entire groups of persons (*prima facie*), most Member States are reluctant to make use of this possibility. Moreover, Article 1C of the Convention, which makes an explicit reference to the possibility of withdrawing refugee status, is rarely applied by the Member States.

2.3. Temporary protection is sometimes criticised by those who consider that in certain Member States it is implemented as an instrument that can be used to circumvent or even evade the obligations flowing from the Geneva Convention. There is indeed a real risk that the situation could get out of control. The European Union's responsibility is crucial, and it must manifest its intention to ensure, by means of its legislative instruments, that that is not its objective.

2.4. The concept and legal framework for temporary protection in the event of a mass influx has been developed in recent history and varies between the European Union Member States. Most have provided in their legislation for the possibility of establishing temporary protection schemes either by statute or by subordinate instruments, circulars or ad hoc decisions. Certain of them do not have the expression 'temporary protection' as such, but in reality the residence documents that are issued and the link with the asylum system have the same practical effect. Systems also vary in terms of the maximum duration of temporary protection (ranging from six months to one, two, three, four or even five years maximum). Certain Member States provide for the possibility of suspending the examination of asylum requests during the temporary protection period; others do not. The chief differences lie in the welfare rights and benefits granted to persons enjoying temporary protection. Certain Member States allow the right to employment and family reunification; others do not. Certain Member States provide that the benefit of temporary protection may not be enjoyed at the same time by an asylum-seeker: applicants must opt for one or the other. Other Member States make no provision for such an incompatibility.

2.5. This situation was observed recently on the occasion of the Kosovo conflict in spring 1999. There are variations between national measures relating to Kosovars evacuated on humanitarian grounds, asylum-seekers, Kosovars already on the territory before the evacuations began, and the benefits granted, but there are also many common elements. It was also observed that national legal frameworks for temporary protection were imperfect, incomplete and sometimes put in place rather hastily on a purely ad hoc basis.

2.6. At international level, the UNHCR Programme Executive Committee adopted a number of instruments as references for the international community: EXCOM No. 19 (XXXI) of 1980 on Temporary Refuge, No. 22 (XXXII) of 1981 on Protection of Asylum-Seekers in Situations of Large-Scale Influx, No. 71 (XLIV) of 1993, No. 74 (XLV) of 1994 and No. 85 (XLIX) of 1998 on international protection. In 1994, the Office of the High Commissioner presented the Executive Committee with a note on international protection, which is still a point of reference. The Council of Europe also began work at the beginning of 1999 on a Recommendation on temporary protection; it was adopted by the Committee of Ministers on 3 May 2000.

3.   The Union *acquis* regarding temporary protection

3.1. In the context of the Maastricht Treaty, the European Union Member States adopted two instruments – a Council Resolution of 25 September 1995 on burden-sharing with regard to the admission and residence of displaced persons on a temporary basis, based on Article K.1 of the Union Treaty, and a Council Decision of 4 March 1996 on an alert and emergency procedure for burden-sharing with regard to the admission and residence of displaced persons on a temporary basis, based on Article K.3(2)(a). The ground for these instruments was the influx of displaced persons from former Yugoslavia in the early 1990s, many of them from Bosnia-Herzegovina. They were never implemented, not even in the context of the Kosovo crisis in spring 1999. Before that, at Copenhagen on 2 June 1993, the Council had paid brief attention to the question of displaced persons from Yugoslavia (6712/93, Press 90).

3.2. The Kosovo conflict in 1999 prompted the Member States to take additional national measures and to engage in what was a difficult coordination progress. In April 1999, in response to the influx of Kosovars and the need, acknowledged by the UNHCR in Geneva on 6 April to undertake humanitarian evacuations beyond the region of first reception, the Member States, at a special Council meeting (Justice and Home Affairs) in Luxembourg on 7 April 1999, had difficulties reaching agreement on the coordination of the reception of the persons concerned. But the Presidency conclusions recognised that, for humanitarian reasons and to avoid destabilising individual host countries in the region of origin, it could be necessary to give protection and assistance on a temporary basis to displaced persons outside the region of origin. Humanitarian evacuations were to be based on the voluntary reception of displaced persons. The principle of family unity was to be applied. On 27 May 1999, the Council adopted conclusions on displaced persons in Kosovo, addressing protection questions in greater detail. The Council acknowledged the ongoing, indeed the intensified, need to give these people temporary protection and welcomed the Member States' offers. It gives a general indication as to the level of protection and social rights. It envisages the possibility of meeting, if necessary, to study needs in terms of responses to the crisis itself and of reception, having regard to the evaluation made by the UNHCR. The temporary protection scheme was brought to an end by the Member States without coordination.

3.3. At the beginning of April 1999 the Commission rapidly amended a proposal for a joint action on the reception and voluntary repatriation of refugees, displaced persons and asylum-seekers, presented in February 1998. On 26 April 1999 this enabled the Council, acting on the basis of Article K.3 of the Union Treaty, to adopt a joint action 'establishing projects and measures to provide practical support in relation to the reception and voluntary repatriation of refugees, displaced persons and asylum seekers, including emergency assistance to persons who have fled as a result of recent events in Kosovo'. On this basis, the EU provided financing up to approximately EUR 17 million for projects relating to the reception and voluntary return of Kosovars.

4. **Work in the European Union context**

4.1. On 5 March 1997 the Commission sent the Council a proposal for a joint action based on Article K.3(2)(b) of the Union Treaty concerning temporary protection of displaced persons. The proposal contained definitions, general provisions, the establishment of temporary protection regimes, the revision and/or phasing out of temporary protection regimes, assistance to Member States which are particularly affected, residence permits, family reunification, employment and social security, housing, welfare benefits and education, asylum, exclusion clauses, implementing measures, and long-term protection measures. The draft received a favourable opinion in the European Parliament on 23 October 1997, with requests for amendments.

4.2. On 24 June 1998, to reflect the Council's discussions, in particular on the question of solidarity and certain amendments put forward by the European Parliament, the Commission presented an amended proposal for a joint action with a second proposal for a joint action, separate from but parallel to the first, concerning solidarity in the admission and residence of beneficiaries of the temporary protection of displaced persons. The two joint actions were intended to come into force at the same time. The new proposal incorporated many of the comments of the Member States and certain of the amendments put forward by the European Parliament so as to improve the proposal and speed up the process of reaching a consensus for the adoption of the joint actions on temporary protection. It set a maximum duration for temporary protection schemes. On 25 November 1998, Parliament again gave a favourable opinion on the Commission proposals, with requests for amendments.

4.3. The UNHCR described the 1997 proposal as balanced and as providing a constructive basis for action. It expressed a preference for a maximum duration of temporary protection of three to five years, in order to clarify the link with the Geneva Convention and welcomed the level of rights granted to persons enjoying temporary protection. The 1998 revised proposal was welcomed by the UNHCR, which observed that there had been many improvements over the 1997 proposal.

4.4. At the beginning of 1999, the Commission and the Council observed that discussions were in deadlock, in particular on the solidarity question. The German Presidency presented the informal Council meeting (JHA) in Berlin with a paper on burden-sharing in matters of the admission and residence of displaced persons and the idea of double voluntary action by host states and the persons received. This principle was well received and the Member States and the Commission agreed to continue working on it. On 1 May 1999, the Commission proposal lapsed on legal grounds when the new Treaty came into force. To implement items 10 to 12 of the Council conclusions of 27 May 1999 on displaced persons in Kosovo, the Member States and the Commission pursued the discussion under the Finnish Presidency on all questions relating to temporary protection and solidarity in the light of the experience of the Member States in response to the Kosovo crisis.

5. The objective of the Commission proposal

5.1. With this proposal for a Directive, the Commission is pursuing the following aims:

(1) implementing the Treaty, the Vienna Action Plan, the Presidency conclusions of the Tampere special European Council and the scoreboard presented to the Council and Parliament in March 2000;

(2) avoiding a total bottleneck in national asylum systems in the event of a mass influx, which would have negative effects on the Member States, the persons concerned and other persons seeking protection outside the context of the mass influx, and thereby supporting the viability of the common European asylum system;

(3) making immediate protection and fair rights available to the persons concerned;

(4) clarifying the link between temporary protection and the Geneva Convention, safeguarding the full application of the Convention;

(5) contributing to achieving balance between the efforts made by the Member States to receive the persons concerned by offering coordination facilities in the event of a mass influx in the European Union and in implementing temporary protection;

(6) to give practical expression to solidarity in the reception of the persons concerned by means of financial solidarity and the double voluntary action in the reception of them.

5.2. To achieve these aims, the Commission is presenting a 'package' in a single Directive, based on Article 63(2)(a) and (b) of the Treaty, containing definitions corresponding to the Treaty's objectives and minimum standards for temporary protection in the event of a mass influx, which should promote a balance between the efforts made by the Member States to receive the persons concerned and to bear the consequences. Transposal of the Directive will require either the adoption or the maintenance of national provisions of primary or secondary legislation making it possible to apply temporary protection in the event of a mass influx of displaced persons in accordance with the Directive from the time when the mass influx is declared. Solidarity mechanisms will be activated automatically (fuller explanation at point 6).

5.3. The Directive provides expressly that temporary protection is without prejudice to recognition of refugee status under the Geneva Convention, to make it clear from the outset that the aim is not to derogate from or circumvent the Member States' international obligations. It also makes clear that it is in the very nature of minimum standards that the Member States may introduce or maintain more favourable conditions for persons enjoying temporary protection. Lastly, as the Kosovo crisis revealed, the link with the United Nations High Commissioner for Refugees is a vital element in assessing the situation and questions of protection. Moreover the persons concerned by temporary protection in the event of a mass influx may be within the UNHCR's mandate. The Directive recognises this fact and provides for regular consultations for the establishment, implementation and termination of temporary protection.

5.4. The maximum duration of temporary protection in the event of a mass influx is a crucial component of the system, especially if access to the asylum procedure is temporarily postponed. In 1998 the Commission proposed a maximum period of three years, possibly to be extended to five years. But there seems to be some reluctance to accept this period in several Member States. The Commission is accordingly making a new proposal for a maximum period of two years, which is a reasonable and workable period. If there is no prospect of a qualified majority in favour of terminating temporary protection as explained at point 5.6, it should automatically lapse after two years. In any event, temporary protection could be terminated at any time.

5.5. The core provisions of the Directive concern the method for activating and terminating temporary protection. First, since there can be no pre-determined quantitative criteria for declaring that there is a mass influx, there will have to be a joint decision making the declaration. But this decision will have to be taken on the basis of an examination of specified questions, including those related to the solidarity issue. This decision on a matter of implementation is reserved for the Council on account of the special nature of temporary protection and of the fact that it is impossible to pre-determine the quantitative criteria to define a mass influx of displaced persons. The decision will require a qualified majority, in view of its importance and of the need to ensure that a sufficient number of Member States agree to activating the mechanism. The same applies to termination, which must also be based on an examination of specified questions. The Directive defines the content of the decision and its effects. As soon as the Member States have agreed to activate the mechanism, they must all implement temporary protection in accordance with the Directive. The Commission has also sought to simplify the decision-making procedure in relation to its 1998 proposals and to make the mechanism easier to understand. Within the maximum period of the temporary protection scheme, renewals are automatic.

5.6. The level of the Member States' obligations towards beneficiaries has to meet a number of constraints. First, they must be fair – they must reflect Europe's humanitarian traditions – and the persons concerned may well include many refugees within the meaning of the Geneva Convention. Second, they must be attractive enough to ensure that there is no excess of asylum applications. The level proposed by the Commission in this proposal for a Directive retains the ambitions of the original proposals of 1997 and 1998, though it reflects discussions that have taken place in the Council and Parliament. It also reflects its careful review of the measures taken by the Member States in relation to the Kosovars who were given temporary protection. The Member States' first obligation towards beneficiaries of temporary protection must be to issue a residence document in good and due form, valid for the entire temporary protection. Following the discussions of the last three years and the experience of Kosovo, the Directive does not determine the precise period of validity of residence documents. But the treatment given to persons enjoying temporary protection must be that set by the minimum standards, irrespective of the duration of the residence document or documents. If persons came from countries subject to a visa requirement, the Directive provides for simplification of formalities and for visas to be issued free of charge. The Commission has incorporated an amendment from Parliament concerning information for beneficiaries: it is important that they should be familiar with the different rights given to them, the provisions governing access to the asylum procedure and the provisions governing the expiry of the temporary protection. The Commission confirms the importance it attaches to persons enjoying temporary protection being given access to employment on the same terms as recognised refugees. This is an obligation that will reduce their dependence on assistance schemes and facilitate voluntary return programmes. Access to employment can also be a valuable way of making temporary protection more attractive than the asylum procedure. The Directive also imposes obligations regarding housing and accommodation, welfare or subsistence assistance, medical or other assistance, education and training. In its proposal on family reunification the Commission stated that the question of preserving family unity in the context of temporary protection would be addressed by a specific proposal rather than the general proposal. Given the limited pre-defined duration of temporary protection, the Commission feels it is necessary to concentrate on the family as already constituted in the country of origin but separated by the circumstances of the mass influx. A broad concept of the family can be posited. This corresponds to the Member States' practice in relation to the Kosovars. But the right provided for here is more limited than the right provided for by the family reunification Directive. Moreover the Commission cannot deny that the political conditions for proposing a broader approach to family reunification for persons enjoying temporary protection than proposed here do not seem to be met. It would like to link recognition of a specific situation and the right to lead a normal family life that is secured by the European Human Rights Convention and is therefore available also to persons enjoying temporary protection, as indicated in the Council of Europe Recommendation adopted by the Committee of Ministers on 15 December 1999 on family reunion for refugees and other persons in need of international protection (R(99)23). Special attention has been paid in this Directive to the situation of children, unaccompanied minors and persons with special needs, particularly those suffering severe traumas. The Directive provides for the non-discriminatory application of obligations towards persons enjoying temporary protection. The Directive does not address the question of free movement of persons enjoying temporary protection and accordingly does not specifically regulate the taking back of a person enjoying temporary protection in an initial Member State and residing unlawfully in a second. For one thing, the existing rules governing the taking back of a person residing unlawfully in a Member State and holding a residence document in another must be simply applicable. For another, the Commission will in due course present proposals for measures concerning the free movement of third-country nationals in the Member States and the conditions governing them.

5.7. The provisions relating to access to the asylum procedure must be taken as an opportunity to clarify once and for all the link between temporary protection in the event of a mass influx and the Geneva Convention. The Commission considers that these provisions must be short but establish strong principles. Access to the procedure must be explicitly guaranteed. But it is necessary to respect the way in which the Member States choose to confront the mass influx in their management of the system. The Directive imposes no obligation on Member States as to whether or not to introduce mechanisms for suspending the examination of applications, whether or not to prohibit the combined status of asylum-seeker and beneficiary of temporary protection and so on. Suspension may be an unavoidable procedure for the Member States most affected by the influx. Non-combination of statuses may be a further factor making temporary protection more attractive and lightening the burden of asylum applications. But the Directive must determine the conditions that absolutely secure access to the procedure for those who so wish. The national provisions transposing the Directive will presumably differ while being constructed on a strong common principle.

5.8. As in the case of access to the asylum procedure, the question of returns and of measures after temporary protection must be governed by simple principles and minimum standards within the scope of Article 63 of the Treaty. After the end of the temporary protection, the ordinary law on protection and the entry and residence of foreign nationals must apply. A variety of scenarios are conceivable:

– Member States must examine asylum applications from those who wish to lodge them;

– if they are rejected, subsidiary protection or an order to leave the territory may be available, depending on the personal situation of the applicant or the situation of his country of origin;

– in the absence of an asylum application, the ordinary law governing the residence of foreign nationals applies;

– in the event of new entries in the Member States' territory, the ordinary law of asylum and the entry and residence of foreign nationals will apply;

– resettlement programmes may be adopted by the Member States.

The Directive provides for standards for the implementation of this basic principle, the response to specific situations and the establishment of voluntary return programmes.

5.9. The implementation of temporary protection in the European Union requires tools to facilitate coordination between Member States. The Directive accordingly provides for administrative cooperation between the Member States in liaison with the Commission. The Commission's intention is to call regular meetings, following any decision to activate temporary protection, of a coordination group to which each Member State would send a representative. If necessary the group will be called to meetings up to a year after the end of the temporary protection. It will consider any question concerning the application of the temporary protection that may be raised by the chair or the representatives of the Member States. The group may consult any relevant organisation whenever it feels the need.

5.10. The Directive specifies the grounds for exclusion from temporary protection of persons who do not deserve it and the conditions for their application.

5.11. Before going into greater detail about the solidarity mechanism, the Commission would recall that the causes of a mass influx of displaced persons lie in event affecting the Union's external relations, its common foreign and security policy and its security and defence identity. Community humanitarian aid is also involved. Upstream of any crisis the European Union has early-warning capacities and participates in measures to prevent and manage crises. In relation to Justice and Home Affairs in particular, the point is to boost the Union's external action by incorporating these questions into the definition and implementation of other policies and actions. Temporary protection in the event of a mass influx thus becomes a component of a coherent and more and more efficient set of Union capacities for action, offering the greatest possible ability to tackle the causes of a mass influx and take crisis action through local measures or post-crisis action, notably in terms of returns. This does not release the Member States from their obligations to protect (point 4 of the Tampere conclusions). But the Member States can rely on a whole range of instruments in the implementation of which the Commission is ready to play its full role, within the areas in which it has power. Its proposal for a Rapid Reaction Facility is conceived in this spirit.

6. Solidarity

6.1. As with its revised proposals for joint action of 1998, the Commission acknowledges the link between temporary protection in the event of a mass influx of displaced persons and solidarity. This solidarity must be capable of being expressed through a clear, transparent and predictable financial mechanism. The Commission also considers, given the background, that the question of physical distribution must be settled by the Community legislation. This is something that the Member States have called for, mainly those most affected by mass influxes in recent years. But only a physical distribution based on the voluntary action of the Member States and the displaced persons themselves will found a consensus in the European Union.

6.2. Financial solidarity

The draft Directive provides expressly for a financial solidarity mechanism in the simple form of a reference to the Council Decision establishing a European Refugee Fund. The Commission, acting under Article 63(2) of the Treaty, adopted this proposal for a Council Decision on 14 December 1999. Apart from structural measures to support reception, integration and voluntary return, the Fund is to finance emergency measures in the event of a mass influx of displaced persons in the European Union. The proposal has been well received, and negotiations are approaching the final stages in the Council. Parliament approved it on 11 April 2000. The reference to the ERF is adequate since it creates a direct link without unnecessary repetitions and has no effect on the Fund's operating rules. Under these rules it will be possible to finance the eligible structural and emergency measures provided for by the Directive. The Fund is to be given EUR 216 million over five years (36 for 2000, 45 each year thereafter, EUR 10 million of that for emergency measures).

6.3. Solidarity in physical reception

Physical reception must be secured, without prejudice to the Member States' international obligations as to non-refoulement, of course, and must express the will of the States and the consent to be received by a Member State of beneficiaries who are not yet in that State. States indicate their reception availabilities, but voluntary action cannot have the effect of generating an obligation to make offers on a scale that must be determined in detail. Voluntary action here can take place in two stages: at the time the mass influx is declared and subsequently, during the temporary protection period, if a Member State still needs to call in the solidarity of other Member States. In this case, there is provision for cooperation between Member States and for a few operational principles for its implementation. The normal Community principle is reception in a spirit of Community solidarity. Consequently, discussions and offers must be incorporated into the preparation of the Council Decision activating temporary protection, and the offers must then be annexed to the actual Decision in the form of Statements by the Member States. But if the flexibility of these principles was still inadequate, an exceptional possibility of not applying physical distribution must be provided for. Reasons must then be given. This complies scrupulously with the voluntary action of the Member States and their international obligations and allows a flexible reaction to the different types of mass influx that might occur (humanitarian evacuations are not the only situation, for example), while setting it within a Community regulatory framework.

7.   **The choice of legal basis**

7.1. The choice of legal basis is consistent with the amendments made to the Treaty establishing the European Community by the Amsterdam Treaty, which entered into force on 1 May 1999. Article 63(2) provides that the Council is to adopt measures relating to refugees and displaced persons, notably in the following areas: minimum standards for giving temporary protection to displaced persons from third countries who cannot return to their country of origin (a) and promoting a balance of effort between Member States in receiving and bearing the consequences of receiving refugees and displaced persons (b). Article 63 is accordingly the proper legal basis for a proposal for minimum standards regarding temporary protection based on solidarity between Member States and accompanied by measures to balance the efforts of the Member States.

7.2. The proposed Directive is to be adopted by the procedure of Article 67 of the Treaty, whereby 'During a transitional period of five years following the entry into force of the Treaty of Amsterdam, the Council shall act unanimously on a proposal from the Commission or on the initiative of a Member State and after consulting the European Parliament'. Title IV of the EC Treaty is not applicable in the United Kingdom and Ireland, unless those Member States decide otherwise in accordance with the procedure laid down in the Protocol on the position of the United Kingdom and Ireland annexed to the Treaties. Title IV of the EC Treaty is likewise not applicable in Denmark, by virtue of the Protocol on the position of Denmark annexed to the Treaties.

8. Subsidiarity and proportionality: justification and value added

8.1. The insertion of the new Title IV (Visas, asylum, immigration and other policies related to free movement of persons) in the Treaty establishing the European Community, demonstrates the will of the High Contracting Parties to confer powers in these matters on the European Community. But the European Community does not have exclusive powers here, and consequently, even with the political will to implement a common policy on asylum and immigration, it must act in accordance with Article 5 of the EC Treaty, that is to say if and to the extent that the objectives of the proposed action cannot be sufficiently achieved by the Member States and can therefore, by reason of the scale or effects of the proposed action, be better achieved by the Community. The proposed Directive satisfies these criteria.

8.2. *Subsidiarity*
The establishment of an area of freedom, security and justice entails the adoption of measures relating to asylum and to refugees and displaced persons. The specific objective of this initiative is to lay down minimum standards for giving temporary protection in the event of a mass influx of displaced persons and promoting a balance of efforts between the Member States in receiving such persons and bearing the consequences thereof. These standards and measures must be capable of being applied through minimum mechanisms and principles in all the Member States. The situation regarding the grant of temporary protection varies from one Member State to another. Minimum Community standards have to be laid down by the kind of action proposed here. They will help to limit the possibility that third-country nationals will decide on their country of destination merely on the basis of the more generous conditions available there. Moreover, solidarity can best be organised at European level. Lastly, the durable absence of European rules on temporary protection would have a negative effect on the effectiveness of other instruments relating to asylum.

8.3. *Proportionality*
The form taken by Community action must be the simplest form allowing the proposal to attain its objective and be implemented as efficiently as possible. In this spirit, the legal instrument chosen is a Directive, which allows minimum standards to be laid down while

leaving to the national authorities the choice of the most appropriate form and methods for implementing it in their national legal order and general context. Moreover, the proposed Directive does not set out to lay down standards relating, for example, to the interpretation of the Geneva Convention, subsidiary protection or other aspects of the right of residence of foreign nationals, on which there will be other proposals. It concentrates on a set of minimum standards that are strictly necessary for the coherence of the planned action.

Part 2
MIGRATION

Chapter 2.1
LONG-TERM RESIDENTS

COUNCIL DIRECTIVE 2003/109/EC
of 25 November 2003
concerning the status of third-country nationals who are long-term residents[1]

THE COUNCIL OF THE EUROPEAN UNION,
Having regard to the Treaty establishing the European Community, and in particular Article 63(3) and (4) thereof,
Having regard to the proposal from the Commission,[2]
Having regard to the opinion of the European Parliament,[3]
Having regard to the opinion of the European Economic and Social Committee,[4]
Having regard to the opinion of the Committee of the Regions,[5]

Whereas:

(1) With a view to the progressive establishment of an area of freedom, security and justice, the Treaty establishing the European Community provides both for the adoption of measures aimed at ensuring the free movement of persons, in conjunction with flanking measures relating to external border controls, asylum and immigration, and for the adoption of measures relating to asylum, immigration and safeguarding the rights of third-country nationals.

(2) The European Council, at its special meeting in Tampere on 15 and 16 October 1999, stated that the legal status of third-country nationals should be approximated to that of Member States' nationals and that a person who has resided legally in a Member State for a period of time to be determined and who holds a long-term residence permit should be granted in that Member State a set of uniform rights which are as near as possible to those enjoyed by citizens of the European Union.

(3) This Directive respects the fundamental rights and observes the principles recognised in particular by the European Convention for the Protection of Human Rights and Fundamental Freedoms and by the Charter of Fundamental Rights of the European Union.

(4) The integration of third-country nationals who are long-term residents in the Member States is a key element in promoting economic and social cohesion, a fundamental objective of the Community stated in the Treaty.

---

[1] OJ L 16, 23.1.2004, p. 44.
[2] OJ C 240 E, 28.8.2001, p. 79.
[3] OJ C 284 E, 21.11.2002, p. 102.
[4] OJ C 36, 8.2.2002, p. 59.
[5] OJ C 19, 22.1.2002, p. 18.

(5) Member States should give effect to the provisions of this Directive without discrimination on the basis of sex, race, colour, ethnic or social origin, genetic characteristics, language, religion or beliefs, political or other opinions, membership of a national minority, fortune, birth, disabilities, age or sexual orientation.

(6) The main criterion for acquiring the status of long-term resident should be the duration of residence in the territory of a Member State. Residence should be both legal and continuous in order to show that the person has put down roots in the country. Provision should be made for a degree of flexibility so that account can be taken of circumstances in which a person might have to leave the territory on a temporary basis.

(7) To acquire long-term resident status, third-country nationals should prove that they have adequate resources and sickness insurance, to avoid becoming a burden for the Member State. Member States, when making an assessment of the possession of stable and regular resources may take into account factors such as contributions to the pension system and fulfilment of tax obligations.

(8) Moreover, third-country nationals who wish to acquire and maintain long-term resident status should not constitute a threat to public policy or public security. The notion of public policy may cover a conviction for committing a serious crime.

(9) Economic considerations should not be a ground for refusing to grant long-term resident status and shall not be considered as interfering with the relevant conditions.

(10) A set of rules governing the procedures for the examination of application for long-term resident status should be laid down. Those procedures should be effective and manageable, taking account of the normal workload of the Member States' administrations, as well as being transparent and fair, in order to offer appropriate legal certainty to those concerned. They should not constitute a means of hindering the exercise of the right of residence.

(11) The acquisition of long-term resident status should be certified by residence permits enabling those concerned to prove their legal status easily and immediately. Such residence permits should also satisfy high-level technical standards, notably as regards protection against falsification and counterfeiting, in order to avoid abuses in the Member State in which the status is acquired and in Member States in which the right of residence is exercised.

(12) In order to constitute a genuine instrument for the integration of long-term residents into society in which they live, long-term residents should enjoy equality of treatment with citizens of the Member State in a wide range of economic and social matters, under the relevant conditions defined by this Directive.

(13) With regard to social assistance, the possibility of limiting the benefits for long-term residents to core benefits is to be understood in the sense that this notion covers at least minimum income support, assistance in case of illness, pregnancy, parental assistance and long-term care. The modalities for granting such benefits should be determined by national law.

(14) The Member States should remain subject to the obligation to afford access for minors to the educational system under conditions similar to those laid down for their nationals.

(15) The notion of study grants in the field of vocational training does not cover measures which are financed under social assistance schemes. Moreover, access to study grants may be dependent on the fact that the person who applies for such grants fulfils on his/her own the conditions for acquiring long-term resident status. As regards the issuing of study grants, Member States may take into account the fact that Union citizens may benefit from this same advantage in the country of origin.

(16) Long-term residents should enjoy reinforced protection against expulsion. This protection is based on the criteria determined by the decisions of the European Court of Human Rights. In order to ensure protection against expulsion Member States should provide for effective legal redress.

(17) Harmonisation of the terms for acquisition of long-term resident status promotes mutual confidence between Member States. Certain Member States issue permits with a permanent or unlimited validity on conditions that are more favourable than those provided for by this Directive. The possibility of applying more favourable national provisions is not excluded by the Treaty. However, for the purposes of this Directive, it should be provided that permits issued on more favourable terms do not confer the right to reside in other Member States.

(18) Establishing the conditions subject to which the right to reside in another Member State may be acquired by third-country nationals who are long-term residents should contribute to the effective attainment of an internal market as an area in which the free movement of persons is ensured. It could also constitute a major factor of mobility, notably on the Union's employment market.

(19) Provision should be made that the right of residence in another Member State may be exercised in order to work in an employed or self-employed capacity, to study or even to settle without exercising any form of economic activity.

(20) Family members should also be able to settle in another Member State with a long-term resident in order to preserve family unity and to avoid hindering the exercise of the long-term resident's right of residence. With regard to the family members who may be authorised to accompany or to join the long-term residents, Member States should pay special attention to the situation of disabled adult children and of first-degree relatives in the direct ascending line who are dependent on them.

(21) The Member State in which a long-term resident intends to exercise his/her right of residence should be able to check that the person concerned meets the conditions for residing in its territory. It should also be able to check that the person concerned does not constitute a threat to public policy, public security or public health.

(22) To avoid rendering the right of residence nugatory, long-term residents should enjoy in the second Member State the same treatment, under the conditions defined by this Directive, they enjoy in the Member State in which they acquired the status. The granting of benefits

under social assistance is without prejudice to the possibility for the Member States to withdraw the residence permit if the person concerned no longer fulfils the requirements set by this Directive.

(23) Third-country nationals should be granted the possibility of acquiring long-term resident status in the Member State where they have moved and have decided to settle under comparable conditions to those required for its acquisition in the first Member State.

(24) Since the objectives of the proposed action, namely the determination of terms for granting and withdrawing long-term resident status and the rights pertaining thereto and terms for the exercise of rights of residence by long-term residents in other Member States, cannot be sufficiently achieved by the Member States and can therefore, by reason of the scale and effects of the action, be better achieved by the Community, the Community may adopt measures, in accordance with the principle of subsidiarity as set out in Article 5 of the Treaty. In accordance with the principle of proportionality, as set out in that Article, this Directive does not go beyond what is necessary to achieve those objectives.

(25) In accordance with Articles 1 and 2 of the Protocol on the position of the United Kingdom and Ireland, annexed to the Treaty on European Union and to the Treaty establishing the European Community, and without prejudice to Article 4 of the said Protocol, these Member States are not participating in the adoption of this Directive and are not bound by or subject to its application.

(26) In accordance with Articles 1 and 2 of the Protocol on the position of Denmark, annexed to the Treaty on European Union and the Treaty establishing the European Community, Denmark does not take part in the adoption of this Directive, and is not bound by it or subject to its application,

HAS ADOPTED THIS DIRECTIVE:

CHAPTER I
General Provisions

Article 1
Subject matter

This Directive determines:

(a) the terms for conferring and withdrawing long-term resident status granted by a Member State in relation to third country nationals legally residing in its territory, and the rights pertaining thereto; and

(b) the terms of residence in Member States other than the one which conferred long-term status on them for third-country nationals enjoying that status.

Article 2
Definitions

For the purposes of this Directive:

(a) 'third-country national' means any person who is not a citizen of the Union within the meaning of Article 17(1) of the Treaty;

(b) 'long-term resident' means any third-country national who has long-term resident status as provided for under Articles 4 to 7;

(c) 'first Member State' means the Member State which for the first time granted long-term resident status to a third country national;

(d) 'second Member State' means any Member State other than the one which for the first time granted long-term resident status to a third-country national and in which that long-term resident exercises the right of residence;

(e) 'family members' means the third-country nationals who reside in the Member State concerned in accordance with Council Directive 2003/86/EC of 22 September 2003 on the right to family reunification;[6]

(f) 'refugee' means any third-country national enjoying refugee status within the meaning of the Geneva Convention relating to the Status of Refugees of 28 July 1951, as amended by the Protocol signed in New York on 31 January 1967;

(g) 'long-term resident's EC residence permit' means a residence permit issued by the Member State concerned upon the acquisition of long-term resident status.

Article 3
Scope

1. This Directive applies to third-country nationals residing legally in the territory of a Member State.

2. This Directive does not apply to third-country nationals who:

(a) reside in order to pursue studies or vocational training;

(b) are authorised to reside in a Member State on the basis of temporary protection or have applied for authorisation to reside on that basis and are awaiting a decision on their status;

(c) are authorised to reside in a Member State on the basis of a subsidiary form of protection in accordance with international obligations, national legislation or the practice of the Member States or have applied for authorisation to reside on that basis and are awaiting a decision on their status;

(d) are refugees or have applied for recognition as refugees and whose application has not yet given rise to a final decision;

(e) reside solely on temporary grounds such as au pair or seasonal worker, or as workers posted by a service provider for the purposes of cross-border provision of services, or as cross-border providers of services or in cases where their residence permit has been formally limited;

(f) enjoy a legal status governed by the Vienna Convention on Diplomatic Relations of 1961, the Vienna Convention on Consular Relations of 1963, the Convention of 1969 on

---

[6] OJ L 251, 3.10.2003, p. 12.

Special Missions or the Vienna Convention on the Representation of States in their Relations with International Organisations of a Universal Character of 1975.

3. This Directive shall apply without prejudice to more favourable provisions of:

(a) bilateral and multilateral agreements between the Community or the Community and its Member States, on the one hand, and third countries, on the other;

(b) bilateral agreements already concluded between a Member State and a third country before the date of entry into force of this Directive;

(c) the European Convention on Establishment of 13 December 1955, the European Social Charter of 18 October 1961, the amended European Social Charter of 3 May 1987 and the European Convention on the Legal Status of Migrant Workers of 24 November 1977.

CHAPTER II
Long-term Resident Status in a Member State

Article 4
Duration of residence

1. Member States shall grant long-term resident status to third-country nationals who have resided legally and continuously within its territory for five years immediately prior to the submission of the relevant application.

2. Periods of residence for the reasons referred to in Article3(2)(e) and (f) shall not be taken into account for the purposes of calculating the period referred to in paragraph 1. Regarding the cases covered in Article 3(2)(a), where the third country national concerned has acquired a title of residence which will enable him/her to be granted long-term resident status, only half of the periods of residence for study purposes or vocational training may be taken into account in the calculation of the period referred to in paragraph 1.

3. Periods of absence from the territory of the Member State concerned shall not interrupt the period referred to in paragraph1 and shall be taken into account for its calculation where they are shorter than six consecutive months and do not exceed in total 10 months within the period referred to in paragraph 1.

In cases of specific or exceptional reasons of a temporary nature and in accordance with their national law, Member States may accept that a longer period of absence than that which is referred to in the first subparagraph shall not interrupt the period referred to in paragraph 1. In such cases Member States shall not take into account the relevant period of absence in the calculation of the period referred to in paragraph 1.

By way of derogation from the second subparagraph, Member States may take into account in the calculation of the total period referred to in paragraph 1 periods of absence relating to secondment for employment purposes, including the provision of cross-border services.

Article 5
Conditions for acquiring long-term resident status

1. Member States shall require third-country nationals to provide evidence that they have, for themselves and for dependent family members:

(a) stable and regular resources which are sufficient to maintain himself/herself and the members of his/her family, without recourse to the social assistance system of the Member State concerned. Member States shall evaluate these resources by reference to their nature and regularity and may take into account the level of minimum wages and pensions prior to the application for long-term resident status;

(b) sickness insurance in respect of all risks normally covered for his/her own nationals in the Member State concerned.

2. Member States may require third-country nationals to comply with integration conditions, in accordance with national law.

Article 6
Public policy and public security

1. Member States may refuse to grant long-term resident status on grounds of public policy or public security. When taking the relevant decision, the Member State shall consider the severity or type of offence against public policy or public security, or the danger that emanates from the person concerned, while also having proper regard to the duration of residence and to the existence of links with the country of residence.

2. The refusal referred to in paragraph 1 shall not be founded on economic considerations.

Article 7
Acquisition of long-term resident status

1. To acquire long-term resident status, the third-country national concerned shall lodge an application with the competent authorities of the Member State in which he/she resides. The application shall be accompanied by documentary evidence to be determined by national law that he/she meets the conditions set out in Articles 4 and 5 as well as, if required, by a valid travel document or its certified copy. The evidence referred to in the first subparagraph may also include documentation with regard to appropriate accommodation.

2. The competent national authorities shall give the applicant written notification of the decision as soon as possible and in any event no later than six months from the date on which the application was lodged. Any such decision shall be notified to the third-country national concerned in accordance with the notification procedures under the relevant national legislation. In exceptional circumstances linked to the complexity of the examination of the application, the time limit referred to in the first subparagraph may be extended.

In addition, the person concerned shall be informed about his/ her rights and obligations under this Directive. Any consequences of no decision being taken by the end of the period provided for in this provision shall be determined by national legislation of the relevant Member State.

3. If the conditions provided for by Articles 4 and 5 are met, and the person does not represent a threat within the meaning of Article 6, the Member State concerned shall grant the third-country national concerned long-term resident status.

Article 8
Long-term resident's EC residence permit

1. The status as long-term resident shall be permanent, subject to Article 9.

2. Member States shall issue a long-term resident's EC residence permit to long-term residents. The permit shall be valid at least for five years; it shall, upon application if required, be automatically renewable on expiry.

3. A long-term resident's EC residence permit may be issued in the form of a sticker or of a separate document. It shall be issued in accordance with the rules and standard model as set out in Council Regulation (EC) No. 1030/2002 of 13 June 2002 laying down a uniform format for residence permits for third-country nationals.[7] Under the heading 'type of permit', the Member States shall enter 'long-term resident – EC'.

Article 9
Withdrawal or loss of status

1. Long-term residents shall no longer be entitled to maintain long-term resident status in the following cases:
   (a) detection of fraudulent acquisition of long-term resident status;
   (b) adoption of an expulsion measure under the conditions provided for in Article 12;
   (c) in the event of absence from the territory of the Community for a period of 12 consecutive months.

2. By way of derogation from paragraph 1(c), Member States may provide that absences exceeding 12 consecutive months or for specific or exceptional reasons shall not entail withdrawal or loss of status.

3. Member States may provide that the long-term resident shall no longer be entitled to maintain his/her long-term resident status in cases where he/she constitutes a threat to public policy, in consideration of the seriousness of the offences he/ she committed, but such threat is not a reason for expulsion within the meaning of Article 12.

4. The long-term resident who has resided in another Member State in accordance with Chapter III shall no longer be entitled to maintain his/her long-term resident status acquired in the first Member State when such a status is granted in another Member State pursuant to Article 23.

---

[7] OJ L 157, 15.6.2002, p. 1.

In any case after six years of absence from the territory of the Member State that granted long-term resident status the person concerned shall no longer be entitled to maintain his/her long term resident status in the said Member State.

By way of derogation from the second subparagraph the Member State concerned may provide that for specific reasons the long-term resident shall maintain his/her status in the said Member State in case of absences for a period exceeding six years.

5. With regard to the cases referred to in paragraph 1(c) and in paragraph 4, Member States who have granted the status shall provide for a facilitated procedure for the re-acquisition of long-term resident status.

The said procedure shall apply in particular to the cases of persons that have resided in a second Member State on grounds of pursuit of studies. The conditions and the procedure for the re-acquisition of long-term resident status shall be determined by national law.

6. The expiry of a long-term resident's EC residence permit shall in no case entail withdrawal or loss of long-term resident status.

7. Where the withdrawal or loss of long-term resident status does not lead to removal, the Member State shall authorise the person concerned to remain in its territory if he/she fulfils the conditions provided for in its national legislation and/or if he/she does not constitute a threat to public policy or public security.

Article 10
Procedural guarantees

1. Reasons shall be given for any decision rejecting an application for long-term resident status or withdrawing that status. Any such decision shall be notified to the third-country national concerned in accordance with the notification procedures under the relevant national legislation. The notification shall specify the redress procedures available and the time within which he/she may act.

2. Where an application for long-term resident status is rejected or that status is withdrawn or lost or the residence permit is not renewed, the person concerned shall have the right to mount a legal challenge in the Member State concerned.

Article 11
Equal treatment

1. Long-term residents shall enjoy equal treatment with nationals as regards:
    (a) access to employment and self-employed activity, provided such activities do not entail even occasional involvement in the exercise of public authority, and conditions of employment and working conditions, including conditions regarding dismissal and remuneration;
    (b) education and vocational training, including study grants in accordance with national law;

(c) recognition of professional diplomas, certificates and other qualifications, in accordance with the relevant national procedures;

(d) social security, social assistance and social protection as defined by national law;

(e) tax benefits;

(f) access to goods and services and the supply of goods and services made available to the public and to procedures for obtaining housing;

(g) freedom of association and affiliation and membership of an organisation representing workers or employers or of any organisation whose members are engaged in a specific occupation, including the benefits conferred by such organisations, without prejudice to the national provisions on public policy and public security;

(h) free access to the entire territory of the Member State concerned, within the limits provided for by the national legislation for reasons of security.

2. With respect to the provisions of paragraph 1, points (b), (d), (e), (f) and (g), the Member State concerned may restrict equal treatment to cases where the registered or usual place of residence of the long-term resident, or that of family members for whom he/she claims benefits, lies within the territory of the Member State concerned.

3. Member States may restrict equal treatment with nationals in the following cases:

(a) Member States may retain restrictions to access to employment or self-employed activities in cases where, in accordance with existing national or Community legislation, these activities are reserved to nationals, EU or EEA citizens;

(b) Member States may require proof of appropriate language proficiency for access to education and training. Access to university may be subject to the fulfilment of specific educational prerequisites.

4. Member States may limit equal treatment in respect of social assistance and social protection to core benefits.

5. Member States may decide to grant access to additional benefits in the areas referred to in paragraph 1. Member States may also decide to grant equal treatment with regard to areas not covered in paragraph 1.

Article 12
Protection against expulsion

1. Member States may take a decision to expel a long-term resident solely where he/she constitutes an actual and sufficiently serious threat to public policy or public security.

2. The decision referred to in paragraph 1 shall not be founded on economic considerations.

3. Before taking a decision to expel a long-term resident, Member States shall have regard to the following factors:

(a) the duration of residence in their territory;

(b) the age of the person concerned;

(c) the consequences for the person concerned and family members;

(d) links with the country of residence or the absence of links with the country of origin.

4. Where an expulsion decision has been adopted, a judicial redress procedure shall be available to the long-term resident in the Member State concerned.

5. Legal aid shall be given to long-term residents lacking adequate resources, on the same terms as apply to nationals of the State where they reside.

Article 13
More favourable national provisions

Member States may issue residence permits of permanent or unlimited validity on terms that are more favourable than those laid down by this Directive. Such residence permits shall not confer the right of residence in the other Member States as provided by Chapter III of this Directive.

CHAPTER III
Residence in the Other Member States

Article 14
Principle

1. A long-term resident shall acquire the right to reside in the territory of Member States other than the one which granted him/her the long-term residence status, for a period exceeding three months, provided that the conditions set out in this chapter are met.

2. A long-term resident may reside in a second Member State on the following grounds:
    (a) exercise of an economic activity in an employed or self-employed capacity;
    (b) pursuit of studies or vocational training;
    (c) other purposes.

3. In cases of an economic activity in an employed or self-employed capacity referred to in paragraph 2(a), Member States may examine the situation of their labour market and apply their national procedures regarding the requirements for, respectively, filling a vacancy, or for exercising such activities.

For reasons of labour market policy, Member States may give preference to Union citizens, to third-country nationals, when provided for by Community legislation, as well as to third country nationals who reside legally and receive unemployment benefits in the Member State concerned.

4. By way of derogation from the provisions of paragraph 1, Member States may limit the total number of persons entitled to be granted right of residence, provided that such limitations are already set out for the admission of third-country nationals in the existing legislation at the time of the adoption of this Directive.

5. This chapter does not concern the residence of long-term residents in the territory of the Member States:
    (a) as employed workers posted by a service provider for the purposes of cross-border provision of services;

(b) as providers of cross-border services. Member States may decide, in accordance with national law, the conditions under which long-term residents who wish to move to a second Member State with a view to exercising an economic activity as seasonal workers may reside in that Member State. Cross-border workers may also be subject to specific provisions of national law.

6. This Chapter is without prejudice to the relevant Community legislation on social security with regard to third country nationals.

Article 15
Conditions for residence in a second Member State

1. As soon as possible and no later than three months after entering the territory of the second Member State, the long-term resident shall apply to the competent authorities of that Member State for a residence permit.

Member States may accept that the long-term resident submits the application for a residence permit to the competent authorities of the second Member State while still residing in the territory of the first Member State.

2. Member States may require the persons concerned to provide evidence that they have:
(a) stable and regular resources which are sufficient to maintain themselves and the members of their families, without recourse to the social assistance of the Member State concerned. For each of the categories referred to in Article 14(2), Member States shall evaluate these resources by reference to their nature and regularity and may take into account the level of minimum wages and pensions;
(b) sickness insurance covering all risks in the second Member State normally covered for its own nationals in the Member State concerned.

3. Member States may require third-country nationals to comply with integration measures, in accordance with national law. This condition shall not apply where the third-country nationals concerned have been required to comply with integration conditions in order to be granted long-term resident status, in accordance with the provisions of Article 5(2). Without prejudice to the second subparagraph, the persons concerned may be required to attend language courses.

4. The application shall be accompanied by documentary evidence, to be determined by national law, that the persons concerned meets the relevant conditions, as well as by their long-term resident permit and a valid travel document or their certified copies.

The evidence referred to in the first subparagraph may also include documentation with regard to appropriate accommodation. In particular:
(a) in case of exercise of an economic activity the second Member State may require the persons concerned to provide evidence:
(i) if they are in an employed capacity, that they have an employment contract, a statement by the employer that they are hired or a proposal for an employment contract, under the conditions provided for by national legislation. Member States shall determine which of the said forms of evidence is required;

(ii) if they are in a self-employed capacity, that they have the appropriate funds which are needed, in accordance with national law, to exercise an economic activity in such capacity, presenting the necessary documents and permits;

(b) in case of study or vocational training the second Member State may require the persons concerned to provide evidence of enrolment in an accredited establishment in order to pursue studies or vocational training.

Article 16
Family members

1. When the long-term resident exercises his/her right of residence in a second Member State and when the family was already constituted in the first Member State, the members of his/her family, who fulfil the conditions referred to in Article 4(1) of Directive 2003/86/EC shall be authorised to accompany or to join the long-term resident.

2. When the long-term resident exercises his/her right of residence in a second Member State and when the family was already constituted in the first Member State, the members of his/her family, other than those referred to in Article 4(1) of Directive 2003/86/EC may be authorised to accompany or to join the long-term resident.

3. With respect to the submission of the application for a residence permit, the provisions of Article 15(1) apply.

4. The second Member State may require the family members concerned to present with their application for a residence permit:

(a) their long-term resident's EC residence permit or residence permit and a valid travel document or their certified copies;

(b) evidence that they have resided as members of the family of the long-term resident in the first Member State;

(c) evidence that they have stable and regular resources which are sufficient to maintain themselves without recourse to the social assistance of the Member State concerned or that the long-term resident has such resources and insurance for them, as well as sickness insurance covering all risks in the second Member State. Member States shall evaluate these resources by reference to their nature and regularity and may take into account the level of minimum wages and pensions.

5. Where the family was not already constituted in the first Member State, Directive 2003/86/EC shall apply.

Article 17
Public policy and public security

1. Member States may refuse applications for residence from long-term residents or their family members where the person concerned constitutes a threat to public policy or public security.

When taking the relevant decision, the Member State shall consider the severity or type of offence against public policy or public security committed by the long-term resident or his/her family member(s), or the danger that emanates from the person concerned.

2. The decision referred to in paragraph 1 shall not be based on economic considerations.

Article 18
Public health

1. Member States may refuse applications for residence from long-term residents or their family members where the person concerned constitutes a threat to public health.

2. The only diseases that may justify a refusal to allow entry or the right of residence in the territory of the second Member State shall be the diseases as defined by the relevant applicable instruments of the World Health Organisation's and such other infectious or contagious parasite-based diseases as are the subject of protective provisions in relation to nationals in the host country. Member States shall not introduce new more restrictive provisions or practices.

3. Diseases contracted after the first residence permit was issued in the second Member State shall not justify a refusal to renew the permit or expulsion from the territory.

4. A Member State may require a medical examination, for persons to whom this Directive applies, in order to certify that they do not suffer from any of the diseases referred to in paragraph 2. Such medical examinations, which may be free of charge, shall not be performed on a systematic basis.

Article 19
Examination of applications and issue of a residence permit

1. The competent national authorities shall process applications within four months from the date that these have been lodged.

If an application is not accompanied by the documentary evidence listed in Articles 15 and 16, or in exceptional circumstances linked with the complexity of the examination of the application, the time limit referred to in the first subparagraph may be extended for a period not exceeding three months. In such cases the competent national authorities shall inform the applicant thereof.

2. If the conditions provided for in Articles 14, 15 and 16 are met, then, subject to the provisions relating to public policy, public security and public health in Articles 17 and 18, the second Member State shall issue the long-term resident with a renewable residence permit. This residence permit shall, upon application, if required, be renewable on expiry. The second Member State shall inform the first Member State of its decision.

3. The second Member State shall issue members of the long-term resident's family with renewable residence permits valid for the same period as the permit issued to the long-term resident.

Article 20
Procedural guarantees

1. Reasons shall be given for any decision rejecting an application for a residence permit. It shall be notified to the third country national concerned in accordance with the notification procedures under the relevant national legislation. The notification shall specify the possible redress procedures available and the time limit for taking action.

Any consequences of no decision being taken by the end of the period referred to in Article 19(1) shall be determined by the national legislation of the relevant Member State.

2. Where an application for a residence permit is rejected, or the permit is not renewed or is withdrawn, the person concerned shall have the right to mount a legal challenge in the Member State concerned.

Article 21
Treatment granted in the second Member State

1. As soon as they have received the residence permit provided for by Article 19 in the second Member State, long-term residents shall in that Member State enjoy equal treatment in the areas and under the conditions referred to in Article 11.

2. Long-term residents shall have access to the labour market in accordance with the provisions of paragraph 1.

Member States may provide that the persons referred to in Article 14(2)(a) shall have restricted access to employed activities different than those for which they have been granted their residence permit under the conditions set by national legislation for a period not exceeding 12 months.

Member States may decide in accordance with national law the conditions under which the persons referred to in Article 14(2)(b) or (c) may have access to an employed or self-employed activity.

3. As soon as they have received the residence permit provided for by Article 19 in the second Member State, members of the family of the long-term resident shall in that Member State enjoy the rights listed in Article 14 of Directive 2003/86/EC.

Article 22
Withdrawal of residence permit and obligation to readmit

1. Until the third-country national has obtained long-term resident status, the second Member State may decide to refuse to renew or to withdraw the resident permit and to oblige the person concerned and his/her family members, in accordance with the procedures provided for by national law, including removal procedures, to leave its territory in the following cases:
    (a) on grounds of public policy or public security as defined in Article 17;
    (b) where the conditions provided for in Articles 14, 15 and 16 are no longer met;

(c) where the third-country national is not lawfully residing in the Member State concerned.

2. If the second Member State adopts one of the measures referred to in paragraph 1, the first Member State shall immediately readmit without formalities the long-term resident and his/her family members. The second Member State shall notify the first Member State of its decision.

3. Until the third-country national has obtained long-term resident status and without prejudice to the obligation to readmit referred to in paragraph 2, the second Member State may adopt a decision to remove the third-country national from the territory of the Union, in accordance with and under the guarantees of Article 12, on serious grounds of public policy or public security.

In such cases, when adopting the said decision the second Member State shall consult the first Member State. When the second Member State adopts a decision to remove the third-country national concerned, it shall take all the appropriate measures to effectively implement it. In such cases the second Member State shall provide to the first Member State appropriate information with respect to the implementation of the removal decision.

4. Removal decisions may not be accompanied by a permanent ban on residence in the cases referred to in paragraph 1(b) and (c).

5. The obligation to readmit referred to in paragraph 2 shall be without prejudice to the possibility of the long-term resident and his/her family members moving to a third Member State.

Article 23
Acquisition of long-term resident status in the second Member State

1. Upon application, the second Member State shall grant long-term residents the status provided for by Article 7, subject to the provisions of Articles 3, 4, 5 and 6. The second Member State shall notify its decision to the first Member State.

2. The procedure laid down in Article 7 shall apply to the presentation and examination of applications for long-term resident status in the second Member State. Article 8 shall apply for the issuance of the residence permit. Where the application is rejected, the procedural guarantees provided for by Article 10 shall apply.

CHAPTER IV
Final Provisions

Article 24
Report and rendez-vous clause

Periodically, and for the first time no later than 23 January 2011, the Commission shall report to the European Parliament and to the Council on the application of this Directive in the Member States and shall propose such amendments as may be necessary. These proposals for amendments shall be made by way of priority in relation to Articles 4, 5, 9, 11 and to Chapter III.

Article 25
Contact points

Member States shall appoint contact points who will be responsible for receiving and transmitting the information referred to in Article 19(2), Article 22(2) and Article 23(1). Member States shall provide appropriate cooperation in the exchange of the information and documentation referred to in the first paragraph.

Article 26
Transposition

Member States shall bring into force the laws, regulations and administrative provisions necessary to comply with this Directive by 23 January 2006 at the latest. They shall forthwith inform the Commission thereof.

When Member States adopt these measures, they shall contain a reference to this Directive or shall be accompanied by such reference on the occasion of their official publication. The methods of making such reference shall be laid down by Member States.

Article 27
Entry into force

This Directive shall enter into force on the day of its publication in the Official Journal of the European Union.

Article 28
Addressees

This Directive is addressed to the Member States in accordance with the Treaty establishing the European Community.

EXPLANATORY MEMORANDUM

1. Context

1.1 The European Council, at its special meeting in Tampere on 15 and 16 October 1999, acknowledged the need to ensure fair treatment of third-country nationals who reside legally on the territory of its Member States. It declared that a more vigorous integration policy should aim at granting them rights and obligations comparable to those of EU citizens.[8] It should also enhance non-discrimination in economic, social and cultural life and develop measures against racism and xenophobia.

---

[8] Presidency Conclusions, point 18.

1.2. The European Council also acknowledged that the legal status of third-country nationals should be approximated to that of Member States' nationals, and decided to pay special attention to the situation of third-country nationals settled on a long-term basis. It declared that a person who has resided legally in a Member State for a period of time to be determined and who holds a long-term residence permit, should be granted in that Member State a set of uniform rights which are as near as possible to those enjoyed by EU citizens; e.g. the right to reside, receive education and work as an employee or self-employed person, as well as the principle of non-discrimination *vis-à-vis* citizens of the State of residence. It endorsed the objective that long-term legally resident third-country nationals be offered the opportunity to obtain the nationality of the Member State in which they are resident.[9]

1.3. In December 1999, when presenting its first initiative relating to legal immigration – the proposal for a Council Directive on the right to family reunification[10] – the Commission announced that it was planning to commence and pursue work on legal immigration by way of follow-up to the conclusions of the Tampere European Council so as to exploit all the possibilities offered by Title IV of the Treaty establishing the European Community. It stated its intention of addressing the question of the legal situation of third-country nationals holding a long-term resident's permit and its desire to give full effect to Article 63(4) of the Treaty establishing the European Community relating to the rights of third-country nationals residing legally in a Member State to reside in another Member State.

1.4. This intention was also declared in the Scoreboard to review progress on the creation of an area of freedom, security and justice in the European Union, approved by the Council on 27 March 2000.[11] The Commission presented the Council (JAI) meeting of 30 November and 1 December 2000.[12] The intention was again confirmed in the Communication on a Community immigration policy[13] presented by the Commission in November 2000, where it looks at all the questions related to immigration in aggregate terms, given the complexity of immigration policy and its impact on a wide range of fields (social, economic, legal and cultural).

1.5. With this proposal, the Commission is giving practical expression to its intention and to its commitment to a matter that is crucial in terms of securing the genuine integration of third-country nationals settled on a long-term basis in the territory of the Member States. The proposal is part of a broader effort on immigration which the Commission has been making for several years now and which is worth recalling here. Before the Amsterdam Treaty entered into force in 1998, the Commission presented its proposal for a Council Regulation (EC) amending Regulation (EEC) No 1408/71 on the application of social security schemes to employed persons and their families moving within the Community to extend it to third-country nationals.[14]

---

[9] Presidency Conclusions, point 21.
[10] COM(1999)638 final, 1.12.1999, adopted as Council Directive (2003) 86, OJ L 251/12, 3.10.2003.
[11] COM(2000)167 final/2, 13.4.2000.
[12] COM(2000)782 final, 30.11.2000.
[13] COM(2000)757 final, 22.11.2000.
[14] OJ C 6, 10.1.1998 p. 15.

In 1999, it presented a proposal extending the freedom to provide cross-border services to third-country nationals established within the Community,[15] along with a proposal for a Directive on the posting of workers who are third-country nationals for the provision of cross-border services.[16] These three proposals are now on the Council's table. Since the Amsterdam Treaty came into force, the Commission has presented the proposal for a Directive on the right to family reunification,[17] the European Parliament gave its Opinion on 6 September, and the Commission immediately responded with an amended proposal,[18] now also on the Council's table.

1.6. The Charter of Fundamental Rights of the European Union,[19] solemnly proclaimed by the European Parliament, the Council of the Union and the European Commission at Nice in December 2000, should also be mentioned in this context. The Charter constitutes the very essence of the European acquis in terms of fundamental rights.

Respecting the principle of universalism, most of the rights enumerated in the Charter are conferred on all persons regardless of their nationality or place of residence; the Charter thus enshrines a number of rights conferred on the nationals of the Member States and on third-country nationals residing there. To that extent it reflects the European Union's traditions and positive attitude to equal treatment of citizens of the Union and third-country nationals.

1.7. The Commission has also considered the question of the rights inherent in freedom of movement and residence for citizens of the Union with a view to matching them more closely to the new legal and political environment flowing from citizenship of the Union. The Commission's intention is that the movement of citizens between Member States should be on much the same basis as when citizens change their residence or job within their own Member State. Supplementary administrative or statutory obligations should be kept to the minimum needed by the specific fact of being a non-national. To that end, as it undertook in the communication on the follow-up to the recommendations of the High-Level Panel on the Free Movement of Persons[20] and in accordance with the Scoreboard, the Commission will be presenting a fresh proposal for a Directive recasting the existing legislation in a single instrument with the primary objective of facilitating freedom of movement and residence, reducing bureaucracy, better regulating the status of family members of citizens of the Union and defining the possibilities for refusing or withdrawing the right of residence. The proposal will be brought forward in the first half of 2001.

2. International legal context

2.1. Internationally, ILO Convention No. 97 introduces obligations to secure equal treatment for migrant workers in a wide range of respects and to ensure security of residence after five

---

[15] OJ C 67, 10.3.1999, p. 17; amended proposal, OJ C 311 E, 31.10.2000, p. 197.

[16] OJ C 67, 10.3.1999, p. 12; amended proposal, OJ C 311 E, 31.10.2000, p. 187.

[17] COM(1999)638 final, 1.12.1999, adopted as Council Directive (2003) 86, OJ L 251/12, 3.10.2003.

[18] COM(2000)624 final, 10.10.2000.

[19] OJ C 364, 18.12.2000, p. 1.

[20] COM(1998)403 final, 1.7.1998.

years, even where an employment contract is terminated. In 1990 the United Nations adopted an International Convention on the Protection of the Rights of all Migrant Workers and Members of their Families, which is not yet in force. It has not yet been ratified by any of the Union Member States.

2.2. At European regional level, the Social Charter of 1961 applies to all the Member States, and the 1996 Charter to only some of them. Migrant workers enjoy equal treatment with nationals in economic and social matters. They also enjoy all employment protection rights. The Council of Europe's European Convention on Establishment, signed in 1955, applies solely on the basis of reciprocity, but it constitutes a valuable precedent since it secures equal treatment in a variety of respects. Migrant workers are offered security of residence after five years, and other migrants enjoy this after ten years. It also creates a link between the duration of residence and stronger protection against expulsion and offers major procedural guarantees. Lastly, the European Convention on the legal status of migrant workers of 1977 supplies a useful basis for the protection of civil, economic and social rights of migrants. But this Convention has been ratified by only six Member States.

2.3. Recently, the Committee of Ministers of the Council of Europe adopted a Recommendation on the security of residence of long-term immigrants. Long-term status should be granted to third-country nationals after five years' residence, or at any rate no more than ten years. They would then enjoy equal treatment with nationals in wide-ranging fields such as access to employment, housing, social protection and participation in local public life. They should enjoy enhanced protection against expulsion in proportion to the duration of their residence in the territory, having regard to the decisions given by the European Court of Human Rights.

3. **The national situation**

3.1. The national legislation of all the Union Member States provides for specific and more favourable legal treatment of third-country nationals who have resided in their territory for some time. In fourteen of them this is established by statute; in the other by administrative practice. Third-country nationals must first show that they have been settled on a long-term basis in the host Member State, then that State gives them the means of fully integrating into their new society by conferring a series of rights on them. While the legitimacy of a specific status for long-term residents is apparently uncontested, the criteria for its acquisition and the scope and determination of the rights conferred vary from one State to another. The study undertaken by the University of Nijmegen at the Commission's request[21] highlighted the fact that, while national bodies of legislation have their own specific features, there are numerous points of convergence, in particular they all take account of the length of time for which links have been established in the host country and how close they are.

3.2. The status of long-term residents in the Member States is often evidenced by a residence permit that is either permanent or of unlimited validity or else by an establishment permit.

---

[21] K. Groenendijk, E. Guild, R. Barzilay, The legal status of third-country nationals who are long-term residents in a Member State of the European Union, University of Nijmegen, April 2000.

The first criterion for the acquisition of such secure residence permits is the period of legal residence of the third-country nationals in the territory.

The period varies from two to fifteen years; eight Member States grant long-term resident status after five years' continuous legal residence. For members of a long-term resident's family or for refugees, certain Member States grant the status after shorter periods of residence. Other criteria are also applied: the persons concerned must not constitute an actual threat to public order or national security and in general must have an adequate income or be employed. Where these criteria are met, long-term resident status is automatic in eleven Member States; in the others, the administration has a degree of discretion.

3.3. The period of validity of the status and of the residence permit that goes with it tends to vary. The status is generally permanent, whereas the permit must be renewed. Certain States, at the time of renewal, check whether the conditions on the basis of which the status was acquired are still valid. But this is a minority position, since in most Member States the residence permit is renewed automatically. Where the status is withheld, the Member States provide for administrative or judicial redress procedures.

3.4. In thirteen Member States permanent residence status entails unrestricted access to the employment market. Long-term residents have access to social benefits and social assistance on the same terms as nationals in most Member States. Some States reserve access to social assistance for their nationals alone. Access to both primary and secondary education is on a non-discriminatory basis in most Member States. But university tuition fees may be higher and access to study grants may be more difficult for third-country nationals, even if they are long-term residents.

3.5. Five Member States provide that long-term residents may vote and stand as candidates at municipal elections. Two others confer this right on the basis of the principle of reciprocity.

3.6. Regarding withdrawal of the status, all the Member States provide for it in the event of fraud or prolonged absence from the territory. The great majority do not consider unemployment or inadequate resources as valid grounds for withdrawal.

3.7. Permanent or long-term resident status is a status that helps to offer those concerned legal certainty, so that they enjoy enhanced protection against expulsion. The longer the period of residence, the greater the violation of public order must be. Certain Member States operate a kind of tariff system, matching the term of imprisonment to the period of residence. Others confine expulsion orders to certain offences (such as drug-trafficking, organised crime, terrorism). And certain States refer to the criteria of Council Directive 64/221/EEC on the coordination of special measures concerning the movement and residence of foreign nationals which are justified on grounds of public policy, public security or public health[22] or those used by the European Court of Human Rights in decisions on Article 8 of the European Convention for the Protection of Human Rights and Fundamental Freedoms. In some Member States, certain categories of long-term residents enjoy absolute protection

---

[22] OJ 56, 4.4.1964, p. 850/64.

against expulsion (persons born in the territory of the Member State, persons resident for more than twenty years, minors).

4. Work in the European Union context

4.1. The special treatment available for third-country nationals who were long-term residents was already visible in the European Union before the entry into force of the Amsterdam Treaty. In 1996 the Council, on a French initiative, adopted a Resolution on the status of third-country nationals residing on a long-term basis in the territory of the Member States,[23] which was the first attempt to approximate national legislation in this field. Apart from the fact that it had no mandatory legal force, the Resolution generated no progress beyond a stock-taking of existing national legislation. In its report to the Commission dated 18 March 1997, the High-Level Group on the free movement of persons stated that the situation of third-country nationals residing legally in a Member State could be improved. In the communication of 1 July 1997 (*supra*), the Commission took stock of measures taken in response to the recommendation, highlighting its proposal of 12 November 1997 for amendment of Regulation (EEC) No. 1408/71 as regards its extension to nationals of third countries.[24]

4.2. In 1997, the Commission presented a proposal for a Convention on the admission of third-country nationals.[25] It provided for a special status for third-country nationals residing on a long-term basis, including the possibility of settling in another Member State to study or work. The aim was to provide input for a debate on immigration questions prior to the entry into force of the Amsterdam Treaty and the large-scale institutional changes flowing from it. In an introductory statement the Commission announced its intention of presenting a new draft in the form of a Directive as soon as the new treaty was in force. The European Parliament's Opinion on the proposal for an admission Convention[26] wished the situation of long-term residents to be treated separately from the instruments on the admission of third-country nationals.

4.3. On 5 and 6 October 2000 the French Presidency organised a seminar in Paris on the integration of third-country nationals residing legally. The purpose of the seminar was to launch a debate between representatives of the Member States and the Community institutions, experts from international and non-governmental organisations and academic circles on means of promoting a vigorous policy on the integration of third-country nationals in the European Union. The study on the legal status of long-term residents conducted by the University of Nijmegen at the Commission's request was presented and discussed there.

4.4. Following this seminar, the French Presidency presented a draft set of Council conclusions on the conditions for harmonising the status of third-country nationals resident on a long-term basis. Initial technical discussions in working parties highlighted the Member States' interest in the topic but, mainly for timetable reasons, no agreement emerged. The Ministers

---

[23] Resolution of 4 March 1996, OJ C 80, 18.3.1996.

[24] OJ C 6, 10.1.1998, p. 15.

[25] OJ C 337, 7.11.1997, p. 9.

[26] Minutes of sitting of 10 February 1999, PE 276.722.

discussed the question at the Council meeting (Justice and Home Affairs) on 30 November and 1 December 2000.

4.5. During the preparatory work on the proposal, the Office of the United Nations Commissioner for Refugees, non-governmental organisations were sounded out. As a result of these soundings, the results of the Paris seminar and the Council's discussions on the French Presidency's draft Conclusions, the Commission had an overview of the question of the status of long-term residents.

5. Objectives and overview of the proposal

5.1. As the Communication on Community immigration policy[27] states, 'it is ... essential to create a welcoming society and to recognise that integration is a two-way process involving adaptation on the part of both the immigrant and of the host society. The European Union is by its very nature a pluralistic society enriched by a variety of cultural and social traditions, which will in the future become even more diverse.

There must, therefore be respect for cultural and social differences but also of our fundamental shared principles and values: respect for human rights and human dignity, appreciation of the value of pluralism and the recognition that membership of society is based on a series of rights but brings with it a number of responsibilities for all of its members be they nationals or migrants. The provision of equality with respect to conditions of work and access to services, together with the granting of civic and political rights to longer-term migrant residents brings with it such responsibilities and promotes integration'.

5.2. To permit fair treatment of third-country nationals and promote their full integration, as called for by the Tampere European Council, the Commission considers that there should be a common status of long-term resident so that all third-country nationals residing legally can acquire it and enjoy it on much the same terms in all the Member States. Criteria must therefore be determined for the acquisition of the status and the rights that go with it, on the basis of equal treatment with citizens of the Union in the spirit of the Tampere conclusions. For the sake of certainty as to the law governing third-country nationals, it is essential that acquisition of the status should not be left to Member States' discretion where the conditions are actually met.

5.3. The status will be available to all third-country nationals who reside legally in the territory of a Member State on a long-term basis. This category covers refugees with recognised status under the Geneva Convention and third-country nationals who are members of the family of a citizen of the Union. The only excluded categories are those who are not intending to actually settle, in particular persons resident in order to study or to engage in a seasonal occupation and those enjoying temporary protection. Lastly, persons enjoying a subsidiary or additional form of protection are not within the scope of the proposal as these concepts have not been harmonised in the Community.

---

[27] COM(2000)757 final, 22.11.2000.

5.4. Long-term residents enjoying the status will enjoy equal treatment in a series of respects, ranging from access to employment and self-employed activity to education and vocational training and social protection and assistance. They will also have enhanced protection against expulsion.

5.5. Although the importance of voting rights and access to nationality for the integration of third-country nationals who are long-term residents is now generally acknowledged, the EC Treaty provides no specific legal basis for it. On voting rights, Community involvement is provided for only as regards municipal and European elections and only for citizens of the Union. Access to nationality is a matter reserved solely for national powers. This proposal accordingly does not address these two aspects, though it is true that the Tampere European Council endorsed 'the objective that long-term legally resident third-country nationals be offered the opportunity to obtain the nationality of the Member State in which they are resident'.[28]

5.6. The Commission considers that full integration also entails the right for long-term residents to reside in other Member States and that the time has come to implement Article 63(4) of the EC Treaty. A genuine area of freedom, security and justice, a fundamental objective of the European Union, is unthinkable without a degree of mobility for third-country nationals residing there legally, and particularly for those residing on a long-term basis. It must also be stressed that Article 45 of the Charter of Fundamental Rights of the European Union confirms that 'freedom of movement and residence may be granted, in accordance with the Treaty establishing the European Community, to nationals of third-countries legally resident in the territory of a Member State'.

5.7. The Commission is aware of the importance of the task it has set itself; there are no relevant provisions in Community law as it stands. Third-country nationals holding a residence permit do not currently have the right of residence in another Member State. The Schengen acquis merely gives them the right to move for up to three months in the Member States where the Schengen acquis applies. Free movement does not entail the possibility of residing in another Member State for study purposes. The proposal to extend freedom to provide cross-border services to third-country nationals established in the Community does not address the question of residence but only freedom to provide services. Consequently, third-country nationals wishing to settle in another Member State will have to go through all the formalities imposed on first-time immigrants and will not be eligible for favourable treatment, even if they are long-term residents in a Member State.

5.8. This situation is discriminatory in relation to citizens of the Union who, under the Treaty and the current secondary legislation, enjoy the freedom of movement of persons. Nor does it match the demands of an employment market that is in a process of far-reaching change, where greater flexibility is needed. The evolution of the employment market in the Union is highlighting employment shortages in certain sectors of the economy. Third-country nationals who are long-term residents may be ready and willing to relocate either in order to put their vocational skills to work in another Member State or to escape unemployment in the Member State where they reside. The mobility of long-term residents can thus make for better utilisation

---

[28] Presidency Conclusions, point 21.

of employment reserves available in different Member States. At a time when several Member States are engaging in international competition to attract specialists, notably in information technology, the possibility of acquiring long-term resident status and therefore of residing in any of the Member States will make the prospect of settling in the European Union on a long-term basis all the more attractive.

5.9. The acquisition of long-term resident status is an essential instrument for integrating persons who are planning to settle on a long-term basis in the Union. This proposal for a Directive preserves a very tight link between actual legal residence in a Member State and acquisition of long-term resident status; putting down roots in a Member State is regarded as a *sine qua non* for acquiring the status provided for by the Directive, which establishes equal treatment with nationals of the Member State in a wide range of aspects of economic and social life and offers the possibility of residing in other Union Member States. There are admittedly categories of third-country nationals, such as researchers, sportsmen and women or artists, who, without wishing to settle on a long-term basis, may wish to enjoy mobility in the Member States. Securing that mobility is a challenge that the Union must take up if it is to remain internationally competitive and be attractive to such categories. This proposal is a first step towards giving effect to Article 63(4) of the EC Treaty, which can be used as a legal basis for other specific instruments for the mobility of third-country nationals not wishing to settle on a long-term basis. In its proposals on the admission of third-country nationals for the purposes of working in an employed or self-employed capacity, studying or vocational training or non-gainful activities, the Commission will provide as necessary for appropriate forms of mobility between Union Member States.

6.   Choice of legal basis

6.1. The choice of legal basis is consistent with the changes made to the EC Treaty by the Amsterdam Treaty, which entered into force on 1 May 1999. Article 63(3)(a) of the EC Treaty provides that the Council is to adopt measures relating to 'conditions of entry and residence, and standards on procedures for the issue by Member States of long-term visas and residence permits, including those for the purpose of family reunion'. Article 63(4) provides that the Council is to adopt 'measures defining the rights and conditions under which nationals of third countries who are legally resident in a Member State may reside in other Member States'.

6.2. These Articles constitute the legal basis for a proposal laying down the conditions for acquisition of long-term resident status by third-country nationals who reside in the territory of a Member State and the conditions on which persons holding that status enjoy the right of residence in another Member State.

6.3. The proposal for a Directive must be adopted by the procedure of Article 67 of the Treaty: the Council acts unanimously on a proposal from the Commission or at the initiative of the Member States after consulting the European Parliament. Title IV of the EC Treaty does not apply to the United Kingdom and Ireland unless those Member States decide otherwise in accordance with the Protocol on the position of the United Kingdom and Ireland annexed to the Treaties. Likewise, Title IV does not apply to Denmark by virtue of the Protocol on the position of Denmark, annexed to the Treaties.

7. Subsidiarity and proportionality

7.1. The new Title IV on visas, asylum, immigration and other policies related to free movement of persons, inserted in the Treaty establishing the European Community, confers powers on these matters on the European Community. These powers must be exercised in accordance with Article 5 of the EC Treaty, i.e. if and in so far as the objectives of the proposed action cannot be sufficiently achieved by the Member States and can therefore, by reason of the scale or effects of the proposed action, be better achieved by the Community. The proposed Directive respects these criteria.

7.2. Subsidiarity

The primary objective of this initiative is to grant a status to third-country nationals who are long-term residents in the territory of a Member State in accordance with criteria that are common to all the Member States. This objective satisfies the requirements of the establishment of an area of freedom, security and justice, which entails the adoption of common rules governing immigration policy. Common criteria can be determined only at Community level. The second objective is to determine the conditions in which such persons may exercise their right of residence in another Member State. This entails determining rules that are common to all the Member States to ensure that the right of residence is effective; such rules can be determined only at Community level.

7.3. Proportionality

The form of Community action must be the simplest that will enable the objective of the proposal to be attained and effectively implemented. In this spirit, the legal instrument chosen is a Directive, laying down general principles but leaving the Member States to which it is addressed the choice of the most appropriate form and methods for giving effect to these principles in their national legal system and general context. The proposed Directive merely determines the conditions for the acquisition of long-term resident status having effect at European level, since the person enjoying it will have the right of residence in another Member State, leaving it up to the Member States, if they wish, to determine more favourable conditions for the acquisition of a permanent status applying solely in the national context.

Chapter 2.2
EMPLOYMENT AND SELF-EMPLOYMENT (proposal)

COUNCIL DIRECTIVE
On the conditions of entry and residence of third-country nationals for the purpose of paid employment and self-employment economic activities[1]

THE COUNCIL OF THE EUROPEAN UNION,
Having regard to the Treaty establishing the European Community, and in particular Article 63 (3)(a) thereof,
Having regard to the proposal from the Commission,
Having regard to the opinion of the European Parliament,
Having regard to the opinion of the Economic and Social Committee,
Having regard to the opinion of the Committee of the Regions,

Whereas:

(1) With a view to the progressive establishment of an area of freedom, security and justice, Article 63(3) (a) of the Treaty provides that the Council is to adopt measures on immigration policy relating to the conditions of residence, and standards on procedures for the issue by Member States of residence permits.

(2) The European Council, at its special meeting in Tampere on 15 and 16 October 1999, acknowledged the need for approximation of national legislation on the conditions for admission and residence of third-country nationals and it requested to this end rapid decisions by the Council, on the basis of proposals by the Commission.

(3) Regulation of immigration for the purpose of exercising activities as an employed or self-employed person is a cornerstone of immigration policy and the development of a coherent Community immigration policy could not succeed without specifically addressing this issue at Community level.

(4) All Member States have regulated access of third-country nationals to work with detailed national administrative rules. If it is to operate successfully, a Community policy in this field should be put in place progressively. As a first step the aim should be to lay down certain common definitions, criteria and procedures, which give a common legal frame to the discretion of Member States.

(5) The newly established Community rules should be based on concepts, which have already been successfully applied in Member States.

---

[1] COM (2001)386 final.

(6) In an increasingly global labour market and faced with shortage of skilled labour in certain sectors of the labour market the Community should reinforce its competitiveness to recruit and attract third-country workers, when needed. This should be facilitated by administrative simplification and by facilitating access to relevant information. Transparent and harmonised rules on the conditions under which third country nationals may enter and stay in the Community to pursue economic activities, and their rights, should be laid down.

(7) Provision for a single national application procedure leading to one combined title, encompassing both residence and work permit within one administrative act, should contribute to simplifying and harmonising the diverging rules currently applicable in Member States.

(8) The chief criterion for admitting third-country nationals to activities as an employed person should be a test demonstrating that a post cannot be filled from within the domestic labour market. The chief criterion for admitting third-country nationals to activities as a self-employed person should be a test demonstrating an added value for employment or the economic development of the host Member State.

(9) Several ways and options for verifying fulfilment of these criteria in the form of individual or horizontal assessments should provide a flexible frame allowing all interested parties including Member States to react flexibly to changing economic and demographic circumstances.

(10) Member States should be allowed to apply horizontal measures, such as ceilings or quotas, limiting the admission of third-country nationals.

(11) Whenever Member States adopt national provisions as provided for by this Directive, they should comply with certain procedural and transparency requirements and in particular an obligation to notify their provisions to the Commission, in order to allow for an exchange of views, further consideration and complementary action within the context of an open coordination mechanism on Community immigration policy.

(12) Member States should lay down rules on penalties applicable to infringements of the provisions of this Directive and ensure that they are implemented. Those penalties must be effective, proportionate and dissuasive.

(13) This Directive respects the fundamental rights and observes the principles recognised in particular by the Charter of Fundamental Rights of the European Union.

(14) In accordance with the principles of subsidiarity and proportionality as set out in Article 5 of the Treaty, the objectives of the proposed action, namely the determination of a harmonised legal framework at Community level concerning the conditions of entry and residence of third-country nationals for the purpose of paid employment and self-employed economic activities and of the procedures for the issue by Member States of the relevant permits cannot be sufficiently achieved by the Member States and can therefore, by reason of the scale and effect of the action, be better achieved by the Community. This Directive confines itself to the minimum required to achieve those objectives and does not go beyond what is necessary for that purpose,

HAS ADOPTED THIS DIRECTIVE:

CHAPTER I
General Provisions

Article 1

The purpose of the Directive is:

(a) to determine the conditions of entry and residence of third-country nationals for the purpose of paid employment and self-employed economic activities; and

(b) to determine standards on procedures for the issue by a Member State of permits to third-country nationals to enter and reside in its territory and to exercise activities as an employed or self-employed person.

Article 2

For the purposes of this Directive:

(a) 'third-country national' means any person who is not a citizen of the Union within the meaning of Article 17(1) of the Treaty, including stateless persons;

(b) 'activity as an employed person' means any remunerated economic activity for and under the direction of another person;

(c) 'activity as a self-employed person' means any remunerated economic activity, which is not accomplished for and under the direction of another person;

(d) 'residence permit – worker' means a permit or authorisation issued by the authorities of a Member State allowing a third-country national to enter and reside in its territory and to exercise activities as an employed person;

(e) 'residence permit – self-employed person' means a permit or authorisation issued by the authorities of a Member State allowing a third-country national to enter and reside in its territory and to exercise activities as a self-employed person;

(f) 'seasonal workers' means third-country nationals who retain their legal domicile in a third country but are employed in the territory of a Member State in a sector of activity dependent on the passing of the seasons, under a fixed-term contract for a specific job;

(g) 'transfrontier workers' means third-country nationals resident in the frontier zone of a neighbouring country who are employed in the frontier zone of an adjacent Member State and who return to the frontier zone of the neighbouring country each day or at least once a week;

(h) 'intra-corporate transferees' means third-country nationals working within a single legal entity and being temporarily transferred into the territory of a Member State, either to the principal place of business or to an establishment of that legal entity, provided that they have worked for the legal entity concerned for at least the 12-month period immediately preceding the transfer;

(i) 'trainees' means third-country nationals whose presence in the territory of a Member State is strictly limited in duration and is closely connected with increasing their skills and qualifications in their chosen profession before returning to their own country to pursue their career.

Article 3

1. The provisions of this Directive shall apply to third-country nationals, except where provisions that are more favourable apply under:

(a) bilateral or multilateral agreements concluded between the Community, or the Community and its Member States, on the one hand, and third countries on the other hand;

(b) bilateral or multilateral agreements concluded between one or more Member States and third countries.

2. The provisions of this Directive shall not apply to the exercise of activities which are directly linked to the supply of goods or services from third countries to the Community, as long as third-country nationals carrying out these activities do not stay for more than three months in the Community.

3. The provisions of this Directive shall not apply to:

(a) third-country nationals established within the Community who are posted to another Member State for the purpose of providing cross-border services or who provide cross border services;

(b) third-country nationals staying in a Member State as applicants for asylum, under subsidiary forms of protection or under temporary protection schemes;

(c) third-country nationals whose residence is not legal and whose deportation has been suspended for factual or legal reasons;

(d) third-country nationals who are family members of citizens of the Union who have exercised their right to free movement within the Community;

(e) third-country nationals staying in a Member State under family reunification rules.

4. In the absence of specific provisions of Community law, Member States may maintain or introduce more favourable provisions regarding the following categories of person:

(a) researchers and academic specialists;

(b) priests and members of religious orders;

(c) sport professionals;

(d) artists;

(e) journalists;

(f) representatives of non-profit making organisations.

CHAPTER II
Entry and Residence for the Purpose of Paid Employment

Section 1
General rules

Article 4

1. Member States shall only authorise third-country nationals to enter and reside in their territory for the purpose of exercising activities as an employed person where a 'residence permit – worker' has been issued by the competent authorities of the Member State concerned in accordance with this Directive.

2. A 'residence permit – worker' shall only be issued if, after verification of the particulars and documents, it appears that the applicant fulfils the requirements for obtaining a 'residence permit – worker' in accordance with Articles 5 and 6, subject to any limitations imposed by a Member State in accordance with Articles 26, 27 and 28.

3. When handling an application, the competent authorities shall comply with the procedural safeguards provided for in Article 29.

Article 5

1. In order to obtain a 'residence permit – worker', a third-country national intending to exercise activities as an employed person in a Member State shall apply to the competent authority of the Member State concerned. The future employer of a third-country national shall have the right to submit an application on behalf of the third-country national applicant.

2. Applications for a 'residence permit – worker' shall be submitted via the representation of a Member State competent for the country of legal residence of the applicant or directly in the territory of the Member State concerned, if the applicant is already resident or legally present there.

3. The application shall be accompanied by the following particulars and documents:
    (a) name and address of the applicant and the employer;
    (b) a valid work contract or a binding offer of work in the Member State concerned, covering the term of the residence permit applied for;
    (c) description of the envisaged activities as an employed person in the Member State concerned;
    (d) appropriate evidence of fulfilment of the requirement laid down in Article 6(1) as provided for in paragraphs 2 to 5 there;
    (e) if required by the Member State concerned, a certificate or adequate proof of good character and conduct and a health certificate;
    (f) valid passport or equivalent travel documents and, if appropriate, evidence of valid residence title;
    (g) documents proving the skills which are necessary for the performance of the envisaged activities and evidence of fulfilment of all the conditions applicable to nationals of the Member State concerned for the exercise of the relevant activity as an employed person;
    (h) evidence of having sufficient resources to support the applicant and his/her family members so as to avoid becoming a burden on the social assistance system of the host Member State for the duration of their stay and of having a sickness insurance covering all risks in the host Member State. Those resources shall be deemed sufficient where they are at, or above, the threshold below which the host Member State may grant social assistance to its nationals. Where this criterion is not applicable, the applicant's resources shall be deemed sufficient where they are no less than the amount of the minimum social security pension paid by the host Member State;
    (i) proof of payment of the fee for handling the application.

4. Third-country nationals who have been legally resident in a Member State and who have legally exercised activities there as an employed person for more than three years over the

preceding five years shall not be required to provide evidence of fulfilment of the requirement laid down in Article 6(1) when submitting an application for a 'residence permit –
worker' in that Member State.

Article 6

1. When submitting an application in accordance with Article 5, it must be demonstrated
that a job vacancy in that Member State cannot be filled in the short term by any of the
following categories:

(a) citizens of the Union;

(b) third-country nationals who are family members of citizens of the Union who have
exercised their right to free movement within the Community;

(c) third-country nationals already enjoying full access to the national labour market
concerned under the agreements referred to in Article 3(1);

(d) third-country nationals already enjoying access to the national labour market concerned under existing national legislation or under Community legislation;

(e) third-country nationals who are legally resident in a Member State and who are and
have been legally exercising activities as an employed person in that Member State for more
than three years; or

(f) third-country nationals who have been legally resident in that Member State and who
have legally exercised activities as an employed person in that Member State for more than
three years over the preceding five years.

2. The requirement laid down in paragraph 1 shall be deemed to be fulfilled if a specific job
vacancy has been made public via the employment services of several Member States for a
period of at least four weeks, and in particular, when appropriate, by means of the European
Employment Services (EURES) network established by Commission Decision 93/569/EEC,[2]
and if no acceptable job application has been received from persons listed in paragraph 1 or
from third-country nationals who are citizens of countries with which accession negotiations have been started. The published job vacancy shall contain realistic, reasonable and
proportionate requirements for the offered post. This shall be checked and scrutinised by the
competent authorities when evaluating an application for a residence permit submitted in
accordance with Article 5.

3. Member States may adopt national provisions according to which the requirement laid
down in paragraph 1 is deemed to be fulfilled for a specific number of jobs, in a specific
sector, for a limited time-period and, if appropriate, in a specific region without the need for
an individual assessment. The national provisions shall lay down in detail the criteria according to which applications for work permits shall be ranked when the number of applications received outnumber the published number of jobs. Member States shall consider in the
first place applications from citizens of countries with which accession negotiations have
been started.

4. Member States may adopt national provisions according to which the requirement laid
down in paragraph 1 is deemed to be fulfilled if the annual income offered to a third-country
national exceeds a defined threshold.

---

[2] OJ L 274, 6.11.1993, p. 32.

5. Member States may adopt national provisions according to which the requirement laid down in paragraph 1 is deemed to be fulfilled for a specific third-country national, if a defined amount of money has been paid by the future employer of that person to the competent authorities. The money received from the employer shall be spent for measures promoting the integration of third-country nationals or for vocational training purposes.

Article 7

1. A 'residence permit – worker' shall be issued for a predetermined period. The initial 'residence permit – worker' granted shall be valid for a period of up to three years to be determined in accordance with national legislation. It shall be renewable for periods of up to three years, to be determined in accordance with national legislation, on application by the holder, to be submitted at least three months before the expiry date and after consideration by the competent authority of a file containing updated information on the items enumerated in Article 5(3) and in particular detailed information on the activities exercised as an employed person.

2. Applicants for renewal who have been holding a 'residence permit – worker' in the Member State concerned for more than three years shall not be required to provide evidence of fulfilment of the requirement laid down in Article 6(1).

Article 8

A 'residence permit – worker' shall initially be restricted to the exercise of specific professional activities or fields of activities. It may also be restricted to the exercise of activities as an employed person in a specific region. After three years, it shall not be subject to these restrictions.

Article 9

1. After a 'residence permit – worker' has been issued, its holder shall notify to the competent authorities any changes to the information provided in accordance with Article 5(3). If these changes relate to points (b) or (c) of Article 5(3) they shall be subject to the approval of the competent authority of the Member State concerned.

2. During the period of validity of a 'residence permit – worker', competent authorities shall not consider changes that relate to Article 5(3)(d).

Article 10

1. The competent authorities shall revoke a 'residence permit – worker' which has been fraudulently acquired.

2. The competent authorities may suspend or revoke a 'residence permit – worker' where the particulars supporting the application as provided for in Article 5 are incorrect or have not been amended in accordance with Article 9. The competent authorities may also suspend or revoke a 'residence permit – worker' when such measure is considered necessary

for reasons of public policy or public security by the Member State concerned in accordance with Article 27.

3. Unemployment in itself shall not constitute a sufficient reason for revoking a 'residence permit – worker' unless the period of unemployment exceeds the following duration:

(a) three months within a 12-month period, for holders of a 'residence permit – worker' who have legally exercised activities as employed or self-employed persons in the Member State concerned for less than two years;

(b) six months within a 12-month period, for holders of a 'residence permit – worker' who have legally exercised activities as employed or self-employed persons in the Member State concerned for two years or more.

Article 11

1. During the period of its validity, a 'residence permit – worker' shall entitle its holder at a minimum to the following:

(a) entry to the territory of the Member State issuing the 'residence permit – worker';

(b) re-entry to the territory of the Member State issuing the 'residence permit – worker' after temporary absence;

(c) passage through other Member States in order to exercise the rights under points (a) and (b);

(d) residence in the Member State issuing the 'residence permit – worker';

(e) exercise of the activities authorised under the 'residence permit – worker';

(f) enjoyment of equal treatment with citizens of the Union at least with regard to:

(i) working conditions, including conditions regarding dismissals and remuneration;

(ii) access to vocational training necessary to complement the activities authorised under the residence permit;

(iii) recognition of diplomas, certificates and other qualifications issued by a competent authority;

(iv) social security including healthcare;

(v) access to goods and services and the supply of goods and services made available to the public, including public housing;

(vi) freedom of association and affiliation and membership of an organisation representing workers or employers or of any organisation whose members are engaged in a specific occupation, including the benefits conferred by such organisations.

2. Member States may restrict the rights conferred under paragraph 1(f)(ii) to third-country nationals who have been staying or who have the right to stay in their territory for at least one year.

They may restrict the rights conferred under paragraph 1(f)(v) with respect to public housing to third-country nationals who have been staying or who have the right to stay in their territory for at least three years.

3. After the expiry of a 'residence permit – worker' and following their return to a third country, former holders of a 'residence permit – worker' shall have the right to request and obtain the payment of the contributions made by them and by their employers into public

pension schemes during the period of validity of the 'residence permit – worker', provided that:

(a) the applicant cannot or will not obtain payment of a Member State pension under national law or under the agreements referred to in Article 3(1), when residing in a third country;

(b) the applicant is unable, under national law or the agreements referred to in Article 3(1), to transfer pension rights to a scheme of the third country where applicant resides;

(c) the applicant formally waives all rights/claims acquired under the national pension scheme concerned;

(d) the application is submitted from a third country.

Section 2
Rules for specific categories

Article 12

1. Seasonal workers may be granted a 'residence permit – seasonal worker' for up to six months in any calendar year, after which they shall return to a third country. The provisions of Section 1 shall apply *mutatis mutandis* to such permit.

A 'residence permit – seasonal worker' shall not be extended to cover a total period exceeding the six-month period. Member States may issue up to five 'residence permits – seasonal worker' covering up to five subsequent years within one administrative act ('multi-annual residence permit – seasonal worker').

2. Member States may ask applicants or their future employers to deposit a security, which shall be repayable on the return of the seasonal worker to a third country.

Article 13

Transfrontier workers may be granted a 'permit – transfrontier worker'. The provisions of Section 1, with the exception of Article 11(1)(d), shall apply *mutatis mutandis* to such permit.

Article 14

1. Intra-corporate transferees may be granted a 'residence permit – intra-corporate transferee'.

The provisions of Section 1 shall apply *mutatis mutandis* to such permit. However, applicants for a 'residence permit – intra-corporate transferee' shall not be required to provide evidence of fulfilment of the requirement laid down in Article 6(1). Instead, applicants shall demonstrate that they fulfil the criteria set out in paragraph 2 of this Article.

2. Intra-corporate transferees shall either be:

(a) 'key personnel', that is to say persons working in a senior management or executive position within a legal entity, receiving general supervision or instructions principally from the board of directors or stockholders of the business or their equivalent. The functions of key personnel can include: directing the establishment or a department or sub-division of the establishment; supervising and controlling the work of other supervisory, professional or managerial employees; and/or having the authority personally to engage and dismiss personnel, or to recommend such engagement or dismissal, or other personnel actions; or

(b) 'specialists', that is to say persons possessing uncommon knowledge essential to the establishment's service, research equipment, techniques or management.

In assessing such knowledge, account will be taken not only of knowledge specific to the establishment, but also of whether the person has a high level of qualification referring to a type of work or trade requiring specific technical knowledge.

3. The initial period of validity of the 'residence permit – intra-corporate transferee' shall be equal to the duration applied for, subject to a maximum period of validity of five years.

Article 15

1. Trainees may be granted a 'residence permit – trainee'.

The provisions of Section 1 shall apply *mutatis mutandis* to such permit. However, applicants for a 'residence permit – trainee' shall not be required to provide the evidence of fulfilment of the requirement laid down in Article 6(1). Instead, applicants shall demonstrate that the envisaged activity is strictly limited in duration and is closely connected with increasing their skills and qualifications.

2. The overall validity of a 'residence permit – trainee' shall not exceed one year. This period may be extended exclusively for the time needed to obtain a professional qualification recognised by the Member State concerned in the sphere of activity of the trainee.

Article 16

1. Third-country nationals pursuing activities as an employed person in the context of youth exchange or youth mobility schemes, including 'au pairs', may be granted a 'residence permit – youth exchange/au pair'.

The provisions of Section 1 shall apply *mutatis mutandis* to such permit. However, applicants for a 'residence permit – youth exchange/au pair' shall not be required to provide evidence of fulfilment of the requirement laid down in Article 6(1). Instead, applicants shall demonstrate that the envisaged activity is strictly limited in duration and connected with a youth exchange or youth mobility scheme officially recognised by the Member State concerned.

2. The overall validity of a 'residence permit – youth exchange/au pair' shall not exceed one year. This period may be extended exceptionally if a youth exchange or youth mobility scheme officially recognised by a Member State provides for that possibility.

3. Member States may ask applicants or their future employers to deposit a security, which shall be repayable on the return to a third country.

CHAPTER III
Entry and Residence for the Purpose of Exercising Self-employed Economic Activities

Article 17

1. Member States shall only authorise third-country nationals to enter and reside in their territory for the purpose of exercising activities as self-employed persons where a 'residence permit – self-employed person' has been issued by the competent authorities of the Member State concerned in accordance with this Directive.

2. A 'residence permit – self-employed person' shall only be issued if, after verification of the particulars and documents, it appears that the applicant fulfils the requirements for obtaining a 'residence permit – self-employed person' in accordance with Articles 18 and 19, subject to any limitations imposed by a Member State in accordance with Articles 26, 27 and 28.

3. When handling an application, the competent authorities shall comply with the procedural safeguards provided for in Article 29.

Article 18

1. In order to obtain a 'residence permit – self-employed person', a third-country national intending to exercise activities as a self-employed person in a Member State shall apply to the competent authority of the Member State concerned.

2. Applications for a 'residence permit – self-employed person' shall be submitted via the representation of a Member State competent for the country of legal residence of the applicant or directly in the territory of the Member State concerned, if the applicant is already resident or legally present there.

3. The application shall be accompanied by the following particulars and documents:
   (a) name and address of the applicant and of the location of exercise of the envisaged activities as a self-employed person;
   (b) detailed business plan covering the time-period for which a 'residence permit – self-employed person' is requested;
   (c) evidence that the applicant has sufficient financial means, including own resources, in accordance with the business plan and, if applicable, evidence of investment of the required minimum investment sum including financial guarantees;
   (d) appropriate evidence of fulfilment of the requirement laid down in Article 19(1);
   (e) if required by the Member State concerned, a certificate or adequate proof of good character and conduct and a health certificate;
   (f) valid passport or equivalent travel documents and, if appropriate, evidence of valid residence title;
   (g) documents proving the skills which are necessary for the performance of the envisaged activities and evidence of fulfilment of all the conditions applicable to nationals of the Member State concerned for the exercise of the relevant activity as a self-employed person;

(h) evidence of having sufficient resources to support the applicant and his/her family members so as to avoid becoming a burden on the social assistance system of the host Member State for the duration of their stay and of having a sickness insurance covering all risks in the host Member State. Those resources shall be deemed sufficient where they are at, or above, the threshold below which the host Member State may grant social assistance to its nationals. Where this criterion is not applicable, the applicant's resources shall be deemed sufficient where they are no less than the amount of the minimum social security pension paid by the host Member State;

(i) proof of payment of the fee for handling the application.

4. Third-country nationals who have been legally resident in a Member State and who have legally exercised activities there as a self-employed person for more than three years over the preceding five years shall not be required to provide evidence of fulfilment of the requirement laid down in Article 19(1) when submitting an application for a 'residence permit – self-employed person' in that Member State.

Article 19

1. When submitting an application in accordance with Article 18, it must be demonstrated that the envisaged activities as a self-employed person will create an employment opportunity for the applicant and will have a beneficial effect on employment in the Member State concerned or on the economic development of that Member State.

2. Member States may adopt national provisions according to which the requirement laid down in paragraph 1 is deemed to be fulfilled, or not fulfilled, for specific activities as a self-employed person in specific sectors and, if appropriate, in a specific region without the need for an individual assessment.

3. Member States may adopt national provisions according to which the requirement laid down in paragraph 1 is deemed to be fulfilled for specific activities as a self-employed person in specific sectors and, if appropriate, in a specific region if an applicant invests a defined minimum amount of own resources.

Article 20

1. A 'residence permit – self-employed person' shall be issued for a predetermined period. The initial 'residence permit – self-employed person' granted shall be valid for a period of up to three years to be determined in accordance with national legislation. It shall be renewable for periods of up to three years, to be determined in accordance with national legislation, on application by the holder, to be submitted at least three months before the expiry date and after consideration by the competent authority of a file containing updated information on the items enumerated in Article 18(3), and in particular detailed information on the activities exercised as a self-employed person.

2. Applicants for renewal who have been holding a 'residence permit – self-employed person' in the Member State concerned for more than three years shall not be required to provide evidence of fulfilment of the requirement laid down in Article 19(1).

Article 21

A 'residence permit – self-employed person' shall initially be restricted to the exercise of specific activities as a self-employed person or to specific fields of activities. It may also be restricted to the exercise of activities as a self-employed person in a specific region. After three years it shall not be subject to these restrictions.

Article 22

1. After a 'residence permit – self-employed person' has been issued, its holder shall notify to the competent authorities any changes to the information provided in accordance with Article 18(3). If these changes relate to points (b) or (c) of Article 18(3) they shall be subject to the approval of the competent authority of the Member State concerned.

2. During the period of validity of a 'residence permit – self-employed person', competent authorities shall not consider changes that relate to point (d) of Article 18(3).

Article 23

1. The competent authorities shall revoke a 'residence permit – self-employed person' which has been fraudulently acquired.

2. The competent authorities may suspend or revoke a 'residence permit – self-employed person' where the particulars supporting the application as provided for in Article 18 are incorrect or have not been amended in accordance with Article 22. The competent authorities may also suspend or revoke a 'residence permit – self-employed person' when such measure is considered necessary for reasons of public policy or public security by the Member State concerned in accordance with Article 27.

3. Commercial difficulties shall not constitute a sufficient reason for revoking a 'residence permit – self-employed person' unless the period during which the holder is not able to meet the costs of living in accordance with Article 18(3)(h) exceeds the following period:
   (a) three months within a 12-month period, for holders of a 'residence permit – self-employed person' who have legally exercised activities as employed or self-employed persons in the Member State concerned for less than two years;
   (b) six months within a 12-month period, for holders of a 'residence permit – self-employed person' who have legally exercised activities as employed or self-employed persons in the Member State concerned for two years or more.

Article 24

The rules set out in Article 11 shall also apply to holders of a 'residence permit – self-employed person'.

CHAPTER IV
Horizontal Provisions

Article 25

Member States may request applicants to pay fees for handling applications in accordance with this Directive. The level of fees shall be proportionate and may be based on the service actually provided.

Article 26

Member States may decide to adopt national provisions limiting the issuing of permits in accordance with this Directive to a set ceiling or suspending or halting the issuing of these permits for a defined period, taking into account the overall capacity to receive and to integrate third-country nationals on their territory or in specific regions thereof. These national provisions shall state in detail which groups of persons are covered by, or exempted from, the measure. If these national provisions impose ceilings, they shall lay down in detail the criteria according to which applications for permits in accordance with this Directive shall be ranked when the number of applications received exceeds the set ceilings.

Article 27

Member States may refuse to grant or to renew, or may revoke, permits in accordance with this Directive on grounds of public policy, public security or public health. The grounds of public policy or public security shall be based exclusively on the personal conduct of the third-country national concerned. Public health shall not be invoked by Member States as a reason for revoking or not renewing a residence permit solely on the ground of illness or disability suffered after the issue of the residence permit.

Article 28

This Directive is without prejudice to the application of national legislation regulating the access of third-country nationals to employment in the public service or to activities which in that Member State are connected, even occasionally, with the exercise of official authority.

CHAPTER V
Procedure and Transparency

Article 29

1. Member States shall ensure that a decision to grant, modify or renew a permit in accordance with this Directive, is adopted and communicated to the applicant at the latest within 180 days after receipt of the application. Decisions on an application submitted in accordance with Articles 14, 15 and 16 shall be adopted and communicated to the applicant within 45 days after its receipt.

2. Every Member State shall make public the average time necessary for its authorities to issue, modify or renew permits in accordance with this Directive and inform applicants thereof upon receipt of an application.

3. If the information supporting the application is inadequate, the competent authorities shall notify the applicant of the additional detailed information that is required. The period referred to in paragraph 1 shall be suspended until the authorities have received the additional information required.

4. Any decision not to grant, modify or renew a permit in accordance with the application and any decision suspending or withdrawing a permit shall contain a statement of reasons based upon objective and verifiable criteria on which the decision is based. The person concerned shall have the right to apply to the courts of the Member State concerned and shall be informed of the time limits allowed for applying for such remedies.

Article 30

When Member States choose to adopt national measures in accordance with Article 6(3), (4) or (5); Article 19(2) and (3), or Article 26, the following rules shall apply:

(a) the Member State shall base its national provisions on the criteria listed in the relevant provisions of this Directive;

(b) the national provisions shall include a statement of reasons based upon objective and verifiable criteria;

(c) the national provisions shall be subject to regular review at national level to ascertain whether it is justifiable under this Directive that the national provisions be maintained unchanged;

(d) the national provisions shall be made public in advance of their entry into force;

(e) the Member State shall notify the national provisions to the Commission and they shall submit to the Commission an annual report on the application of those national provisions.

Article 31

Each Member State shall ensure that an exhaustive and regularly updated set of information concerning the conditions of entry and stay of third-country nationals to its territory for the purpose of pursuing activities as an employed or self-employed person is made available to the general public.

CHAPTER VI
Final Provisions

Article 32

The Member States shall give effect to the provisions of this Directive without discrimination on the basis of sex, race, colour, ethnic or social origin, genetic characteristics, language, religion or beliefs, political or other opinions, membership of a national minority, fortune, birth, disabilities, age or sexual orientation.

Article 33

Member States shall lay down the rules on penalties applicable to infringements of the national provisions adopted pursuant to this Directive and shall take all measures necessary to ensure that they are implemented. The penalties provided for must be effective, proportionate and dissuasive. The Member States shall notify those provisions to the Commission by the date specified in Article 35 at the latest and shall notify it without delay of any subsequent amendment affecting them.

Article 34

By 31 December 2007 at the latest, the Commission shall report to the European Parliament and the Council on the application of this Directive in the Member States and propose amendments if appropriate.

Article 35

Member States shall adopt and publish, before 1 January 2004, the provisions necessary to comply with this Directive. They shall forthwith inform the Commission thereof. They shall apply those provisions from 1 January 2004. When Member States adopt those provisions, they shall contain a reference to this Directive or be accompanied by such a reference on the occasion of their official publication. Member States shall determine how such reference is to be made.

Article 36

This Directive shall enter into force on the twentieth day following that of its publication in the Official Journal of the European Communities.

Article 37

This Directive is addressed to the Member States.

Explanatory Memorandum

1. **Conditions of entry and residence of third-country nationals for the purpose of paid employment and self-employed economic activities**

According to the mandate given by the Tampere European Council of October 1999 and in line with the 'Scoreboard to review progress on the creation of an area of "freedom, security and justice" in the European Union',[3] the Commission is due to adopt in 2001 a proposal for a Directive dealing with 'the conditions of entry and residence of third-country nationals for the purpose of paid employment and self-employed economic activities'.

---

[3] COM(2000)167 final of 24.3.2000 as updated by COM(2001)278 of 23.5.2001.

In its recent Communication on a Community Immigration Policy (COM(2000)757 of 22 November 2000) the Commission has suggested to follow a 'two-tier approach': To define a common legal framework on admission of economic migrants and to launch an open coordination mechanism on Community immigration policy. In its Communication the Commission has already set out the main aims and principles upon which the common legal framework should be based:

Transparency and rationality: laying down clearly the conditions under which third-country nationals may enter and stay in the EU as employed or self-employed workers, setting out their rights and obligations and ensuring that they have access to this information and that there are mechanisms in place to see that it is applied fairly.

Differentiating rights according to length of stay: the aim should be to give a secure legal status for temporary workers who intend to return to their countries of origin, while at the same time providing a pathway leading eventually to a more permanent status for those who wish to stay and who meet certain criteria.

Clear and simple procedures: application procedures should be clear and simple.

Respect for the domestic labour market situation: the principle that a post can only be filled with a third-country worker after a thorough assessment of the domestic labour market situation (unless international obligations and commitments of the EU and its Member States already provide otherwise) is currently applied in all Member States and it is not intended to touch this principle.

Availability of information: more extensive use of new communications technology could be used to provide information on job opportunities, conditions of work, etc.

Assist industry: in order to allow European industry, particularly small and medium-sized industries, to recruit − in cases where there is a demonstrated economic need for workers in a specific sector or for a specific job which cannot be filled from within the EU labour market − successfully and quickly from third countries, employers need a practical tool for demonstrating that there is a concrete shortage on the EU labour market.

As indicated in this Communication, the issues addressed in this legal proposal will also need to be the subject of further policy consideration and complementary action within the context of an open coordination mechanism on Community immigration policy. This mechanism is going to be made operational in a specific Commission Communication on an open method of coordination for the Community immigration policy, presented in parallel with this proposal.

2. Background and compatibility with other initiatives

In June 2000, a comparative study on the admission of third-country nationals for paid employment and self-employed economic activities was submitted to the Commission services. It illustrates that currently the rules on admission of third-country nationals to work in the EU differ from Member State to Member State. Both third-country nationals wishing to be admitted to work in the EU and EU employers in need of third-country workers are confronted with sometimes highly complex national administrative rules and procedures and there are only a few common rules and principles applicable in all Member States.

In November 2000, the Commission issued its Communication on a Community Immigration Policy which already outlined the main policy lines this proposal is following.

Compatibility with other initiatives:

This proposal has been drafted to be fully compatible with and complementary to the recently proposed draft Directive on long-term resident third-country nationals.[4] Whilst workers and self-employed persons newly arrived in the EU will be covered by the specific legal regime proposed in this proposal, the 'horizontal' provisions of the proposed Directive on long-term resident third-country nationals would apply if these third-country workers have fulfilled the conditions and have applied for long-term resident status in accordance with the proposed long-term residents Directive.

The proposal has also been drafted to be fully compatible with the commitments undertaken by the EC and its Member States under the WTO Agreement on Trade in Services (GATS), and to further facilitate the trade in services which has already been committed to in this context.

In accordance with the 'Scoreboard to review progress on the creation of an area of "freedom, security and justice" in the European Union', further legislative initiatives concerning the conditions of entry and residence for the purpose of study or vocational training and unpaid activities are to be prepared and to be adopted by the Commission shortly.

3.   The objectives of the proposal

With this proposal for a Directive, the Commission is pursuing the following aims:

1. laying down common definitions, criteria and procedures regarding the conditions of entry and residence of third-country nationals for the purpose of paid employment and self-employed economic activities, based on concepts, which have already been successfully applied in Member States;

2. laying down common criteria for admitting third-country nationals to employed activities and self-employed economic activities ('*economic needs test*' and '*beneficial effects test*') and opening different options for demonstrating compliance with these criteria;

3. providing procedural and transparency safeguards, in order to assure a high level of legal certainty and information for all interested actors on Member State rules and administrative practice in the field of entry and residence of third-country nationals for the purpose of paid employment and self-employed economic activities;

4. providing a single national application procedure leading to one combined title, encompassing both residence and work permit within one administrative act, in order to simplify and harmonise the diverging rules currently applicable in Member States;

---

[4] Proposal for a Council Directive concerning the status of third-country nationals who are long-term residents (COM(2001)127 final of 13.3.2001).

5. providing rights to third-country nationals whilst respecting Member States discretion to limit economic migration: If third-country workers and self-employed persons fulfil all the conditions set out in Chapters II and III they shall be admitted, unless Member States impose limitations in accordance with Chapter IV (e.g. national ceilings or limitations based on reasons of public policy, public security or public health);

6. providing a flexible framework allowing all interested parties, including Member States, to react quickly to changing economic and demographic circumstances and opening the possibility of having an exchange of views on the experiences of Member States in the application of this Directive within an open coordination mechanism on Community immigration policy;

7. adding real meaning to the commitments that the EC and its Member States have undertaken in the context of the WTO GATS Agreement;

8. acknowledging Member States' right to limit admission of third-country nationals under the terms of this proposal, if a Member State considers that it is necessary to apply horizontal measures (e.g. ceilings or quota) to that effect.

4. The choice of the legal basis

The choice of the legal basis is consistent with the changes made to the EC Treaty by the Amsterdam Treaty, which entered into force on 1 May 1999. Article 63(3) of the EC Treaty provides that the Council is to adopt *'measures on immigration policy within the following areas: (a) conditions of entry and residence, and standards on procedures for the issue by Member States of long-term visas and residence permits'*.

Regulation of immigration for the purpose of exercising employed or self-employed economic activities is a cornerstone of immigration policy and the development of a coherent Community immigration policy is impossible without addressing 'the conditions of entry and residence of third-country nationals for the purpose of paid employment and self-employed economic activities'. Article 63(3)(a) is, accordingly, the proper legal basis for this proposal.

This proposal for a Directive must be adopted by the procedure of Article 67 of the Treaty: the Council acts unanimously on a proposal from the Commission or at the initiative of the Member States after consulting the European Parliament. This proposal is based on Title IV of the EC Treaty, which does not apply to the United Kingdom and Ireland unless those Member States decide otherwise in accordance with the Protocol on the position of the United Kingdom and Ireland annexed to the Treaties. Likewise, Title IV does not apply to Denmark by virtue of the Protocol on the position of Denmark, annexed to the Treaties.

5. Subsidiarity and proportionality: justification and value added

The new Title IV on visas, asylum, immigration and other policies related to free movement of persons, inserted in the Treaty establishing the European Community, confers powers on these matters on the European Community. These powers must be exercised in accordance with Article 5 of the EC Treaty, i.e. if and in so far as the objectives of the proposed action cannot be sufficiently achieved by the Member States and can, therefore, by reason of the scale or effects of the proposed action, be better achieved by the Community. The proposed Directive respects these criteria.

Subsidiarity
The primary objective of this initiative is to determine a harmonised legal frame at EU level concerning the conditions of entry and residence of third-country nationals for the purpose of paid employment and self-employed economic activities and of the procedures for the issue by Member States of pertinent permits. Currently national administrative rules and procedures regulating this field differ widely between Member States. Taking into account the significant divergence of national provisions and regulatory approaches in Member States, the establishment of a harmonised legal frame can only be achieved at Community level.

Proportionality
The form of Community action must be the simplest that will enable the objective of the proposal to be attained and effectively implemented. In this spirit, the legal instrument chosen is a Directive, laying down general principles but leaving the Member States to which it is addressed the choice of the most appropriate form and methods for giving effect to these principles in their national legal system and general context. The proposed Directive determines common definitions, criteria and procedures regarding the conditions of entry and residence of third-country nationals for the purpose of paid employment and self-employed economic activities, whilst leaving a high level of discretion with Member States.

Financial and administrative consequences of the proposal on national governments, local authorities, economic stakeholders and citizens
According to the above-mentioned comparative study on the admission of third-country nationals for paid employment and self-employed economic activities, the rules on admission of third-country nationals to work in the EU differ from Member State to Member States.

Both third-country nationals wishing to be admitted to work in the EU and EU employers in need of third-country workers are confronted with sometimes highly complex national administrative rules and procedures and there are only a few common rules and principles applicable in all Member States.

The proposed creation of a single national application procedure leading to one combined title, encompassing both residence and work permit within one administrative act, will contribute to simplifying and harmonising the diverging rules currently applicable in Member States. For Member States this creation of a single procedure may be an incentive to streamline their internal administration and to avoid duplication of work. Third-country national wishing to exercise economic activities in the EU and future employer of third-country national will directly benefit from a 'one-stop shop procedure'.

Both the proposed common criteria for admitting third-country nationals to employed activities and self-employed economic activities ('*economic needs test*' and '*beneficial effects test*') and the proposed procedural and transparency safeguards will assure a high level of legal certainty, transparency and information for all interested actors. This will be of specific value to economic stakeholders and third-country workers.

National governments (competent authorities) will be allowed to ask for proportionate fees for their activities. These fees may be based on the principle of the service actually provided, thus assuring that the newly established procedures will neither become a financial burden on national administrations, nor an undue burden for those benefiting from the permits issued.

Chapter 2.3
STUDENTS & VOLUNTEERS

COUNCIL DIRECTIVE
on the conditions of entry and residence of third-country nationals for the purpose of studies, vocational training or voluntary service[1]

THE COUNCIL OF THE EUROPEAN UNION,
Having regard to the Treaty establishing the European Community, and in particular points 3(a) and 4 of the first subparagraph of Article 63 thereof,
Having regard to the proposal from the Commission,
Having regard to the Opinion of the European Parliament,
Having regard to the Opinion of the Economic and Social Committee,
Having regard to the Opinion of the Committee of the Regions,

Whereas:

(1) For the gradual establishment of an area of freedom, security and justice, the Treaty establishing the European Community provides for measures to be adopted in the fields of asylum, immigration and the protection of the rights of third-country nationals.

(2) Point 3(a) of the first subparagraph of Article 63 of the Treaty provides that the Council is to adopt measures on immigration policy relating to conditions of entry and residence, and standards on procedures for the issue by Member States of long-term visas and residence permits.

(3) At its special meeting at Tampere on 15 and 16 October 1999, the European Council acknowledged the need for approximation of national legislation on the conditions for admission and residence of third country nationals and asked the Council to rapidly adopt decisions on the basis of proposals by the Commission.

(4) One of the objectives of European Community action in education is to promote Europe as a whole as a world centre of excellence for studies and vocational training. Promoting the mobility of third-country nationals to Europe for the purpose of studies, vocational training or voluntary service is a key factor in that strategy. The approximation of the Member States' national legislation on conditions of entry and residence is part of this.

---

[1] COM(2002)548 final; NB: political agreement only (reached on 30 March 2004); formal agreement expected for the autumn of 2004; the recital may be re-shuffled; the final numbers of the articles may be re-arranged, and also the final text may ever so slightly differ from the text included in this Volume.

(5) Migration for the purpose of studies, vocational training or voluntary service, which is by definition temporary and does not depend on the employment-market situation in the host country, constitutes a form of mutual enrichment for the migrants concerned, their country of origin and the host country and helps to promote better familiarity between cultures.

(6) The new Community rules are based on definitions of student, trainee, educational establishment, vocational training scheme and volunteer already in use in European law, in particular in the various Community programmes to promote the mobility of the relevant persons (Socrates, European Voluntary Service, etc.).

(7) The term admission covers the entry and residence of third country nationals for the purposes set by this Directive.

(8) In order to allow the initial entry to their territory, Member States can issue in a timely manner a residence permit or, if they issue residence permits exclusively on their territory, a visa.

(9) The duration and other conditions of preparatory courses for students covered by the present Directive should be determined by Member States in accordance with their national legislation.

(10) The admission of third country nationals who intend to carry out specialisation studies in the field of Medicine should be determined by the Member States.

(11) Admission for the purposes set by this Directive may be refused on duly justified grounds. In particular, admission could be refused if a Member State considers, according to an assessment based on facts, that the third-country national concerned is a potential threat to public policy or public security. The notion of public policy may cover a conviction for committing a serious crime. In this context it has to be noted that the notion of public policy and public security covers also cases in which a third country national belongs or has belonged to an association which supports terrorism, supports or has supported such an association, or has or had extremist aspirations.

(12) The mobility of students who are third-country nationals studying in several Member States must be facilitated, as must the admission of third-country nationals participating in Community programmes to promote mobility within and towards Europe for the purpose of studies, vocational training or voluntary service.

(13) In case of doubts concerning the grounds of the application, Member States could require all the evidence which is necessary to assess its coherence, in particular on the basis of the applicant's proposed studies, in order to fight against abuse and misuse of the procedure set by this Directive.

(14) The evidence of acceptance of a student in an establishment of higher education could include, among other possibilities a letter or certificate confirming his /her enrolment.

(15) To reflect the cost of training and the fact that more and more people have to work to help pay for it, third-country nationals admitted for study purposes should be given limited access to the employment market.

(16) The principle of the access of students to the labour market, under the conditions set out in this Directive should be a general rule; however, in exceptional circumstances Member States should be able to examine the situation of their national labour markets.

(17) The notion of prior authorisation includes also the granting of work permits to the students who wish to exercise an economic activity.

(18) This Directive should not affect the national legislation in the area of part-time work.

(19) Provision should be made for fast-track admission procedures for study purposes, in particular in cases involving mobility in the context of partnerships organised between European and third-country educational establishments or of pupil exchange schemes managed by accredited organisations in the Member States.

(20) Efforts must be made to secure transparency to ensure that third-country nationals have access to information on educational or vocational training establishments and courses that are open to them in the European Community.

(21) Each Member State should ensure that the fullest possible set of regularly updated information is made available to the general public, notably on the Internet, as regards the establishments defined in this Directive, courses of study to which third-country nationals may be admitted and the conditions and procedures for entry and residence in its territory for these purposes.

(22) Fellowships may be taken into account in the assessment of the availability of sufficient resources.

(23) The Member States should give effect to the provisions of this Directive without discrimination on the basis of sex, race, colour, ethnic or social origin, genetic characteristics, language, religion or beliefs, political or other opinions, membership of a national minority, fortune, birth, disabilities, age or sexual orientation.

(24) This Directive respects the fundamental rights and observes the principles recognised by the Charter of Fundamental Rights of the European Union.

(25) The objectives of the proposed action, namely the establishment of a harmonised Community legal framework for the conditions for entry and residence of third-country nationals in the territory of the Member States for a period exceeding three months for the purposes of studies, vocational training or voluntary service, and for the procedures for issuing residence permits allowing them to enter and reside in the Member States for those purposes, cannot be sufficiently achieved by the Member States and can, by reason of the scale or effects of the proposed action, be better achieved by the Community in accordance with the subsidiarity principle declared by Article 5 of the Treaty. In accordance with the proportionality principle declared by Article 5, this Directive does not go beyond what is necessary to achieve these objectives.

(26) This Directive should not affect in any circumstances the application of Council Regulation 1030/2002 of 13 June 2002 laying down a uniform format for residence permits for third-country nationals.

(27) Third country nationals who fall under the categories of unremunerated trainees and volunteers who are considered, by virtue of their activities or the kind of compensation or remuneration received, as workers under national legislation should not be covered by the scope of this Directive.

(28) Under Articles 1 and 2 of the Protocol on the position of Denmark annexed to the Treaty on European Union and the Treaty establishing the European Community, Denmark does not participate in the adoption of this Directive. The Directive will therefore not be binding in Denmark nor applicable there,

HAS ADOPTED THIS DIRECTIVE:

CHAPTER I
General Provisions

Article 1
Subject-matter

The purpose of this Directive is to determine:

a) the conditions for admission of third-country nationals to the territory of the Member States for a period exceeding three months for the purpose of studies, pupil exchange unremunerated training or voluntary service;

b) rules concerning the procedures for admitting third-country nationals to the territory of the Member States for those purposes.

Article 2
Definitions

For the purposes of this Directive:

a) 'third-country national' means any person who is not a citizen of the European Union within the meaning of Article 17(1) of the Treaty;

b) 'student' means a third-country national accepted by an establishment of higher education and admitted to the territory of a Member State to pursue as his / her main activity a full-time course of study leading to a higher education qualification recognised by the Member State, including diplomas, certificates or doctoral degrees in an establishment of higher education which may cover a preparatory course prior to such education according to national legislation;

c) 'school pupil' means a third-country national admitted to the territory of a Member State to follow a recognised programme of secondary education in the context of an exchange scheme operated by an organisation recognised for the purpose by the Member State in accordance with its regulations or administrative practice;

d) 'unremunerated trainee' means a third-country national who has been admitted to the territory of a Member State for a training period without remuneration, in accordance with national law;

e) 'establishment' means a public or private establishment recognised by the host Member State and /or whose courses of study are recognised in accordance with its regulations or administrative practice for the purposes set out in this Directive;

f) 'voluntary service scheme' means a programme of activities of practical solidarity, based on a State or a Community scheme, pursuing objectives of general interest;

g) 'residence permit' means any authorisation issued by the authorities of a Member State allowing a third country national to stay legally in its territory, in accordance with the provisions of Article 1 (2) (a) of Council Regulation (EC) 1030/2002 of 13 June 2002 laying down a uniform format for residence permits for third country nationals.

Article 3
Scope

1. This Directive applies to third-country nationals who apply to be admitted to the territory of a Member State for the purposes of studies.

Member States may also decide to apply this directive to third country nationals who apply to be admitted for the purposes of pupil exchange, unremunerated training or voluntary service.

2. The provisions of this Directive do not apply to:

a) third-country nationals residing in a Member State as asylum-seekers, or under subsidiary forms of protection or under temporary protection schemes;

b) third-country nationals whose expulsion has been suspended for reasons of fact or of law;

c) third-country nationals who are members of the family of Union citizens who have exercised their right to free movement in the Community;

d) third-country nationals who enjoy long-term resident status in a Member State in accordance with Council Directive 2003/109/EC of 25.11.2003 on status of third country nationals who are long-term residents[2] and exercise their right to reside in another Member State in order to study or receive vocational training.

e) third country nationals qualified under the national legislation of the Member State concerned as workers or self- employed persons.

Article 4
More favourable provisions

1. This Directive is without prejudice to more favourable provisions of:

a) bilateral or multilateral agreements between the Community or the Community and its Member States and one or more third countries; or

b) bilateral or multilateral agreements between one or more Member States and one or more third countries.

2. This Directive is without prejudice to the right of Member States to adopt or maintain provisions that are more favourable to the persons to whom it applies.

---

[2] Ed: OJ L 16, 23.1.2004, p. 44.

CHAPTER II
Conditions of Admission

Article 5
Principle

The admission of a third country national under this Directive is subject to the verification of documentary evidence showing that he/she meets the conditions laid down in Article 6 and whichever of Article 7, 8, 9, 10 or 11 applies to the relevant category.

Article 6
General conditions

1. A third country national who applies to be admitted for the purposes set out in Articles 7-11 shall:

a) present a valid travel document, as determined by the national law. Member States may require the period of the validity of the travel document to cover at least the duration of the planned stay;

b) if he /she is a minor under the national law of the host Member State, present a parental authorisation for the planned stay;

c) have sickness insurance in respect of all risks normally covered for its own nationals in the Member State concerned;

d) not be regarded as a threat to public policy, public security or public health.

e) provide proof, if the Member State so requests, that he / she has paid the fee for handling the application on the basis of Article 20 of this Directive.

2. Member States shall facilitate the admission procedure for the third-country nationals covered by Articles 7 to 11 who participate in Community programmes enhancing mobility towards or within the European Union.

Article 7
Specific conditions for students

1. In addition to the general conditions stipulated in Article 6, a third country national who applies to be admitted for study purposes shall:

a) have been accepted by an establishment of higher education to follow a course of study;

b) provide evidence requested by a Member State that during his/her stay he /she will have sufficient resources to cover his /her subsistence, study and return travel costs. Member States shall make public the minimum monthly resources required for the purpose of this provision, without prejudice to individual examination of each case;

c) provide evidence , if the Member State so requires, of sufficient knowledge of the language of the course followed by the student;

d) provide evidence, if the Member State so requires, that he/she has paid the fees charged by the establishment.

2. Students who automatically qualify for sickness insurance in respect of all risks normally covered for the nationals of the Member State concerned as a result of enrolment at an establishment shall be presumed to meet the condition of Article 6(1)(c).

Article 8
Mobility of students

1. Without prejudice to Articles 12(2), 15 and 18(2), a third-country national who has already been admitted as a student and applies to follow in another Member State part of the studies already commenced, or complement them with a related course of study in another Member State, shall be admitted by the latter Member State within a period that does not hamper the pursuit of the relevant studies, whilst leaving the competent authorities sufficient time to process the application, if he /she:

a) meets the conditions laid down by Articles 6 and 7 in relation to that Member State; and

b) has sent, with his /her application for admission, full documentary evidence of his /her academic record and evidence that the course he /she wishes to follow genuinely complements the one he /she has completed; and

c) participates in a Community or bilateral exchange programme or has been admitted as a student in a Member State for no less than two years.

2. The requirements referred to in paragraph 1c shall not apply in the case where the student, in the framework of his /her programme of studies has compulsorily to attend a part of his / her courses in an establishment of another Member State.

3. The competent authorities of the first Member State shall, at the request of the competent authorities of the second Member State provide the appropriate information in relation to the stay of the third country national student 6n the territory of the first Member State.

Article 9
Specific conditions for school pupils participating in an exchange scheme

1. Subject to Article 3, a third country national who applies to be admitted in a pupil exchange scheme shall, in addition to the general conditions stipulated in Article 6:

a) not be below the minimum age nor above the maximum age set by the Member State concerned;

b) provide evidence of acceptance to a secondary education establishment;

c) provide evidence of participation in a recognised pupil exchange scheme programme operated by an organisation recognised for that purpose by the Member State concerned in accordance with its regulations or administrative practice;

d) provide evidence that the pupil exchange organisation accepts responsibility for him / her throughout his /her period of presence in the territory of the Member State concerned, in particular as regards subsistence, study, health-care and return travel costs;

e) be accommodated throughout his / her stay by a family meeting the conditions set by the Member State concerned and selected in accordance with the rules of the pupil exchange scheme in which he / she is participating.

2. Member States may confine the admission of school pupils participating in an exchange scheme to nationals of third countries which offer the same possibility for their own nationals.

Article 10
Specific conditions for unremunerated trainees

Subject to Article 3, a third country national who applies to be admitted as an unremunerated trainee, shall, in addition to the general conditions stipulated in Article 6:

a) have signed a training agreement, approved if need be by the relevant authority in the Member State concerned in accordance with its regulations or administrative practice, for an unremunerated placement with a public- or private-sector enterprise or vocational training establishment recognised by the Member State in accordance with its regulations or administrative practice;

b) provide evidence requested by a Member State that during his/her stay he/she will have sufficient resources to cover his / her subsistence, training and return travel costs. The Member States shall make public the minimum monthly resources required for the purpose of this provision, without prejudice to individual examination of each case;

c) receive, if the Member State so requires, basic language training so as to acquire the knowledge needed for the purposes of the placement.

Article 11
Specific conditions for volunteers

Subject to Article 3, a third country national who applies to be admitted in a voluntary service scheme shall, in addition to the general conditions stipulated in Article 6:

a) not be below the minimum age nor above the maximum age set by the Member State concerned;

b) produce an agreement with the organisation responsible in the Member State concerned for the voluntary service scheme in which he/she is participating, giving a description of tasks, the conditions in which he/she is supervised in the performance of those tasks, his/her working hours, the resources available to cover his travel, subsistence, accommodation costs and pocket money throughout his/her stay and, if appropriate, the training he will receive to help him/her perform his/her service;

c) provide evidence that the organisation responsible for the voluntary service scheme in which he /she is participating has subscribed a third-party insurance policy and accepts full responsibility for him/her throughout his/her stay, in particular as regards his/her subsistence, health-care and return travel costs;

d) and, if the host Member State specifically requires it, receive a basic introduction to the language, history and political and social structures of that Member State.

CHAPTER III
Residence Permits

Article 12
Resident permit issued to students

1. A residence permit shall be issued to the student for a period of at least one year and renewable if the holder continues to meet the conditions of Articles 6 and 7. Where the duration of the course of study is less than one year, the permit shall be valid for the duration of the course.

2. Without prejudice to Articles 16, renewal of a residence permit may be refused or the permit may be withdrawn if the holder:

a) does not respect the limits imposed on access to economic activities under Article 17 of this Directive;

b) does not make acceptable progress in his/her studies in accordance with national legislation or administrative practice.

Article 13
Resident permit issued to school pupil

A residence permit issued to school pupils shall be issued only for a period of no more than one year.

Article 14
Resident permit issued to unremunerated trainees

The period of validity of a residence permit issued to unremunerated trainees shall correspond to the duration of the placement or for a maximum of one year. In exceptional cases, it may be renewed, once only and exclusively for such time as is needed to acquire a vocational qualification recognised by a Member State in accordance with its regulations or administrative practice, provided the holder still meets the conditions laid down in Articles 6 and 10.

Article 15
Residence permit issued to volunteers

A residence permit issued to volunteers shall be issued only for a period of no more than one year.

In exceptional circumstances, if the duration of the relevant programme is longer than one year, the duration of the validity of the residence permit may correspond to the period concerned.

Article 16
Withdrawal or non-renewal of residence permits

1. Member States may withdraw or refuse to renew a residence permit issued on the basis of this Directive when it has been fraudulently acquired or wherever it appears that the holder did not meet or no longer meets the conditions for entry and residence provided for by Article 6 and whichever of Articles 7 to 11 inclusive applies to the relevant category.

2. Member States may withdraw or refuse to renew a residence permit on grounds of public policy, public security or public health.

CHAPTER IV
Treatment of the Third-country Nationals Concerned

Article 17
Economic activities by students

1. Outside their study time and subject to the rules and conditions applicable to the relevant activity in the host Member State, students shall be entitled to be employed and may be entitled to exercise self – employed economic activity. The situation of the labour market in the said Member State may be taken into account.

Where necessary, Member States shall grant students and/or employers prior authorization in accordance with national legislation.

2. Each Member State shall determine the maximum number of hours per week or days or months per year allowed for such an activity, which shall not be less than 10 hours per week, or the equivalent in days or months per year.

3. Access to economic activities for the first year of residence may be restricted by the host Member State.

4. Member States may require students to report, in advance or otherwise, to an authority designated by them, that they are engaging in an economic activity. Their employers may also be subject to a reporting obligation, in advance or otherwise.

CHAPTER V
Procedure and Transparency

Article 18
Procedural guarantees and transparency

1. A decision on an application for obtaining or renewing a residence permit shall be adopted and the applicant shall be notified of it within a period that does not hamper the pursuit of the relevant studies, whilst leaving the competent authorities sufficient time to process the application.

2 If the information supplied in support of the application is inadequate the consideration of the application may be suspended and the competent authorities shall inform the applicant what further information they need.

3. Any decision rejecting an application for a residence permit shall be notified to the third-country national concerned in accordance with the notification procedures under the relevant national legislation. The notification shall specify the possible redress procedures available and the time limit for taking action.

4. Where an application is rejected, or a residence permit, issued in accordance with this Directive, is withdrawn, the person concerned shall have the right to mount a legal challenge before the authorities of the Member State concerned.

Article 19

Fast-track procedure for issuing residence permits or visas to student and school pupils

An agreement on the establishment of a fast-track admission procedure allowing residence permits or visas to be issued in the name of the third-country national concerned may be concluded between the authority of a Member State with responsibility for the entry and residence of students or school pupils who are third-country nationals and an establishment of higher education or an organization operating pupil exchange schemes which has been recognised for this purpose by the Member State concerned in accordance with its regulations or administrative practice.

Article 20

Fees

Member States may request applicants to pay fees for handling applications in accordance with this Directive.

CHAPTER VI

Final Provisions

Article 21

Reporting

Periodically, and for the first time no later than three years after the period determined by Article 22, the Commission shall report to the European Parliament and the Council on the application of this Directive in the Member States and propose amendments if appropriate.

Article 22

Transposal

Member States shall bring into force the provisions necessary to comply with this Directive no later than twenty – four months after the date of entry into force of this Directive. They shall forthwith inform the Commission thereof.

When Member States adopt those provisions, they shall contain a reference to this Directive or be accompanied by such a reference on the occasion of their official publication. Member States shall determine how such reference is to be made.

Article 23

(Derogation)

By way of derogation from the provisions set out in Chapter III, Member States are not obliged to issue permits in accordance with this Directive in the form of a residence permit for a period of up to two years, after the period determined by Article 22 expires.

Article 24
(Time derogation)

Without prejudice to Article 4 (2) second subparagraph of the Council Directive 2003/109/ EC of 25 November 2003, concerning the status of third country nationals who are long term residents, Member States shall not be obliged to take into account the time during which the student, exchange pupil, unremunerated trainee or volunteer has resided as such in their territory for the purpose of granting further rights under national law to the said third country nationals.

Article 25
Entry into force

This Directive shall enter into force on the twentieth day following its publication in the Official Journal of the European Union.

Article 29
Addressees

This Directive is addressed to the Member States.

EXPLANATORY MEMORANDUM

1. Context

1.1. In accordance with the objectives set by the Scoreboard to review progress in the creation of an area of freedom, security and justice in the European Union,[3] the European Commission is presenting a proposal for a directive on the conditions of entry and residence of third-country nationals for the purpose of studies, vocational training or voluntary service. This proposal completes the set of initiatives already presented on immigration for the purposes of employment[4] and family reunification[5] to harmonise national legislation on conditions of entry and residence of third-country nationals with a view to establishing a full legal framework governing admission on the basis of the purpose of the stay. It has been decided that there will not be a proposal governing the admission of third-country nationals for other purposes not provided for in the other proposals for directives, to constitute the parallel to Directive 90/364/EEC of 28 June 1990 on the right of residence[6] of Community nationals not enjoying the right under other provisions of Community law. The fact is that the admission

---

[3] Six-monthly updating, first half of 2002, COM(2002)261, p. 23.

[4] Proposal for a Council Directive on the conditions of entry and residence of third-country nationals for the purpose of paid employment and self-employed economic activities (COM(2001)386).

[5] Proposal for a Council Directive on the right to family reunification (COM(1999)638) and amended proposals (COM(2000)624 and COM(2002)225) adopted as Council Directive (2003) 86, OJ L 251/12, 3.10.2003.

[6] OJ L 180, 13.7.1990, p. 26.

of the relatively low number of people falling in this category can be dealt with adequately by the Member States' domestic law at the current stage of approximation of immigration legislation. If the need for common rules is felt in the future, the Commission will be able to exercise it's right of initiative and amplify the legislation.

The Commission has now presented all the immigration policy proposals needed for the implementation of Article 63(3)(a) and (4) of the Treaty establishing the European Community, as amended by the Amsterdam Treaty. The mandate given by point 20 of the conclusions of the Tampere European Council on 15 and 16 October 1999 ('The European Council acknowledges the need for approximation of national legislations on the conditions for admission and residence of third country nationals [and] requests to this end rapid decisions by the Council, on the basis of proposals by the Commission') has thus been carried out on the Commission's side.

1.2. The specific feature of migration for the purpose of studies, vocational training or voluntary service is that it is by definition temporary and that it does not depend on the labour market situation in the host country. It constitutes a form of mutual enrichment for the migrants who benefit directly from it, both for their country of origin and for the host country, while helping to improve mutual familiarity between cultures. The admission of third-country nationals for training purposes has therefore traditionally been looked on favourably, particularly as regards students in higher education, as can be seen in the Resolution on the admission of third-country nationals to the territory of the Member States for study purposes[7] adopted by the Council on 30 November 1994 in the justice and home affairs cooperation established by the Maastricht Treaty. Certain Member States apply policies that are more and more attractive to students from third countries.

1.3. The number of students benefiting from international exchanges is now greater than ever, and demand for international education and student mobility is growing constantly. One of the objectives of European Community action on education and international relations is to promote the Member States together as a world centre of excellence for education and to share knowledge better around the world as a means of helping to disseminate the values of human rights, democracy and the rule of law. In their Joint Declaration at Bologna on 19 June 1999, the Education Ministers of 29 European States declared that 'The vitality and efficiency of any civilisation can be measured by the appeal that its culture has for other countries. We need to ensure that the European higher education system acquires a world-wide degree of attraction equal to our extraordinary cultural and scientific traditions'. As certain experiences have shown, welcoming large numbers of third-country nationals into Europe's educational establishments, especially at master's and doctorate levels, can have a beneficial effect on the quality and dynamism of Europe's own training systems. Establishments will have an incentive to develop more and more high-quality courses meeting the demand for internationalisation in education and for greater student mobility. This proposal for a directive has been designed to ensure that the harmonisation of national legislation in the Member States governing the conditions of entry and residence of third-country nationals for the purpose of studies contributes to the attainment of these objectives by promoting their admission. It thus makes an indirect contribution to the objective of developing quality

---

[7] OJ C 274, 19.9.1996, p. 10.

education set by Article 149 of the EC Treaty and, along with the proposal for establishing the Erasmus World programme,[8] fits into the strategy of stepping up cooperation with third countries in higher education proposed by the Commission in its communication of 18 July 2001.[9]

1.4. Many Member States more and more often provide certain third-country nationals with the opportunity to remain after their training as workers, at least for a limited period, so as to remedy shortages of skilled manpower. Changes from student to worker status are envisaged for third-country nationals in the proposal for a directive on the conditions of entry and residence of third-country nationals for the purpose of paid employment and self-employed economic activities,[10] Article 5 of which allows residence permit applications to be lodged 'directly in the territory of the Member State concerned, if the applicant is already resident or legally present there'. But the wish to promote the admission of third-country nationals for the purpose of studies requires the Union and the Member States to take flanking measures to avoid amplifying the South-North brain drain, which has already acquired unprecedented proportions. These measures form part of the partnership with countries of origin called for by the conclusions of the Tampere European Council among other measures needed for the establishment of a comprehensive policy on migration and should deal by way of priority with action on the commitment given by the Community and the Member States in the third subparagraph of Article 13(4) of the Cotonou Agreement of 23 June 2000 that they would see that in vocational training schemes in the Member States national and regional cooperation programmes would be oriented towards vocational integration of ACP nationals in their country of origin.

1.5. The wish to promote the admission of third-country nationals for the purpose of studies or vocational training must be accompanied by a constant concern to safeguard public policy and public security. On this point the proposal contains provisions that are broad enough to leave the Member States with the room for manoeuvre they need to refuse admission or terminate the stay of a third-country national who constitutes a threat to public policy and public security (Articles 6 and 16(2)). The fact that the various types of residence permit covered by the proposal have a general maximum period of validity of one year, except in special cases, or must be renewed every year will make it easier for Member States to exercise strict control.

2.   Background and compatibility of the proposal with other commission initiatives

2.1. The objective pursued by this proposal for a directive has already been covered, in whole or in part, by a number of European instruments or initiatives. Apart from the 1994 Council Resolution on the admission of third-country nationals for study purposes (see point 1.2, *supra*), the 1997 Commission proposal for a Council Act establishing the Convention on rules for the admission of third-country nationals in the Member States[11] contained

---

[8] Proposal for a European Parliament and Council Decision establishing a programme for the enhancement of quality in higher education and the promotion of intercultural understanding through cooperation with third countries (COM(2002)401).

[9] COM(2001)385.

[10] COM(2001)386.

[11] OJ C 337, 7.11.1997, p. 9.

provisions relating to admission for study and vocational training purposes and other purposes, but no action was taken on it because of the entry into force of the Amsterdam Treaty.

2.2 The Commission asked the International Centre for Migration Policy Development (ICMPD) for a comparative law study by way of input for the preparatory work on this proposal for a directive. The findings were published by the Official Publications Office of the European Communities in 2001 as 'Admission of third country nationals to an EU Member State for the purposes of study or vocational training and admission of persons not gainfully employed'. The Commission also engaged in wide-ranging consultations on the basis of an internal discussion paper. Apart from bilateral consultations with delegations of officials from administrative bodies in the Member States, the opinions of many representative organisations in the fields of education, vocational training, voluntary service and migration and of the social partners were sought both in Europe and in its Member States. The results helped make it possible to enrich and improve the proposal substantially on many points.

3. **Objectives and overview of the proposal**

3.1. The proposal distinguishes four categories of third-country nationals: students, school pupils, unremunerated trainees and people doing voluntary service (volunteers).

Admission for study purposes mainly concerns higher education, as it is well known that this is where international mobility is most common and admission for the purpose of vocational training concerns the acquisition of occupational skills in a public- or private-sector enterprise or vocational training establishment. Provisions have been made in the proposal for a directive to promote secondary school pupil exchanges between the European Union and non-member countries to stimulate the discovery of European culture by young people from non-member countries, especially as they might subsequently be tempted to return to their host Member State to pursue their studies in higher education. The proposal also contains provisions for volunteers, who sometimes have difficulty obtaining a residence permit since, as they are not workers (being unremunerated), nor students (not being enrolled in an educational establishment), they are sometimes regarded as not belonging to any specific category of migrants.

3.2. Apart from the general conditions for admission, the proposal lays down the specific conditions for admission of each of the four categories. They have been drafted as objectively as possible to promote admission on the grounds set out at points 1.2 and 1.3 while preserving the Member States' room for discretion. The main criterion for admission of third-country nationals for purposes of study, vocational training or voluntary service must be, apart from an assurance that they have adequate resources to cover their needs during their stay, admission to an educational establishment, participation in a pupil exchange scheme programme, a vocational training contract or participation in a voluntary service scheme, as the case may be. As regards the resources criterion, it is proposed that for students and trainees the Member States should publish the minimum monthly financial resources required. The resources of school pupils and volunteers are a matter for their host family or voluntary service organisation, which must meet their needs.

3.3 Mobility of students between Member States must be facilitated so that the European Union can reflect the reality of the growing internationalisation of education. Two situations need to be distinguished: first, the situation of third-country nationals admitted to the European Union for the purpose of studies, in respect of whom Article 8 of this proposal acknowledges, once they have been admitted a first time to a Member State, the right to reside in another Member State to pursue part of the course they have started or to take a further course, provided they meet specific conditions; and second, the situation of third-country nationals who already reside in the European Union for whom this proposal contains no provisions, since Article 16(1) of the proposal for a directive on the status of third-country nationals who are long-term residents allows them, once they have acquired long-term resident status (i.e. after five years' uninterrupted lawful residence), the right to reside in another Member State for study or vocational training purposes. The proposal also contains a provision to facilitate the admission of third-country nationals participating in Community programmes to encourage mobility towards or within the European Union (Article 6(2)).

3.4. To reflect the cost of training and the fact that more and more people have to work to help pay for it, the proposal gives students generally and unremunerated trainees limited access to the employment market up to a maximum number of weekly hours to be set by each Member State at between 10 and 20 hours, while allowing the Member States to insist that those concerned make a declaration of their working activity so that compliance with this limit can be monitored.

3.5. The proposal also contains procedural provisions. In particular, it allows applicants other than holders of short-stay visas to apply for their residence permit locally. Apart from the maximum time allowed for issuing residence permits and visas, which, assuming the application is fully in order, is 90 days, the proposal provides a basis for the good practices of certain Member States which expedite the procedures for admitting students and school pupils and provides for their generalisation across the European Union by means of agreements to be concluded between the Member States' immigration authorities and educational establishments or exchange organisations. To promote in third countries education and vocational training possibilities available in Europe, Member States are asked to make efforts at transparency so as to ensure that third-country nationals can have access in their countries of origin to information about education and vocational training establishments and programmes open to them in the Member States and the conditions and procedures for admission to the territory.

4. Choice of legal basis

4.1. The legal basis for the proposal has been selected on the basis of its purpose, which is to lay down the conditions and procedures for entry and residence by third-country nationals in the territory of the Member States for the purpose of studies, vocational training or voluntary service. It does not concern the conditions for admission to education establishments or vocational training schemes, which remain the responsibility of the Member States and possibly of the relevant establishments, authorities or firms themselves. This directive will not require the Member States to open up their education or vocational training schemes to third-country nationals where they are currently excluded, nor to establish one or other kind of vocational training scheme to which it applies which they do not already have (such as on-the-job training in firms). Article 63(3)(a) and (4) of the EC Treaty, as amended by the Amsterdam Treaty, which entered into force on 1 May 1999, provides that the Council is to adopt measures relating to immigration policy in the following areas:

'(a) conditions of entry and residence, and standards on procedures for the issue by Member States of long-term visas and residence permits, including those for the purpose of family reunion', and this has been taken as the legal basis.

4.2. This proposal must therefore be adopted by the procedure of Article 67 of the EC Treaty: the Council acts unanimously on a proposal from the Commission or the initiative of a Member State after consulting the European Parliament. Since it is based on Title IV of the Treaty, Denmark will not participate in the adoption of the directive, which will not be binding on it or applicable to it by virtue of Articles 1 and 2 of the Protocol on the position of Denmark annexed to the Union and EC Treaties. Nor will it apply to the United Kingdom or Ireland by virtue of Articles 1 and 2 of the Protocol on the position of the United Kingdom and Ireland, unless they decide otherwise in accordance with the procedure determined by that Protocol.

5. Subsidiarity and proportionality

5.1. The European Community does not have exclusive powers under Title IV (Visas, asylum, immigration and other policies related to free movement of persons) of the EC Treaty and therefore, in accordance with the subsidiarity and proportionality principles, can act only if and to the extent that the objectives of the proposed action cannot be sufficiently achieved by the Member States and can therefore, by reason of the scale or effects of the proposed action, be better achieved by the Community, and the Community action may not go beyond what is necessary to achieve the objectives of the Treaty. The proposal for a directive meets these requirements.

5.2. The conditions of entry and residence of third-country nationals for the purpose of studies or vocational training currently diverge widely between the Member States. The first objective of this directive, which is to establish a harmonised Community legal framework for the conditions for entry and residence of third-country nationals in the territory of the Member States for a period exceeding three months for those purposes, and for the procedures for issuing residence permits and visas allowing them to enter and reside in the Member States for those purposes, cannot be sufficiently achieved by the Member States. Moreover, the promotion of the European Union as a whole as a world centre of excellence for education and vocational training, to which this proposal contributes, can obviously be better attained at Community level than at national level.

5.3. The proposed instrument is a directive that lays down general principles and leaves it up to the addressee Member States to choose the most appropriate form and methods for implementing many points of it in their domestic law in the domestic context. The proposal refers to Member States' own rules and regulations and administrative practice as regards the definition of establishment of higher, professional or secondary education or vocational training and requirements for accreditation or similar and the determination of the language schools and courses for which third-country nationals can apply. Certain conditions, such as proof of payment of enrolment fees demanded by the establishment and fees for processing applications for residence permits and applicants' language skills, are not mandatory but left to the discretion of the Member States (Article 6(1)(c) and (d), Article 10(c) and Article 11(d)). Account has been taken of the fact that in some countries health-care insurance is available automatically to those who enroll at an educational establishment (Article 7(2)).

Lastly, the financial resources that students or unremunerated trainees may be required to have are not determined by the directive, the Member States simply being required to publish the minimum amount that they determine. Out of the same concern for flexibility, other conditions are not determined by the directive but left to the Member States' discretion (such as those relating to age limits of school pupils and volunteers). As regards fast-track procedures, the directive likewise merely sets a general framework within which the relevant authorities of the Member States and educational establishments and pupil exchange organisations may agree on procedures for issuing residence permits, in particular the shortened time-spans applicable here.

Chapter 2.4
VICTIMS OF TRAFFICKING

COUNCIL DIRECTIVE
on the short-term residence permit issued to victims of action to facilitate illegal immigration or trafficking in human beings who cooperate with the competent authorities[1]

THE COUNCIL OF THE EUROPEAN UNION,
Having regard to the Treaty establishing the European Community, and in particular Article 63(3) thereof,
Having regard to the proposal from the Commission,
Having regard to the Opinion of the European Parliament,
Having regard to the Opinion of the Economic and Social Committee,
Having regard to the Opinion of the Committee of the Regions,

Whereas:

(1) The framing of a common immigration policy, including the definition of the conditions of entry and residence for foreigners and measures to combat illegal immigration, is a constituent element of the European Union's objective of creating an area of freedom, security and justice.

(2) At its special meeting in Tampere on 15 and 16 October 1999, the European Council expressed its determination to tackle illegal immigration at source, for example by targeting those who engage in trafficking of human beings and the economic exploitation of migrants. It called on the Member States to concentrate their efforts on detecting and dismantling criminal networks while protecting the rights of victims.

(3) An indication of the growing concern about this phenomenon at international level was the adoption by the United Nations General Assembly of a Convention against Transnational Organised Crime, supplemented by a Protocol to Prevent, Suppress and Punish Trafficking in Persons, especially Women and Children, and a Protocol Against the Smuggling of Migrants by Land, Sea and Air. These were signed by the Community and the fifteen Member States in December 2000.

---

[1] COM(2002)71 final. This Directive has been formally adopted on 29 April 2004.

See also the Council Framework Decision on Strengthening of the penal framework to prevent the facilitation of unauthorised entry, transit and residence – (JHA) No. 946/2002 – Official Journal L328, 5 December 2002; and the Council Directive Defining the facilitation of unauthorised entry, transit and residence – (EC) No. 90/2002 – Official Journal L328, 5 December 2002.

(4) At European Community level, several instruments are in the process of being adopted to define the offences of facilitating illegal immigration and trafficking in human beings.[2]

(5) This Directive introduces a residence permit intended for the victims of these offences, which offers a sufficient incentive to them to cooperate with the competent authorities while including certain conditions to safeguard against abuse.

(6) To this end, it is necessary to define the short-term residence permit, to lay down the criteria for issuing it, the conditions of residence and the grounds for non-renewal and withdrawal.

(7) Victims must be informed of the possibility of obtaining this residence permit and be given a period in which to reflect on their position. This should help put them in a position to reach a well-informed decision as to whether or not to cooperate with the police and judicial authorities (in view of the risks this may entail), so that they cooperate freely and hence more effectively. Given the extreme vulnerability of victims' situation they must have access to the assistance and care they require.

(8) Confronted with a victim who clearly intends to cooperate and whose presence the judicial authority regards as useful to the proceedings, the competent administrative authority will issue a short-term residence permit for six months, renewable for six month periods.

(9) To enable victims to gain their independence and not return to the criminal network, the residence permit shall allow the holder to have access to the labour market and pursue vocational training and education. For the same reasons, the Member States may make the issue of the permit conditional on victims' participation in programmes aimed at integrating them or preparing them for assisted return.

(10) This Directive is without prejudice to other provisions on the protection of victims, witnesses or persons who are particularly vulnerable. Nor does it detract from the prerogatives of the Member States as regards the right of residence granted on humanitarian or other grounds.

(11) This Directive respects fundamental rights and complies with the principles recognised for example by the Charter of Fundamental Rights of the European Union.

(12) The objective of introducing a short-term residence permit for victims who lodge a complaint or cooperate in the fight against traffickers or smugglers cannot be achieved adequately by Member States. Indeed, the criminal organisations operate by definition on an international scale. In order to fight against this phenomenon, an increasing number of Member States have introduced residence permits for those cooperating with the judicial authorities, with positive results. It would, however, be wrong if disparities between measures in different states were to lead to a shift in the activities of international networks to those

---

[2] Ed.: Council Directive 2002/90/EC on defining the facilitation of unauthorised entry, transit and residence, OJ L 328, 5.12.2002; Council Framework Decision of 19.7.2002 on combating trafficking in human beings, OJ L 203, 1.8.2002, p. 1.

Member States where they faced fewer difficulties and risks. As the objectives pursued, in view of the extent of the action, can be better achieved at the Community level, the Community can take measures in accordance with the subsidiarity principle as laid down in Article 5 of the Treaty. In accordance with the proportionality principle, as laid down in the same Article, the directive does not go beyond what is necessary to achieve these goals.

HAS ADOPTED THIS DIRECTIVE:

CHAPTER I
General Provisions

Article 1
Purpose

The purpose of this Directive is to introduce a short-term residence permit for third-country nationals who are victims of offences constituted by the action to facilitate illegal immigration or by trafficking in human beings (hereafter referred to as 'victims') who cooperate in the fight against the perpetrators of these offences.

Article 2
Definitions

For the purposes of this Directive:

(a) 'third-country national' means any person who is not a citizen of the Union within the meaning of Article 17(1) of the treaty, including stateless persons;

(b) 'action to facilitate illegal immigration' means the offences defined in Articles 1 and 2 of the Council Directive 2002/90/EC on defining the facilitation of unauthorised entry, transit and stay;[3]

(c) 'trafficking in human beings' means the offences defined in Articles 1, 2 and 3 of the Council Framework Decision of 19.7.2002 on combating trafficking in human beings;[4]

(d) 'measure to enforce an expulsion order' means any measure taken by a Member State to enforce the decision of an administrative authority ordering the expulsion of a third-country national;

(e) 'short-term residence permit' means any permit or authorisation issued by a Member State in accordance with its legislation, allowing a victim to reside in its territory in order to cooperate with the competent authorities.

Article 3
Scope

1. This Directive shall apply to victims, as referred to in Article 1, having reached the age of majority.

---

[3] Ed.: OJ L 328, 5.12.2002.
[4] Ed.: OJ L 203, 1.8.2002.

2. Member States may decide to apply the provisions of this Directive to minors who fulfil certain conditions laid down in their national law.

Article 4
Safeguard

This Directive shall be without prejudice to the protection extended to refugees, to beneficiaries of subsidiary protection and persons seeking international protection under international refugee law and without prejudice to other human rights instruments.

Article 5
Non-discrimination

Member States shall apply this Directive without discrimination on the grounds of sex, race, colour, ethnic or social origin, genetic characteristics, language, religion or belief, political or other opinion, membership of a national minority, wealth, birth, disability, age or sexual orientation.

Article 6
More favourable provisions

The provisions of this Directive shall not affect any laws, regulations or administrative provisions laid down by a Member State which would be more favourable to the persons covered by this Directive.

CHAPTER II
Procedure for Issuing the Short-term Residence Permit

Article 7
Information given to the victims

Persons who are identified by the competent authorities as victims within the meaning of Article 1 shall immediately be informed of the possibility of obtaining the short-term residence permit provided for by this Directive.

The information shall be provided by the authorities responsible for the investigation or prosecution, an association or a non-governmental organisation.

Article 8
Reflection period

1. Victims shall be granted a reflection period of 30 days to take the decision to cooperate with the competent authorities. This period starts from the moment they sever relations with those suspected of committing the offences referred to in Article 2(b) and (c).

2. During this period and while awaiting the decision of the authority responsible for the investigation or prosecution in accordance with Article 10(1), they shall have access to the

assistance and care referred to in Article 9 and it shall not be possible to enforce any expulsion order against them.

3. The reflection period shall not create any entitlement to residence under this Directive.

4. The State may at any time terminate the reflection period if the person has renewed contact with the authors of the offences referred to in Article 2(b) and (c) or for reasons relating to the protection of public order and national security.

Article 9
Assistance and care

1. Without prejudice to the application of measures relating to the protection of victims and witnesses, Member States shall ensure that victims have access to suitable accommodation, emergency medical and psychological treatment and medical care that cannot be postponed, and to the necessary support in the form of social welfare and means of subsistence if they do not have sufficient resources. They shall attend to the special needs of the most vulnerable.

2. Member States shall provide victims with free legal aid and translation and interpreting services.

Article 10
Issue and renewal of the residence permit

1. The authority responsible for the investigation or prosecution shall decide on the following matters, at the latest ten days after the expiry of the 30-day reflection period:
   (a) whether the presence of the victim is useful;
   (b) whether the victim has shown a clear intention to cooperate substantiated, for example, by an initial, material declaration to the authorities responsible for the investigation or prosecution, or the lodging of a complaint, or any other act provided for by the Member State's legislation;
   (c) whether the victim has severed all relations with those suspected of acts that might be included among the offences referred to in Article 2.

2. The short-term residence permit shall be issued if:
   (a) the authority responsible for the investigation or prosecution rules favourably on the criteria listed in paragraph 1;
   (b) there are no objections on the grounds of the protection of public order and national security.

3. The short-term residence permit shall be valid for six months. It shall be renewed for periods of six months if the conditions set out in paragraph 2 continue to be satisfied.

4. When Member States grant a short term permit to a person identified as a victim of one of the offences referred to under Article 2(b) and (c) with member of his/her family or persons treated as members of his/her family, they shall take this element into account when examining the possibility of granting them a residence permit on humanitarian grounds.

Article 11
Format of the residence permit

The short-term residence permit may be issued in the form of a sticker or a separate document. It shall be issued according to the rules and standard format laid down in Council Regulation No 1030/2002 laying down a uniform format for residence permits for third-country nationals.[5] Under the heading 'Type of permit' Member States shall enter the words 'Short term residence permit'.

CHAPTER III
Conditions of Residence

Article 12
Work, training and education

The Member States shall authorise the holders of a short-term residence permit to have access to the labour market, vocational training and education.

Article 13
Medical and psychological care

1. Member States shall ensure that holders of a short-term residence permit have access to primary medical care, in addition to the assistance and care referred to in Article 9.

2. Member States shall meet to the special needs of victims, such as pregnant women, the disabled or victims of rape or other forms of sexual violence and, if Member States take advantage of the option provided in Article 3(2), minors.

Article 14
Victims who are minors

If Member States take advantage of the option provided in Article 3(2), the following provisions shall apply:
  a) Member States shall take due account of the best interests of the child when applying the provisions of this Directive. They shall ensure that the procedure is appropriate to the age and maturity of the child. In particular, if they consider that it is in the best interest of the child, they may extend the reflection period.
  b) Member States shall ensure that minors have access to the educational system under the same conditions as nationals. Member States may stipulate that such access must be limited to the public education system.
  c) Besides, in the case of victims who are unaccompanied minors, Member States shall take the necessary steps to establish their identity and the fact that they are unaccompanied.

They shall make every effort to locate their families as quickly as possible and take the necessary steps immediately to ensure legal representation, including representation in criminal proceedings, if necessary.

---

[5] Ed.: OJ L 157, 15.6.2002.

Article 15
Rehabilitation programmes for victims

Member States may make the issue of short-term residence permits conditional upon the victims' participation in a programme aimed either at their integration in the host country and, where appropriate, vocational training, or their assisted return to the country of origin or another country willing to accept them.

CHAPTER IV
Non-renewal and Withdrawal

Article 16
Non-renewal

1. The short-term residence permit shall not be renewed if the conditions of Article 10(2) cease to be satisfied, if a judicial decision has terminated the proceedings or, if relevant, the beneficiary does not take part in the rehabilitation programme referred to in Article 15.

2. When the short-term residence permit expires ordinary aliens law shall apply. If victims submit an application for another type of residence permit, Member States shall take account of their cooperation when considering their applications.

Article 17
Withdrawal

The short-term residence permit may be withdrawn at any time:
(a) if the holder has renewed contacts with those suspected of committing the offences in question, or
(b) if the judicial authority considering the case believes that the victim's cooperation or complaint is fraudulent or wrongful, or
(c) for reasons relating to the protection of public order and national security.

CHAPTER V
Final Provisions

Article 18
Penalties

Member States shall determine the system of penalties applying to violations of the national provisions enacted pursuant to this Directive and shall take all necessary measures to ensure the implementation of these provisions. The penalties envisaged must be effective, proportionate and deterrent. Member States shall communicate these provisions to the Commission at the latest by the date specified in Article 21. Any later amendment affecting these provisions shall be communicated without delay.

Article 19
Exchange of information

Every year the Member States shall communicate up-to-date information to the Commission on the following:

(a) the number of short-term residence permits issued, the proceedings initiated and their outcome;

(b) the rehabilitation programmes referred to in Article 15, together with an assessment of their effectiveness in rehabilitating victims.

Article 20
Report

1. No later than 30 June 2007, the Commission shall report to the European Parliament and the Council on the application of this Directive in the Member States and propose any amendments that are necessary. The Member States shall send the Commission any information relevant to the preparation of this report.

2. After presenting the report referred to in paragraph 1, the Commission shall report to the European Parliament and the Council at least every three years on the application of this Directive in the Member States.

Article 21
Transposal

The Member States shall bring into force the laws, regulations and administrative provisions necessary to comply with this Directive no later than 30 June 2003. They shall immediately inform the Commission accordingly.

When the Member States adopt these measures, they shall contain a reference to this Directive or shall be accompanied by such a reference when they are officially published. The precise nature of such a reference shall be decided by the Member States.

Article 22
Entry into force

This Directive shall enter into force on the twentieth day following its publication in the Official Journal of the European Communities.

Article 23
Addressees

This Directive is addressed to the Member States.

EXPLANATORY MEMORANDUM

1. Background

This Directive is a response to a problem that is causing mounting concern: the increase in illegal immigration, particularly in its two most odious forms, namely the growth of networks of smugglers acting for non-humanitarian reasons and the exploitation of foreign nationals in the form of trafficking in human beings.

1.1. *Nature of the phenomenon*

Although accurate figures are hard to come by, given that this is by definition a clandestine activity, research and field reports[6] suggest that illegal immigration is growing at international and European level. EU Member States are increasingly affected. The most common form involves transnational criminal networks operating for profit, displaying complete disregard for human dignity and endangering the lives of their victims.

Facilitating illegal immigration and trafficking in human beings are two separate offences in law, but experience suggests that in practice they often overlap. There are cases of migrants exploited on their journey to pay the price demanded by the smuggler, of others condemned to servitude to repay their debt once they arrive in their country of destination and others who believe they have found a way of earning a better living in a more developed country only to find themselves the victims of sexual or other forms of exploitation.

There are a number of other distinctive characteristics which justify the measures proposed to combat this phenomenon. Because this sort of immigration is illegal the victims do not have the right papers and their situation is to say the least insecure.

Even though they are victims of the crimes referred to above, they will not usually dare to report the matter to the authorities in the country where they find themselves, for fear of being immediately returned to their country of origin because of their illegal status. This means going back to square one, with the added misfortune of having failed in their attempt to leave. They will usually keep the details of their experience to themselves, thus failing to prevent other victims from falling into the same trap. Added to this is the fear of retaliation by the criminals, either directly against the victims or against their families and relations in the country of origin.

While this situation is unsatisfactory for the victims it is equally so for the authorities of the Member States trying to combat illegal immigration and expose and disband the networks involved. Victims may remain underground or be swiftly deported, but either way they do not disclose the invaluable information they have gained from their situation and what they have seen and heard. Yet this is precisely the sort of information the authorities responsible for investigating and prosecuting such crimes need to obtain in order to be able to combat them effectively. If the victims can be persuaded to cooperate with the authorities it may be possible to extract the different pieces of information in their possession (names, addresses,

---

[6] IOM, UNHCR and OSCE conducted several studies on this subject. The French Presidency has also organised a seminar on illegal immigration networks on 20-21 July 2000.

organisations, etc.). The more this cooperation serves the interests of the victim, the better they will be as a source of information. It is therefore necessary to offer incentives to victims to cooperate, and the incentives must be tailored to their concerns.

1.2.   *Provisions adopted by the Member States*

These considerations have prompted several Member States to try in recent years to step up the fight against the perpetrators of these crimes by turning to their victims. Belgium in 1994, Italy and the Netherlands in 1998 and Spain in 2000 amended their domestic legislation or regulations to promote the recovery and reintegration of victims, to enable victims to cooperate with the authorities pursuing the investigation or prosecution by supplying information, or to lay charges against the people suspected of these crimes, respectively. In the meantime, victims are given a residence permit, possibly after a reflection period if the permit is issued in exchange for actual cooperation with the authorities. Victims also receive help with housing, daily subsistence, medical care, etc. Where necessary they will be covered by the ordinary legislation on witness protection.

One point to note is that the first three Member States to adopt such provisions targeted trafficking in human beings, whereas Spain, the most recent country to introduce such measures, also included illegal immigration, illegal trafficking in labour and exploitation through prostitution. Most of the other Member States will issue residence permits on humanitarian grounds where such circumstances require it.

1.3.   *The United Nations Convention and Protocols*

While the Member States were upgrading their legal arsenal to reflect their desire to tackle this issue, the United Nations opened its Convention Against Transnational Organised Crime for signature in Palermo in December 2000, together with the additional Protocol to Prevent, Suppress and Punish Trafficking in Persons, especially Women and Children, and the Protocol Against the Smuggling of Migrants by Land, Sea and Air. The Convention was adopted by the UN General Assembly and signed by 135 countries. The Protocols were signed by 93 and 89 countries respectively. The Convention and Protocols define the offences in question, but the limitations of an international framework covering the countries of departure, transit and destination are clearly apparent in the restricted legal scope of the articles dealing with the protection of victims of trafficking.

1.4.   *The Community response*

This matter has also been dealt with by different Community institutions on several occasions since the late 1980s.

In 1989, the European Parliament adopted a Resolution on the exploitation of prostitution and the traffic in human beings, calling on the Member States to ensure that victims could lodge a complaint without fear of immediate deportation.[7] This was followed in 1993 by a Resolution on trade in women, which called for the formulation of a policy to combat illegal immigration and a legal right to residence and protection for migrant women when they are witnesses before, during and after legal proceedings against trade in human beings, as well

---

[7] Resolution A2-52/89, 14 April 1989, OJ C 120, 16 May 1989, p. 352 ff., in particular point 8.2.

as permission for victims of this international trade to remain in the Member States' territory, especially when their repatriation might pose a threat to their personal safety or expose them to renewed exploitation.[8] The adoption of measures to ensure the safety and dignity of victims in cases where they report their exploiters to the police, by guaranteeing them the right to bring civil proceedings, a temporary residence permit for humanitarian reasons and protection as witnesses, during and after the trial, all featured in a 1996 Resolution on trafficking in human beings.[9]

In the same year, the Commission referred explicitly to a temporary residence permit in its Communication on trafficking in women for the purpose of sexual exploitation.

It specifically mentioned 'the issue of a temporary permit of stay for victims prepared to act as witnesses in judicial proceedings and ... proper coordination between judicial and police authorities to avoid expulsion without consultation'.[10] The European Parliament Resolution on the matter listed specific measures to be taken: temporary residence status, social, health and psychological care, work permit and training opportunities during the period of stay, etc.[11]

Continuing the approach outlined in its 1996 Communication, the Commission presented another Communication two years later on further actions in the fight against trafficking in women.[12] It stressed the close interaction between the need for an immigration policy that catered for the situation of the victims of trafficking and the question of increasing the powers of the courts to sentence traffickers, reiterating the connection between improving prosecutions of traffickers and the possibility of allowing victims to remain in the host country and receive help there. Citing experience in Belgium, Italy and the Netherlands, the Commission expressed its belief that more should be done in this area by all Member States and announced that a proposal would be presented for legislation on temporary residence permits for victims prepared to give evidence, drawing on recent experience of national provisions in order to avoid the risk of any future measures being abused.

There has also been increased involvement by the Council. Under the Dutch Presidency, a Ministerial Declaration was adopted in The Hague on 26 April 1997, which included the idea of temporary residence status among the measures aimed at encouraging victims to go to the police and give evidence. Temporary residence status also featured in the Joint Action of 24 February 1997 adopted by the Council on the basis of Article K.3 of the Treaty on European Union, concerning action to combat trafficking in human beings and sexual exploitation of children.[13]

---

[8] Resolution B3-1264, 1283 and 1309/93, 16 September 1993, OJ C 268, 4 October 1993, p. 141 ff., in particular points 2 and 10.

[9] Resolution A4-0326/95, 18 January 1996, OJ C 032, 5 February 1996, p. 88 ff., in particular point 25.

[10] Commission Communication to the Council and the European Parliament on trafficking in women for the purpose of sexual exploitation, 20 November 1996, COM(96)567 final.

[11] Resolution A4-0372/1997 on the Commission Communication to the Council and the European Parliament on trafficking in women for the purpose of sexual exploitation, 16 December 1997.

[12] COM(1998)726, 9 December 1998.

[13] OJ L 63, 4 March 1997, p. 2 ff.

The Community has not only issued formal documents; it has launched Stop, an incentive and exchange programme for people responsible for combating trade in human beings and the sexual exploitation of children. It was set up in 1996 for a period of five years, which was then extended for a further two years. It complements the Daphne programme of Community action (2000-2003) on preventive measures to fight violence against children, young persons and women.

With the Treaty of Amsterdam having conferred powers in immigration matters on the Community, the Tampere European Council on 15 and 16 October 1999 set out the measures intended to facilitate the creation of an area of freedom, security and justice. Point 3 of the Conclusions of the Tampere European Council refers to the need 'to stop illegal immigration and to combat those who organise it and commit related international crimes', while point 23 expresses the determination 'to tackle at its source illegal immigration, especially by combating those who engage in trafficking in human beings and economic exploitation of migrants'.

Finally, this legislative proposal was announced in the recent Communication from the Commission on a common policy on illegal immigration.[14] Among the measures aimed at preventing and combating illegal immigration, set out here, the Commission indicated that it would present a legislative proposal on short-term residence permits for victims of trafficking who are prepared to cooperate in investigations and criminal proceedings against their exploiters.

2.   Aim: to step up the fight against illegal immigration

The aim of the present proposal for a Directive is to strengthen the instruments for combating illegal immigration by introducing a residence permit for the victims of action facilitating illegal immigration and trafficking in human beings, subject to conditions designed to encourage them to cooperate with the competent authorities against those suspected of committing the crimes in question. The proposal has been prepared on the basis of a thorough examination of the legislation and practice of the Member States, the replies to the questionnaire which the Commission sent to the Member States in Spring 2000 and the consultations in the European crime prevention forum of 30 October 2001.

2.1.   *A residence permit subject to conditions designed to encourage cooperation with the authorities*

The permit would be issued to victims, defined as adults (or possibly minors who fulfil certain conditions laid down by domestic law) who are third-country nationals and have suffered harm directly caused by action to facilitate illegal immigration or trafficking in human beings. When the police come into contact with people who might reasonably be regarded as victims, they will inform them of the existence of the temporary residence permit. Victims who effectively break off all relations with the suspected criminals will be granted a 30-day reflection period in which to decide, on the basis of all the facts, whether or not to take their cooperation with the police and judicial authorities any further.

---

[14] COM(2001)672 final, in particular point 4.7.2.

During this reflection period the Member State will allow victims to receive aid according to their needs (housing, medical and psychological care, social assistance if necessary), which should help them to regain the material and psychological autonomy needed to take the decision to cooperate. At the same time, the authority responsible for the investigation and prosecution (the judicial authorities or the police, depending on the Member State in question) will determine whether the presence of the victims is useful for the investigation or for prosecuting the suspects.

This authority will also have to decide whether victims are really prepared to cooperate and whether they have genuinely severed their links with the suspects. Cooperation may take various forms, from simply providing information or lodging a complaint to giving evidence in a trial.

If these three conditions are met and the victim does not pose a threat to public order or national security, the short-term residence permit will be issued for six months.

This permit gives access to the labour market, education and vocational training. It also gives victims greater access to medical care. The Member States may arrange for victims to follow an integration programme with a view to settling there or returning to their country of origin.

The residence permit may be renewed under the same conditions as it was issued. It will not be renewed if a judicial decision has been reached terminating the proceedings. At this point, the normal aliens legislation will apply. If victims apply for a residence permit on other grounds the Member State will take their cooperation in the criminal proceedings into account when considering the application.

Conversely, the short-term residence permit may be withdrawn from victims who are found to have renewed contacts with the suspects or who have not genuinely cooperated.

2.2.   *Victims of action facilitating illegal immigration and trafficking in human beings*

2.2.1.   From trafficking in women and children to trafficking in human beings
This proposal for a Directive is aimed at the victims of the offences of facilitating illegal immigration and trafficking in human beings. As we have seen from the various measures and different ways of looking at the issue prior to this proposal, the target group first consisted predominantly of women who were the victims of trafficking in human beings. This was because at that time they accounted for the majority of victims. Children were soon added to the target group, as it became clear that they, too, were affected by this phenomenon in large numbers. Then the definition was widened to trafficking in human beings, to include all those who might be affected. From victims of trafficking to victims of action to facilitate illegal immigration.

2.2.2.   From victims of trafficking to victims of action to facilitate illegal immigration
To put in the same text victims of action to facilitate illegal immigration and victims of trafficking in human beings reflects the fact that these two crimes are two particularly odious forms of a more general problem: the increase in illegal immigration. An instrument that

applies to both types of offence is likely to be more effective than one that targets only one of them. Hence the scope of this proposed Directive. Moreover, the two offences have certain factors in common, and victims often experience both in turn.

However, it should be clear that the notion of victim is to be understood in the precise and specific sense of Article 1. Although the notion of victim of trafficking in human beings does not present any difficulties (featuring as it does in the UN Protocol to Prevent, Suppress and Punish Trafficking in Persons, especially Women and Children), the concept of 'victim of action to facilitate illegal immigration' has a very specific meaning, in that it does not cover all those who seek assistance in illegal immigration, only those who might be reasonably regarded as victims, who have suffered harm (which is why it does not feature in the UN Protocol Against the Smuggling of Migrants by Land, Sea and Air). The concept, as mentioned in Article 1, covers persons who have suffered harm, for example having their lives endangered or physical injury.

2.3. *Not a victim protection or witness protection measure*

This proposal for a Directive is concerned with a residence permit and defines the conditions for its issue. In this sense, and to the extent that certain provisions on the conditions of residence constitute protective measures (starting with the residence permit itself, which offers *de facto* 'protection' against deportation), the proposal may appear to serve to protect victims. This is not, however, the case: the proposed Directive introduces a residence permit and is not concerned with protection of either witnesses or victims. This is neither its aim nor its legal basis. Victim protection and witness protection are matters of ordinary national or European law.

At the European level, the framework decision of 15 March 2001 on the status of victims in criminal proceedings[15] sets out the rules concerning the right to receive information and the specific assistance to be given to victims, as well as the right to compensation. It foresees that each Member State shall ensure that victims who are particularly vulnerable can benefit from specific treatment. Each Member State shall also guarantee a suitable level of protection to the victims and, if necessary, to their family or to persons treated as members of their family where the competent authorities consider that there is a serious risk of reprisals or firm evidence of serious intent to interfere with their privacy.

The Council in its Resolution of 23 November 1995 on the protection of witnesses in the framework of the fight against international organised crime[16] calls on the Member States to ensure proper and effective protection of witnesses before, during and after trials. Such protection must also be extended if necessary to the parents, children and other close relatives of witnesses.

3. **The choice of legal basis**

The choice of legal basis is consistent with the changes made to the Treaty establishing the European Community by the Treaty of Amsterdam, which came into force on 1 May 1999.

---

[15] OJ L 82, 22 March 2001, p. 1.
[16] OJ C 327, 7 December 1995, p. 5.

Article 63(3) of the EC Treaty states that the Council is to adopt 'measures on immigration policy within the following areas:

(a) conditions of entry and residence… ;

(b) illegal immigration and illegal residence'. This Article is the legal basis for a proposal for a Directive which would define the conditions of issue, the terms of residence and the grounds for withdrawal or non-renewal of a residence permit issued to people whose administrative situation is irregular or precarious.

The purpose of the proposed Directive is to introduce a residence permit, with the aim of enhancing measures to combat illegal immigration. The text is not intended to incriminate networks of organised crime or to arrange protection for victims or witnesses. The proposal does not regulate these aspects, even though they are to some extent related to the subject matter of the text.

The proposed Directive must be adopted by the procedure provided for in Article 67 of the Treaty: the Council must act unanimously on a proposal from the Commission or on the initiative of a Member State, after consulting the European Parliament. Title IV of the EC Treaty does not apply to the United Kingdom or Ireland, unless these States decide otherwise, under the arrangements set out in the Protocol on the position of the United Kingdom and Ireland, annexed to the Treaties. Nor does Title IV apply to Denmark, in accordance with the Protocol on the position of Denmark, annexed to the Treaties.

4. Subsidiarity and proportionality: justification and added value

The inclusion in the Treaty establishing the European Community of the new Title IV on visas, asylum, immigration and other policies related to free movement of persons attributed certain powers in these fields to the European Community. These must be exercised in accordance with Article 5 of the EC Treaty, that is if and insofar as the objectives of the proposed action cannot be sufficiently achieved by the Member States and can therefore, by reason of the scale or effects of the proposed action, be better achieved by the Community. The proposal for a Directive satisfies these criteria.

Subsidiarity
The prime objective of the proposed Directive is to tighten up measures against illegal immigration by introducing a short-term residence permit for victims of action to facilitate illegal immigration or trafficking in human beings who cooperate with the authorities. Certain Member States already have such measures, although they differ enormously from one State to the next. Others make no such provision in their legislation. These disparities have the undesirable effect of diverting the activity of criminal organisations to those countries where the risks are lowest. This suggests the need for harmonised rules, which can only be agreed at Community level.

Proportionality
The form of Community action must be the simplest that will enable the objective of the proposal to be attained and effectively implemented. In this spirit, the legal instrument chosen is a Directive, laying down general principles but leaving the Member States to which it is addressed the choice of the most appropriate form and methods for giving effect to these

principles in their national legal system and general context. The proposed Directive sets out common definitions and confines itself to defining the criteria for issuing the short-term residence permit, laying down the terms of residence granted to the holders and the grounds for non-renewal or withdrawal. Member States remain free to enact more favourable conditions for victims.

Chapter 2.5
FAMILY REUNIFICATION

COUNCIL DIRECTIVE 2003/86/EC
of 22 September 2003
on the right to family reunification[1]

THE COUNCIL OF THE EUROPEAN UNION,
Having regard to the Treaty establishing the European Community, and in particular Article 63(3)(a) thereof,
Having regard to the proposal from the Commission,[2]
Having regard to the opinion of the European Parliament,[3]
Having regard to the opinion of the European Economic and Social Committee,[4]
Having regard to the opinion of the Committee of the Regions,[5]

Whereas:

(1) With a view to the progressive establishment of an area of freedom, security and justice, the Treaty establishing the European Community provides both for the adoption of measures aimed at ensuring the free movement of persons, in conjunction with flanking measures relating to external border controls, asylum and immigration, and for the adoption of measures relating to asylum, immigration and safeguarding the rights of third country nationals.

(2) Measures concerning family reunification should be adopted in conformity with the obligation to protect the family and respect family life enshrined in many instruments of international law. This Directive respects the fundamental rights and observes the principles recognised in particular in Article 8 of the European Convention for the Protection of Human Rights and Fundamental Freedoms and in the Charter of Fundamental Rights of the European Union.

(3) The European Council, at its special meeting in Tampere on 15 and 16 October 1999, acknowledged the need for harmonisation of national legislation on the conditions for admission and residence of third country nationals.

In this context, it has in particular stated that the European Union should ensure fair treatment of third country nationals residing lawfully on the territory of the Member States and

---

[1] OJ L 251, 3.10.2003, p. 12. This Directive is subject to an ECJ procedure; see p. 26.
[2] OJ C 116 E, 26.4.2000, p. 66, and OJ C 62 E, 27.2.2001, p. 99.
[3] OJ C 135, 7.5.2001, p. 174.
[4] OJ C 204, 18.7.2000, p. 40.
[5] OJ C 73, 26.3.2003, p. 16.

that a more vigorous integration policy should aim at granting them rights and obligations comparable to those of citizens of the European Union. The European Council accordingly asked the Council rapidly to adopt the legal instruments on the basis of Commission proposals. The need for achieving the objectives defined at Tampere have been reaffirmed by the Laeken European Council on 14 and 15 December 2001.

(4) Family reunification is a necessary way of making family life possible. It helps to create socio-cultural stability facilitating the integration of third country nationals in the Member State, which also serves to promote economic and social cohesion, a fundamental Community objective stated in the Treaty.

(5) Member States should give effect to the provisions of this Directive without discrimination on the basis of sex, race, colour, ethnic or social origin, genetic characteristics, language, religion or beliefs, political or other opinions, membership of a national minority, fortune, birth, disabilities, age or sexual orientation.

(6) To protect the family and establish or preserve family life, the material conditions for exercising the right to family reunification should be determined on the basis of common criteria.

(7) Member States should be able to apply this Directive also when the family enters together.

(8) Special attention should be paid to the situation of refugees on account of the reasons which obliged them to flee their country and prevent them from leading a normal family life there. More favourable conditions should therefore be laid down for the exercise of their right to family reunification.

(9) Family reunification should apply in any case to members of the nuclear family, that is to say the spouse and the minor children.

(10) It is for the Member States to decide whether they wish to authorise family reunification for relatives in the direct ascending line, adult unmarried children, unmarried or registered partners as well as, in the event of a polygamous marriage, minor children of a further spouse and the sponsor. Where a Member State authorises family reunification of these persons, this is without prejudice of the possibility, for Member States which do not recognise the existence of family ties in the cases covered by this provision, of not granting to the said persons the treatment of family members with regard to the right to reside in another Member State, as defined by the relevant EC legislation.

(11) The right to family reunification should be exercised in proper compliance with the values and principles recognised by the Member States, in particular with respect to the rights of women and of children; such compliance justifies the possible taking of restrictive measures against applications for family reunification of polygamous households.

(12) The possibility of limiting the right to family reunification of children over the age of 12, whose primary residence is not with the sponsor, is intended to reflect the children's

capacity for integration at early ages and shall ensure that they acquire the necessary education and language skills in school.

(13) A set of rules governing the procedure for examination of applications for family reunification and for entry and residence of family members should be laid down. Those procedures should be effective and manageable, taking account of the normal workload of the Member States' administrations, as well as transparent and fair, in order to offer appropriate legal certainty to those concerned.

(14) Family reunification may be refused on duly justified grounds. In particular, the person who wishes to be granted family reunification should not constitute a threat to public policy or public security. The notion of public policy may cover a conviction for committing a serious crime. In this context it has to be noted that the notion of public policy and public security covers also cases in which a third country national belongs to an association which supports terrorism, supports such an association or has extremist aspirations.

(15) The integration of family members should be promoted. For that purpose, they should be granted a status independent of that of the sponsor, in particular in cases of break-up of marriages and partnerships, and access to education, employment and vocational training on the same terms as the person with whom they are reunited, under the relevant conditions.

(16) Since the objectives of the proposed action, namely the establishment of a right to family reunification for third country nationals to be exercised in accordance with common rules, cannot be sufficiently achieved by the Member States and can therefore, by reason of the scale and effects of the action, be better achieved by the Community, the Community may adopt measures, in accordance with the principle of subsidiarity as set out in Article 5 of the Treaty. In accordance with the principle of proportionality as set out in that Article, this Directive does not go beyond what is necessary in order to achieve those objectives.

(17) In accordance with Articles 1 and 2 of the Protocol on the position of the United Kingdom and Ireland, annexed to the Treaty on European Union and to the Treaty establishing the European Community and without prejudice to Article 4 of the said Protocol these Member States are not participating in the adoption of this Directive and are not bound by or subject to its application.

(18) In accordance with Article 1 and 2 of the Protocol on the position of Denmark, annexed to the Treaty on European Union and the Treaty establishing the European Community, Denmark does not take part in the adoption of this Directive, and is not bound by it or subject to its application,

HAS ADOPTED THIS DIRECTIVE:

CHAPTER I
General Provisions

Article 1

The purpose of this Directive is to determine the conditions for the exercise of the right to family reunification by third country nationals residing lawfully in the territory of the Member States.

Article 2

For the purposes of this Directive:

(a) 'third country national' means any person who is not a citizen of the Union within the meaning of Article 17(1) of the Treaty;

(b) 'refugee' means any third country national or stateless person enjoying refugee status within the meaning of the Geneva Convention relating to the status of refugees of 28 July 1951, as amended by the Protocol signed in New York on 31 January 1967;

(c) 'sponsor' means a third country national residing lawfully in a Member State and applying or whose family members apply for family reunification to be joined with him/her;

(d) 'family reunification' means the entry into and residence in a Member State by family members of a third country national residing lawfully in that Member State in order to preserve the family unit, whether the family relationship arose before or after the resident's entry;

(e) 'residence permit' means any authorisation issued by the authorities of a Member State allowing a third country national to stay legally in its territory, in accordance with the provisions of Article 1(2)(a) of Council Regulation (EC) No. 1030/2002 of 13 June 2002 laying down a uniform format for residence permits for third country nationals;[6]

(f) 'unaccompanied minor' means third country nationals or stateless persons below the age of eighteen, who arrive on the territory of the Member States unaccompanied by an adult responsible by law or custom, and for as long as they are not effectively taken into the care of such a person, or minors who are left unaccompanied after they entered the territory of the Member States.

Article 3

1. This Directive shall apply where the sponsor is holding a residence permit issued by a Member State for a period of validity of one year or more who has reasonable prospects of obtaining the right of permanent residence, if the members of his or her family are third country nationals of whatever status.

2. This Directive shall not apply where the sponsor is:

(a) applying for recognition of refugee status whose application has not yet given rise to a final decision;

(b) authorised to reside in a Member State on the basis of temporary protection or applying for authorisation to reside on that basis and awaiting a decision on his status;

---

[6] OJ L 157, 15.6.2002, p. 1.

(c) authorised to reside in a Member State on the basis of a subsidiary form of protection in accordance with international obligations, national legislation or the practice of the Member States or applying for authorisation to reside on that basis and awaiting a decision on his status.

3. This Directive shall not apply to members of the family of a Union citizen.

4. This Directive is without prejudice to more favourable provisions of:
  (a) bilateral and multilateral agreements between the Community or the Community and its Member States, on the one hand, and third countries, on the other;
  (b) the European Social Charter of 18 October 1961, the amended European Social Charter of 3 May 1987 and the European Convention on the legal status of migrant workers of 24 November 1977.

5. This Directive shall not affect the possibility for the Member States to adopt or maintain more favourable provisions.

CHAPTER II
Family Members

Article 4

1. The Member States shall authorise the entry and residence, pursuant to this Directive and subject to compliance with the conditions laid down in Chapter IV, as well as in Article 16, of the following family members:
  (a) the sponsor's spouse;
  (b) the minor children of the sponsor and of his/her spouse, including children adopted in accordance with a decision taken by the competent authority in the Member State concerned or a decision which is automatically enforceable due to international obligations of that Member State or must be recognised in accordance with international obligations;
  (c) the minor children including adopted children of the sponsor where the sponsor has custody and the children are dependent on him or her. Member States may authorise the reunification of children of whom custody is shared, provided the other party sharing custody has given his or her agreement;
  (d) the minor children including adopted children of the spouse where the spouse has custody and the children are dependent on him or her. Member States may authorise the reunification of children of whom custody is shared, provided the other party sharing custody has given his or her agreement. The minor children referred to in this Article must be below the age of majority set by the law of the Member State concerned and must not be married.

By way of derogation, where a child is aged over 12 years and arrives independently from the rest of his/her family, the Member State may, before authorising entry and residence under this Directive, verify whether he or she meets a condition for integration provided for by its existing legislation on the date of implementation of this Directive.

2. The Member States may, by law or regulation, authorise the entry and residence, pursuant to this Directive and subject to compliance with the conditions laid down in Chapter IV, of the following family members:

(a) first-degree relatives in the direct ascending line of the sponsor or his or her spouse, where they are dependent on them and do not enjoy proper family support in the country of origin;

(b) the adult unmarried children of the sponsor or his or her spouse, where they are objectively unable to provide for their own needs on account of their state of health.

3. The Member States may, by law or regulation, authorise the entry and residence, pursuant to this Directive and subject to compliance with the conditions laid down in Chapter IV, of the unmarried partner, being a third country national, with whom the sponsor is in a duly attested stable long-term relationship, or of a third country national who is bound to the sponsor by a registered partnership in accordance with Article 5(2), and of the unmarried minor children, including adopted children, as well as the adult unmarried children who are objectively unable to provide for their own needs on account of their state of health, of such persons. Member States may decide that registered partners are to be treated equally as spouses with respect to family reunification.

4. In the event of a polygamous marriage, where the sponsor already has a spouse living with him in the territory of a Member State, the Member State concerned shall not authorise the family reunification of a further spouse.

By way of derogation from paragraph 1(c), Member States may limit the family reunification of minor children of a further spouse and the sponsor.

5. In order to ensure better integration and to prevent forced marriages Member States may require the sponsor and his/her spouse to be of a minimum age, and at maximum 21 years, before the spouse is able to join him/her.

6. By way of derogation, Member States may request that the applications concerning family reunification of minor children have to be submitted before the age of 15, as provided for by its existing legislation on the date of the implementation of this Directive. If the application is submitted after the age of 15, the Member States which decide to apply this derogation shall authorise the entry and residence of such children on grounds other than family reunification.

CHAPTER III
Submission and Examination of the Application

Article 5

1. Member States shall determine whether, in order to exercise the right to family reunification, an application for entry and residence shall be submitted to the competent authorities of the Member State concerned either by the sponsor or by the family member or members.

2. The application shall be accompanied by documentary evidence of the family relationship and of compliance with the conditions laid down in Articles 4 and 6 and, where applicable, Articles 7 and 8, as well as certified copies of family member(s)' travel documents.

If appropriate, in order to obtain evidence that a family relationship exists, Member States may carry out interviews with the sponsor and his/her family members and conduct other investigations that are found to be necessary.

When examining an application concerning the unmarried partner of the sponsor, Member States shall consider, as evidence of the family relationship, factors such as a common child, previous cohabitation, registration of the partnership and any other reliable means of proof.

3. The application shall be submitted and examined when the family members are residing outside the territory of the Member State in which the sponsor resides.

By way of derogation, a Member State may, in appropriate circumstances, accept an application submitted when the family members are already in its territory.

4. The competent authorities of the Member State shall give the person, who has submitted the application, written notification of the decision as soon as possible and in any event no later than nine months from the date on which the application was lodged.

In exceptional circumstances linked to the complexity of the examination of the application, the time limit referred to in the first subparagraph may be extended. Reasons shall be given for the decision rejecting the application. Any consequences of no decision being taken by the end of the period provided for in the first subparagraph shall be determined by the national legislation of the relevant Member State.

5. When examining an application, the Member States shall have due regard to the best interests of minor children.

CHAPTER IV
Requirements for the Exercise of the Right to Family Reunification

Article 6

1. The Member States may reject an application for entry and residence of family members on grounds of public policy, public security or public health.

2. Member States may withdraw or refuse to renew a family member's residence permit on grounds of public policy or public security or public health.

When taking the relevant decision, the Member State shall consider, besides Article 17, the severity or type of offence against public policy or public security committed by the family member, or the dangers that are emanating from such person.

3. Renewal of the residence permit may not be withheld and removal from the territory may not be ordered by the competent authority of the Member State concerned on the sole ground of illness or disability suffered after the issue of the residence permit.

Article 7

1. When the application for family reunification is submitted, the Member State concerned may require the person who has submitted the application to provide evidence that the sponsor has:

(a) accommodation regarded as normal for a comparable family in the same region and which meets the general health and safety standards in force in the Member State concerned;

(b) sickness insurance in respect of all risks normally covered for its own nationals in the Member State concerned for himself/herself and the members of his/her family;

(c) stable and regular resources which are sufficient to maintain himself/herself and the members of his/her family, without recourse to the social assistance system of the Member State concerned. Member States shall evaluate these resources by reference to their nature and regularity and may take into account the level of minimum national wages and pensions as well as the number of family members.

2. Member States may require third country nationals to comply with integration measures, in accordance with national law.

With regard to the refugees and/or family members of refugees referred to in Article 12 the integration measures referred to in the first subparagraph may only be applied once the persons concerned have been granted family reunification.

Article 8

Member States may require the sponsor to have stayed lawfully in their territory for a period not exceeding two years, before having his/her family members join him/her.

By way of derogation, where the legislation of a Member State relating to family reunification in force on the date of adoption of this Directive takes into account its reception capacity, the Member State may provide for a waiting period of no more than three years between submission of the application for family reunification and the issue of a residence permit to the family members.

CHAPTER V
Family Reunification of Refugees

Article 9

1. This Chapter shall apply to family reunification of refugees recognised by the Member States.

2. Member States may confine the application of this Chapter to refugees whose family relationships predate their entry.

3. This Chapter is without prejudice to any rules granting refugee status to family members.

Article 10

1. Article 4 shall apply to the definition of family members except that the third subparagraph of paragraph 1 thereof shall not apply to the children of refugees.

2. The Member States may authorise family reunification of other family members not referred to in Article 4, if they are dependent on the refugee.

3. If the refugee is an unaccompanied minor, the Member States:

(a) shall authorise the entry and residence for the purposes of family reunification of his/her first-degree relatives in the direct ascending line without applying the conditions laid down in Article 4(2)(a);

(b) may authorise the entry and residence for the purposes of family reunification of his/her legal guardian or any other member of the family, where the refugee has no relatives in the direct ascending line or such relatives cannot be traced.

Article 11

1. Article 5 shall apply to the submission and examination of the application, subject to paragraph 2 of this Article.

2. Where a refugee cannot provide official documentary evidence of the family relationship, the Member States shall take into account other evidence, to be assessed in accordance with national law, of the existence of such relationship. A decision rejecting an application may not be based solely on the fact that documentary evidence is lacking.

Article 12

1. By way of derogation from Article 7, the Member States shall not require the refugee and/or family member(s) to provide, in respect of applications concerning those family members referred to in Article 4(1), the evidence that the refugee fulfils the requirements set out in Article 7.

Without prejudice to international obligations, where family reunification is possible in a third country with which the sponsor and/or family member has special links, Member States may require provision of the evidence referred to in the first subparagraph.

Member States may require the refugee to meet the conditions referred to in Article 7(1) if the application for family reunification is not submitted within a period of three months after the granting of the refugee status.

2. By way of derogation from Article 8, the Member States shall not require the refugee to have resided in their territory for a certain period of time, before having his/her family members join him/her.

CHAPTER VI
Entry and Residence of Family Members

Article 13

1. As soon as the application for family reunification has been accepted, the Member State concerned shall authorise the entry of the family member or members. In that regard, the Member State concerned shall grant such persons every facility for obtaining the requisite visas.

2. The Member State concerned shall grant the family members a first residence permit of at least one year's duration.

This residence permit shall be renewable.

3. The duration of the residence permits granted to the family member(s) shall in principle not go beyond the date of expiry of the residence permit held by the sponsor.

Article 14

1. The sponsor's family members shall be entitled, in the same way as the sponsor, to:
    (a) access to education;
    (b) access to employment and self-employed activity;
    (c) access to vocational guidance, initial and further training and retraining.

2. Member States may decide according to national law the conditions under which family members shall exercise an employed or self-employed activity. These conditions shall set a time limit which shall in no case exceed 12 months, during which Member States may examine the situation of their labour market before authorising family members to exercise an employed or self-employed activity.

3. Member States may restrict access to employment or self-employed activity by first-degree relatives in the direct ascending line or adult unmarried children to whom Article 4(2) applies.

Article 15

1. Not later than after five years of residence, and provided that the family member has not been granted a residence permit for reasons other than family reunification, the spouse or unmarried partner and a child who has reached majority shall be entitled, upon application, if required, to an autonomous residence permit, independent of that of the sponsor.

Member States may limit the granting of the residence permit referred to in the first sub-paragraph to the spouse or unmarried partner in cases of breakdown of the family relationship.

2. The Member States may issue an autonomous residence permit to adult children and to relatives in the direct ascending line to whom Article 4(2) applies.

3. In the event of widowhood, divorce, separation, or death of first-degree relatives in the direct ascending or descending line, an autonomous residence permit may be issued, upon application, if required, to persons who have entered by virtue of family reunification. Member States shall lay down provisions ensuring the granting of an autonomous residence permit in the event of particularly difficult circumstances.

4. The conditions relating to the granting and duration of the autonomous residence permit are established by national law.

CHAPTER VII
Penalties and Redress

Article 16

1. Member States may reject an application for entry and residence for the purpose of family reunification, or, if appropriate, withdraw or refuse to renew a family member's residence permit, in the following circumstances:
(a) where the conditions laid down by this Directive are not or are no longer satisfied. When renewing the residence permit, where the sponsor has not sufficient resources without recourse to the social assistance system of the Member State, as referred to in Article 7(1)(c), the Member State shall take into account the contributions of the family members to the household income;
(b) where the sponsor and his/her family member(s) do not or no longer live in a real marital or family relationship;
(c) where it is found that the sponsor or the unmarried partner is married or is in a stable long-term relationship with another person.

2. Member States may also reject an application for entry and residence for the purpose of family reunification, or withdraw or refuse to renew the family member's residence permits, where it is shown that:
(a) false or misleading information, false or falsified documents were used, fraud was otherwise committed or other unlawful means were used;
(b) the marriage, partnership or adoption was contracted for the sole purpose of enabling the person concerned to enter or reside in a Member State.

When making an assessment with respect to this point, Member States may have regard in particular to the fact that the marriage, partnership or adoption was contracted after the sponsor had been issued his/her residence permit.

3. The Member States may withdraw or refuse to renew the residence permit of a family member where the sponsor's residence comes to an end and the family member does not yet enjoy an autonomous right of residence under Article 15.

4. Member States may conduct specific checks and inspections where there is reason to suspect that there is fraud or a marriage, partnership or adoption of convenience as defined by paragraph 2. Specific checks may also be undertaken on the occasion of the renewal of family members' residence permit.

Article 17

Member States shall take due account of the nature and solidity of the person's family relationships and the duration of his residence in the Member State and of the existence of family, cultural and social ties with his/her country of origin where they reject an application, withdraw or refuse to renew a residence permit or decide to order the removal of the sponsor or members of his family.

Article 18

The Member States shall ensure that the sponsor and/or the members of his/her family have the right to mount a legal challenge where an application for family reunification is rejected or a residence permit is either not renewed or is withdrawn or removal is ordered.

The procedure and the competence according to which the right referred to in the first subparagraph is exercised shall be established by the Member States concerned.

CHAPTER VIII
Final Provisions

Article 19

Periodically, and for the first time not later than 3 October 2007, the Commission shall report to the European Parliament and the Council on the application of this Directive in the Member States and shall propose such amendments as may appear necessary. These proposals for amendments shall be made by way of priority in relation to Articles 3, 4, 7, 8 and 13.

Article 20

Member States shall bring into force the laws, regulations and administrative provisions necessary to comply with this Directive by not later than 3 October 2005. They shall forthwith inform the Commission thereof.

When Member States adopt these measures, they shall contain a reference to this Directive or be accompanied by such a reference on the occasion of their official publication. The methods of making such reference shall be laid down by the Member States.

Article 21

This Directive shall enter into force on the day of its publication in the Official Journal of the European Union.

Article 22

This Directive is addressed to the Member States in accordance with the Treaty establishing the European Community.

A.   As provided for by COM(1999)638 final

1.   **Towards a common european policy on immigration of third-country nationals: family reunification**

1.1. One of the amendments made by the Amsterdam Treaty which entered into force on 1 May 1999 requires that an area of freedom, security and justice be established progressively. The Treaty establishing the European Community now accordingly provides for the adoption of measures relating to free movement of persons, in conjunction with flanking measures relating to border controls, asylum, immigration and the protection of the rights of third-country nationals. The immigration measures provided for by Article 63(3) and (4) concern the conditions for entry and residence and the issuance by Member States of visas and long-term residence permits, illegal immigration and illegal residence, including the repatriation of illegal residents, and the rights of third-country nationals legally resident in a Member State to reside in another Member State, and the conditions under which they may do so.

It is therefore possible for the European Community[7] to adopt measures concerning the entry and residence of third-country nationals in the Member States, this being a matter which, prior to the entry into force of the Amsterdam Treaty, was governed by Title VI of the Treaty on European Union before it was amended and was only partly covered by Community powers.[8]

1.2. The European Council, at its special meeting in Tampere on 15 and 16 October 1999, acknowledged the need for harmonisation of national legislation on the conditions for admission and residence of third-country nationals, to be based on a common evaluation both of social and demographic trends within the Union and of the situation in countries of origin. The European Council accordingly asked the Council to rapidly adopt decisions on the basis of Commission proposals. These decisions were to take account not only of the absorption capacity of each Member State but also their historical and cultural links with countries of origin.[9]

1.3. The identification of guiding principles to serve as a basis for a common immigration policy is an important task and the Commission's intention is to give it its fullest attention. The Commission considers that the zero immigration mentioned in past Community discussion of immigration was never realistic and never really justified.

The policy has never been fully implemented as such, and there are a number of reasons for that: not just that, in the short and medium term, immigration facilities such as family reuni-

---

[7] Three Member States (the United Kingdom, Ireland and Denmark) enjoy a special status under the Protocols annexed to the Treaty.

[8] It should be emphasised that, even before the Amsterdam Treaty entered into force, the list of non-member countries whose nationals had to have a visa in order to cross external borders and measures relating to visas in cases of a sudden influx were already within Community powers.

[9] Presidency Conclusions, point 20.

fication could not and should not be interrupted but also that there were branches of industry that were short of manpower. Moreover, the Member States wished to remain open to the outside world, and in particular to maintain their privileged relationships with certain non-member countries. In the longer term, there are demographic factors such as the ageing of the population, with all that this entails in terms of welfare protection and the funding of pension schemes.

1.4. It is true that the current employment market situation does not give the Community the grounds for operating an entry and residence policy of the very open kind that prevailed in the 1950s and 1960s. But the unemployment rate is not the only factor underlying immigration policy: specific sectors of business activity may well be short of skilled and qualified staff. More generally, a common immigration policy at European level will need to be flexible so that it can reflect the manifold dimensions of migratory flows, be they economic, social, cultural or historical, relating both to host countries and to countries of origin.

1.5. The Commission, following up directly the conclusions of the Tampere European Council, is planning to begin and pursue work on legal immigration so as to exploit every opportunity offered by Title IV of the EC Treaty. In the medium term it will tackle all aspects of entry and residence of third-country nationals in turn, and particularly entry and residence for the purposes of study, of salaried and self-employed occupations and unpaid activities. The Commission is also planning to look into the legal position of third-country nationals holding a long-term residence permit, and into the application of Article 63(4) (rights of third-country nationals residing lawfully in one Member State to reside in another Member State).

2.   Entry and residence for the purposes of family reunification

2.1. For some years now, entry and residence for the purposes of family reunification have been the chief form of legal immigration of third-country nationals. Family immigration is predominant in virtually all the OECD countries, in particular Canada and the United States; the same applies in the Union Member States, even though the figures vary from one to another. Family immigration refers both to family reunification *stricto sensu* – where family members join the head of family who is already a resident – and family formation, where family ties come about after the head of family entered the host country.

2.2. Beyond the purely quantitative importance of this form of legal immigration, family reunification is a necessary way of making a success of the integration of third-country nationals residing lawfully in the Member States. The presence of family members makes for greater stability and deepens the roots of these people since they are enabled to lead a normal family life.

3.   The international legal framework

3.1. The rules governing family reunification are substantially outside the scope of national legislation, being laid down by international instruments. The Universal Declaration of Human Rights and the International Covenants of 1966 on Civil and Political Rights and on Economic and Social Rights recognise that the family is the natural and fundamental unit of society and is entitled to the fullest possible protection by society and the State. Convention No. 143 of the International Labour Organisation, ratified by Italy, Portugal and Sweden, calls on States to facilitate family reunification of all migrant workers residing lawfully in their territory.

3.2. The International Convention on the protection of the rights of all migrant workers and members of their families, adopted by the General Assembly of the United Nations in December 1990, provides that 'States Parties shall take measures that they deem appropriate and that fall within their competence to facilitate the reunification of migrant workers with their spouses or persons who have with the migrant worker a relationship that, according to applicable law, produces effects equivalent to marriage, as well as with their minor dependent unmarried children'.

The Convention describes the areas in which members of the family of a migrant worker are to enjoy the same treatment as nationals: access to education, to vocational training, to health and welfare services and to cultural life. States must also endeavour to facilitate the teaching of the local language and their mother tongue and culture for the children of migrant workers. In the case of the death of a migrant worker or dissolution of marriage, the State of employment must favourably consider granting family members of that migrant worker residing in that State on the basis of family reunification an authorisation to stay; the State of employment shall take into account the length of time they have already resided in that State. Members of the family to whom such authorisation is not granted shall be allowed before departure a reasonable period of time in order to enable them to settle their affairs in the State of employment. The Convention has not yet entered into force as the requisite number of ratifications has not been reached; no member State has ratified the Convention yet.

3.3. The 1951 Convention relating to the Status of Refugees makes no provision for family reunification. But the principle was recognised in the Final Act of the Conference that adopted it. The Executive Committee of the Office of the High Commissioner for Refugees (HCR) has repeatedly reminded States that the principle of unity of the family has been proclaimed in the international human rights instruments and that Governments must take the requisite measures to ensure that the unity of the family is preserved. Regarding the definition of the family and its members, the HCR Executive Committee has argued for a pragmatic, flexible approach that has regard to factors of physical, financial and psychological dependence of the central parents/children nucleus.[10]

3.4. In the context of the international legal framework, mention must be made of the Convention on the Rights of the Child of 20 November 1989. This Convention requires States to ensure that the child is not separated from its parents. Every application to leave or enter a country for the purposes of family reunification must be dealt with in a positive, humane and expeditious manner. In all decisions concerning the child, his superior interests are the paramount consideration.

3.5. Among European legal instruments relevant to family reunification, the European Convention for the Protection of Human Rights and Fundamental Freedoms of 1950 is espe-

---

[10] Conclusions Nos. 9 (XXVIII), 24 (XXXII), 84 (XLVIII) and 85 (XLIX) and Conclusions of 50th session (1999).

cially important. Article 8 secures the right to respect for private and family life; Article 12 secures the right to marry and found a family.

There is a long line of cases decided by the Court interpreting the Convention. The Court has not deduced that there is an unlimited right to family reunification of the members of the family of a third-country national lawfully settled in a Member State, nor absolute protection against separation from members of the family in the event of expulsion, unless a normal family life is impossible in the country of origin. But the Court's decisions put limits on the discretionary exercise of the powers of public authorities regarding controls on entry into the territory and in the event of expulsion.

3.6. Two European instruments apply specifically to family reunification – the European Social Charter and the European Convention of 1997 on the Legal Status of Migrant Workers. The Parties to the European Social Charter undertake to facilitate as far as possible the family reunification of a migrant worker authorised to settle in their territory so as to ensure the effective exercise of the right of migrant workers and their families to protection and assistance. The European Convention of 1977 on the Legal Status of Migrant Workers provides that the spouse and unmarried children are authorised to join the migrant worker already residing in the territory of a Contracting Party. But there are two limits to the scope of this Convention: it applies only to employed workers, and only to workers who are nationals of a Contracting Party. The Convention has not been ratified by all the Member States.

4.   The situation at national level

4.1. It should be noted that protection of the family is a principle explicitly upheld by the constitutional provisions in several Member States, notably Germany, Greece, Portugal and Italy. The Member States recognise either a right to family reunification, or the discretionary possibility of allowing family reunification, depending on the category and the legal status of third-country nationals. Only one Member State applies a policy of quotas to applications for admission of family members.

4.2. The exercise of this right is, however, subject to conditions, such as respect for public policy and public security, the availability of adequate accommodation and resources, and in some cases even a qualifying period. The legislation and practice of the Member States vary widely on these matters.

4.3. Regarding accommodation, some Member States require a resident who wishes to receive his family to have adequate accommodation to house them in acceptable conditions. This conditions is fixed in different ways depending on the Member State. In Germany, the accommodation must be equivalent to social housing. In France, Portugal and the Netherlands, it must be equivalent to the normal accommodation occupied by nationals. Other criteria such as size, hygiene and safety may be applied (Greece, Italy, Austria, United Kingdom). Spain and Luxembourg do not apply predefined rules and consider situations case by case. The adequate accommodation condition is not imposed in Belgium, Denmark, Finland or Sweden.

4.4. The resources criterion is also subject to divergent interpretations. Resources must be equivalent to the minimum wage in France, Portugal and Spain. They must be no less than the minimum social-security pension in Germany and the Netherlands. The United Kingdom requires that there be no demand on public funds, and Denmark requires the resident to satisfy the needs of the members of his family. France and the Netherlands further require that resources be permanent and stable. Austria requires family members to have social insurance. The adequate resources condition is not imposed in Belgium, Finland, Luxembourg or Sweden.

4.5. Certain Member States impose a qualifying period on newly admitted third-country nationals. The duration varies, from one year in France and Spain to three years in Denmark and five years in Greece. The other Member States impose no formal qualifying period, but the waiting time before family reunification can be long because examination of the application takes so long. The effect of the quota scheme in Austria is that the waiting time may last several years.

4.6. Differences are also encountered as regards the family members who are admitted to join the resident head of family, the age of children allowed to be reunited and the admission of unmarried partners.

4.7. Third-country nationals recognised as refugees in accordance with Article 1(A) of the 1951 Geneva Convention relating to the status of refugees enjoy better family reunification terms in certain Member States: they are exempt from the resources and accommodation conditions, there is no qualifying period and the right to family reunification sometimes extends beyond the nuclear family.

5. The rules of community law on family reunification

5.1. Community law already contains provisions relating to family reunification of third-country nationals. The instruments governing free movement for Union citizens within the European Community apply to family members whether they are Community or third-country nationals. A Union citizen exercising the right to free movement may be accompanied or joined by his family; the terms for integration of the family in the host country are the *sine qua non* for the exercise of free movement in objective conditions of freedom and dignity.

5.2. The right to be accompanied or joined by the family is conferred on Union citizens who establish themselves in another Member State to exercise a gainful activity, whether they are employed workers[11] or self-employed.[12] The family members retain the right to reside in the host country, on certain conditions, where the Union citizen on whom they depend has ceased working.[13] In addition, the right to family reunification is enjoyed by Union citizens other than employed or self-employed workers who also enjoy the right to free movement, provided they have adequate resources and sickness insurance cover.[14]

---

[11] Regulation (EEC) No. 1612/68, 15.10.1968 (OJ L 257, 19.10.1968 p. 2).

[12] Directive 73/148/EEC, 21.5.1973 (OJ L 172, 28.6.1973, p. 14).

[13] Regulation (EEC) No. 1251/70, 29.6.1970 (OJ L 142, 30.6.1970, p. 24), and Directive 75/34/EEC, 17.12.1974 (OJ L 14, 20.1.1975, p. 28).

[14] Directive 90/364/EEC, 28.6.1990 (OJ L 180, 13.7.1990, p. 26) and Directive 90/365/EEC, 28.6.1990 (OJ L 180, 13.7.1990, p. 28).

5.3. The family members to whom this applies are the spouse and dependent relatives in the descending and ascending lines.[15] Students may be accompanied or joined by their spouse and dependent children only if they can show that they have adequate resources and sickness insurance cover.[16] These rules also apply to nationals of the European Economic Area pursuant to the Agreement of 2 May 1992.

5.4. The rights of family members are derived rights flowing from those enjoyed by the Union citizen enjoying the right to free movement, so family members are given a residence document valid on the same terms as the document issued to the person on whom they are dependent. The Member States may impose limits on the exercise of the admission and residence rights of family members on grounds of public policy, domestic security and public health.[17] Community rules also allow the spouse and children to have access to employment, even if they do not have the nationality of a Member State.

5.5. Apart from the situation of third-country nationals who are family members of a Union citizen exercising his right to free movement, Community law contains no rules on family reunification of third-country nationals, of refugees or of other categories of migrants. This is the direct consequence of the absence of a Community legal basis prior to the entry into force of the Amsterdam Treaty on 1 May 1999.

6.   **Work in the European Union**

6.1. The importance of family reunification had already been recognised in the European Union by Council activities before the Amsterdam Treaty came into force. Family reunification was a priority topic in the programme of harmonisation of immigration policies adopted by the Ministers responsible for immigration and approved by the European Council at Maastricht in 1991.

6.2. In 1993, the Ministers responsible for immigration adopted a Resolution on the harmonisation of national policies on family reunification.[18] This instrument of soft law sets out the principles which should govern the Member States' national policies (family members eligible for admission, conditions for entry and residence). It concerns the family reunification of third-country nationals residing in the territory of the Member States on a basis offering the prospect of durable residence; it does not deal with the family reunification of Union citizens or of third-country nationals who have obtained refugee status.

6.3. The relevant Council bodies have continued to pay special attention to family reunification; the topic has always been on the Council agenda, even before the Amsterdam Treaty came into force, in the form of exchanges of views, information gathering, background

---

[15] Regarding Union citizens who settle in another Member State to engage in a gainful activity, it is also provided that Member States must support the admission of other family members if in the country of origin they are dependent on the migrant worker or live under his roof. See Commission proposals for amendment of Regulation (EEC) No. 1612/68 in OJ C 344, 12.11.1998, p. 9).

[16] Directive 93/96/EEC, 29.10.1993 (OJ L 317, 18.12.1993, p. 59).

[17] Directive 64/221/EEC, 25.2.1964 (OJ 56, 4.4.1964, p. 850/64).

[18] Document SN 282/1/93 WGI 1497 REV 1.

documents and discussion of proposals, during the Dutch, Luxembourg, British and Austrian Presidencies.

6.4. In December 1997, the Council adopted a Resolution on measures to combat marriages of convenience.[19] It does not directly concern family reunification, but it is related; it concerns measures to combat or repress possible circumventions of the rules on entry and residence by means of marriages of convenience.

6.5. In 1997, the Commission presented a proposal for a Convention on rules for the admission of third-country nationals to the Member States.[20] The aim was to provide input for the debate on immigration questions before the Amsterdam Treaty came into force with all the major institutional changes that followed it. In a preliminary declaration the Commission stated its intention of presenting a new draft directive after the entry into force of the new Treaty. The object here was to preserve the benefit of discussions on the substance of the text when producing a Community legal instrument.

6.6. Following the entry into force of the Amsterdam Treaty and the insertion of a new Title IV in the Treaty establishing the European Community, relating to visas, asylum, immigration and other policies related to the free movement of persons, the Commission feels the time has come to give practical form to the commitment entered into in 1997 and present a new proposal regarding family reunification in the form of a Community legal instrument.

6.7. This sits well with the Council and Commission Plan of Action of 3 December 1998[21] on how best to implement the provisions of the Treaty of Amsterdam on an area of freedom, security and justice. Under this Plan, an instrument on the legal status of legal immigrants is to be adopted within two years of the entry into force of the Treaty, and rules on the conditions of entry and residence, and standards on procedures for the issue by Member States of long-term visas and residence permits, including those for the purposes of family reunion are to be prepared within five years. This confirms the attention paid by the Council and the Commission to these topics. Lastly, it will be remembered that the Vienna European Council on 11 and 12 December 1998 urged the Council to continue work on, among other things, the rules applicable to third-country nationals.[22]

6.8. It is also useful to recall that at the Cologne European Council meeting on 3-4 June 1999, the Heads of State and Government decided that a Charter of Fundamental Rights of the European Union should be drawn up. This Charter should bring together the fundamental rights applying on a Union wide basis in order to raise their profile. Its scope should not only be limited to the citizens of the union. Nevertheless, to date; no decision has been taken concerning the legal scope and the enforceable value of the Charter.

6.9. In the course of preparatory work for the presentation of the proposal, there have been consultations to sound out the Office of the High Commissioner for Refugees and non-

---

[19] OJ C 382, 16.12.1997, p. 1.
[20] OJ C 337, 7.11.1997, p. 9.
[21] OJ C 19, 23.1.1999, p. 1.
[22] Presidency Conclusions, Vienna, 11 and 12 December 1998, point 85.

governmental organisations active in this area. By taking account of work done by the Council on family reunification and of the European Parliament's Opinion on the proposal for a Convention on admission, the Commission has been able to base its decision on a full overview of the problem of family reunification.

7. Objective of the commission proposal

7.1. At its special meeting at Tampere on 15 and 16 October 1999,[23] the European Council reiterated that the European Union must offer fair treatment to third-country nationals residing lawfully in the territory of its Member State. It also recognised that a more dynamic integration policy should aim to offer them rights and obligations comparable to those enjoyed by Union citizens.

7.2. To attain this objective, the Commission considers it necessary to allow third-country nationals residing lawfully in the territory of the Member States to enjoy the right to family reunification, subject to certain conditions. This is indispensable if these people are to lead a normal family life and will help them to integrate into society in the Member States. To ensure that they can look forward to being treated in the same way as Union citizens, the proposal for a directive is based on certain provisions of existing Community law as regards the family reunification of Union citizens who exercise their right to free movement.

7.3. Respect for family life applies to all third-country nationals, irrespective of their reasons for opting to live in the territory of the Member States (employment, self-employed activity, studies, etc.). The scope of the proposed directive is not confined to certain categories of third-country nationals. The sole criterion is lawful residence. Refugees and persons enjoying subsidiary protection are eligible for respect for family life only via reunification in a country in which they can lead a normal family life together after being forced to flee their country of origin, such flight often being the cause of separation of members of a family. In these specific circumstances, the directive provides for specific treatment in terms of the preconditions for reunification (accommodation, resources, qualifying period) and of the family members eligible for reunification.

7.4. Ultimately, the proposed directive seeks to harmonise the legislation of the Member States for two main reasons. Third-country nationals are to be eligible for broadly the same family reunification conditions, irrespective of the Member State in which they are admitted for residence purposes. And the possibility that the choice of the Member State in which a third-country national decides to reside will be based on the more generous terms offered there must be restricted.

7.5. The situation of family members of Citizens of the Union who reside in the country of their nationality and who did not exercise their right of freedom of movement is only governed by national law. Since they did not exercised their right to freedom of movement, in the past it has been considered that it was a pure internal situation falling under Member States competences. Thus, a difference exists depending on whether the Union citizen exercises or not his right to free movement. The Commission considers that an appropriate solu-

---

[23] Presidency Conclusions, point 18.

tion has to be found to avoid this difference and to fill the legal gap. It is thus proposed to remove this difference and give the Union citizens full access to existing Community law.

In this exercise, the Commission is nonetheless conscious that existing Community law does not cater for all the situations foreseen in this directive proposition. On one point, the disposition concerning the autonomous residence permit, the proposition offers to family members of third-country nationals more favorable conditions, in the current state of community law on free movement, than to those being family members of Union citizens. On a medium-term basis, in the framework of future initiatives in the domain of free movement, the Commission will see to maintain a balance between the legal situation of Union citizens and their family members and third-country nationals.

8. Choice of legal basis

8.1. The choice of legal basis is consistent with the amendments made to the Treaty establishing the European Community by the Amsterdam Treaty, which entered into force on 1 May 1999. Article 63(3)(a) of the EC Treaty now provides that the Council is to adopt measures relating to conditions of entry and residence, and standards for the issue of long-term visas and residence permits, including those for the purposes of family reunion.

8.2. That Article is accordingly the natural legal basis for a proposal that establishes family reunification as a right of third-country nationals already residing in the territory of a Member State, determines the conditions of entry of members of his family and establishes certain elements of the legal status of those family members.

8.3. The proposal for a directive falls to be adopted by the procedure of Article 67 of the Treaty, whereby, during a transitional period of five years, the Council is to act unanimously on a proposal from the Commission or on the initiative of a Member State, after consulting the European Parliament. Title IV of the EC Treaty is not applicable to the United Kingdom and Ireland unless the two countries decide otherwise in accordance with the procedure laid down in the Protocol on the position of the United Kingdom and Ireland annexed to the Treaties. Title IV of the EC Treaty is not applicable to Denmark by virtue of the Protocol on the position of Denmark annexed to the Treaties.

9. Subsidiarity and proportionality: justification and value added

9.1. The insertion of the new Title IV (visa, asylum, immigration and other policies related to free movement of persons) in the EC Treaty is evidence of the desire of the High Contracting Parties to confer powers on the European Community in these matters.

9.2. But the Community does not have exclusive powers here; consequently, even if there is the political will to implement a common policy on asylum and immigration, it must still act in accordance with Article 5 of the Treaty, in other words if and in so far as the objectives of the planned action cannot be sufficiently achieved by the Member States and can therefore, by reason of the scale or effects of the planned action, be better achieved by the Community. The proposal for a directive satisfies these criteria.

9.3. *Subsidiarity*

An area of freedom, security and justice entails common rules on immigration policy. The object of this proposal is to establish a right to family reunification that can be exercised in accordance with common criteria in all the Member States; this will improve certainty as to the law for third-country nationals. The situation regarding entry and residence for family members of third-country nationals varies from one Member State to another. Common criteria for the Community must be set by action of the kind proposed. Common criteria will also help to ensure that third-country nationals are less likely to select their country of destination purely on the basis of the more generous conditions available to them there.

9.4. *Proportionality*

The form of the Community action must be the simplest that will enable the proposal's objectives to be attained effectively. In this spirit, the legal instrument chosen is a directive, which would set the guiding principles while leaving the Member States to which it is addressed free to choose the form and methods for the implementation of these principles in their legal systems and national context.

Moreover, the proposal for a directive does not set out to settle the legal situation of all third-country nationals residing lawfully in the territory of the Member States, leaving the Member States free to determine rules governing persons whose residence permit is valid for less than one year.

B.   As provided for by COM(2000)624 final

1.   **Background**

On 1 December 1999 the Commission adopted a proposal for a Council Directive on the right to family reunification (COM(1999)638 final – 1999/0258 (CNS)). The proposed directive is based on Article 63 of the EC Treaty and introduces a right to family reunification for third-country nationals legally residing on the territory of a Member State. It lays down the conditions for exercising this right to obtain authorisation for the entry and residence of family members who are nationals of third countries.

The proposal was sent to the Council, the European Parliament, the Economic and Social Committee and the Committee of the Regions. The Economic and Social Committee was consulted by the Council on 10 February 2000 and delivered its Opinion on 25 May 2000. By letter dated 11 February 2000, the Council consulted Parliament in accordance with Article 67 of the EC Treaty. Parliament referred the proposal to its Committee on Citizens' Freedoms and Rights, Justice and Home Affairs for an in-depth examination and to its Committee on Legal Affairs and the Internal Market for an opinion. The Committee on Citizens' Freedoms and Rights, Justice and Home Affairs, after receiving and examining the Legal Committee's opinion adopted on 17 April 2000, adopted its own report on 13 July 2000. On 6 September 2000, Parliament adopted its Opinion in plenary, approving the Commission proposal subject to amendments and calling on the Commission to amend its proposal accordingly, in accordance with Article 250(2) of the EC Treaty.

2. **The amended proposal**

Parliament supports the general thrust and main objectives of the Commission's proposal, in particular the introduction of a right to family reunification for third-country nationals who are already resident. It adopted 17 amendments. The Commission can accept most of them in full or in part or, in some cases, subject to a change of wording. The amendments are completely in line with the Commission's approach and complement and enrich the directive.

One amendment restricts the scope of the directive. It excludes persons enjoying a subsidiary form of protection and calls for the adoption without delay of a proposal on their admission and residence. The Commission accepts this amendment and has changed the relevant articles accordingly. It considers that persons in this category must have the right to family reunification and need protection; however, it recognises that the absence of a harmonised concept of subsidiary protection at Community level constitutes an obstacle to their inclusion in the proposed directive.

The Conclusions of the Tampere European Council of 15 and 16 October 1999 specify that '[refugee status] should also be completed with measures on subsidiary forms of protection offering an appropriate status to any person in need of such protection'. To that end, the Scoreboard presented by the Commission in March 2000 and endorsed by the Council envisages the adoption before 2004 of a proposal on the status of persons enjoying subsidiary forms of protection. The Commission intends to make such a proposal next year, which could also cover family reunification for this category of third-country nationals.

2.1. *Amendments accepted in full or in part*[24]

---

[24] Included in *The Migration Acquis Handbook* (The Hague, 2001), pp. 208-219.

Chapter 2.6
SOCIAL SECURITY

COUNCIL REGULATION
No. 859/2003 of 14 May 2003
extending the provisions of Regulation (EEC) No. 1408/71 and Regulation (EEC) No.
574/72 to nationals of third countries who are not already covered by those provisions
solely on the ground of their nationality[1]

THE COUNCIL OF THE EUROPEAN UNION,
Having regard to the Treaty establishing the European Community and in particular Article
63, point 4 thereof,
Having regard to the proposal from the Commission,[2]
Having regard to the opinion of the European Parliament,[3]

Whereas:

(1) As its special meeting in Tampere on 15 and 16 October1999, the European Council
proclaimed that the European Union should ensure fair treatment of third country nationals
who reside legally in the territory of its Member States, grant them rights and obligations
comparable to those of EU citizens, enhance non-discrimination in economic, social and
cultural life and approximate their legal status to that of Member States'nationals.

(2) In its resolution of 27 October 1999,[4] the European Parliament called for prompt action
on promises of fair treatment for third-country nationals legally resident in the Member
States and on the definition of their legal status, including uniform rights as close as possible
to those enjoyed by the citizens of the European Union.

(3) The European Economic and Social Committee has also appealed for equal treatment of
Community nationals and third-country nationals in the social field, notably in its opinion of
26 September 1991 on the status of migrant workers from third countries.[5]

(4) Article 6(2) of the Treaty on European Union provides that the Union shall respect fundamental rights, as guaranteed by the European Convention on the Protection of Human
Rights and Fundamental Freedoms signed in Rome on 4 November 1950 and as they result
from the constitutional traditions common to the Member States, as general principles of
Community law.

---

[1] OJ L 124, 20.5.2003, p. 1.
[2] OJ C 126 E, 28.5.2002, p. 388.
[3] Opinion of 21 November 2002 (not yet published in the Official Journal).
[4] OJ C 154, 5.6.2000, p. 63.
[5] OJ C 339, 31.12.1991, p. 82.

(5) This Regulation respects the fundamental rights and observes the principles recognised in particular by the Charter of Fundamental Rights of the European Union, in particular the spirit of its Article 34(2).

(6) The promotion of a high level of social protection and the raising of the standard of living and quality of life in the Member States are objectives of the Community.

(7) As regards the conditions of social protection of third country nationals, and in particular the social security scheme applicable to them, the Employment and Social Policy Council argued in its conclusions of 3 December 2001 that the coordination applicable to third-country nationals should grant them a set of uniform rights as near as possible to those enjoyed by EU citizens.

(8) Currently, Council Regulation (EEC) No. 1408/71 of 14 June 1971 on the application of social security schemes to employed persons and their families moving within the Community,[6] which is the basis for the coordination of the social security schemes of the different Member States, and Council Regulation (EEC) No. 574/72 of 21 March 1972, laying down the procedure for implementing Regulation (EEC) No. 1408/71,[7] apply only to certain third-country nationals. The number and diversity of legal instruments used in an effort to resolve problems in connection with the coordination of the Member States' social security schemes encountered by nationals of third countries who are in the same situation as Community nationals give rise to legal and administrative complexities. They create major difficulties for the individuals concerned, their employers, and the competent national social security bodies.

(9) Hence, it is necessary to provide for the application of the coordination rules of Regulation (EEC) No. 1408/71 and Regulation (EEC) No. 574/72 to third-country nationals legally resident in the Community who are not currently covered by the provisions of these Regulations on grounds of their nationality and who satisfy the other conditions provided for in this Regulation; such an extension is in particular important with a view to the forthcoming enlargement of the European Union.

(10) The application of Regulation (EEC) No. 1408/71 and Regulation (EEC) No. 574/72 to these persons does not give them any entitlement to enter, to stay or to reside in a Member State or to have access to its labour market.

(11) The provisions of Regulation (EEC) No. 1408/71 and Regulation (EEC) No. 574/72 are, by virtue of this Regulation, applicable only in so far as the person concerned is already legally resident in the territory of a Member State. Being legally resident is therefore a prerequisite for the application of these provisions.

---

[6] OJ L 149, 5.7.1971, p. 2; Regulation last amended by Regulation (EC) No. 1386/2001 of the European Parliament and of the Council (OJ L 187, 10.7.2001, p. 1).

[7] OJ L 74, 27.3.1972, p. 1; Regulation last amended by Commission Regulation (EC) No. 410/2002 (OJ L 62, 5.3.2002, p. 17).

(12) The provisions of Regulation (EEC) No. 1408/71 and Regulation (EEC) No. 574/72 are not applicable in a situation which is confined in all respects within a single Member State. This concerns, *inter alia*, the situation of a third country national who has links only with a third country and a single Member State.

(13) The continued right to unemployment benefit, as laid down in Article 69 of Regulation (EEC) No. 1408/71, is subject to the condition of registering as a job-seeker with the employment services of each Member State entered. Those provisions may therefore apply to a third-country national only provided he/she has the right, where appropriate pursuant to his/her residence permit, to register as a job-seeker with the employment services of the Member State entered and the right to work there legally.

(14) Transitional provisions should be adopted to protect the persons covered by this Regulation and to ensure that they do not lose rights as a result of its entry into force.

(15) To achieve these objectives it is necessary and appropriate to extend the scope of the rules coordinating the national social security schemes by adopting a Community legal instrument which is binding and directly applicable in every Member State which takes part in the adoption of this Regulation.

(16) This Regulation is without prejudice to rights and obligations arising from international agreements with third countries to which the Community is a party and which afford advantages in terms of social security.

(17) Since the objectives of the proposed action cannot be sufficiently achieved by the Member States and can therefore, by reason of the scale or effects of the proposed action, be better achieved at Community level, the Community may take measures in accordance with the principle of subsidiarity enshrined in Article 5 of the Treaty. In compliance with the principle of proportionality as set out in that Article, this Regulation does not go beyond what is necessary to achieve these objectives.

(18) In accordance with Article 3 of the Protocol on the position of the United Kingdom and Ireland annexed to the Treaty on the European Union and to the Treaty establishing the European Community, Ireland and the United Kingdom gave notice, by letters of 19 and 23 April 2002, of their wish to take part in the adoption and application of this Regulation.

(19) In accordance with Articles 1 and 2 of the Protocol on the position of Denmark annexed to the Treaty on the European Union and to the Treaty establishing the European Community, Denmark is not taking part in the adoption of this Regulation and is not therefore bound by or subject to it,

HAS ADOPTED THIS REGULATION:

Article 1

Subject to the provisions of the Annex to this Regulation, the provisions of Regulation (EEC) No. 1408/71 and Regulation (EEC) No. 574/72 shall apply to nationals of third countries who are not already covered by those provisions solely on the ground of their nationality, as well as to members of their families and to their survivors, provided they are legally resident in the territory of a Member State and are in a situation which is not confined in all respects within a single Member State.

Article 2

1. This Regulation shall not create any rights in respect of the period before 1 June 2003.

2. Any period of insurance and, where appropriate, any period of employment, self-employment or residence completed under the legislation of a Member State before 1 June 2003 shall be taken into account for the determination of rights acquired in accordance with the provisions of this Regulation.

3. Subject to the provisions of paragraph 1, a right shall be acquired under this Regulation even if it relates to a contingency arising prior to 1 June 2003.

4. Any benefit that has not been awarded or that has been suspended on account of the nationality or the residence of the person concerned shall, at the latter's request, be awarded or resumed from 1 June 2003, provided that the rights for which benefits were previously awarded did not give rise to a lump sum payment.

5. The rights of persons who prior to 1 June 2003, obtained the award of a pension may be reviewed at their request, account being taken of the provisions of this Regulation.

6. If the request referred to in paragraph 4 or paragraph 5 is lodged within two years from 1 June 2003, rights deriving from this Regulation shall be acquired from that date and the provisions of the legislation of any Member State on the forfeiture or lapse of rights may not be applied to the persons concerned.

7. If the request referred to in paragraph 4 or paragraph 5 is lodged after expiry of the deadline referred to in paragraph 6, rights not forfeited or lapsed shall be acquired from the date of such request, subject to any more favourable provisions of the legislation of any Member State.

Article 3

This Regulation shall enter into force on the first day of the month following its publication in the Official Journal of the European Union.

This Regulation shall be binding in its entirety and directly applicable in the Member States in accordance with the Treaty establishing the European Community.

ANNEX

SPECIAL PROVISIONS REFERRED TO IN ARTICLE 1

I. **Germany**

In the case of family benefits, this Regulation shall apply only to third-country nationals who are in possession of a residence permit meeting the definition in German law of the 'Aufenthaltserlaubnis' or 'Aufenthaltsberechtigung'.

II. **Austria**

In the case of family benefits, this Regulation shall apply only to third-country nationals who fulfil the conditions laid down by Austrian legislation for permanent entitlement to family allowances.

EXPLANATORY MEMORANDUM

1. **General Comments**

1.1. *The background*

The purpose of this proposal is to extend Regulation (EEC) No 1408/71 to nationals of third countries. It replaces the Commission's proposal of 12 November 1997[8] which is withdrawn. Regulation (EEC) No. 1408/71[9] provides for Community coordination of the Member States' social security schemes. This Regulation currently applies to Community nationals and certain categories of nationals of third countries.

The Commission proposal of 12 November 1997 was designed to address the requirement of equal treatment of Community citizens and third country nationals legally resident in the Community. In addition, its objective was to simplify the rules by reducing the number of national and international instruments governing the coordination of social security schemes for this category of persons, which should considerably reduce the administrative costs. These grounds are still valid. The objective of equal treatment has been confirmed by the Community institutions since the Commission introduced the proposal.

The European Council, at its special meeting in Tampere on 15 and 16 October 1999, acknowledged the need to ensure fair treatment of third-country nationals who reside legally on the territory of its Member States. It declared that a more vigorous integration policy should aim at granting them rights and obligations comparable to those of EU citizens.

---

[8] OJ C 6, 10.01.1998, p. 15.

[9] Regulation (EEC) No. 1408/71 of the Council of 14 June 1971 on the application of social security schemes to employed persons and their families moving within the Community, OJ L 149, 5.7.1971, p. 2. Regulation updated by Regulation (EC) No. 118/97 (OJ L 28, 30.1.1997, p. 1) and last amended by Regulation (EC) No. 1386/2001 of the European Parliament and of the Council of 5 June 2001 (OJ L 187, 10.7.2001, p. 1).

This policy should also enhance non-discrimination in economic, social and cultural life and develop measures against racism and xenophobia. The European Council also acknowledged that the legal status of third-country nationals should be approximated to that of Member States' nationals.[10] Subsequently, the European Social Agenda annexed to the conclusions of the Nice European Council of December 2000 included a commitment to a more vigorous integration policy for third-country nationals who reside legally on the territory of the Union.

In its Resolution of 27 October 1999, the European Parliament called for prompt action on promises of fair treatment for third-country nationals legally resident in the Member States and on the definition of their legal status, including uniform rights as close as possible to those enjoyed by the citizens of the European Union.[11]

Following the entry into force of the Amsterdam Treaty and in line with the conclusions of the Tampere European Council, the Commission presented a proposal for a Council Directive concerning the status of third-country nationals who are long-term residents,[12] whose second part concerns the conditions under which long-term residents may take up residence in another Member State to work, study or for other purposes. This proposal implies extension an of the scope of Regulation No. 1408/71 in the framework of the Commission's commitment to ensure the genuine integration of third-country nationals who have settled long-term on the territory of the Member States and to offer equal treatment to long-term residents in the field of social protection.

The extension of Regulation (EEC) No. 1408/71 is also designed to encourage worker mobility. In its Communication of 28 June 2000[13] on the Social Policy Agenda, the Commission recalled the need to extend Regulation (EEC) No. 1408/71 to third-country nationals, in particular to encourage worker mobility. To this end, and in particular with a view to promoting new European labour markets which are open to all, with access for all, the Communication from the Commission of 28 February 2001[14] also called for support for mobility for third-country nationals.

Finally, the Charter of Fundamental Rights of the European Union, solemnly proclaimed in December 2000 at Nice by the European Parliament, the Council of the European Union and the European Commission, enshrines a certain number of rights which are recognised both in respect of nationals of the Member States and nationals of third countries resident in the Member States.

1.2. *Choice of the legal basis*
The Council has discussed the choice of the legal basis to be used for extending Regulation (EEC) No. 1408/71 to third-country nationals. The Commission's initial proposal of 12

---

[10] Conclusions of the Presidency, points 18 and 21.
[11] OJ C 154, 5 June 2000, p. 63.
[12] OJ C 240 E of 28 August 2001, p. 79.
[13] COM(2000)379, 28 June 2000.
[14] COM(2001)116, 28 February 2001

November 1997 took the legal basis of Regulation (EEC) No. 1408/71 itself, i.e. Articles 51 and 235, now 42 and 308, of the EC Treaty.

Following the entry into force of the Amsterdam Treaty and the new provisions of Title IV of the Treaty and in the light of the recent case law of the Court of Justice (cf. in particular the judgment of 11 October 2001 in *Khalil* (C-95/99)), it was necessary to reexamine the legal basis initially proposed. It emerged that, in the present case, Article 63(4) on the conditions of entry and residence of third-country nationals in the Community would constitute an appropriate legal basis for the application and coordination of the social security schemes of the Member States to all third-country nationals who satisfy the substantive conditions of Regulation No. 1408/71 and who are currently excluded on grounds of their nationality.

In its conclusions of 3 December 2001 the Council agreed on the possibility of using Article 63(4) of the EC Treaty as a legal basis for such an extension. It also considered that the coordination applicable to third-country nationals should grant them a set of uniform rights as close as possible to those enjoyed by the citizens of the European Union. The Laeken European Council of 14 and 15 December 2001 took note of the political agreement concerning the extension of the coordination of social security schemes to third country nationals and invited the Council to adopt the necessary rules as soon as possible (see point 29 of the Conclusions of the Presidency).[15]

In this context, the Commission considers it appropriate to make a new proposal with Article 63(4) of the EC Treaty as the legal basis. This amended proposal will enable the Council to continue its work and the European Parliament can be consulted afresh. Article 63(4) was introduced by the Amsterdam Treaty. It stipulates that the Council must adopt 'measures defining the rights and conditions under which nationals of third countries who are legally resident in a Member State may reside in other Member States'. The coordination of social security schemes is certainly a factor if nationals of third countries are to reside in another Member State or to move within the Community.

The proposal for a regulation must be adopted under the procedure referred to in Article 67 of the Treaty: the Council acts unanimously on a proposal from the Commission or on the initiative of a Member State and after consulting the European Parliament. Title IV of the EC Treaty does not apply to the United Kingdom and Ireland, unless these countries decide otherwise in accordance with the procedures laid down in the Protocol on the Position of the United Kingdom and Ireland annexed to the Treaties. Neither does Title IV apply to Denmark, pursuant to the Protocol on the position of Denmark, annexed to the Treaties.

1.3. *Subsidiarity and proportionality*

The European Community's powers must be exercised in compliance with Article 5 of the EC Treaty, i.e. only if and insofar as the objectives of the proposed action cannot be sufficiently achieved by the Member States and can therefore, by reason of the scale or effects of the proposed action, be better achieved by the Community. This proposal for a regulation meets these criteria.

---

[15] Point 29 of the Presidency conclusions.

A binding rule in the form of a regulation is proportionate to the objective pursued. It is necessary to guarantee equal treatment in the field of coordination of the Member States' social security schemes between Community nationals and the nationals of third countries and to simplify and clarify the legal rules applicable in this area to members of this latter category who are not already covered by Regulation (EEC) No. 1408/71. A regulation is the instrument which was considered most appropriate for achieving this objective.

Chapter 2.7
MUTUAL RECOGNITION ON EXPULSION

COUNCIL DIRECTIVE 2001/40/EC
of 28 May 2001
on the mutual recognition of decisions on the expulsion of third country nationals[1]

THE COUNCIL OF THE EUROPEAN UNION,
Having regard to the Treaty establishing the European Community, and in particular Article 63(3) thereof,
Having regard to the initiative of the French Republic,[2]
Having regard to the opinion of the European Parliament,[3]

Whereas:

(1) The Treaty stipulates that the Council is to adopt measures on immigration policy within areas comprising conditions of entry and residence as well as illegal immigration and illegal residence.

(2) The Tampere European Council on 15 and 16 October 1999 reaffirmed its resolve to create an area of freedom, security and justice. For that purpose, a common European policy on asylum and migration should aim both at fair treatment of third country nationals and better management of migration flows.

(3) The need to ensure greater effectiveness in enforcing expulsion decisions and better cooperation between Member States entails mutual recognition of expulsion decisions.

(4) Decisions on the expulsion of third country nationals have to be adopted in accordance with fundamental rights, as safeguarded by the European Convention for the Protection of Human Rights and Fundamental Freedoms of 4 November 1950, in particular Articles 3 and 8 thereof, and the Geneva Convention relating to the Status of Refugees of 28 July 1951 and as they result from the constitutional principles common to the Member States.

(5) In accordance with the principle of subsidiarity, the objective of the proposed action, namely cooperation between Member States on expulsion of third country nationals, cannot be sufficiently achieved by the Member States and can therefore, by reason of the effects of the envisaged action, be better achieved by the Community. This Directive does not go beyond what is necessary to achieve that objective.

---

[1] OJ L 149, 2.6.2001, p. 34.
[2] OJ C 243, 24.8.2000, p. 1.
[3] Opinion delivered on 13 March 2001 (not yet published in the Official Journal).

(6) In accordance with Article 3 of the Protocol on the position of the United Kingdom and Ireland annexed to the Treaty on European Union and the Treaty establishing the European Community, the United Kingdom has given notice by letter of 18 October 2000 of its wish to take part in the adoption and application of this Directive.

(7) In accordance with Articles 1 and 2 of the Protocol on the position of Denmark annexed to the Treaty on European Union and the Treaty establishing the European Community, Denmark is not participating in the adoption of this Directive, and is therefore not bound by it or subject to its application. Given that this Directive aims to build upon the Schengen acquis under the provisions of Title IV of the Treaty establishing the European Community, in accordance with Article 5 of the above-mentioned Protocol, Denmark will decide within a period of six months after the Council has adopted this Directive whether it will transpose this decision into its national law.

(8) As regards the Republic of Iceland and the Kingdom of Norway, this Directive constitutes a development of the Schengen acquis within the meaning of the agreement concluded on 18 May 1999 between the Council of the European Union and those two States. As a result of the procedures laid down in the agreement, the rights and obligations arising from this Directive should also apply to those two States and in relations between those two States and the Member States of the European Community to which this Directive is addressed,

HAS ADOPTED THIS DIRECTIVE:

Article 1

1. Without prejudice to the obligations arising from Article 23 and to the application of Article 96 of the Convention implementing the Schengen Agreement of 14 June 1985, signed at Schengen on 19 June 1990, hereinafter referred to as the 'Schengen Convention', the purpose of this Directive is to make possible the recognition of an expulsion decision issued by a competent authority in one Member State, hereinafter referred to as the 'issuing Member State', against a third country national present within the territory of another Member State, hereinafter referred to as the 'enforcing Member State'.

2. Any decision taken pursuant to paragraph 1 shall be implemented according to the applicable legislation of the enforcing Member State.

3. This Directive shall not apply to family members of citizens of the Union who have exercised their right of free movement.

Article 2

For the purposes of this Directive,
   (a) 'third country national' shall mean anyone who is not a national of any of the Member States;
   (b) 'expulsion decision' shall mean any decision which orders an expulsion taken by a competent administrative authority of an issuing Member State;

(c) 'enforcement measure' shall mean any measure taken by the enforcing Member State with a view to implementing an expulsion decision.

Article 3

1. The expulsion referred to in Article 1 shall apply to the following cases:

(a) a third country national is the subject of an expulsion decision based on a serious and present threat to public order or to national security and safety, taken in the following cases:
 – conviction of a third country national by the issuing Member State for an offence punishable by a penalty involving deprivation of liberty of at least one year,
 – the existence of serious grounds for believing that a third country national has committed serious criminal offences or the existence of solid evidence of his intention to commit such offences within the territory of a Member State.

Without prejudice to Article 25(2) of the Schengen Convention, if the person concerned holds a residence permit issued by the enforcing Member State or by another Member State, the enforcing State shall consult the issuing State and the State which issued the permit. The existence of an expulsion decision taken under this point shall allow for the residence permit to be withdrawn if this is authorised by the national legislation of the State which issued the permit;

(b) a third country national is the subject of an expulsion decision based on failure to comply with national rules on the entry or residence of aliens.

In the two cases referred to in (a) and (b), the expulsion decision must not have been rescinded or suspended by the issuing Member State.

2. Member States shall apply this Directive with due respect for human rights and fundamental freedoms.

3. This Directive shall be applied without prejudice to the provisions of the Convention Determining the State Responsible for Examining Applications for Asylum Lodged in one of the Member States of the European Communities and readmission agreements between Member States.

Article 4

The Member States shall ensure that the third country national concerned may, in accordance with the enforcing Member State's legislation, bring proceedings for a remedy against any measure referred to in Article 1(2).

Article 5

Protection of personal data and data security shall be ensured in accordance with Directive 95/46/EC of the European Parliament and of the Council of 24 October 1995 on the protection of individuals with regard to the processing of personal data and on the free movement of such data.[4] Without prejudice to Articles 101 and 102 of the Schengen Convention, per-

---

[4] OJ L 281, 23.11.1995, p. 31.

sonal data files shall be used in the context of this Directive only for the purposes laid down therein.

Article 6

The authorities of the issuing Member State and of the enforcing Member State shall make use of all appropriate means of cooperation and of exchanging information to implement this Directive.

The issuing Member State shall provide the enforcing Member State with all documents needed to certify the continued enforceability of the decision by the fastest appropriate means, where appropriate in accordance with the relevant provisions of the SIRENE Manual.

The enforcing Member State shall first examine the situation of the person concerned to ensure that neither the relevant international instruments nor the national rules applicable conflict with the enforcement of the expulsion decision. After implementation of the enforcement measure, the enforcing Member State shall inform the issuing Member State.

Article 7

Member States shall compensate each other for any financial imbalances which may result from application of this Directive where expulsion cannot be effected at the expense of the national(s) of the third country concerned.

In order to enable this Article to be implemented, the Council, acting on a proposal from the Commission, shall adopt appropriate criteria and practical arrangements before 2 December 2002. These criteria and practical arrangements shall also apply to the implementation of Article 24 of the Schengen Convention.

Article 8

1. Member States shall bring into force the laws, regulations and administrative provisions necessary to comply with this Directive not later than 2 December 2002. They shall forthwith inform the Commission thereof. When Member States adopt these measures, they shall contain a reference to this Directive or shall be accompanied by such reference on the occasion of their official publication. The methods of making such reference shall be laid down by Member States.

2. Member States shall communicate to the Commission the text of the main provisions of domestic law which they adopt in the field governed by this Directive.

Article 9

This Directive shall enter into force the day of its publication in the Official Journal of the European Communities.

Article 10

This Directive is addressed to the Member States, in accordance with the Treaty establishing the European Community.

Part 3

MISCELLANEOUS

Chapter 3.1
OTHER RELEVANT INSTRUMENTS

Apart from the instruments, the Directives in particular, contained in this Volume, reference should also be made to some other relevant instruments as well as to Communications.[1]

3.1.a LEGISLATION[2]

Entry

– Unaccompanied minors who are nationals of third countries – *Council Resolution – Official Journal C221, 19 July 1997;*

– Establishment of 'Eurodac' for the comparison of fingerprints for the effective application of the Dublin Convention – *Council Regulation (EC) No. 2725/2000 – Official Journal L316, 15 December 2000;*

– Freedom of movement with a long stay visa – *Council Regulation (EC) No. 1091/2001 – Official Journal L150, 6 June 2001;*

– Certain rules to implement Regulation (EC) No. 2725/2000 concerning the establishment of 'Eurodac' for the comparison of fingerprints for the effective application of the Dublin Convention – *Council Regulation (EC) No. 407/2002 – Official Journal L62, 5 March 2002;*

– Strengthening of the penal framework to prevent the facilitation of unauthorised entry, transit and residence – *Council Framework Decision (JHA) No. 946/2002 – Official Journal L328, 5 December 2002;*

– Defining the facilitation of unauthorised entry, transit and residence – *Council Directive (EC) No. 90/2002 – Official Journal L328, 5 December 2002;*

– Obligation of carriers to communicate passenger data – *initiative for a Council Directive No. 10079/03, 3 June 2003;*

---

[1] Many of the instruments mentioned here, as well as earlier texts, proposals, Joint Actions and so on, can be found in *The Asylum Acquis Handbook* (The Hague 2000), *The Migration Acquis Handbook* (The Hague, 2001) and/or *The Migration Acquis 2002 Update* (The Hague/Vienna, 2002).

[2] For an overview of the (legal) differences between Directives, Regulations, Framework Decisions, Resolutions, Recommendations and so on, see e.g. Staples in *The Asylum Acquis Handbook*, pp. 37-46.

–   Requirement for the competent authorities of the Member States to stamp systematically the travel documents of third country nationals when they cross the external borders – *proposal for a Council Regulation – COM (2003) 664 final – Commission position on European Parliament amendments on 21 April 2004;*

–   Specific procedure for admitting third-country nationals for purposes of scientific research – *proposal for a Council Recommendation – COM (2004) 178-2 final – discussion at the Council on 18 May 2004;*

–   Admission of third-country nationals to carry out scientific research in the European Community – *proposal for a Council Recommendation – COM (2004) 178-3 final; political agreement reached on 8 June 2004;*

–   Uniform short-stay visas for researchers from third countries travelling within the European Community for the purpose of carrying out scientific research (proposal) – *proposal for a Council Recommendation – COM (2004) 178-4 final – discussion at the Council on 18 May 2004.*

Stay

–   Harmonized application of the definition of the term 'refugee' in Article 1 of the Geneva Convention of 28 July 1951 relating to the status of refugee – *Joint Position (JHA) No. 196/1996 – Official Journal L63, 13 March 1996;*

–   Minimum guarantees for asylum procedure – *Council Resolution – Official Journal C274, 19 September 1996;*

–   Decision of the Committee set up by Article 18 of the Dublin Convention concerning the transfer of responsibility for family members in accordance with Article 3(4) and Article 9 of that Convention – *Decision No. 1/2000 – Official Journal L281, 7 November 2000;*

–   Conditions in which third-country nationals shall have the freedom to travel in the territory of the Member States for periods not exceeding three months, introducing a specific travel authorisation and determining the conditions of entry and movement for periods not exceeding six months – *proposal for a Council Directive – COM (2001) 388 final – Committee of Regions opinion on 13 March 2002;*

–   Uniform format for residence permits for third-country nationals – *Council Regulation (EC) No. 1030/2002 – Official Journal L157, 15 June 2002;*

–   Creation of a immigration liaison officers network – *Council Regulation (EC) No. 377/ 2004 – Official Journal L64, 2 March 2004;*

–   The right of citizens of the Union and their family members to move and reside freely within the territory of the Member States – *Directive of the European Parliament and of the Council (EC) No.38/2004 – Official Journal L158, 30 April 2004.*

Return

–   Specimen bilateral readmission agreement between a Member State and a third country – *Council Recommendation – Official Journal C274, 19 September 1996;*

–   Standard travel document for the expulsion of third-country nationals – *Council Recommendation – Official Journal C274, 19 September 1996;*

–   Carrier penalties – supplementing the provisions of Article 26 of the Convention implementing the Schengen Agreement of 14 June 1985 – *Council Directive (EC) No. 51/2001 – Official Journal L187, 10 July 2001;*

–   European arrest warrant and the surrender procedures between Member States – *Council Framework Decision No. 584 (JHA) – Official Journal L190, 18 July 2002;*

–   Return Action Programme – *14673/02 – adopted by the Council on 28 November 2002;*

–   Assistance in cases of transit through the territory of one or more Member States in the context of removal measures taken by Member States against third-country nationals – *initiative for a Council Directive No.10909/03, 3 July 2003;*

–   Assistance in cases of transit by land in the context of removal measures taken by Member States against third-country nationals – *initiative for a Council Directive No. 11419/03, 14 July 2003;*

–   Organisation of joint flights for removals of third-country nationals illegally present in the territory of two or more Member States – *initiative for a Council Decision – Official Journal C223, 19 September 2003;*

–   Assistance in cases of transit for the purposes of removal by air – *Council Directive (EC) No. 110/2003 – Official Journal L321, 6 December 2003;*

–   Agreement between the European Community and the Government of the Hong Kong Special Administrative Region of the People's Republic of China on the readmission of persons residing without authorisation – *Official Journal L17, 24 January 2004;*

–   Criteria and practical arrangements for the compensation of the financial imbalances resulting from the application of Council Directive 2001/40/EC on the mutual recognition of decisions on the expulsion of third country nationals – *Council Decision (EC) No. 191/2004 – Official Journal L60, 27 February 2004;*

–   European Agency for the Management of Operational Co-operation at the External Borders – *proposal for a Council Regulation – COM (2003) 687 final – Commission position on European Parliament amendments on 9 March 2004.*

EU – wide programmes

– Establishing a programme for financial and technical assistance to third countries in the areas of migration and asylum (AENEAS) – *Regulation of the European Parliament and of the Council No. 491/2004 – Official Journal L80, 18 March 2004;*

– European Refugee Fund (proposal for the period 2005-2010) – *Council Decision – COM (2004) 102 final – political agreement reached on 8 June 2004;*[3]

3.1.b   COMMUNICATIONS[4]

– Communication on immigration and asylum policies – *COM (1994) 23 final – European Parliament resolution on 21 September 1995;*

– Commission Working Document – The relationship between safeguarding internal security and complying with international protection obligations and instruments – *COM (2001) 743 final – Committee of Regions opinion on 16 May 2002;*[5]

– Proposal for a comprehensive plan to combat illegal immigration and trafficking of human beings in the European Union – *Official Journal C142, 14 June 2002;*

– Communication – Towards a common asylum procedure and a uniform status, valid throughout the Union, for persons granted asylum – *COM (2000) 755 final – European Parliament resolution on 3 October 2001;*

– Communication on a Community immigration policy – *COM (2000) 757 final – European Parliament resolution on 3 October 2001;*[6]

– Communication on a common policy on illegal immigration – *COM (2001) 672 final – Council Conclusions on 15 October 2002;*[7]

– Green Paper on a Community return policy on illegal residents – *COM (2002) 175 final – European Economic and Social Committee opinion on 11 December 2002;*[8]

– Communication on the common asylum policy and the Agenda for protection – *COM (2003) 152 final – transmission to European Parliament on 26 March 2003;*

---

[3] Under the 'Return Action Plan' funds will also be made available for the return of e.g. rejectees; see for instance 8541/04 MIGR31.

[4] This overview is listed in a chronological order of agreement, which does not necessarily amount to the chronological order of publication.

[5] See also van Krieken/Ungureanu, *Migration Acquis Update* (MAU) The Hague/Vienna, spring 2002, p. 290 ff.

[6] Included in *The Migration Acquis Handbook* (MAH), The Hague, 2001, p. 11 ff.

[7] MAU, p. 193 ff.

[8] Idem, p. 242 ff.

– Communication – The future of the European Employment Strategy (EES) A strategy for full employment and better jobs for all – *COM (2003) 6 final – Committee of Regions position on 10 April 2003;*

– Communication on the Common Asylum Policy, introducing an open coordination method – *COM (2001) 710 final – Economic and Social Committee opinion on 29 May 2003;*

– Communication on an open method of coordination for the Community Immigration Policy – *COM (2001) 387 final – European Parliament resolution on 19 June 2003;*[9]

– Communication on undeclared work – *COM (1998) 219 final – Council resolution on 20 October 2003;*[10]

– Communication to present an Action plan for the collection and analysis of Community Statistics in the field of migration – *COM (2003) 179 final – European Parliament resolution on 6 November 2003;*

– Communication on integrating migration issues in the European Union's relations with third countries – migration and development – report on the effectiveness of financial resources available at community level for repatriation of immigrants and rejected asylum seekers, for management of external borders and for asylum and migration projects in third countries – *COM (2002) 703 final – European Parliament resolution on 15 January 2004;*

– Communication on the development of a common policy on illegal immigration, smuggling and trafficking of human beings, external borders and the return of illegal residents – *COM (2003) 323 final – European Parliament resolution on 15 January 2004;*

– Communication on immigration, integration and employment – *COM (2003) 336 final – Committee of regions opinion on 11 February 2004;*

– Communication – Towards more accessible, equitable and managed asylum systems – *COM(2003) 315 final – European Parliament resolution on 1 April 2004;*

– Communication – Development of the Schengen Information System II and possible synergies with a future Visa Information System (VIS) – *COM (2003) 771 – Council conclusions on 29 April 2004;*

– Communication – Area of freedom, security and justice: Assessment of the Tampere programme and future orientation – *COM (2004) 401 final – Commission adoption on 2 June 2004;*

---

[9] Idem, p. 265 ff.
[10] Idem, p. 74 ff.

–   Communication on the managed entry in the EU of persons in need of international protection and the enhancement of the protection capacity of regions of origin – 'improving access to durable solutions' – *COM (2004) 410 final – Commission adoption on 6 June 2004.*

–   Communication on a more efficient common European Asylum System – the single procedure as the next step – *July 2004.*

Chapter 3.2
DEFINITIONS[1]

Term	Definition
Return	Comprises the process of going back to one's country of origin, transit or another third country, including preparation and implementation. The return may be voluntary or enforced.
Illegal resident	Any person who does not, or no longer, fulfil the conditions for presence in, or residence on the territory of the Member State of the European Union.
Illegal entrant	Any person who does not fulfil the conditions for entry in the territory of the Member States of the European Union.
Voluntary return	The assisted or independent departure to the country of origin, transit or another third country based on the will of the returnee.
Forced return	The compulsory return to the country of origin, transit or another third country, on the basis of an administrative or judicial act.
Readmission	Act by a state accepting the re-entry of an individual (own nationals, third-country nationals or stateless persons), who has been found illegally entering to, being present in or residing in another state.
Readmission agreement	Agreement setting out reciprocal obligations on the contracting parties, as well as detailed administrative and operational procedures, to facilitate the return and transit of persons who do not, or no longer fulfil the conditions of entry to, presence in or residence in the requesting state.

---

[1] These definitions have been agreed upon by the Council 'Return Action Programme' (November 2002). It represents a first list of common interpretation of terms. For other definitions see Batey's extensive glossary in *The Migration Aqcuis Handbook* (The Hague, 2001) pp. 415-429.

Term	Definition
Expulsion	Administrative or judicial act, which states – where applicable – the illegality of the entry, stay or residence or terminates the legality of a previous lawful residence, e.g., in case of criminal offences.
Expulsion order	Administrative or judicial decision to lay the legal basis for the expulsion.
Detention pending removal	Act of enforcement, deprivation of personal liberty for return enforcement purposes within a closed facility.
Detention order	Administrative or judicial decision which forms the legal basis for the detention pending removal.
Removal	Act of enforcement, which means the physical transportation out of the country.
Removal order	Administrative or judicial decision to lay the legal basis for the removal. (in some legal systems synonymous with expulsion order).
Legal re-entry	Admission of a third-country national or stateless person to the territory of the Member State of the European Union after prior departure.
Rejection	Refusal of entry to a state.
Transit	Passage through a country while travelling from a country of departure to the country of destination.

Chapter 3.3
THE 2004 EU CONSTITUTION

The following sets out the migration and asylum related Articles of the EU Constitution, following agreement on the Constitution at the EU summit on June 18, 2004. This agreement concluded the Intergovernmental Conference (IGC) which had been convened in October 2003.

The text is consolidated on the basis of the legal experts' revised text of the Constitution drawn up initially by the constitutional Convention (doc. IGC 50/03), including the relevant corrections to that document made later (doc. IGC 50/03 cor 7), plus the substantive amendments to that text agreed by the EU leaders in the IGC (docs. (IGC 81/04 and 85/04).

The IGC has made some substantive amendments to the draft Constitution, E.G.: Article III- 158, as well as other articles in the JHA realm, like III-170, III-171, III-172, III-174 and III-175. The final numbering of the Articles of the Constitution will undoubtedly be different from the ones indicated below following the substantive changes made at the IGC and the forthcoming legal experts' revisions.

The official signature ceremony is planned to take place before the end of 2004 according to the conclusions of the June 2004 EU summit meeting (European Council).[1]

CHAPTER IV
Area of Freedom, Security and Justice

Section 1
General provisions

Article III-158
(IGC amendment to paragraph 1)

1. The Union shall constitute an area of freedom, security and justice with respect for fundamental rights and the different legal traditions and systems of the Member States.

2. It shall ensure the absence of internal border controls for persons and shall frame a common policy on asylum, immigration and external border control, based on solidarity between Member States, which is fair towards third-country nationals. For the purpose of this chapter, stateless persons shall be treated as third-country nationals.

---

[1] See the remarks by Steve Peers, Professor of Law, University of Essex, June 24, 2004, on www.statewatch.org.

3. The Union shall endeavour to ensure a high level of security by measures to prevent and combat crime, racism and xenophobia, and measures for coordination and cooperation between police and judicial authorities and other competent authorities, as well as by the mutual recognition of judgments in criminal matters and, if necessary, the approximation of criminal laws.

4. The Union shall facilitate access to justice, in particular by the principle of mutual recognition of judicial and extrajudicial decisions in civil matters.

Article III-159

The European Council shall define the strategic guidelines for legislative and operational planning within the area of freedom, security and justice.

Article III-160

Member States' national Parliaments shall ensure that the proposals and legislative initiatives submitted under Sections 4 and 5 of this Chapter comply with the principle of subsidiarity, in accordance with the arrangements laid down by the Protocol on the application of the principles of subsidiarity and proportionality.

Article III-161

Without prejudice to Articles III-265 to III-267, the Council of Ministers may, on a proposal from the Commission, adopt European regulations or decisions laying down the arrangements whereby Member States, in collaboration with the Commission, conduct objective and impartial evaluation of the implementation of the Union policies referred to in this Chapter by Member States' authorities, in particular in order to facilitate full application of the principle of mutual recognition. The European Parliament and Member States' national Parliaments shall be informed of the content and results of the evaluation.

Article III-162

A standing committee shall be set up within the Council in order to ensure that operational cooperation on internal security is promoted and strengthened within the Union. Without prejudice to Article III-247, it shall facilitate coordination of the action of Member States' competent authorities. Representatives of the Union bodies, offices and agencies concerned may be involved in the proceedings of this committee. The European Parliament and Member States' national parliaments shall be kept informed of the proceedings.

Article III-163

This Chapter shall not affect the exercise of the responsibilities incumbent upon Member States with regard to the maintenance of law and order and the safeguarding of internal security.

Article III-164

The Council shall adopt European regulations to ensure administrative cooperation between the relevant departments of the Member States in the areas covered by this Chapter, as well as between those departments and the Commission. It shall act on a Commission proposal, subject to Article III-165, and after consulting the European Parliament.

Article III-165

The acts referred to in Sections 4 and 5 of this Chapter, together with the European regulations referred to in Article III-164 which ensure administrative cooperation in the areas covered by these Sections, shall be adopted:
(a) on a proposal from the Commission, or
(b) on the initiative of a quarter of the Member States.

Section 2
Policies on border checks, asylum and immigration

Article III-166

1. The Union shall develop a policy with a view to:
(a) ensuring the absence of any controls on persons, whatever their nationality, when crossing internal borders;
(b) carrying out checks on persons and efficient monitoring of the crossing of external borders;
(c) the gradual introduction of an integrated management system for external borders.

2. For this purpose, European laws or framework laws shall establish measures concerning:
(a) the common policy on visas and other short-stay residence permits;
(b) the controls to which persons crossing external borders are subject;
(c) the conditions under which nationals of third countries shall have the freedom to travel within the Union for a short period;
(d) any measure necessary for the gradual establishment of an integrated management system for external borders;
(e) the absence of any controls on persons, whatever their nationality, when crossing internal borders.

3. This Article shall not affect the competence of the Member States concerning the geographical demarcation of their borders, in accordance with international law.

Article III-167

1. The Union shall develop a common policy on asylum, subsidiary protection and temporary protection with a view to offering appropriate status to any third-country national requiring international protection and ensuring compliance with the principle of *non-refoulement*. This policy must be in accordance with the Geneva Convention of 28 July

1951 and the Protocol of 31 January 1967 relating to the status of refugees and other relevant treaties.

2. For this purpose, European laws or framework laws shall lay down measures for a common European asylum system comprising:
    (a) a uniform status of asylum for nationals of third countries, valid throughout the Union;
    (b) a uniform status of subsidiary protection for nationals of third countries who, without
obtaining European asylum, are in need of international protection;
    (c) a common system of temporary protection for displaced persons in the event of a
massive inflow;
    (d) common procedures for the granting and withdrawing of uniform asylum or subsid-
iary protection status;
    (e) criteria and mechanisms for determining which Member State is responsible for con-
sidering an application for asylum or subsidiary protection;
    (f) standards concerning the conditions for the reception of applicants for asylum or
subsidiary protection;
    (g) partnership and cooperation with third countries for the purpose of managing inflows
of people applying for asylum or subsidiary or temporary protection.

3. In the event of one or more Member States being confronted by an emergency situation
characterised by a sudden inflow of nationals of third countries, the Council, on a proposal
from the Commission, may adopt European regulations or decisions comprising provisional
measures for the benefit of the Member State(s) concerned. It shall act after consulting the
European Parliament.

Article III-168

1. The Union shall develop a common immigration policy aimed at ensuring, at all stages,
the efficient management of migration flows, fair treatment of third-country nationals residing legally in Member States, and the prevention of, and enhanced measures to combat,
illegal immigration and trafficking in human beings.

2. To this end, European laws or framework laws shall establish measures in the following
areas:
    (a) the conditions of entry and residence, and standards on the issue by Member States of
long-term visas and residence permits, including those for the purpose of family reunion;
    (b) the definition of the rights of third-country nationals residing legally in a Member
State, including the conditions governing freedom of movement and of residence in other
Member States;
    (c) illegal immigration and unauthorised residence, including removal and repatriation
of persons residing without authorisation;
    (d) combating trafficking in persons, in particular women and children.

3. The Union may conclude agreements with third countries for the readmission of third-
country nationals who do not or who no longer fulfil the conditions for entry, presence or
residence in the territory of one of the Member States.

4. European laws or framework laws may establish measures to provide incentives and support for the action of Member States with a view to promoting the integration of third-country nationals residing legally in their territories, excluding any harmonisation of the laws and regulations of the Member States.

5. This Article shall not affect the right of Member States to determine volumes of admission of third-country nationals coming from third countries to their territory in order to seek work, whether employed or self-employed.

Article III-169

The policies of the Union set out in this Section and their implementation shall be governed by the principle of solidarity and fair sharing of responsibility, including its financial implications, between the Member States. Whenever necessary, the acts of the Union adopted pursuant to this Section shall contain appropriate measures to give effect to this principle.

Chapter 3.4
INDEX[1]

---

[1] Prepared by Cristian Cartis. Remarks and suggestions are welcome at press@asser.nl

T·M·C·ASSER PRESS

THE HAGUE — THE NETHERLANDS

Related titles by
Peter J. van Krieken

THE ASYLUM ACQUIS HANDBOOK

The Foundation for a Common European Asylum Policy

The Hague, 2000, ISBN 90-6704-122-x, 360 pp., hardcover
URL: www.asserpress.nl/cata/asylum/fra.htm

THE MIGRATION ACQUIS HANDBOOK

The Foundation for a Common European Migration Policy

The Hague, 2001, ISBN 90-6704-130-0, 432 pp., hardcover
URL: www.asserpress.nl/cata/migration/fra.htm

HEALTH, MIGRATION AND RETURN

A Handbook for a Multidisciplinary Approach

The Hague, 2001, ISBN 90-6704-128-9, 464 pp., hardcover
URL: www.asserpress.nl/cata/health/fra.htm

Distributed for T.M.C.ASSER PRESS by CAMBRIDGE UNIVERSITY PRESS:

Cambridge University Press
Customer Service Department
Shaftesbury Road
Cambridge, CB2 1BR, United Kingdom
Tel. +44(1223)326050 / Fax +44(1223)326111
Email: directcustserve@cambridge.org
www.cambridge.org/uk

Cambridge University Press
100 Brook Hill Drive
West Nyack, NY 10994
USA
Tel.+1(845)3537500
Fax +1(845)3534141
www.cambridge.org/us

T·M·C·ASSER PRESS

THE HAGUE — THE NETHERLANDS

Related titles by
Peter J. van Krieken

REFUGEE LAW IN CONTEXT:
THE EXCLUSION CLAUSE

The Hague, 1999, ISBN 90-6704-118-1, 344 pp., hardcover
URL: www.asserpress.nl/cata/refugee/fra.htm

TERRORISM
AND THE INTERNATIONAL LEGAL ORDER
With Special Reference to the UN, the EU
and Cross-border Aspects

The Hague, 2002, ISBN 90-6704-148-3, 482 pp., hardcover
URL: www.asserpress.nl/cata/terrorism/fra.htm

Distributed for T.M.C. ASSER PRESS by CAMBRIDGE UNIVERSITY PRESS:

Cambridge University Press
Customer Service Department
Shaftesbury Road
Cambridge, CB2 1BR, United Kingdom
Tel. +44(1223)326050 / Fax +44(1223)326111
Email: directcustserve@cambridge.org
www.cambridge.org/uk

Cambridge University Press
100 Brook Hill Drive
West Nyack, NY 10994
USA
Tel. +1(845)3537500
Fax +1(845)3534141
www.cambridge.org/us